北京外国语大学2021年"中青年卓越人才支持计划"和
一般规划教材项目（2022JCB01）

翻译专业基础课系列教材

英汉双向交替口译基础

主　编◎王颖冲
编　者◎周思蕊　卢青亮　朱　珠

ENGLISH AND CHINESE
CONSECUTIVE
INTERPRETING:
A PRACTICAL GUIDE

华东师范大学出版社
·上海·

图书在版编目（CIP）数据

英汉双向交替口译基础 / 王颖冲主编；王健卿副主编. -- 上海：华东师范大学出版社，2024. -- ISBN 978-7-5760-5250-3

Ⅰ．H315.9

中国国家版本馆CIP数据核字第20245KR019号

英汉双向交替口译基础

主　　编　王颖冲
项目编辑　张　婧　袁一萐
特约审读　张　锷
责任校对　曹一凡　时东明
装帧设计　俞　越

出版发行　华东师范大学出版社
社　　址　上海市中山北路3663号　邮编 200062
网　　址　www.ecnupress.com.cn
电　　话　021-60821666　行政传真 021-62572105
客服电话　021-62865537　门市（邮购）电话 021-62869887
地　　址　上海市中山北路3663号华东师范大学校内先锋路口
网　　店　http://hdsdcbs.tmall.com

印　刷　者　上海展强印刷有限公司
开　　本　787毫米×1092毫米　1/16
印　　张　18
字　　数　350千字
版　　次　2024年12月第1版
印　　次　2024年12月第1次
书　　号　ISBN 978-7-5760-5250-3
定　　价　59.80元

出版人　王　焰

（如发现本版图书有印订质量问题，请寄回本社客服中心调换或电话021-62865537联系）

前　言

一、本书的编写背景

语言交流诞生于人类社会形成之初，不同部落族群的交互则催生了对口译的需求，以服务于宗教传播、商贾往来、技术交流等，而早期的口译活动也远远早于文字的记载。随着国家与民族的诞生，口译在外交礼节、战争谈判、国际贸易、文化传播等方面也一直发挥着不可替代的桥梁作用。

全球化时代下，不同国家和民族之间的交流日趋频繁，在政治、经济、社会、文化、科技、环境等方面的交融也愈发紧密。加拿大作家玛格丽特·阿特伍德（Margaret Atwood）曾说："War is what happens when language fails.（语言的尽头便是战争的开端。）"如今，国际性和区域性组织、跨国企业、多边贸易越来越多，各方之间的沟通合作、利益分配、矛盾消除都有赖于口译。如果翻译不力或出现误解和误译，就可能耽误议程，甚至激化冲突。大到一个国家或民族，小至一个企业或个人，都是如此。可以说，口译工作是实现双赢、互联互通、构建人类命运共同体的必要工具。

随着中国在全球舞台上的崛起，对外交流与合作的需求越来越大，具备跨文化能力的外语人才是不同民族与文化之间相互理解与合作的桥梁。与此同时，党的二十大精神强调了社会主义核心价值观和中华优秀传统文化的传承与发展，通过外语来"讲好中国故事"对世界了解中国至关重要。这些都对新一代的翻译学习者提出了更高的要求。那么如何从一般的外语学习者过渡到口译学习者，通过翻译实践来加强民族交往、促进文化交流与融合呢？英汉口译教材可以帮助学生分步拆解、专项训练，掌握交替口译中的基本技能，了解不同翻译目的和场合的需求差异，培养跨文化意识和交际能力。

本书是英汉、汉英双向的口译入门教材，适用于本科翻译专业（BTI）和英语专业的口译基础课程。课程一般面向本科三年级学生，部分院校也会在本科二年级或四年级时开设。目前，少量高校的口译课分类比较细致，按形式可分为联络口译、交替传译、同声传译、视译等，按方向可分为英译汉、汉译英和双向口译，按领域可分为外交口译、医疗口译、商务口译等，按难易程度可分为基础课、进阶课、模拟会议等。但是，大部分高校的课程设置没有划分得这么细，许多时候会将各类口译课程合并为一两门来教授，由于课时量不足且课程进度较快，给师生都带来了巨大的挑战。例如，有的高校只有一门口译课，同时包含了英汉、汉英双向口译的相关内容，分别选用两本或多本教材。这样做在教学思路、课时分配和授课进度等方面往往存在问题，而本书所设计的同步训练则照顾到了这类需求，也便于对比和反思两种翻译方向下口译学习的重难点异同，互相促进。当然，它的语料也可以拆分为英译汉和汉译英两部分，不影响其应用于两门独立的课程。

除了口译入门阶段常用的日常对话和生活场景，我们针对教育、科技、经济、环保、社会等重点发展领域，在教材中加入了相关的词汇和说明，帮助学生掌握这些领域的基础性专业知识。汉译英的素材包含了以历史文化、发展成就、国家政策和社会问题为主题的内容，培养学生的爱国情怀，使学生在口译实践中更好地理解和传递国家的核心价值观，推动文明之间的对话和交流。英译汉的素材引导学生体验两种不同文化背景下的思维方式、价值观念和社会习俗，培养学生的国际视野和包容性，促进不同文化间的和谐共存。

口译要求学生具备扎实的语言基础、广博的知识储备、强大的逻辑思维和快速反应的能力，而口译教材也需要为此服务，促进学生的全面发展，逐步增强自信。本教材鼓励学生们开展团队合作，通过资料共享、同伴评议、模拟会议等形式分工协作，培养有效沟通、化解冲突的能力，成为合格的团队成员，这对于其未来的职业规划具有重要意义。

二、本书的编写特色

本书考虑到课上和课下衔接的问题，对于教学活动、自主练习、小组练习的组织方式都有详细的描述，希望能够手把手带学生入门口译。对于授课教师来说，它也可以指导组织基础课的教学，包括如何在课堂引导学生高效、有理有据地进行同伴评议，如何策划课后作业并持续激励学生练习和自我反思。作为入门教材，《英汉双向交替口译基础》一书具有以下几大特色：

第一，材料难度适宜。 有的教材追求真实会议和演讲的音频，这类素材的语言自然地道，语音有地域和个人特色，语调抑扬顿挫，语速平稳中不失节奏感，而且是实战中经常会遇到的场景，对进阶型学习者来说的确是很理想的素材。但是，这类材料的句式往往复杂多样，用词灵活，对初学者而言难度太高，甚至经常出现整段听完不知所云的情况，这样容易打击学习者的自信心，而自信心对于口译来说恰恰是极为重要的。因此，我们在选取材料时不一味追求现场感，而希望它们的适用性更广。本书的练习从简短对话、慢速英语，逐渐过渡到根据演讲文稿改编后由专人朗读的音频，到后期才会使用真实演讲和会议的音频素材。

第二，能够授人以渔。 一本教材再好，其包含的内容也是有限的，且原本时效性强的素材很快会过时，而口译学习需要长期、大量的训练，以量变促成质变。在信息时代，上网寻找视听资源很容易，各类新闻、访谈、演讲和会议的视频层出不穷，但是学生仍然普遍觉得很难找到适合自己的练习材料。这说明互联网时代海量的信息反而让筛选和判断成了一项考验。授人以鱼不如授人以渔，本书旨在帮助师生根据不同的外语水平、口译基础、训练主题和目标来选材。同时，我们也介绍了一些拓展思路和"改造"素材的方法，比如：如何利用普通的听力材料来做口译练习，二者的训练侧重又有何不同；如何利用软件调整音频的速率以适应不同阶段的训练;如何利用语音识别技术将文字材料生成音频,用于自主口译训练等。

第三,适用于教师授课,尤其是帮助非口译专业的教师来上好这门课。2022年时,全国开设翻译专业的院校已高达206所,不少院校的英语专业也开设了口译课程,但却面临翻译师资不足、专业的口译教师严重缺乏的问题,因此部分课程需要由文学、语言学、区域与国别研究方向的英语教师担纲。相比传统的理论阐释和词句分析,本书的讲解部分更注重口译实操和课堂活动。课后作业的设计丰富多样,包括传话、复述、主旨口译、数字口译、公共演讲、模拟会议等,还提供了学生转写录音的注意事项、撰写口译日志的模板等。

第四,以夯实语言基本功和培养口译技能为主,将专题知识融入其中。许多口译教材以不同领域来划分章节,例如旅游、教育、妇女儿童、人口与家庭、经贸、科技、环境、外交、医药、文化等,涵盖社会发展的方方面面。这类材料有助于扩大学生的阅读面和词汇量,提高综合运用英语的能力,但是对于口译初学者来说往往较难内化。在实操的过程中,许多学生受制于专题知识和词汇量的不足,容易在字词层面卡壳,不能做到"听意不听词",难以通过阐释、转换、省略等灵活的表达方式来传达主旨、实现交际意图。因此,本书以口译技能为主线,将领域知识融入不同的篇章练习中。

第五,结合一线译员的工作经验,紧跟时代和技术的发展。编者具有丰富的口译教学和会议口译经历,能够提供一手的实战经验。本书也涉及远程会议和人工智能时代口译行业的发展,以适应不断变化的新形势和新问题。例如,在线口译课程需要什么样的设备、系统和软件,线上线下混合教学如何开展,在线模拟会议如何筹备。当代译者应该顺应时代、克服困难、善用技术,而不是抗拒变化。不管是远程会议、语音识别,还是在线语料库,都可以成为译前准备和临场应对的利器。

虽然本书的定位是入门教材,但对于学有余力的同学,它也提供了足够的拓展训练资源。例如,有的篇章是演讲的节选,但书中提供了原始视频、音频或文稿的题目,同学们可以自行完成全篇的练习。有的篇章改编自多个素材,而我们也提供了背景说明,不管是作为译前准备还是译后的延伸阅读都很合适。每个专题选用若干篇英译汉和汉译英实践材料,大部分英文素材来自原始的音频和文字素材,大部分中文素材整合了多篇公开发表的材料,以保证语言的地道性。选材尽量覆盖不同专题领域,旨在为学生提供更多有关该专题的知识、信息、词语和表达方式。使用本教材时,教师也可以自行检索相关主题,节选部分片段作为阅读材料,这样可以把听、说、读、译有机地结合起来,既训练学生的口头表达能力、口译实践能力,又帮助他们增加知识储备、扩大词汇量,并提高英语综合运用能力。

三、本书的结构

本书分为十五章。前两章为口译准备,明确口译学习的目的、流程和要点;第三至第七章为无笔记训练,分项突破听辨、记忆和逻辑分析三大技能,这也是口译入门阶段最重要的环节;第八至第十章为口译笔记,主要分为笔记法和数字口译两大专项;第十一章至第十五章为非语言技能,包括公共演讲、跨文化意识、临场应变、模拟会议的组织,以及技术在口译实战中的运用。章节架构的思路基本按照口译教学的逻辑和教学周的进度,每一章都涵盖了英汉和汉英两个翻译方向,师生可以根据不同的课型自由选择和组合。

本书集口译理论、技巧、实践与评估为一体,每一章的内部可分为主题技能讲解、专项练习、段落练习和篇章练习。学生使用时可以先通读相关的口译理论和技巧讲解,对主题章节的教学意图和重难点形成大致的了解。讲解部分并非纯理论介绍,大部分章节也包含了翻译任务的实例,指出教学过程中常见的困难和错误,提供教师评价与分析,帮助同学们对什么是好的译法形成直观的印象。接着,学生通过书中专项练习和段落练习集中强化相关的技能,根据每次的技能目标有的放矢,提高训练效率。最后,每个章节都配有英译汉和汉译英的语料,淡化单个技能,落实到篇章训练,注重口译任务的综合性和评价的整体性,包括语言能力、心理素质、交流技巧和灵活机动的能力等。篇章练习包含了主题介绍、背景信息和重要词汇表,避免学生"打无准备之仗",也符合实战口译时的译前准备流程。有的练习虽然没有提供主题介绍,但音频的开篇不需要翻译,只是作为进入主题的过渡与译者的心理准备阶段,而学生在听到提示音后才开始翻译。完成口译训练后,学生可以在复盘时重新回顾理论讲解部分,分析本次训练的得失和未来改进的对策,从而在认知上实现螺旋式上升。

本书除了参考答案,还特设附录部分,包含了口译反思日志的模板及说明、学生口译日志实例等,可以配合课堂练习和课后作业使用。这些辅助材料适用于大部分院校的口译课程,不管是何种翻译方向、翻译主题和进阶程度的课型都可使用。总而言之,口译的提高不在一朝一夕,不可能通过每周课堂的两课时来实现。编者希望大家能够掌握书中介绍的学习方法,通过大量课后练习来内化和夯实这些技能,并有机会在课外实践和未来职业中利用这项专长服务社会、服务于国际传播的伟大事业。

本书的编写受到北京外国语大学"中青年卓越人才支持计划"和一般规划教材项目（2022JCB01）的资助。感谢编辑和王红婴女士的辛勤付出,感谢北京外国语大学的刘畅、向贵凡、章瓦尔、欧阳婉玥等同学提供素材。

目　录

第一章　开始之前的几个问题　/ 1

第一节　初识口译　/ 1
第二节　我的英语不太好,能学习口译吗?　/ 2
第三节　英汉口译和汉英口译哪个更难?　/ 2
第四节　课下我该如何安排自主学习?　/ 4

专项练习　/ 8

第二章　学会沟通　/ 12

第一节　口译员的角色　/ 12
第二节　联络口译的要点　/ 13
第三节　口译中的沟通技巧　/ 13

专项练习　/ 15

第三章　学会听辨(Ⅰ)　/ 24

第一节　听力练习与口译听辨　/ 24
第二节　从语音听辨到语流听辨　/ 25
第三节　口译听辨的练习方法　/ 26

专项练习　/ 28
篇章练习　/ 31

第四章　学会听辨(Ⅱ)　/ 35

第一节　听辨的难点　/ 35
第二节　听辨的方法　/ 39

专项练习　/ 44
篇章练习　/ 46

第五章　学会记忆（I） / 50

第一节　听懂了却记不住？ / 50
第二节　"小组传话"练习 / 53

专项练习 / 54
篇章练习 / 57

第六章　学会记忆（II） / 61

第一节　短期记忆与长期记忆 / 61
第二节　记忆强化的训练方法 / 63

专项练习 / 66
篇章练习 / 70

第七章　逻辑分析 / 74

第一节　逻辑与记忆 / 74
第二节　口译中的逻辑分析 / 75

专项练习 / 80
篇章练习 / 85

第八章　口译笔记（I） / 89

第一节　"脑记"与"笔记" / 89
第二节　口译笔记与精力分配 / 94

专项练习 / 95
篇章练习 / 98

第九章　口译笔记（II） / 105

第一节　口译笔记的特点 / 105
第二节　口译笔记的形式与内容 / 110

专项练习 / 114
篇章练习 / 116

第十章　数字口译　/ 122

第一节　数字口译的特征与类型　/ 122
第二节　数字口译的训练方法　/ 124
第三节　积累核心概念词　/ 125

专项练习　/ 127

篇章练习　/ 131

第十一章　公共演说　/ 136

第一节　口译与公共演说的共性与区别　/ 136
第二节　声音与仪态　/ 137
第三节　心理素质　/ 139

专项练习　/ 141

篇章练习　/ 143

第十二章　跨文化意识　/ 151

第一节　口音与听辨　/ 151
第二节　习语、俚语、谚语的处理　/ 153
第三节　文化专有项　/ 155
第四节　习俗与禁忌　/ 158

专项练习　/ 159

篇章练习　/ 162

第十三章　临场应对　/ 168

第一节　材料问题　/ 168
第二节　讲者问题　/ 170
第三节　译者问题　/ 172
第四节　现场环境问题　/ 175

专项练习　/ 176

篇章练习　/ 178

第十四章　模拟会议　/ 182

　　第一节　模拟会议的组织形式　/ 182
　　第二节　会前准备　/ 183
　　第三节　课堂模拟　/ 184
　　第四节　会后反思　/ 185

专项练习　/ 186

第十五章　技术驱动下的口译学习与口译行业　/ 191

　　第一节　借助语料库的译前准备　/ 191
　　第二节　远程口译　/ 192
　　第三节　语音识别、人工智能与口译行业　/ 195

专项练习　/ 197

参考答案　/ 198

附录　/ 269

　　附录1：口译反思日志模板及说明　/ 269
　　附录2：学生口译日志实例　/ 271

第一章

开始之前的几个问题

第一节 初识口译

1953年，国际会议口译员协会（International Association of Conference Interpreters，简称AIIC）成立后，口译员的社会地位和职业规范进一步确立。受到一些影视剧的影响，有的同学觉得口译员的工作非常光鲜，是一个"金饭碗"。在许多人的印象中，口译员就是"翻译官"，要么坐在"格子间"（booth）里，要么坐在要员身边，从事一些高端会议的交传和同传。由于这类工作要求高、压力大，因此许多人觉得口译的门槛太高，学习时有畏难情绪。但实际上，口译分为很多种类，包括非正式会议场合的交替口译，以及陪同口译、社区口译等形式，学生译员（interpreting trainees）经过一定的训练也能够胜任。

不少行业外的人士觉得口译非常神秘，需要学会速记，或是痴迷于令人赞叹的"天书"笔记。但其实口译笔记和速记在形式、内容和风格上完全不同。而且译员不能依赖笔记，更加需要基于理解，加强脑记，即短期记忆（short-term memory，STM）。有些客观条件下，做笔记还很不方便，例如站立时、陪同行进过程中，或是遇到突发任务来不及准备纸笔时。

还有一些同学认为译员的素质是天生的（Interpreters are born, not taught），而自己不擅长于此。不可否认，一些人在这方面具备天赋，例如短期记忆好、反应敏捷、心理素质佳等，但是对于普通人来说，各类口译技能和外语水平一样，也可以通过训练习得和精进。例如，数字口译对于很多初学者来说都是一道坎儿，他们往往需要踟蹰良久才能小心翼翼憋出一个数字，经常还是错的。但实际上这种转换和排列组合万变不离其宗，译者熟练之后便能脱口而出，从而在听记时把更多的注意力放在数字背后的信息上。

初识口译，我们可能会有诸多不解和误解，但如果我们走近它、了解它，就会发现这项技能并非遥不可及。不管是协助外国游客出行、游览和购物，还是参与国际赛事的志愿者活动，抑或是在各类正式场合承担会议口译，译员都在帮助不同国家和地区的人们实现跨语言、跨文化的交际。因此，口译也常常引发有关"桥梁"（bridge）和"旅行"（travel）的隐喻。

不管你是因为对口译职业心怀向往，还是由于专业培养方案的要求必须修读这门课，心中可能都怀着以下一系列问题：我能学好口译吗？英汉和汉英交替互译时，我应该注意哪些事项？除了教材，我应该选择什么样的材料来练习？我该如何在课下自学、巩固和提高呢？那么现在，就让我们解答这几个问题，开启这场语言、思维和文化激荡的旅行吧。

第二节　我的英语不太好，能学习口译吗？

对于口译来说，"语言能力是首要条件。培养语言能力是口译教学的首要工作"（杨承淑，2005：5）。所有的口译学习者都懂双语，但是其母语和外语的熟练程度各不相同。有的同学语言基础比较薄弱，遇到的挑战就会更大。如果口译的音频难度超越了学生的听力水平，也就是说即便用该音频来做听力理解也有困难，那么译出率就会很低，甚至完全偏离主旨。因此，在一些院校口译课不是必修课，而是有先修要求（prerequisites），例如英语听力达到85分以上、英语口语达到85分以上等，这样的设置也是合理的。不过，即使你的外语能力不够突出，也不一定要将口译拒之门外。事实上，口译学习和英语语言基本功的培养是相辅相成的。口译学习者在平时的练习中不能只练口译，而应该把听、说、读、写、译等语言能力的训练有机地结合起来，在输入和输出的循环往复中提高双语素养。

反过来，如果一个人的双语能力都不错，是不是就"自带"了口译技能，或者学习起来就更省力呢？对于口译学习者而言，语言能力强的确是一项优势，但这并不意味着口译技能也强，就算是出生于跨国家庭的双母语者也不一定能胜任口译。译员还需要具备许多非语言技能，例如良好的记忆力、高效的笔记体系、丰富的背景知识、处变不惊的心理素质等。有些时候，双母语背景甚至还有可能是负面因素。我们在课上曾接触过一些华裔学生，他们的英语和汉语都非常流利，但是在双语转换时仍然面临种种困难，例如译词不达意、表达生硬等。有同学在译后反思中写道："我的中英文听说都没有问题，但是翻译的时候总是别扭。也许是因为平时我都直接用英文或中文来表达一个意思，还不习惯意义的提取和转换。"理解意义（understanding sense）—脱离语言外壳（de-verbalization）—转向到另一种语言表述（reformulation/restoration）是一项不断转换的能力，对于口译来说至关重要，这是可以习得的，而且必须通过针对性的训练才能精进。

第三节　英汉口译和汉英口译哪个更难？

如果教师在班里做一项课前小调查"英译汉难还是汉译英难"，绝大部分同学都会认为汉译英的难度远远高于英译汉。但是，如果将问题进一步细化为"英汉口译难还是汉英口译难"，那么同学们的意见可能会出现分歧。在系统学习之前，你对于这个问题是怎么看的呢？不妨在表1-1中列出两种翻译方向的难点。

表1-1　英汉口译和汉英口译的难点

英汉口译的难点	汉英口译的难点
难点1：	难点1：
难点2：	难点2：

续　表

英汉口译的难点	汉英口译的难点
难点3：	难点3：
难点4：	难点4：
……	……

部分学生觉得汉英口译难度更高，因为英文表达不如说母语流畅，要地道就更难了。另一些同学则认为英汉口译难度更高，因为汉译英时至少能听懂原文的内容，不管译语的质量如何总能想办法表达出来；但英译汉的时候常常听不懂原文，甚至连主旨大意也把握不住，要么模糊处理或省略，要么编译（fabrication），甚至干脆放弃了整个翻译任务。

那么，究竟哪一个更难呢？实际上，两种感受都符合实情。有学生在反思日志中这样写道："英汉口译的目的语是中文，所以如果对源语主题很了解就会如鱼得水；反之如果正好碰到不熟悉的领域，可能就会误译、漏译。汉英口译中一般不会有原文理解的问题，翻译出来也不难，但难在译好、译准。相对而言，汉英口译难易程度的不确定性要小一点。"

如果一项工作需要耗费更多的认知努力，就可以被视作"难度较高"，而口译这样复杂的工作会涉及不同的步骤，例如听力理解、逻辑处理、意义转换、脑记、笔记、口头表达等，各个部分的难度不同，因此合理分配有限的精力至关重要。目前有一些实证研究探索笔译中翻译方向和精力分配的关系，其结果显示"与译入方向相比，学生译者在译出方向的总体注意分配及投入译文产出活动的注意分配均显著更多"（冯佳、王克非，2021：102），这似乎意味着译出难于译入。但是，口译终究不同于笔译：原文转瞬即逝，也无法借助资料或反复思考。在英译汉中，第一遍如果没有听懂原文便没有第二次机会了，纵使译入语是母语也会陷入"无话可说"的僵局。如果听力不过关，理解便构成了英汉口译最大的障碍。

反过来，在汉英口译中，听懂原文的难度相对较低，精力主要分配在信息的逻辑处理与英语的表达方面。在理解的准确性和笔记的完整性相同的情况下，两份译语的质量也可能由于表达的差异而大相径庭，包括基本的语法、用词、句式、流畅度、语言风格的得体程度等，这些就受制于译者的外语水平。总结来说，汉英口译要译出来也许不难，但是要译好不易。正因如此，联合国教科文组织的《内罗毕建议书》（*Recommendation on the Legal Protection of Translators and Translations and the Practical Means to Improve the Status of Translators*）（UNESCO, 1976）曾提出译员应尽量译入母语或与母语相当的语言。其他一些国际组织提出的行业规范也与之类似，包括国际译联的《翻译工作者宪章》（*The Translator's Charter*）、英国翻译协会的《译员职业道德准则手册》（*The Code of Professional Ethics of the Translator's Guide of Great Britain*）等。

每则音频的口译体验与译者个体的语言能力和非语言能力都有关系，在口译学习的各个阶段也有不同的表现形式。在英汉口译方面，初学者和英语基础不够扎实的同学不妨把训练重点放在"听懂"上，即时复述检测听的成果，不断提高英语水平，先不必急于学习记忆、笔记法等口译技巧。而在汉英口译方面，"听懂"的门槛就要低很多，一开始可以多关注译文的完整性、逻辑性和准确性，再训练反应速度、词汇量和句式组织，提高译语的流畅度和地道程度。

第四节　课下我该如何安排自主学习？

口译学习依靠课堂时间是远远不够的，入门阶段该如何在课下自主提高口译能力呢？首先我们可以初步了解译前、译中和译后三个环节及其注意事项。

一、译前：材料的选择

各类教材和翻译资格证考试的教辅为我们的口译练习提供了很好的素材。它们都经过精心筛选和编辑，以适应不同层次学习者的要求。如果你不满足于一两本教材的内容，希望探索如何自主练习，就已经迈出了重要的一步。

海量的网络资源该如何筛选才能提高训练的效率？口译材料讲求循序渐进，并且要符合现阶段的语言和技术水平。初学者可以使用普通听力训练的材料。一般听力考试中的题型大多是单选题、填空题，少数为多选题、连线题。题干和选项基本为学生搭建了语篇框架，即使没有完全听懂内容，靠抓取关键词甚至是猜测也可能做对。但是口译时没有任何现成的框架可依，需要自己梳理信息的逻辑，所以即使是听力考试能得满分的材料，用于口译也不简单。例如，雅思听力考试的第四部分就非常适合我们在入门阶段自主练习。它一般是模拟演讲的开头部分，主题大多为教育、科普、商业类，有一定的专业性，但是没有太多术语，即使有，讲者也会进行解释。音频语速适中、逻辑清晰，中间只有一处很短的暂停，整段只播放一遍，考验学生在学术场景下的理解力以及快速提取关键信息的能力，这些特点都符合口译实战的场景。

许多慢速英语的音频也是很好的口译入门材料。初学者可以使用语速为80—110词/分钟的音频，VOA慢速英语的语速约为95词/分钟，恰好在这个区间。这类广播的主题范围比较广，也能扩大同学们的知识面，例如美国之音的慢速英语（VOA Special English）有健康报道（Health report）、教育报道（Education report）、科技报道（Science report）、经济报道（Economic report）等栏目；英国广播电台的BBC Learning English、环球慢速英语等。VOA常速英语的语速为130—160词/分钟，BBC常速为150—180词/分钟，语速偏快，适合中级以上的学习者。

此外，欧盟口译司的语料库Speech Repository也是很好的素材库（见图1-1）。如果网站无法登录，也可以在其他搜索引擎直接键入"Speech Repository"，就能在各大视频网站找到相关的视频和专辑。该语料库中的演讲、访谈和会议发言按照不同的语种、主题和难度分类，对于初学者很友好，也能循序渐进。

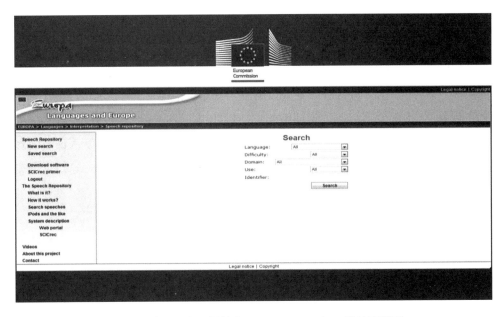

图 1-1　欧盟口译司语料库 Speech Repository 的检索界面

汉英口译的选材标准也是如此，速度宜慢不宜快，题材广泛但不必太专业化。如果没有现成的音频资料，我们也可以请家人、朋友以合适的速度朗读杂志中的文段。如果手头的音频内容不错，但语速偏快，也可以使用音频软件调整速度。例如 Audacity 软件的免费版就可以实现这些简单的编辑功能（见图 1-2），更多操作说明见软件官方网站。

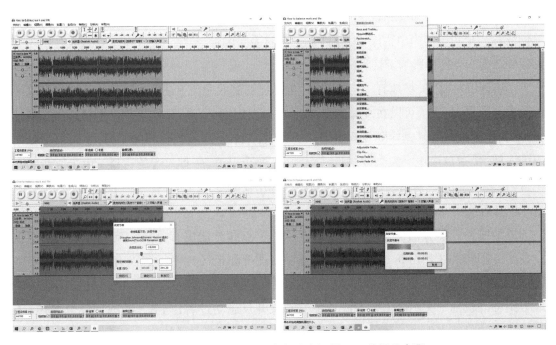

图 1-2　用 Audacity 3.3 将音频速度调慢 10% 的操作步骤

需要指出的是，新闻类音频信息密度高，一句话里面往往就包含了时间、地点、人物、事件等多种要素，对于口译初学者来说难度较大。而多人采访、论辩和讨论的音频由于话轮转换太频繁，也不太适合自学。因此，初学者不妨选择演讲、讲课等单人叙述的音频。

随着口译学习的进阶，材料也需要升级难度。慢速英语即便调整速度后，由于句式和用词都比较简单，其难度也未必能达到训练要求。例如，前述Speech Repository语料库的材料基本都是由专人朗读的教学视频，现场感和实战性比较弱。这时候就需要选择真实场景下的常速演讲，其难点往往不是语速，而在于用词考究、句式多样、专业性高，给口译员带来更大的挑战。我们可以在搜索引擎中键入某个国际会议的名称，选择视频标签，就可以获得大量的会议影音资料。

二、译中：训练的形式与方法

课下的口译训练可以独立完成，也可以通过组成三到五人的小组完成。自主练习时需要自行将音频暂停，在原文说完两三句完整的意思时停顿并开始翻译，不用非得像教材那样在时长非常合适的地方截断。如果是多人的对话，一人说完后就可以暂停并开始口译，即便这一段非常短，也不必拘泥于时长。

一个人练习时间自由，但是也有一些不利因素。首先，练习的材料无法预判，往往拿到就练，其难易程度和背景信息无从知晓；如果自己先听一遍、看一遍，又失去了口译的即时性。其次，放音和暂停会占据一部分精力，而交替口译本身已经涉及了听辨、记忆、笔记、口述等一系列复杂的程序。根据工作记忆容量理论（Baddeley, 2006），人脑对信息加工和储存的记忆系统的容量是有限的，当处理高难度任务的时候，大量信息会占据一部分认知资源，而用于信息加工的认知资源就很有限了。这样的话，要么暂停的地方不太合理，比如在一个单词或者一个句子的当中暂停了，处理下一段时需要倒带，影响训练效率；要么就是因为受到额外任务的干扰而影响了信息的加工处理。

小组训练对时间、场地有一定的要求，但是能够有效避免上述两大问题。为了提高练习的效率和质量，每个人可以在平时独立训练时注意搜集和甄选，每次贡献一则精选出来的材料，负责朗读或放音。这样既发挥了团队的力量，减轻一个人找材料的压力，也可以加强内容的多样性，避免由于个人兴趣总听一个领域、一个渠道、一种口音的材料。由于放音的同学自己已经训练过这份材料，对其重点和难点都比较清楚，进行同伴点评（peer evaluation）时也可以更有建设性，避免泛泛而谈。

由于两种翻译方向的难点不同，其训练的重点和方法也有差异。英汉口译的训练重点在听力理解和逻辑分析（逻辑分析也是帮助理解和记忆），第一遍没有完全听懂也要坚持译出主旨或部分信息，之后可以通过复听两三遍原文来补充和矫正，如若还有不明白的地方则可以求助于文本。但是在吃透原文意义并反思功过后，与其再花时间反复口述，不如多听新的材料来加强英语的输入，提高听力理解。汉英口译的难点主要在表达阶段，因此即使看过原文，甚至是看过参考译文，仍可以反复训练，不断提高英语译文的流利性和准确度。

三、译后：反思与评价

许多同学在听译完一篇材料后会如释重负，巴不得立刻把刚才听到的、说过的内容都抛在脑后，殊不知复盘是抠细节、内化知识点、巩固口译技巧的重要步骤。不愿意反思不只因为这是一项额外的任务，更多时候是因为学生觉得自己的译文"不忍卒听"，笔记"不忍卒读"，不想面对不完美。在这方面大家不必背着包袱，即使是优秀的职业译员也会犯或大或小的错误，译语质量理论上可以不断提高。

根据美国明德大学蒙特雷国际研究院（Middlebury Institute of International Studies at Monterey）白瑞兰（Laura Burian）教授的建议，我们可以填写下面这份口译训练反思表（见表1-2）。

表1-2 口译训练反思表模板

Source text	What I said	I should have said	Diagnosis/Cure
Segmented source text	Including slips of tongue, fillers, pauses, etc.	Reference version	Point out the mistakes, analyze the reasons for the errors and come up with coping methods

反思的目的一方面是搞清楚原文的意义、逻辑和具体表述（见表1-2的第一栏"Source text"），摸索更好的译法（见第三栏"I should have said"）；另一方面是发现自己译语的问题，找出原因并总结今后遇到类似情况时的应对策略（见第四栏"Diagnosis/Cure"）。况且，有的问题是我们在口译时没有觉察到的，因为自我监听（self-monitoring）给译员额外增加了一项任务，在工作记忆容量有限的情况下，有的译者会自动关闭监听机制，导致自己无法察觉到口误、口头禅等问题。

转写译文是复盘工作的重点和基础，即第二栏"What I said"。转写时需要如实记录下自己的口误、重复、填充词（如"嗯""啊""这个""那个"等）、长时间的停顿（可以用省略号标注）等问题，不要"美化"和"简化"自己的译语。现在有一些语音识别的软件和网站能够快速完成转写（例如讯飞听见、迅捷文字语音转换器），但人工校订这一工序绝不能少。一方面这固然是因为现有技术的精度尚有提升的空间，但更重要的是，转写的目的并不是为了获得一份文字稿（如会议纪要），而是为了发现自己译语中形形色色的问题。语音识别技术可以高效地做出一份初稿，但只有亲自转写或校订才能切身体会到那些明显的语法错误、别扭的句式与用词、尴尬的停顿与重复。

译后复盘的另一项工作是评价，包括自我评价和同伴评价。评价不是打一个分，也不是泛泛地说一句"很好""不够好"，而需要在表格第四栏中列出每个语段中遇到的挑战和发生的问题，需要具体情况具体分析。同学们可以从不同方面检视译语的优势与不足，例如信息是否完整，逻辑是否清楚，语法和用词是否准确，语流是否顺畅等，从而订立下一阶段的训练目标。本书附录中的学生反思表范例可以给大家提供参考。可以说，评价的过程是对一次口译训练的总结与升华，以第三方的视角与心态分析得失，这样才能将训练效果最大化。

总而言之，口译学习与实操都需要语言准备、技能准备、心理准备和技术准备。除了上述基本的流程，实际工作场景中还包括关于具体任务的译前准备，比如行业术语与知识、会议背景信息、相关的人名和机构名称等，这些会在第十四单元"模拟会议"里重点介绍。现在我们已经对口译的译前、译中和译后三个环节心中有数，可以开始攻克信息输入中的第一个难关：听辨与理解。

参考文献

Baddeley A. Working Memory: An Overview[M]//Pickering S. Working Memory and Education. New York: Academic Press, 2006: 1-31.

冯佳，王克非. 翻译方向和文本难度对注意分配的影响——基于英/汉翻译的实证证据[J]. 中国外语，2021，18(4): 97-104.

杨承淑. 口译教学研究：理论与实践[M]. 北京：中国对外翻译出版公司，2005.

专项练习

1. 听译与转写

要求：听下面的四个语段，口译并录音，可以做笔记也可以不做。完成后复听自己的录音，并根据模板转写。

英汉段落 1: Health benefits of dance

Dancing is something that humans do when they want to have a good time. It's a universal response to music, found in all cultures. But what's only been discovered recently is that dancing not only makes us feel good, it's also extremely good for our health.

Dancing, like other forms of exercise, releases hormones, such as dopamine, which makes us feel relaxed and happy. And it also reduces feelings of stress or anxiety.

Dancing is also a sociable activity, which is another reason it makes us feel good. One study compared people's enjoyment of dancing at home in front of a video with dancing in a group in a studio. The people dancing in a group reported feeling happier, whereas those dancing alone did not.

英汉段落 2: Climate change

The evidence is everywhere, burning forests in Argentina, massive floods in Bangladesh, drought in Spain. The impacts of climate change are here, and they're getting worse. And according to a landmark United Nations report, not only are some of these impacts worse than previously known; some may already be irreversible. Today's IPCC report is an atlas of human suffering and a damning indictment of failed climate leadership. With fact upon fact, this report reveals how people and the planet are getting clobbered by climate change. The report conducted by a UN panel of more than 200 scientists from over 60 countries emphasized that our warming of the planet is unleashing damages at a pace and intensity that many nations won't be able to handle, and that reducing the pollution that's driving climate change isn't happening nearly fast enough.

英汉段落 3: Hot drinks and cancer

Next time you make yourself a hot cup of tea or coffee, you might want to let it cool down a bit before drinking. Researchers say letting your hot drinks cool off could help you avoid some kinds of cancer.

In fact, the United Nations' cancer research agency decided to list hot drinks with lead, gasoline and exhaust fumes as "possibly carcinogenic". In other words, each one could cause cancer.

Researchers at IARC found evidence that drinks at temperatures above 65 degrees Celsius, when swallowed, can cause cancer of the esophagus. The researchers examined findings from other studies where tea and coffee were often served at 70 degrees Celsius or above. Those studies were completed in Iran, China and South America.

The findings, however, are good news for coffee drinkers. In 1991, the World Health Organization listed coffee as "possibly carcinogenic". WHO officials have since changed their position on that listing. They now suggest that the temperature of your hot drink is a greater risk factor than the actual drink itself.

汉英段落 1: 骑自行车的好处

骑自行车是一项非常好的活动,在锻炼身体的同时也可以带来无尽的乐趣。首先,骑自行车有助于燃烧脂肪,促进排汗,是非常好的有氧运动。这项运动的一个优点是可以锻炼全身的肌肉,包括腿部、背部和肩部。第二,骑车也可以对心情产生积极影响,因为沿途可以欣赏不断变化的风景,有助于减压。压力是许多疾病的诱因,有可能会导致焦虑、抑郁、糖尿病、高血压、消化问题、心血管疾病等。此外,骑自行车也有利于改善大脑功能,骑手需要保持专注,这对大脑也是一种锻炼。

汉英段落2:人工智能

只要提供正确的数据,机器将完全超越人类。一位老师在40年的职业生涯中可能审阅一万篇作文,一名眼科医生大概可以检查5万只眼睛。但在短短几分钟之内,机器就可以审阅百万篇文章或检查数百万只眼睛。对于频繁、大批量的任务,我们无法与机器抗衡。

但有些事情机器却无能为力。它们在解决新情况方面进展甚微。它们还不能处理未曾反复接触过的事情。机器学习致命的局限性在于,它需要从大量已知的数据中总结经验,人类则不然。我们有一种能力,可以把看似毫不相关的事物联系起来,从而解决从未见过的问题。

汉英段落3:高等教育与流动性

在当今中国社会,接受高等教育是社会个体进入更高社会阶层的基本条件。尤其是进入信息时代以后,知识因素成为决定个体发展的主要因素,而学识的多寡与接受教育的程度密不可分。接受过高等教育的人,就有更多的机会实现自我的价值和能力,从而实现"阶级跨越"。处于较低阶层的个体可以在平等的选拔体制中,通过自己的努力提升其社会地位、经济地位、政治地位。因此在中国社会,人们对优质的教育资源十分向往。

2. 译后反思

要求:回顾自己的口译过程,总结六个段落的难点。

英汉段落1	英汉段落2	英汉段落3
难点1:	难点1:	难点1:
难点2:	难点2:	难点2:
难点3:	难点3:	难点3:
难点4:	难点4:	难点4:
……	……	……

续 表

汉英段落1	汉英段落2	汉英段落3
难点1：	难点1：	难点1：
难点2：	难点2：	难点2：
难点3：	难点3：	难点3：
难点4：	难点4：	难点4：
……	……	……

3. 音频编辑技术练习

要求：利用Audacity 3.3练习以下音频编辑的操作：添加单音、剪切、合并、降噪、调快速度、调慢速度。也可以使用Audacity的其他版本或其他音频视频编辑软件进行同样的操作。

第二章
学会沟通

第一节 口译员的角色

口译的目的是促进沟通,其本质是人际交往,只不过恰好双方说两种不同的语言,需要译员从中协调。译者如果听到什么全都照直译出,交际效果未必理想,甚至有可能造成误解。我们不妨先来进行一场头脑风暴。

> 活动 2-1:
> 你觉得在不同的情境下,口译员应该扮演何种角色呢?

大多数同学最先想到的角色可能就是"桥梁",这的确是关于翻译最常见的隐喻。但是,译员的作用恐怕不仅仅是充当"桥梁",否则就将其单一化和简单化了。译者的介入在联络口译(liaison interpreting,也叫"陪同口译")、社区口译(community interpreting)等场景下尤为突出。他们往往还需要扮演助理、讲解员、调解员、谈判专家等多重角色。有的同学在毕业后从事外事和翻译工作,发现职责范围远远超出了口、笔译,还包括前期联络、会务安排、文书函件等各种事宜,因此笑称自己是"打杂"的。从这种意义上来讲,说译员需要什么都懂一点(know something about everything)并不为过。

例如,许多国际课程和培训项目的师生来自不同的国家,全程都需要口译员来从中协调(interpreting for workshop and training)。译者不仅需要熟悉讲稿和幻灯片的内容,即时翻译授课内容,常常还需要解释课程的重难点、维持课堂纪律、安排小组讨论、回收问卷与作业、协助培训师答疑等。译者相当于担任了"助教"和"课代表",实实在在参与了课程内容的建构。还有一个例子来自北京外国语大学的多语言服务中心。它由北京奥组委国际联络部和北京外国语大学共同成立,于2008年7月24日正式运行。中心的工作人员和志愿者们主要通过电话翻译和视频翻译的方式为各国人士提供语言服务,协助解决交通、医疗、警务、生活等方面的沟通问题。在此过程中,他们除了将求助者的话翻译成中文告知相关机构,还会回应求助者的请求,表示关切,进行安抚。

业界和学界对译者角色的认知不断变化,它从"传声筒/管道"(conduit)转变为跨文化交际的促进者和构建者(Angelelli, 2004: 141)。口译员不是完全中立和透明的,他们有必要在跨语际交流遇到障碍时及时介入,提供必要的补充信息和背景知识;或是在双方矛盾升级、谈判无法继续时缓和气氛,化解分歧,甚至增进友谊;还有的口译员因受雇于一方,需要在谈判中站稳立场为己方争取利益,其工作内容远远超出了跨语际转换本身。

第二节 联络口译的要点

初级口译最常见的实践形式是联络口译(liaison interpreting),有时又被称为"短交传"。相较于会议口译中的交替传译,联络口译的每个对话轮持续时间短,内容呈现双向交互性。这种形式常见于旅游、接待、实地考察、交易会等情景中。

联络口译可能为单向口译或双向口译,但考虑到经济成本和口译难度,双向口译相对更常见。例如,外国人来华旅游时通常只会雇佣一名联络口译,作为自己和当地人之间的"传话筒"。译者须同时进行中译英和英译中的双向口译。单向的联络口译最常见于商务洽谈,每名讲话人各自配备一名译员,译员只需单向实现源语到译入语的转换即可。

很多译员初出茅庐时都是从简单的联络口译开始的。尽管它比正式的会议口译难度低,但仍需具备相关常识,特别要注意以下几个方面:

1. 增强记忆力,适应无笔记

联络口译经常用于机场、酒店、宴会等场合,译员经常是在站立甚至是走动中翻译。双方谈话的形式也要求译员在短时间内做出反应,来不及做笔记,所以很多情况下译员必须依靠自己的记忆力进行无笔记交传。

2. 选择合适人称

口译者需要站在发言者的角度口译,使用第一人称,例如"我""我方""我们"等,而非"他"或"他们"。这是初期译员的典型错误之一。

3. 忠实传递讲话者情绪

双方对话中,尤其是在商务会谈等磋商性场合,很多情况下会出现表达情绪的语气词。此时译员需要仔细揣摩讲话者的情绪和意图,原则上应忠实地翻译出讲者情绪,但不必拘泥于原话形式。在特殊场合(如重大冲突)下,译员可能还需充当"调解者"角色,具体会根据实际情景随机应变。

4. 重视礼仪规范

联络口译中译员总是面对面地和外宾接触,其言行举止直接代表了国家形象。礼仪规范主要涵盖三个方面的内容:译员服装、姿态和表情管理,外宾国家文化习俗及禁忌,特殊场合的行为规范(如宴会、使领馆招待会等)。

第三节 口译中的沟通技巧

刘敏华(1993:19)指出:"(口译)教师要时时'忘了'自己曾经读过原文,要在心态上时时'假装'自己听不懂原文,准备好一副'新鲜'的耳朵,听学生是不是把讯息给传达出来了,而不是'检查'他们是不是把原演讲的每个字都译出来了"。因此,在入门阶段最忌讳对着原文或者参考译文来挑刺。

第一，口译注重达旨，而非拘泥于字词。尤其是联络口译，并不一定要把原话逐字翻译出来，在词汇量不足时要善于把握讲者的主要意图来"换言之"，以实现交际目的。例如，有教师在课堂上使用过一篇"妇女儿童"主题的材料，其中有一句是："有的夫妻还有可能在结婚之前就对他们的各自财产进行了公证。"这里面"公证"（notarize）一词对于很多学生来说是生词，如果没有提前准备到，现场容易卡壳。有同学尽力解释成"legally make clear their own respective properties"，尽管不够确切，但至少传达了基本的意思，值得认可。

这一点对于口译评价也具有重要的意义。准备口译素材的人，不管是教师还是朋辈，最好都不要充当语言权威，而要扮演一名知晓双语、略知背景的普通观众，以便设身处地地给译员提供帮助与建议。教师最重要的工作是教方法，而不是纯语言教学的讲词汇、讲语法。如果学生某一处没有听懂选择了中途放弃，点评时不必直接提供所谓的"参考译文"；不妨站在译员的角度，同样在"一知半解"的情况下为其出谋划策，如采用省略、模糊处理、合理猜测等技巧。

第二，沟通除了使用语言符号（verbal signs），还可以借助眼神、手势、现场环境等传达意图。即使完全不使用语言，也有可能依靠非语言符号来实现交际目的。让我们来模拟如下的场景。

> **活动2-2：**
> 假设你目前身处国外却不懂该国语言，步入一家咖啡馆想要一杯热水，你会如何做呢？

这个场景其实许多出国旅行的游客都遇到过。即使游客本人懂英语，所在地也可能并非英语国家，交际对象不一定能用英语对谈。有一位老奶奶便步入咖啡馆，对着店员抱紧双臂做出瑟瑟发抖的样子，然后单手做举杯状，放到嘴边发出"咕嘟咕嘟"的喝水声。店员立刻就明白了老人的意思，给她倒了一杯热水。老奶奶在这里主动扮演了跨文化交际的中介（intercultural agents and active intermediaries）。由此可以看出，肢体语言和现场环境可以为双方提供大量的信息，部分代替语言交流的需求。口译时也是一样，在会议中可以请观众查看幻灯片的特定栏目，在翻译时省略部分复杂的细节；可以引导游客关注指示牌、景点或展品本身的特点，从而略译有关外观、颜色、材质等较难翻译的内容。

第三，口译中可以根据语境和文化需求，酌情删减、增补、阐释和改动，改善沟通效果。除了利用非语言信息来略译和省译，补充说明和阐释也是常见的策略，尤其是在寒暄和开场白这类较为轻松的场合。例如，两个公司之间进行正式的商务洽谈前，一方提到"This is my second visit to ... (company)"，直译为"这是我第二次来到贵公司"。但一些经验丰富的译员则可能补充道："上一次会面是去年八月时来参加ESG的会议。"这是因为译员深知说话人的意图是表明双方的渊源，确立和巩固联系，因此补充了之前会晤的信息来加深印象。

还有一些情况下，照直翻译可能会造成误解或尴尬，需要译者从中微调，优化原文的情感、态度和措辞。让我们来看下面这个例子。

> 活动2-3：
> 两个公司初次洽谈，甲方领导说："I have full confidence in our further cooperation. Actually, our first Asian managing director came from your company."作为翻译你会如何处理？

这句话字面翻译的难度不高，意为"我对我们进一步的合作充满信心。其实我们公司第一位来自亚洲的董事总经理就是从贵公司跳槽来的。"由于是普通寒暄，说话人两句之间并没有特别紧密的联系，只是想表示合作的诚意，以及对对方公司资质的认可。公司之间的人员流动本身是很正常的，但是基于"人往高处走"的原则，说自己公司的员工是从对方公司跳槽过来的略显不妥。此时，有经验的译员会处理为"我们公司第一位来自亚洲的董事总经理就曾经任职于贵公司"，既保全了事实，又优化了表述方式。

当然，译者的上述做法都是基于充分了解双方交际意图的基础之上，不应夹杂个人的情绪和观点、越俎代庖、肆意发挥和演绎，这类编造（fabrication）和根据具体问题酌情处理有着本质的区别。

参考文献

Angelelli C V. Revisiting the Interpreter's Role: A Study of Conference, Court, and Medical Interpreters in Canada, Mexico, and the United States[M]. Amsterdam/Philadelphia: John Benjamins Publishing Company, 2004.

刘敏华. 逐步口译与笔记：理论、实践与教学[M]. 台北：辅仁大学出版社，1993.

专项练习

要求：以3—4人的小组练习以下四则情境对话。每个场景由两人分别扮演中方和外方人士，其余1—2人担任翻译，并在下一个场景轮换。特别注意联络口译中的交际目的与沟通技巧。

1. 商务洽谈

Preview:

Business meeting interpreting is one of the most common topics in liaison interpreting. It is a process between two or more parties (each with its own aims, needs, and viewpoints) that have the objective to discover common ground and reach an agreement to settle a matter of mutual concern, resolve a conflict and exchange value. A complete process of business negotiation usually contains three parts: establishing positions, setting conditions, setting a deal. Interpreting a business negotiation requires adequate preparation of negotiation topics (esp. the company name, technical terms, and specification terms), clear and concise transmission and accurate interpretation of polysemic or rhetorical expressions that might occur to mitigate the negotiation atmosphere. During this process, disagreements may also appear, posing challenges to the crisis handling ability of the interpreters.

Glossary:	
tank top：背心	单品：SKU (stock keeping unit)
hoodie：连帽衫	仓储空间：warehousing space
zip-up top：拉链衫	delivery schedule：交货时间表
经销商：reseller	minimum monthly volume：每月最低交易量
零售商：retailer	即时物流：just-in-time logistics

Text 1: Establishing positions and setting conditions

(P for producer, R for reseller)

P: So let's get started. I've read your proposals, and I understand you're looking for unbranded clothing in a variety of styles.

R: 没错。

P: Meaning T-shirts, tank tops, hoodies, zip-up tops, and long-sleeved tees, right?

R: 对的。

P: Alright. So, my first question is: what kind of volumes are you looking at?

R: 嗯,因为我们是经销商,所以我们重新把它们包装成品牌服饰并出售给零售商。我建议从小额开始,然后逐渐扩大规模。我们希望每件单品先订购500至1 500件,热卖的尺码和颜色多要一些。

P: And that would be per-month, or ...?

R: 我们希望开始的时候能灵活一些。

P: What do you have in mind exactly? I'm not against flexibility, but logistics require a certain amount of forward planning.

R: 那是自然! 有一个问题: 生产和交货情况如何? 您处理订单需要多长时间?

P: It's not completely fixed, but around two weeks. Larger orders can take more time.

R: 没关系。所以现在的状况是这样:我们没有太多的仓储空间,也就意味着无法承诺定期货单。而当库存降到一定程度,匀出空间,我们就需要补货。

P: Hmm ... that's possible. One thing you should know: we won't be able to offer the lowest prices if we can't be sure of your delivery schedule in advance.

R: 我明白。

P: And for every product category, for example short-sleeved T-shirts, how many variations of size and color do you need?

R: 我们需要所有的常见尺寸,从XS(特小)到XXL(特大),每种尺寸16种颜色。如果我们一次订购大约10万件,单件定价最低多少?

P: That depends on whether you can commit to a regular delivery schedule or not. Assuming that you need a flexible schedule, we could offer six dollars per unit for tees and tank tops, and fifteen for hoodies and zip-ups.

R: 如果我们增加订购数量,还能再降价吗?

P: Possibly, but the schedule is more important to us. Supposing you could commit to a minimum monthly volume, we could go down to five-fifty and fourteen.

R: 如果我们承诺六个月的最低订购量,但要求交付时间灵活,能否拿到这个价格?

P: As long as there were some limitations on delivery timing, I think that would be acceptable.

Text 2: Resolving disagreements and setting the deal

R: 咱们来详谈一下关于交付和进度的相关事宜。

P: For us to make this work at the lower price, we'd need to have monthly deliveries, but we could let you adjust the size of the order to some extent, so that you can manage your warehousing space.

R: 我觉得这个方案行不通。因为灵活性对我们而言至关重要,我们的整个模式也正是基于即时物流，所以实在没有办法。

P: Well, in that case, we won't be able to offer you the lower price. I have no problem with flexible deliveries as such, but we can't offer our best prices without a regular commitment on your part.

R: 恕我直言，但这样的想法未免有些目光狭隘，因为我们可能之后每年会有百万量级的订购需求。灵活交付也不意味着我们不会定期下单，只是说需要对时间和数量进行一定的把控。

P: I understand completely, but you need to realize that we have our own logistics issues to deal with. If we don't know exactly when and how big an order will be, that creates costs for us. We're not willing to absorb those costs. I feel that if you need this flexibility, then you should be willing to pay for it. I'm sorry but I have to draw a clear line. It's simply too risky for us to give you what you're asking.

R: 我们似乎陷入了僵局。先休息五分钟好吗？

P: Good idea.

(5 minutes later)

P: Right, I've spoken to a few people and I have a proposal which I hope can achieve a win-win result.

R: 听起来不错。您什么想法？

P: The problem for us is that if you don't maintain a certain monthly volume, we might lose money at lower prices, which obviously we can't do.

R: 当然。

P: So, here's my solution: we have an annual contract with a flexible delivery schedule, but with a minimum volume per-quarter. At the end of the quarter, if you haven't met the volume requirements, you're liable for the difference in price between your orders and the minimum.

R: 基本符合我的想法，但之前我建议签订一份为期六个月的合同，那个方案似乎更好。

P: Well, I want to make this work, but the lower prices only work if we can guarantee orders over a full year. I'll make another offer: you pay five seventy-five for tees and tank tops and fourteen-fifty for hoodies and zip-up tops. Then you can have a six-month contract, with minimum volume per-quarter.

R: 这个方案不错，我需要打电话给团队确认，但我认为应该没问题。

P: Great!

2. 接待和参观

Text 3: Visiting the Temple of Heaven

Preview:

The Temple of Heaven is an Imperial Sacrificial Altar in Beijing. Its overall layout and that of its individual buildings symbolize the relationship between the earth and the heaven — which stands at the heart of Chinese cosmogony, and also the special role played by the emperors within that relationship. The Temple of Heaven is an axial arrangement of Circular Mound Altar to the south open to the sky with the conically roofed Imperial Vault of Heaven immediately to its north. This is linked by a raised sacred way to the circular, three-tiered, conically-roofed Hall of Prayer for Good Harvests further to the north. Here at these places the emperors of the Ming and Qing dynasties offered sacrifices to the heaven and prayed for bumper harvests. To the west is the Hall of Abstinence where the emperor fasted after making sacrifices. Within the complex, there are a total of 92 ancient buildings with 600 rooms. It is the most complete existing imperial sacrificial building complex in China and the world's largest existing building complex for offering sacrifice to the heaven.

Glossary:	
red-eye：红眼航班，指在深夜至凌晨时段运行，并于翌日清晨至早上抵达目的地的航班	故宫：the Forbidden City
长城：the Great Wall	walking encyclopedia：活词典，指知识渊博的人
天坛：Temple of Heaven	全国重点文物保护单位：national key cultural relics protection units
世界文化遗产：World Heritage	圜丘坛：Circular Mound Altar
皇穹宇：Imperial Vault of Heaven	祈年殿：Hall of Prayer for Good Harvests

(A for Ai Linlin, B for Bennett)

A：您好！贝内特先生，欢迎来访北京。我叫艾琳琳，是中国对外文化集团有限公司的副总经理，本次访华行程主要由我来负责接待您。

B: Hello, Miss Ai. We're sorry that the flight was delayed due to stormy weather, at last we had to catch the red-eye at midnight. Apologize for the inconvenience it has caused!

A：您别客气，能够安全抵达就好。

B：Thanks. This is our first visit to Beijing. So apart from work, we'd also expect to get to know this ancient city of great civilization.

A：没问题，这都在我们的安排之中了。的确，北京人杰地灵，历史文化非常丰富，长城、故宫等著名景点您一定早有耳闻。

B：Sure! As there are so many scenic spots in Beijing, we may have to break the journey in a few places to make sure we've got enough energy for the project discussion. I have been longing to visit the Temple of Heaven in Beijing before coming here. Not sure if it can be arranged?

A：别担心，我们会合理安排行程，保证劳逸结合！您若愿意的话，我想把您安排在市中心的王府井希尔顿酒店下榻。开车15分钟即可到我们公司。

B：Very good. Do you have any plans for tonight?

A：今晚7点我们总经理将在公司餐厅设宴为您洗尘，欢迎您的光临，也请您品尝一下最地道的北京果木烤鸭，相信您一定会喜欢。

B：No problem, see you tonight!

(Three days later)

A：昨晚的商谈很愉快，今天我们放松一下，陪您参观一下北京天坛。昨晚我还专门"挑灯夜读"，做足了功课，保证讲解到位。

B：Thank you so much for your thorough preparation. You must have known it inside out now, great that we have a walking encyclopedia here!

A：哈哈，那倒不敢当！入乡随俗，咱们就按照最地道的天坛走法：我们从南门进入，沿轴线一直走便可游览天坛全局。

B：The ancient Chinese architecture is ingenious. That's truly admirable!

A：天坛是现存中国古代规模最大的祭祀建筑群。1961年，天坛被列入第一批全国重点文物保护单位之一；1998年，被列为世界文化遗产。

B：Seems we've come to the right place!

A：当然！天坛被两重坛墙分隔成内坛和外坛，形似"回"字。中国古人相信"天圆地方"，这一理念贯穿在天坛的设计之中。

B：Interesting.

A：天坛的内坛墙周长四千余米，辟有六门。主要建筑都集中在内坛，南有圜丘坛和皇穹宇，北有祈年殿。中间以墙相隔，构成内坛的南北轴线。

B：Chinese architecture values the symmetrical layout. This is quite similar to Western architectural aesthetics.

A：是的。圜丘坛是皇帝举行祭天仪式的地方。这里的栏杆和台阶数要么是9，要么是9的倍数。如果您不相信，可以数一数。

B：So why are they all multiples of 9? What does it mean in Chinese culture?

A：好问题。由于9是十进制中最高的个位数，因此是最神圣的数字，也是中国古代的"阳数之极"。中国皇帝都喜欢数字9，象征着至高皇权、祈求长寿和国运恒昌。

B：Wow! I didn't know that before.

A：对，这就是为什么中国的皇帝穿着九龙皇袍，皇宫建筑的墙面刻印着九龙形象。

B：The wisdom of the ancient Chinese is indeed admirable. They were able to seamlessly integrate the architectural aesthetics with mathematics symbols. It seems that I have to come to China a few more times to gain a deeper understanding of the profoundness of Chinese culture.

3. 医疗口译

Text 4: Seeing the doctor

Preview:

Medical interpreters interpret conversations between doctors, carers, clinicians, and patients in a medical setting. It is one of the most complicated types of liaison interpreting since it requires a general understanding of medical terminology in both languages and cultural factors that could influence communication between doctors and patients. The following passage provides a conversation interpreting practice of OCT eye consulting.

Optical coherence tomography (OCT) is a non-invasive imaging test. OCT uses light waves to take cross-section pictures of your retina. With OCT, your ophthalmologist can see each of the retina's distinctive layers. This allows your ophthalmologist to map and measure their thickness. These measurements help with diagnosis. They also provide treatment guidance for diseases of the retina.

Glossary:	
预防性检查：precautionary check-up	visual field analysis：视野分析（一种眼科检查）
optic nerve：视神经	floaters：飞蚊症
OCT：光学相干断层扫描检查	

(N for nurse, P for patient, D for doctor)

N: Good morning, madam. How may I help you?

P: 早上好。早上9点我约了医生。

N: Have you registered with us earlier?

P: 有的。

N: Please show me your registration card. Or I can search for your details through your mobile number.

P: 好。我的手机号码是178××××3728。

N: OK, I've found your details. You last visited us in August 2021.

P: 没错。

N: You can pay the consultation fee here.

P: 好。这是我的银行卡。

N: Please take a seat, and feel free to help yourself with water, newspapers, etc.

P: 谢谢。

(After 15 minutes, the attendant calls the patient's name, and the patient proceeds to the doctor's cabin.)

P: 早上好,医生。

D: Good morning. How are you doing today?

P: 不错,谢谢。

D: So what brings you here?

P: 我是来做定期检查的。现在没有什么不适,但几年前有位医生建议我每年进行预防性检查。

D: I see that your optic nerve is thicker than normal. That's probably the reason why you were asked to undergo precautionary tests every year. You can have the same two tests today, visual field analysis and OCT. And once you have the two reports, we can meet again in the afternoon.

P: 谢谢您,医生。

(Two hours later, the patient visits the doctor again with the reports.)

D: Everything went well with the tests?

P: 是的,一切顺利。因为我之前也做过测试,所以清楚怎么做。

D: Your reports are absolutely fine. Since these reports have been consistently normal for many years, I think you can now take these tests once in two years, not annually.

P: 好的。

D: In case your eyes get tired quickly, I would recommend an eye drop, which you can use

2-3 times in the day. Our eyes get dry when we stare at the computer screen without blinking for long, a common reason for eye fatigue. This eye drop will lubricate your eyes. Do you've any other questions?

P: 有。我经常看到一些薄薄的、黑色的、波浪似的东西漂浮在眼前，闭上眼睛后也不会消失。这些是什么？它们有害吗？

D: They're called floaters, and most people develop them to a different extent as they age. They're not harmful.

P: 谢谢您，医生。占用您的时间了。

D: You're welcome.

第三章

学会听辨(Ⅰ)

第一节 听力练习与口译听辨

对于英语学习者来说,听力练习一定不陌生。那么你是如何自主练习的呢?相信大多数同学都是按照以下步骤进行的:

(1) 选择发音标准、语言规范、无噪音干扰、语速适中的录音材料;

(2) 预习背景知识,阅读题目,提前了解题目要求关注的信息;

(3) 听的时候往往只需捕捉关键词就足以根据题干抓住采分点,但是对整篇材料的意思未必充分理解;

(4) 对照参考答案,判断自己对听力题所考察内容是否理解正确;

(5) 倘若遇到听力障碍,一般会通过复听和对照录音文本来解决;

(6) 复习听力材料中的生词、表达和其他语言知识,模仿标准发音,将注意力放在语言形式上。

这样的训练模式有助于提高语言能力和答题技巧,可以为我们打下不错的语言基础。但是,口译不光要会做选择、填空和连线题,更重要的是关注连贯的语意,因此我们还需要尝试一些新的训练方式。口译听辨虽然依托于传统的听力训练,但侧重点不同。尤其是译员听后还需要将听到的内容以另一种语言输出,必须同时协调听辨、笔记、输出准备的精力分配,面临的压力更大。

在听力练习中,我们通常只是"被动地听"来完成信息的接收;而在口译中,译员必须积极主动地听。所谓"主动地听",指的是译员不仅需要接收信息,还需要同时对其进行分析、整理、记忆,最好能够根据自己的知识储备和经验预判讲话的走向。在自主练习的时候,如果发现注意力只能牢牢紧跟原文,无法分出一定的精力去主动分析、预判,那么在听完之后脑中往往无法对原文信息构建出清晰的脉络,说不出个"所以然",这就是"被动地听"。如果能将所听内容与大脑中已有的信息进行比较、判断、联想,那么此时就进入了"主动地听"的状态。

口译具有即时性,译员需要在只听一遍的情况下迅速把握讲话者的意思。而听力自主练习中有的学生则依赖复听,甚至是中途暂停、退回重听,这些对于口译学习来说都不是好习惯。

译员与学生练习听力的目标也有所不同。译员的首要任务并非语言学习而是捕捉语意信息，因此不会把注意力放在特定语言表达或是零星的词语上。相反，他们会努力去整体把握，在头脑中形成有逻辑关系、有意义的语意。

此外，口译材料可能不如一般的听力材料来得"理想"，往往措辞欠规范、发音和吐字不够清晰、语速过快或不稳定，有时还会有现场噪音和突发情况的干扰。这些都给口译听辨提出了更高的要求。

第二节　从语音听辨到语流听辨

由于大部分现行主流考试的听力题型设置有局限，真正考查语流听辨的试题占比不足。因此，我们习惯于把注意力放在特定的词语和表达上，而不是把握句子或者段落的整体意思。尤其是遇到那些不熟悉的词时，初学者容易卡在那里，导致后面本应能听懂的内容被忽略了。但如果在训练时能改变这种注意力的分配习惯，把关注点聚焦在"森林"而非"树木"，反而容易捕捉语段的意义。下面这个例子就很典型：

例 3-1

原文：

<u>Seek out content that makes you happy to balance out your newsfeed.</u> This may be images of cute kittens, beautiful landscapes, <u>drool-worthy</u> food videos or something else. You could even follow a social media account dedicated to sharing only happy and positive news.

参考译文：

<u>查阅推送信息时多看那些让你开心的内容</u>，比如可爱的小猫、美丽的风景、<u>令人垂涎的美食视频</u>等。你甚至可以关注一个专门分享正面信息的社交媒体账号。

大家在收听甚至是阅读这段材料时，都可能在画线部分遇到困难。"balance out"是平衡、抵消的意思，但是却不常与"newsfeed"搭配，听到此处时同学们容易停下来斟酌该如何表达。而"drool-worthy"对很多同学来说都是生词。由于过往的学习习惯，人们很可能会反复问自己这是什么，因而忽略了后面的内容。不少人甚至会有冲动想要暂停录音打开词典查一查。但我们一定要冷静，不要把注意力放在一个词或词组上。完整听完这一段，你会发现这两处其实并不妨碍我们理解，因为根据自身刷微博、看朋友圈的经历，结合上下文的"content that makes you happy"及"happy and positive news"，很容易推断出整句的含义，表达的时候也无须拘泥于字面。从认知科学的角度来说，我们之所以能理解整体意思是因为人脑具有"模糊特征摄取"的特点，具备"心理完形"的能力，可以近乎本能地填补原文缺失的信息。通过这个例子，我们发现"语流听辨"并不是一项全新的技能。我们只不过是囿于过往的外语学习方式有些不适应，现在需要调整训练习惯。

由于我们的母语是中文，一般会相信自己的中文听辨没有问题，但事实远非如此。译者可能会遇到一些用词高深却逻辑不清的材料,在这种情况下原文实际想表达的意思往往会被掩藏了起来。

例3-2

原文:

为什么从传播和哲学这两个命题谈起,因为中国的哲学几乎所有西方人都会说太深奥了。而且呢,那么悠久的历史再加上我们的方块儿字这里面会带来传播上的诸多困难。而我今天恰恰想说,在传播中去探讨它当代的应用价值这大概是我们现在很多身处西方的学子能够做的最好的一件事情,因为我们会去在比较文化中感受中国文化。文化其实分两个层面去对它进行一种贡献,一种是文化内涵的研究,第二种是文化外延的传播。研究是逻辑性的内在的稳定的价值,而传播是发散性的外在的实用的价值。

原文核心意义:

中国哲学因为历史悠久和语言障碍很难在西方传播,所以身处西方的中国学子可以通过讨论中国哲学的当代应用价值来帮助传播中国文化。对中国文化的贡献方式有两种,一种是研究其内涵,另一种是传播其实用价值。

学生们在课堂上听完这段材料后普遍反映中文每个字都能听懂,但依然难以理解,甚至连大意都很难记住。实际上,我们可以抛开语言的外壳,提炼大意。从这个例子我们可以看出,汉译英中也要注重把握原文的主要逻辑而不是将注意力放在字词上,否则就会舍本逐末。下面和大家分享两种有效的训练方法,可以帮助调整听力习惯,适应"语流听辨"。

第三节　口译听辨的练习方法

一、无笔记复述

初学者通常进行的听辨训练是"源语复述",也即根据记忆,使用源语言阐述所听内容,无需翻译。这种训练看似简单,却是开展口译活动的基础,着重考查译员的听力、理解、信息归纳和总结能力。复述训练主要分为五步。

1. 材料选择

选择复述文本时可循序渐进,按照120词/分钟的速度,从1分钟的复述练习做起,随后扩展至2分钟、3分钟、4分钟,甚至更长时间。内容可涉及接待、文化、旅游、科技、经贸、外交等各个领域,但要把握"由浅入深"的原则。建议在训练之初选择有故事情节和趣味性的文本,切忌选择艰涩难懂的内容,这样不仅无法达到理想的训练效果,还会打击信心,令人对口译训练产生抗拒情绪。

2. 听力理解

训练时不要使用笔记,集中精力抓取讲话者的关键信息,厘清逻辑顺序。在此过程中,要关注讲者的"思维流动",这有利于构建讲述者心态,实现信息图谱的构建。

3. 口头复述

依据记忆,将刚刚所听到的内容用源语复述出来。这一步骤建议录音,切勿苛求完美,也不要因遗忘细节而停滞不前,导致"因小失大"。应尽量将脑海中短期存留的核心信息元素或片段,通过逻辑、清晰的语言表达出来,不求面面俱到,通顺达意即可。进阶阶段,可以在理解大意的基础上补充细节,使内容更加细致丰满。

4. 复听检查

对照文本仔细回听自己的复述录音,检查两点:第一,复述时间尽量不超过讲话者发言时间;第二,仔细分析遗漏信息的性质和遗忘原因,找到解决方案。

5. 反复练习

按照以上步骤重复,直至能够使用简洁、清晰且准确的语言重现原文逻辑结构和信息内容。

二、主旨口译

第二种训练方法是主旨口译(gist interpreting),也称"要点口译",即先听原文,然后在规定时间内把要点用另一种语言口译出来。20世纪60年代产生于法国高翻学院的释意理论是主旨口译的主要理论依托。释意理论主张译员脱离"源语语言外壳"(de-verbalization),追求原文和译文意义上的等效。这就要求译者脱离讲话者语言形式的束缚,根据自身知识背景把握讲者意图,挖掘其"言外之意",用流畅自然的译入语概括听到的内容,实现原文的交际意图。

主旨口译训练的基本步骤可参照上一小节中讲过的复述训练,但是需将源语信息用译入语进行总结性概述。这里主要须注意以下几点。

1. 充分调动工作记忆

工作记忆(也即短期记忆)是主旨口译的核心训练内容,它不是对信息的机械复制,而是要主动加工、提炼和编码。

2. 抓住主要观点和核心词汇

聪明的译者懂得"四两拨千斤"的艺术,知道如何层层剥开讲者的细节描述,理出逻辑主干和主要论点,通过关键词串联的方式进行记忆。关键词建议选择高度概括且有实质含义的词汇,以求最大程度地将零散信息组织起来,唤醒对相关内容的记忆。这里也可以用到第五章中的"条块信息串联"方法,扩大每个单位的存储容量,实现"记忆扩容"(见第五章第一节)。

3. 把握主线,理清逻辑

做主旨口译时,译者应尽量在脑海中构建叙述主线,在此基础上添加旁枝侧节,形成逻辑清晰、环环相扣的树状图式。随着讲话的不断进行，主要论点不断增加，译者应及时调整篇章逻辑，分清观点之间的主次关系，才能清晰重现原文的情景意义。

4. 大意概括，切忌啰嗦

主旨口译归根结底也是一门"懂得节制"的艺术，不要陷入对细枝末节的赘述之中，这样只会埋没主要论点，令人不知所云。口译时可适当按照逻辑顺序进行信息重组，例如可以一开头先抛出核心论点，之后再详细说明。译语可脱离源语外壳，追求简洁达意，时间一般是原始讲话时长的一半以内。

需要指出的是，口译听辨是传统听力训练的进阶，而非对传统听力练习的否定。一般的听力音频其实也是绝佳的上手素材，只需要按照口译听辨的要求来使用即可，之后可以再过渡到真实的现场材料。经过一段时间的复述和主旨口译练习，大家一定能转换思路，为之后的口译技能学习打下牢固的基础。

专项练习

1. 复述练习

要求：请回顾前面所述听辨训练技巧，听一遍录音后直接用英文进行复述。

(1) Taking a bath in the morning can be refreshing, helping you feel more alert at work. By contrast, a warm bath before going to bed can remove the dirt from the surface of the skin, accelerate blood circulation, relax the muscles of the whole body, eliminate fatigue, and improve sleep quality.

(2) Texting someone back. Changing a lightbulb. Booking your pet's wellness visit. The cumulative mental load of unintentionally stockpiling tiny tasks like these can be distracting and mentally draining. Even manageable duties start to feel overwhelming and suffocating due to their sheer number.

(3) The climate crisis is damaging the health of foetuses, babies and infants across the world. Scientists discovered increased heat was linked to fast weight gain in babies, which increases the risk of obesity in later life. Higher temperatures were also linked to premature birth, which can have lifelong health effects, and to increased hospital admissions of young children.

(4) There are several reasons why wholegrains may work to help people maintain waist size and reduce increases in other risk factors. The presence of dietary fibre in wholegrains can have a satiating effect, and the magnesium, potassium and antioxidants may contribute to lowering blood pressure. Soluble fibre in particular may have a beneficial effect on post-meal blood sugar spikes.

(5) Young people spending hours staring at screens means half the world may need glasses within 30 years. Phone devices and computer screens are to blame for the rising risk of short-sightedness among children and young adults, say scientists. Researchers have found high levels of looking at a phone or tablet are linked with around a 30 percent higher risk of short-sightedness, also known as myopia. But when it is combined with excessive computer use, that risk rises to around 80 percent. Researchers fear that this could mean that by 2050, half the world or five billion people could be short-sighted.

(6) With fashion magazines, advertisements and teenage icons sporting the "latest and greatest" trends, there's a lot of pressure on teenagers to fit the mold, no matter how expensive it might be. For decades, teenage and adolescent boys and girls have used fashion as a social weapon. Bullies will pick out peers that aren't wearing the best brands of clothing and criticize them. There are some tell-tale signs your child might be a victim of fashion bullying. They'll become picky about what clothes they wear and will be very demanding when you take them shopping.

(7) Seasonal affective disorder (SAD) is a type of depression that sets in or starts in the winter months. Unlike other types of depression, it may improve as spring comes on. It is often a cyclical, recurring disorder — you'll feel depression every winter and begin to feel better each spring. SAD depression is caused by lowered levels of serotonin, the mood-affecting brain chemical that is triggered by seasonal changes in daylight. Shorter days may also disrupt the body's biological clock — circadian rhythm — which upsets the balance of melatonin, the hormone which regulates mood and sleep patterns.

(8) Inflammation is part of your body's healing mechanism — the reason why your knee swelled and turned red when you injured it. But this inflammatory repair process can sometimes go awry, lasting too long and harming instead of helping. When inflammation is caused by an ongoing problem, it can contribute to health problems. Over time, inflammation stemming from chronic stress, obesity, or an autoimmune disorder may potentially trigger conditions such

as arthritis, heart disease, or cancer. It may also harm the brain. Researchers have found a link between higher levels of inflammation inside the brain and an elevated risk for cognitive decline and impairment. Regularly adding anti-inflammatory foods to your diet may help to switch off this process.

2. 主旨口译

要求：在无笔记的情况下，译出所听材料的要点（不妨限定自己在30秒内完成翻译）。

英汉段落 1: Keeping cats

China has seen an increase in pet ownership over the years, with people increasingly choosing cats. Globally, though dogs were still more common pets, including the United States and the United Kingdom, cats have emerged as the most popular pet in the European Union lately.

Cats have also turned into a social phenomenon in China and elsewhere, with the felines becoming the subject of viral memes and videos. Many cat lovers online also identify themselves as "cat slaves" and "cat sniffers," publicly professing their pet preference.

Researchers attribute the fast growth of cat pets to the lifestyle in Chinese cities, with some experts also suggesting the feline's popularity is linked with the young generation's pursuit of individuality. Many city dwellers have busy lives and relatively smaller accommodations, thus making cats their ideal companions — it's easy to raise cats, unlike dogs that require more attention and outdoor activities.

英汉段落 2: Self-driving cars

Self-driving cars are expected to be much safer than human-driven ones. But even if the first robot cars hit the roads, most of us probably won't give up driving entirely for at least another 15 or 20 years. In the meantime, driverless cars will gradually take over certain aspects of traditional driving.

Companies have been adding semiautonomous features to cars since the 1990s. Within a few years, cars may be able to determine when an accident is likely and make adjustments to the cabin — moving seats, closing windows, retracting the steering wheel.

英汉段落 3: Attention residue

Thanks to things like time constraints and incessant interruptions, it's not uncommon to find yourself setting aside half-completed tasks in order to deal with something urgent that's come up or has to take priority.

A small piece of your attention is left with the unfinished task, known as attention residue. When you experience attention residue, your brain is working overtime by thinking about the task you're now on, as well as ruminating about the previous task you had to leave unfinished.

If you do have to stop work on a task prematurely, you can decrease the amount of attention residue by writing down the specifics of what's left to finish. This can help decrease rumination and allow you to clear your mind.

汉英段落1：间隔年

间隔年在西方国家非常流行，通常指年轻人在升入大学时或毕业之后进入职场前，规划一次长期的思想文化之旅，去体验一段与之前不同的生活方式。期间，学生离开自己的国家到一个新的环境，或长途旅行，或打工换取旅费，或在公益机构做义工，在探索过程中了解自我、发现兴趣、挖掘潜能，从而在回归后更好地融入社会。

汉英段落2：美国的失业率

2023年，美国的失业率再创新低，超出市场预期。这主要是因为服务业需求的旺盛，包括休闲、娱乐、餐饮等行业吸纳了大量兼职人员。另一方面，老年人参与工作的比率难以恢复，也形成了岗位空缺。不过，我们认为美国失业率仍然会回升，只是时间不如之前预想的那么早。美国经济硬着陆的风险已经大幅下降，但还未完全解除。

汉英段落3：信息革命

当前，随着国际力量的消长变化，全球化发展正处在新的历史转折点上，从以国际贸易驱动为特征的"1.0"版，到以国际金融驱动为特征的"2.0"版，如今全球化正步入以数据要素为主要驱动力的"3.0"版。现在世界各主要经济体都在借助信息技术革命的新浪潮，加快建设和运用互联网，以推动本国经济社会发展，保持或者强化自身整体实力和国际竞争力。

篇章练习

要求：听下面的两个篇章，先不做笔记，用源语复述每个语段的主要内容并录音，注意捕捉并准确复述原语段的关键信息和逻辑结构。完成后再试着翻译这两个篇章。

Text 1: UK sugar tax linked to fall in child hospital admissions for tooth extraction (excerpt)

Preview:

It is established that sugar-sweetened drinks could lead to tooth decay. To reduce sugar consumption, soft drinks industry levy was introduced in 2018 in the UK on the recommendation of the WHO. According to an analysis by researchers at the University of Cambridge, the levy may have saved more than 5,500 hospital admissions for tooth extractions and may have reduced the number of under-18s having a tooth removed due to tooth decay by 12 percent. Even though the researchers cannot say definitively that the soft drinks levy caused this reduction in tooth decay since this is an observational study, they conclude that the study provides evidence of possible benefits to children's health from the UK soft drinks industry levy beyond obesity which it was initially developed to address.

Glossary:	
sugar-sweetened drink：含糖饮料	tooth extraction：拔牙
soft drinks industry levy：软饮料行业税	dental health：牙齿健康

Sugar-sweetened drinks account for around 30 percent of the added sugars in the diets of children aged one to three years and over a half by late adolescence. In England, nearly 90 percent of all tooth extractions in young children are due to decay, resulting in around 60,000 missed school days a year.

The World Health Organization has recommended a tax on sugar-sweetened drinks to reduce sugar consumption, which more than 50 countries have implemented. In March 2016, the UK government announced a soft drinks industry levy or "sugar tax", which aimed to reduce sugar intake by encouraging drinks manufacturers to reformulate their products. The levy was implemented in April 2018.

While the relationship between sugar-sweetened drinks and tooth decay is well established, no studies have used real-world data to examine the relationship between the levy and dental health.

To address this, researchers analyzed hospital admissions data for tooth extractions due to tooth decay in children up to 18 years old in England from January 2014 to February 2020.

Overall, in children aged 18 and under, there was an absolute reduction in hospital admissions of 3.7 per 100,000 population per month compared to if the soft drinks levy had not happened. This equated to a relative reduction of 12 percent compared to if the levy had not been introduced.

Based on a population of nearly 13 million children in England in 2020, the researchers estimated that the reduction avoided 5,638 admissions for tooth decay. Reductions in hospital admissions were greatest in younger children aged up to four years and among children aged five to nine years, with absolute reductions of 6.5 and 3.3 per 100,000 respectively.

Text 2：失眠是如何造成的？

Preview:

除了营养和锻炼，睡眠是健康的三大支柱之一。世界卫生组织建议每天睡7—9小时。然而，每天晚上，世界上有数以亿计的人饱受失眠之苦，约占世界人口的10%—30%。失眠（insomnia）是一种不容易自然地进入睡眠状态的症状，包括难以入睡，或是很难维持较长时间的深度睡眠。失眠一般会伴随着白天精神不佳、嗜睡、易怒，或是抑郁等症状。失眠可能会增加车祸意外的风险，也可能会让人注意力不集中、工作易疲惫及学习效果不佳。那么失眠是如何造成的，又有什么方法来解决失眠问题呢？希望你在本文中找到答案。

Glossary:	
失眠：insomnia	生物钟：biological clock
呼吸系统的：respiratory	肠胃的：gastrointestinal
应激反应系统：stress response system	过度清醒：hyperarousal

是什么导致你晚上睡不着？思考某些深刻的问题？因旅行感到兴奋？或者是因为未完成的工作、即将来临的考试、对家庭聚会的恐惧？对很多人来说，这种压力是暂时的，因为压力来源很快便会消失。但是，如果那个导致你失眠的原因正是"害怕失眠"这一压力本身呢？这个看似无法解决的死循环是失眠问题的核心，而失眠是世界上最常见的睡眠问题。

几乎任何事情都可能导致失眠：打呼噜的伴侣、身体上的疼痛，或者情绪上的困扰。还有像时差这种剥夺睡眠的极端情况，都可能打乱你的生物钟，破坏睡眠时间表。但在大多数情况下，睡眠剥夺是暂时的，最终我们会陷入一种疲劳感。但一些长期症状，如呼吸系统疾病、肠胃问题等，会让我们虽然疲惫却仍无法入眠。随着不眠之夜越来越多，卧室开始与那些未眠夜关联起来，充斥着焦虑感。每到睡觉时间，失眠患者便会感到压力。由于压力太大，患者的大脑开始干涉人体应激反应系统，提高心率和血压，刺激身体进入"过度清醒"状态。这种情况下，大脑会搜索潜在威胁，任何不适或者噪音都变得难以忍受。而当失眠患者最终睡着了，他们的睡眠质量已受到影响。

　　幸好，有些方法可以打破失眠的循环。管理导致"过度清醒"的压力是我们已知的失眠治疗方法之一，而且好的睡眠习惯可以重建你的睡眠时间。确保你的卧室足够黑暗和凉爽，让导致"过度清醒"状态的威胁因素降至最低。你的床只用来睡觉，如果睡不着，可以离开卧室，做一些放松的活动让自己感到倦意，比如阅读、冥想、或者写日记。通过设置规律的休息和清醒时间来调节新陈代谢，以便适应身体生物钟。这个生物钟对光线也很敏感，所以在晚上要避免亮光，这将有助于提醒身体现在是睡觉时间。我们的睡眠和清醒周期是一个微妙的平衡，这个平衡对于维护我们身心健康非常重要。因此，维持稳定的睡眠时间值得我们投入一些时间和精力，但不要浪费睡眠时间来思考这一问题。

第四章

学会听辨（Ⅱ）

第一节 听辨的难点

通过完成上一单元的练习，相信大家对于口译听辨究竟需要"听"什么、"辨"什么已经有了直观感受。但在实践中，你或许还会感到慌乱，无法准确捕捉关键信息，对原文总是似懂非懂。本章将为你总结听辨中的难点，并与你分享相关技巧，教你如何通过训练克服它们。只要经过合理科学的训练，你的听辨能力一定会大有长进。

听辨的首要目的就是为了理解原文。丹尼·吉尔（Gile, 1995）曾提出口译理解方程式：C（理解）= KL（语言知识）+ EKL（言外知识）+ A（分析），其中后三项都服务于"理解"。笔者将听辨的难点分为语言障碍、信息陌生与信息密集三类。

一、语言障碍

语言障碍，顾名思义是指由于自身外语基本功不扎实带来的理解问题，包括词汇、语法、习语等。最常见的困难是生词问题。除了临时准备和会议主题相关的词汇，我们在日常学习中也需要积累一般性词汇，不断扩大词汇量。此外，熟悉句法和固定搭配能让你较为准确地切分意群，减少理解错误。我们先来看看下面这个例子：

例 4-1

原文：

Governments have expanded their ability to police and supervise their populations. Britain has <u>more than 4 million CCTV cameras</u>, one for every 14 people.

参考译文：

各国政府都在加大对民众监管的能力建设。英国安装了<u>超过400万个闭路电视摄像头</u>，即每14个人就有一个摄像头。

这里的"CCTV"实际上是"closed-circuit television"的缩写。部分学生在翻译画线部分时，不假思索地翻译为"超过400万个中央电视台的摄像头"，这与上下文严重不符，尤其是下文还提到了英国。但是学生受限于背景知识，在口译时没能意识到这一问题。另外需要注意的是，如今我们已经不再使用"中央电视台"的说法，而改称"中央广播电视总台"，译作"China Media Group"。

根据我们的教学经验,学生通常都会花大量时间背单词,但不太注重刻意积累固定用法和搭配,而这往往是容易失误的地方,尤其"危险"的是那些由常用词构成的习语。

例4-2

原文:

A new study shows that in a perfect world, indulging in a daily portion of French fries instead of almonds would be a simple choice, and no negative consequences would stem from selecting the salty, deep-fried option. But a Harvard expert says we should take the findings of a new study supporting this scenario with, er, a grain of salt.

参考译文:

一项新研究表明,在理想状态下,人们大可以每天享用一份薯条而不是杏仁(这类健康零食),而这种高盐的油炸食物无伤大雅。但哈佛大学的一位专家指出,对支持这一结果的新研究应持保留态度。

学生在口译这段材料时,第一句话一般不会有重大理解问题,基本能说出大意,但到了第二句,大家的译文就开始变得五花八门了。比如有的学生说道:"但是一位哈佛的专家表示我们应该就盐的摄入量开展一项新的研究。"还有的学生说:"但是一位哈佛的专家认为我们应该开展一项新的研究支持给食物加盐。"学生遇到的问题其实来自最后的"take something with a grain of salt"。毫无疑问他们听懂了"salt"一词,却不知道整个习语的含义,于是连蒙带猜把"盐"与上下文杂糅在一起,闹出了笑话。

习语"take something with a grain of salt"表示对某件事情持保留态度、将信将疑,类似于英文的"doubt"或者"treat something with suspicion"。原文选择这一习语主要是为了与前文"the salty, deep-fried option"构成呼应("salt"呼应"salty"),形成双关,制造诙谐幽默的效果。通过这个案例我们可以看到,熟练掌握习语和固定搭配可以大大帮助译员减少理解错误,这是孤立背单词无法实现的。

二、信息陌生

信息陌生指的是学生由于缺乏语言外知识而无法把握原文的信息。听辨时,如果我们大脑中储存了足够多的背景知识,就可以更轻松地与原文建立关联,减少推理负荷,提高听辨效果。

例4-3

原文:

Until 1868, when the Meiji Era began, Japan had maintained a fiercely isolationist policy that kept it culturally and politically intact for centuries. When the nation finally chose, after a brief internal struggle, to submit to external pressure and open its doors, this largely untouched world of "old Japan" was suddenly subjected to violent upheavals, with the immediate rush to modernize and Westernize.

参考译文：

1868年明治维新之前，日本数百年里都奉行闭关锁国政策，在文化上、政治上不受外界影响。经历了短暂的内部斗争后，日本最终屈服于外界的压力打开了国门。一个几乎未受外部世界影响的"旧日本"突然开始遭受剧烈的动荡，迅速奔向现代化和西方化。

如果你对明治维新时期日本的历史背景有所了解的话，结合语段中的时间节点和"isolationist"的时代描述，便可以推测出"Meiji"这一专有名词的含义。反之，不了解这段历史的学生听到"Meiji"就有些慌乱，多数选择了省译，少数进行了编译，自信心也因此大受影响。

信息陌生同样会对中文原文的听辨构成障碍，包括行业术语、知识原理、社交礼仪套话等。需要注意的是，对于术语的翻译不能仅限于字面，否则可能仍然难以把握语段的内部逻辑。这就是为什么我们强调，译前准备不要只查术语的译法，更应该去探索与之相关的原理。以"外汇储备"一词为例，同学们基本都会提前查一下，知道应该译为"foreign exchange reserve"。但口译不是译单词，讲者可能讨论到外汇储备的主要用途和形式、它的积极影响和消极影响、中国外汇储备的现状等问题。稍微多花一点功夫搞清这些基本的问题，在口译时就能事半功倍，较为轻松地把握语篇的逻辑，至少不至于产出违背常识的译文。

此外，一些话语的内涵、逻辑或是言外之意需要译员具备一定的人生阅历和较高的素养才能听明白。笔者曾经在北京大学举办的一场教育论坛担任译员，会上一位香港知名大学的老校长打趣道，"官越做越大，车越坐越小"。笔者当时并没有真正听懂这句话的内涵，情急之下处理成了"the higher your position, the smaller your car is likely to be"，译文并不理想。之后在午宴期间，笔者得以与这位校长进一步交流。他解释说：在香港，职级较低的官员可能需要搭乘公共交通上班，但随着职级越来越高，高级官员就能享受专车服务。明白了这句话的文化背景之后，我们可以发现译文使用"vehicle"会比"car"更为合适。通过这一案例我们可以认识到，作为中文母语者我们仍然需要不断学习，加强自己的母语功底，同时还需要丰富自身阅历和修养，这样才能真正理解讲者的所指和所思。

为了积累各领域的百科知识，我们鼓励大家平时泛听、泛读，而不是专挑自己感兴趣的内容来听、来看。针对这一问题，小组练习是个不错的方法：即便每个人提供的语料都属于各自最擅长的两三个领域，每次训练话题的丰富性也能大大提高。

三、信息密集

信息密集指的是听辨时大脑信息过载，即所谓的"听三句漏两句"。译员难免会遇到语速较快、信息量较大的材料,这就要求他们对听辨内容做出合理的精力分配:务必抓住主要内容,尽量保留细节,如果无法做到的话要记得"有舍才有得"。请看下面这个例子:

例4-4

原文:

Today, the most innovative leaders aren't the conformers. They're the bold individualists who carve their own paths. So learning to embrace one's inner "badass" is the new key to success. <u>Too often, people are advised or feel pressured to bury the special or quirky aspects of their personalities, recalibrate their speaking or personal styles, or think twice about sharing honest opinions at work in order to demonstrate that they are "a good fit"</u>. But that approach does a disservice to both the employee and the business. Research shows being true to who you are leads to greater professional performance and personal satisfaction and if companies are serious about increasing diversity and inclusion, encouraging everyone to bring their individuality and unvarnished opinions with them is a good start.

参考译文:

如今最具创新精神的领导者不是合群的人。他们是大胆的个人主义者,勇于开辟自己的道路。因此,学会拥抱自己内心的"邪恶"是通往成功的新路径。<u>很多时候,人们会被告诫或是自己觉得有必要掩饰性格中古怪的部分,调整说话风格或个人风格,以及在工作中谨慎表达真实想法,以此显得合群</u>。但这种做法对员工和企业都是有害的。研究表明,忠于自己的内心会提升职场表现和个人满意度。如果公司想要增加多样性和包容性,不妨先鼓励每个人彰显个性、直抒己见。

画线处举了一些具体的例子,语态(are advised or feel pressured to)、用词(recalibrate、quirky)都比较复杂,学生们表示听辨和笔记的难度都很高。但它其实只是该段的一小部分,译员还有更重要的信息需要听辨和处理。为了合理分配精力,我们可以尝试将其简化,因为几项细节都是下文"to demonstrate that they are 'a good fit'"的不同方法。如果有几项没听懂或者没有记下来,可以适当省略,但务必保留之后的概述:"人们为了显得合群不得不谨言慎行。"

汉译英的时候虽然听力理解相对容易一些,但是密集的信息同样会困扰译者。比如下面这个例子就很典型:

例4-5

原文:

12年来,泛北论坛秉持促进泛北部湾区域合作发展的初心,坚持"优势互补、合作共赢、共同繁荣发展"的原则,积极推动泛北合作从倡议走向行动,从共识走向实践,从合作走向共赢,取得了丰硕成果,广泛惠及各国民众,成为中国—东盟全面合作框架下的重要次区域合作,成为中国—东盟最具活力、最富内涵、最有成果的关系之一。

参考译文:

In the past 12 years, the Pan-Beibu Gulf Economic Cooperation Forum is committed to its founding mission of promoting Pan-Beibu Gulf (PBG) economic cooperation as well as to the principle of "complementarity of respective strengths and win-win cooperation for common prosperity and development". The Forum has shifted the focus from consensus to practice and from cooperation to win-win results, and achieved fruitful outcomes to the benefit of people in participating countries. The Forum has become a major sub-regional cooperation platform as well as one of the most dynamic, substantive and fruitful hubs under the framework of China-ASEAN cooperation.

大家如果觉得这段译不出来,千万不要有挫败感,因为我们专门选取了这个高难度例子用于分析汉英口译的理解难点,并不要求初学者去翻译。这句话之所以难,第一是因为专有名词,"泛北论坛"就是"泛北部湾经济合作论坛"的缩写;第二是使用了大量列举,脑记和笔记的压力大;第三是因为四字格,高度概括的同时也提高了信息密集度;第四是因为它构成了很长的流水句,没有明示各层次的逻辑关系。

当然,我们也要明白信息密集是一个相对概念。也许某一材料客观来说信息量并不大,语速也不算快,但由于语言基本功不足、知识储备不足、精力分配不合理,可能主观上会感到信息过载。因此,我们必须认识到听辨的三大难点是一个有机的整体,克服了其中一种,其它几项的挑战也可能随之迎刃而解。

第二节 听辨的方法

一、关注要素

听辨时首先要关注材料的who、what、where、when等这几大要素,因为任何事件的发生都离不开这几项。尤其要注意who,因为有一些专有名词(proper names)有固定的译名,并非直译,例如华裔人士或者香港特别行政区人士的名字。比如,在外媒报道中,腾讯公司创办人马化腾是Pony Ma,百度董事长兼首席执行官李彦宏是Robin Li,美籍华裔女星刘玉玲是Lucy Alexis Liu,而香港特别行政区第五任行政长官林郑月娥是Carrie Lam Cheng Yuet-ngor。还有一些外籍人士出于对中国的友好,也会给自己取一个中文名字,比如哈佛大学第29任校长Lawrence Bacow中文名是白乐瑞,明德大学蒙特雷高级翻译学院的教授Laura Burian中文名是白瑞兰。

与此同理,一些组织机构、活动、会议的名称(what)也不能想当然,必须逐一查阅。比如北京冬奥会官方说法是Beijing 2022 Olympic Winter Games,而北京冬残奥会是Beijing 2022 Paralympic Winter Games。同学们经常会把"Winter"和"Olympic"及"Paralympic"的位置放错。

此外,同名的地名(where)也会成为挑战。比如一位前往剑桥大学演讲的哈佛大学教授在致辞中说"It is a great pleasure for me to travel from the new Cambridge to the old Cambridge"。译员如果不知道哈佛大学坐落于马萨诸塞州的坎布里奇镇(Cambridge, Mass.)与"剑桥"同名,就有可能无法理解这句话的含义。

最后,因为英文是屈折语言,时态变化(when)与语意逻辑是紧密联系在一起的,因此译者必须高度关注时态变化。

例4-6

原文:

Interest rates <u>are</u> still below where they <u>were in 2018 and 2019</u> and yet the economy <u>has recovered</u> so quickly from the recession. I think what we need <u>is</u> a pretty quick move toward normalization, bringing us back to what you might think of as neutral monetary policy, the kind of monetary policy we <u>had prior to the recession</u> and then an assessment as to how much further the Fed <u>will</u> need to tighten.

参考译文:

现在利率仍比2018年、2019年时要低,然而经济已经从衰退中快速恢复。我认为我们需要快速转向常态化,重新实施中性的货币政策,也就是我们在衰退前实施的那种货币政策,然后再来评估美联储未来需要如何进一步收紧。

这段材料中时态仿佛在跳跃着变化,语意是与时态高度捆绑在一起的,如果你没有注意时态,那么自然也就无法正确理解其逻辑。汉语不像英语那样具有明显的时态标记,英译汉中只要抓住了时间状语,理解和输出的难度不大。但是如果上面那段话换成汉译英,同学们往往会暴露出大量的时态问题:忘记使用过去时、滥用完成时、时态与时间状语不匹配等。时态不仅需要在听辨中关注,在后续的笔记训练中也要有恰当的标注方式,否则整段话的信息就可能出错。

二、把握逻辑

在听辨的时候,你很可能无法完全听懂每一个词、每一句话,因此要特别注意把握发言的逻辑(即材料的how和why),从而更好地捕捉重点内容。你在日常学习中需要留意总结一些逻辑词,并熟悉这些逻辑词所释放的信号,它们一旦出现你就能够预判语意的走向。

例 4-7

原文：

Innovation has shifted focus toward crops and areas of the country most negatively affected by climate change and toward more adaptive forms of technology, like heat-resistant seeds. This has all helped farmers adapt. However, the notion that new technology is going to fully mitigate the economic consequences of climate change seems inconsistent with existing data.

参考译文：

创新已经让人们把关注焦点放到了受气候变化影响最严重的作物和地区以及适应性技术，比如耐热种子。这一切都能帮助农民适应气候变化。然而，现有数据并不能证实新技术可以全面减缓气候变化带来的经济后果。

听辨这段材料时，你需要特别留意"However"，因为"However"之后的内容才是讲话者想表达的关键信息。由于是转折的关系，后面的观点和立场也就比较容易推测出来。

此外，在即兴讲话中，由于讲话者没有足够的时间组织严密精准的语言，有可能会出现指代不明的情况。这给译员在短时间内把握逻辑带来不小的挑战，需要译员格外留心。

例 4-8

原文：

There was tremendous strain and stress during the early months of childbirth and into the first year, but in fact, women by and large persisted. It wasn't that the strains and anxieties of childbirth were great because women dropped out. They were great because women stayed in the labour force.

参考译文：

在生育后头几个月和第一年压力尤其大，但事实上女性大体上都坚持下来了。女性并不是因为离职而感到孕产带来的压力和焦虑，她们是因为坚持留在职场而感到压力很大。

这段材料是受访者的即兴回答，部分语言组织得不够严谨。部分同学反映听到最后部分的"they"时有些困惑，不明白指代的是什么，有的学生甚至翻译为"女性能在职场中坚持下来很伟大"。但结合上下文，我们不难推断这里"they"应该是指代"the strains and anxieties of the childbirth"。

在中文讲话中，我们也会遇到指代不明、逻辑不清、冗余重复的情况，这就需要译者快速梳理、删繁就简、组织语言，为听众提供便利。

例 4-9

原文：

就像我们现在年轻人不喜欢中国的文化，我经常给他们举一个我们的真实案例，跟他们讲我们中国的白酒几千年的历史怎么怎么样。他就突然给我来一句，就是在深圳，他说这么深厚的文化和我有什么关系呢？就是完全不在一个对话的平台和语系当中。

参考译文：

For instance, the younger generation are not very interested in traditional Chinese culture. Once in Shenzhen, I tried to introduce to a group of young audience the long history of Chinese *baijiu*. One of them popped out "But why should I care?" In other words, we did not share common grounds to have a meaningful dialogue.

讲者在即兴讲话的过程中，杂糅了不同层级的信息，其人称代词有的泛指年轻人，有的指某次在深圳遇到的一群年轻人，还有的特指提问的那一位年轻人。作为译员，我们需要快速反应、积极思考，为讲者传递其真正想表达的意思。

三、抓大放小

在口译实践中，一些讲话中经常会出现修饰性或列举式的话语，译员在精力有限的情况下可以适当简化甚至省略，把节省下来的精力放在材料的主干信息和逻辑关系上。让我们来看看下面这个例子。

例 4-10

原文：

A summer dilemma worthy of Solomon: how to stay cool in days of high heat and humidity without turning to traditional air conditioning, which consumes vast amounts of electricity and emits potent climate-changing greenhouse gases. The answer potentially involves a new class of solid-state refrigerants that could enable energy-efficient and emission-free cooling.

参考译文：

夏天里有一个只有所罗门才能解决的难题：如何在又热又潮湿的天气下不开空调保持凉爽，因为空调耗电量大还会排放温室气体导致气候变化。答案可能就在一类新型的固态冷冻剂，它制冷能耗低，而且零排放。

有些同学在听到"Solomon"的时候就慌了，心中反复纠结"Solomon"是什么而忘记了听后面的内容。这是古代以色列国王所罗门，智慧过人，擅长给他人提建议。该典故在原文中起到的是修辞效果，并没有实质性的意义。即使省略它，直接译为"夏天有一个难题"，仍

然可以准确把握全段要义。此外,这段里的"traditional"也是一个在实际口译中可以略去的次要信息。再举一例:

例4-11

原文:

一种是"老好人"型老师,对学生非常关心、非常亲切,学生不及格也让他勉勉强强及格,作文或论文质量不太高也给他个好分。再一种是"虎妈"型老师,对学生也很好,但是非常严格,不过没有把学生引到更高一层的学术发展方向上。

参考译文:

One type is the nice-guy teachers. They are caring and loving, and are very lenient in grading (tests and papers). The other type is the tiger-mom teachers. They are nice, too, but strict at the same time. Nevertheless they are not very inspiring academically.

原文中过于细节的列举(比如:学生不及格也让他勉勉强强及格;作文或论文质量不太高也给他个好分)都是为了说明老好人型教师打分不严,概括化的译文反而符合英语简明的风格,其中括号里的内容也可以省略(试比较:They may pass the students even though they should fail the tests, and give pretty good scores to poorly written essays and papers.)。真正需要关注的其实是第二句的逻辑,先是与前一类老师比较异同,然后是一个转折,指出"虎妈"型老师对于学生的学术发展帮助不大。如果我们把所有的精力都放在前面的举例上,后半部分的听辨就可能出现逻辑混乱,或者无法在有限的时间内翻译完。

四、积极推测

倘若遇到陌生的概念或者复杂的信息,除了"听",你也需要唤起其他感官知觉(比如视觉化想象)来帮助你理解、记忆,并且尽力调用大脑中储备的知识去推测新知识。请看下面这个例子:

例4-12

原文:

If you've ever struggled with back pain, you know that it can be surprisingly debilitating, even if the discomfort is short-term. You may find it difficult to grocery shop, do housework, play sports, or even tie your shoelaces. When back pain is chronic, lasting 12 weeks or longer, it can impair quality of life and physical function, and contribute to or worsen stress, anxiety, and depression.

参考译文:

如果你经历过背痛,你就知道它有多折磨人,即使持续时间很短也很痛苦。你可能连买日用品、干家务、做运动甚至系鞋带都有困难。<u>如果是持续12周以上的长期背痛</u>就会影响生活质量和身体功能，并引发或加剧压力、焦虑和抑郁。

这段话里的"debilitating"对大多数同学来说都是生词，但我们可以根据背痛或任何身体部位疼痛的经历来描述病症，在情感态度上与原文不会差得太远；加上后半句的让步逻辑（even if the discomfort is short-term），我们更加可以确定"debilitating"与"discomfort"语义相近。后半部分的"chronic"是常用词，但部分词汇量不足的同学仍然遇到了听辨障碍，所幸下文的定义"lasting 12 weeks or longer"能帮助你推测出意思。

通过这两章的学习，相信你已经了解了听辨中的难点和技巧。不管是有笔记口译还是无笔记口译，听辨的要点都不是孤立的字词，切忌记录下一串名词和动词，却不知道它们彼此之间的联系。如何串成有意义、有条理的意群才是重点。只有养成语流听辨的习惯，抓住主旨与逻辑，才能"得意而忘言"，顺利完成口译任务。

参考文献

Gile D. Basic Concepts and Models in Interpreter and Translator Training [M]. Amsterdam/Philadelphia: John Benjamins Publishing Company, 1995.

专项练习

1. 复述练习

要求：请回顾前面所述的听辨训练技巧，听一遍录音后，用英文进行复述。

(1) One thing that runs through the entire economy is interest rates. And interest rates have gone up incredibly quickly because of what the Fed has already done and what the Fed is expected to continue to do. When interest rates go up, it becomes more attractive for investors to move their money into bonds and out of stocks and that causes stocks to fall.

(2) From ancestry tests to the personal genetic information collected by law enforcement to solve cold cases, the use of DNA-based technologies is expanding rapidly across American society. But while their use is becoming more widespread, the knowledge about how these technologies work and the options people have when confronted with choices about how their own DNA might be used hasn't kept pace.

(3) As food costs continue to rise and a global food crisis looms on the horizon, it's staggering to think that some 30–40 percent of America's food supply ends up in landfills, mostly due to spoilage. At the same time, the World Health Organization estimates that foodborne illness from microbial contamination causes about 420,000 deaths per year worldwide. What if there were a way to package fresh foods that could extend their shelf life and eliminate microbial contamination?

(4) Plant-based proteins are increasingly popular with diners. A good vegan milk needs to look like milk and taste like milk, whether it's a fatty version, preferred by bakers, or a skimmed one, favoured by the health-conscious. And, for coffee-drinkers, it should ideally foam like the stuff from a cow. For years manufacturers have had trouble hacking this delicate imitation game.

(5) The earth's average surface temperature has increased drastically since the start of the Industrial Revolution, but the warming effect seen at the poles is even more exaggerated. While existing climate models consider the increased heating in the Arctic and Antarctic poles, they often underestimate the warming in these regions. This is especially true for climates millions of years ago, when greenhouse gas concentrations were very high. This is a problem because future climate projections are generated with these same models.

2. 主旨口译

要求：在无笔记的情况下译出材料要点，尽量限时在30秒内完成翻译。

英汉段落1: Urban parks

Many American urbanites' experience of nature begins and ends with their city's public park system. Fifty percent of all New Yorkers, for example, report that the only time they spend in a natural environment is in city parks. There are over one million acres of urban parks in the United States, which are as vulnerable to the effects of climate change as wilderness areas, coastlines, and other parts of our national landscape. Fittingly, urban parks are often described as forgotten or invisible infrastructure.

英汉段落2: Bittersweet

What does it mean to have a "bittersweet" state of mind? It has to do with the awareness that life is a mix of joy and sorrow, light and dark, and that everything and everyone you love is impermanent. I first experienced this state of mind when I would listen to sad music. All my life I had this mysterious reaction to sad music; it would make me feel a sense of connection to the people who had known the sorrow that the musician was trying to express. At first, I thought it was just me, but when I started my research, I realized that many musicologists have been studying this because for a long time many people have had this reaction not only to music, but to other aspects of the human experience.

汉英段落1：新质生产力

中国现在追求的是高质量发展而不是量的高速增长。这种高质量发展是由"新质生产力"和创新来推动的。高质量发展并非一蹴而就，而是受内外因素共同影响。从内部来看，中国一直走的是创新驱动的高质量发展之路。从20世纪80年代到21世纪的第一个十年，中国的GDP以超过9%的年均增速增长，在有些年份甚至以两位数的高速增长。尽管中国的农业和工业发展已经达到较高水平，但服务行业的发展仍大有可期。从外部来看，全球紧张局势促使中国聚焦高质量发展，尤其在关键领域实现自主自立，进而获得战略主动权。

汉英段落2：电子商务

随着互联网技术在全球的广泛应用，电子商务已成为"网络经济"时代的重要特征，并为我国尤其是西部地区提供了难得的发展机遇。然而刚刚兴起的西部电子商务发展还很不完善，存在诸多的制约因素。从西部地区电子商务发展的总体概况来看，相比东部地区，其智能手机普及率、企业的信息化应用水平和物流等都相对薄弱。

篇章练习

Text 1: The textile industry

Preview:

The textile industry is huge and extremely important, as we're sure you can imagine. It's an industry that helped countries like India grow a lot economically and it's now worth billions of dollars. We have the pleasure to present to you today the five things you didn't know about the textile industry.

Glossary:	
market cap：市场价值	fiber：纤维
polyester：聚酯纤维，涤纶	nylon：尼龙
apparel：服装	

Number 1. The textile industry is now worth almost $3 trillion. So far, no billionaire or industry has come close to this figure. Since textiles are used so widely, it's no wonder that this industry is one of the most prosperous in the world, along with the food and petrol industries. Today's global clothing and textile industry produces 80 billion garments worldwide every year, employing about 75 million people worldwide. //

Number 2. India's textile market is expected to reach $226 billion market cap by 2023. India is one of the world's biggest textile producers, being number two behind China's textile industry, representing more than 4 percent of the country's total GDP and more than 14 percent of its yearly exports. The industry hires around 105 million people directly and indirectly. The big advantage India holds is the ease of producing a wide range of fibers from natural to synthetic ones, like polyester or nylon. Oh, and guess what? India is also the biggest cotton producer in the world, reaching roughly 6 million kilograms in 2017. //

Number 3. The US is the biggest importer of garments in the world. And who do they import from? Yep, from China. Up to 50 percent of all apparel products sold in the US come from China and the rest from other developing countries that provide cheap workforce like Bangladesh or India. Actually, the textile manufacturing industry in the US has declined by more than 80 percent over the past two decades and they're only justifying it because there's way cheaper labor out there. The US is one of the biggest fashion consumers in the world, with the average American spending roughly up to $1700 a year on clothing. //

Number 4. Technology in textiles is the future of this industry, and it is in every industry known to humans so far. Slowly, but surely, everything became manufactured in factories by machines and computers. We've come a long way over the past 100 years, and nobody plans on stopping. The textile industry has also developed. You can now find all sorts of fibers and fabrics designed for specific activities and types of body. Sports, dancing, running, climbing, swimming, festival costumes and so on are now specially designed and more reliable than ever. Just take a look at crowdfunding websites if you want to see what people develop in this industry. //

Number 5. China is the world's largest textile producer. There's always a one country that provides the whole world with all sorts of things, whether it's food, clothing, electronic components, or natural resources. In the textile industry, China is the world leader exporting all over the world tons of different textiles. India comes in a close second place for both production and exports. The largest Chinese companies that go into the textile industry are owned by the state, so their success helps the economy to grow significantly. Taking into consideration that China is also a big manufacturing country with cheap labor, it's no wonder the country has one of the biggest economies in the world. //

Text 2：2022年北京冬奥志愿者培训

Preview:

北京冬奥会和冬残奥会志愿者为北京、河北两地三个赛区的12个竞赛场馆、3个训练场馆、26个非竞赛场馆，以及其他重点服务设施场所提供服务。服务类别包括对外联络、竞赛运行、媒体运行与转播、场馆运行等十大类。

为了培训好冬奥会志愿者，北京冬奥组委建立了通用培训、专业培训、场馆培训和岗位培训的四阶段培训体系，由志愿者部统筹负责，来提升志愿者服务水平。各志愿者来源高校也根据实际情况制定了个性化通用培训方案。志愿者上岗之后，还需在各场馆或设施正式运行前七天进行场馆和岗位培训。

Glossary:	
北京冬奥组委：Beijing Organizing Committee for the 2022 Olympic and Paralympic Winter Games	志愿者部：Volunteer Department
北京冬奥会和冬残奥会：Beijing 2022 Olympic and Paralympic Winter Games	行为规范：code of conduct
志愿服务精神：volunteerism	

各位志愿者朋友，大家好，欢迎大家再次回到我们志愿者的通用培训。我来自北京冬奥组委志愿者部，在正式跟大家分享行为规范之前，首先想表达一下欢迎大家加入我们北京冬奥会、冬残奥会志愿服务的大家庭。未来这里将是一片舞台，而你们将是志愿服务这个舞台的舞者，你们是主角。亲们，你们准备好了吗？//

你有没有想过幸运的我们在一生之中有几次机会能够代表你自己的国家？2022年的北京冬奥会和冬残奥会给予了我们所有志愿者代表自己国家的机会。你认为你应该怎么做才更好？//

分享冬奥会和冬残奥会志愿服务行为规范之前，我们先要了解一下关于行为规范的概念。什么是行为规范？其实简单来说，就是社会群体或个人在社会生活当中所应该遵循的规则和准则。它根据人们的需求、好恶、价值判断逐步形成，是社会成员在社会活动当中应该遵循的标准或原则。//

奥运会的志愿者站在世界瞩目的舞台之上，除了践行志愿服务精神，我们还要面向世界。在奥运会的赛场上，在我们的颁奖广场上，在我们的各个领域，所有的志愿者都有可能成为主角，从镜头、照片、文章当中传播到全世界，所以在这里你们还要面向全世界。//

就像我一开始说的：这一次你代表着你的国家，所以我们每一个人都要在这个舞台上向来到北京和张家口的客人提供我们卓越的服务。卓越的不仅仅是我们提供的服务，更是我们言谈举止、一言一行当中方方面面的细节。这就有赖于我们落实行动去实践关于行为规范的一些要求。//

第五章

学会记忆（Ⅰ）

第一节　听懂了却记不住？

记忆是口译工作的核心内容之一，对口译效果至关重要。在口译课程中，学生需要有效记忆来处理信息，包括文本解读、意群分离、话语组织等。可惜的是，针对记忆训练的实用性指导教学不足（Ballester & Jimenez, 1992: 238）。本章将引入记忆的基本原理，结合实例具体解读口译中的记忆机制和训练方法。

如果说同声传译中译员运用的是一种"超短期记忆"，对记忆的要求不算太高；那么在正式的交替传译中，讲话人一个语段的长度一般都在一分钟以上。按照一分钟120—180字的正常语速计算，就意味着译员要有很强的记忆力（仲伟合、王斌华，2009: 82）。很多人都认为口译员天生"才智过人"，实际上后天有意识的训练才是增强记忆力的法宝，经年累月的知识储备也会减轻记忆的负担。在此过程中，掌握正确的训练方法和记忆技巧能起到事半功倍的效果。

在口译训练的初始阶段，译员必须首先明确一个问题，即"主干"和"枝叶"的主次和彼此之间的关系。常有学生问："为什么感觉意思大约听懂了，但是根据记下的词却很难记住到底说了什么？"成因就在于舍"主干"而取"枝叶"，本末倒置。有些无笔记的联络口译中，讲话人有时候洋洋洒洒讲两三分钟。在这个过程中，即便是天生记忆能力出众的译员，想要完全复述出讲话细节也很难。如果译员一开始就抱着"完美主义"的心态，容易造成巨大心理负担，也无法关照全局，导致译出的信息支零破碎。字对字的"忠实"翻译会让译员在口译实战中撞头磕脑，唯有厘清逻辑主干，将自己代入讲者身份，将讲话内容融会于胸，继而用流畅地道的译入语传达出来，才能做到与原话内容"神似"。

那么如何做到"既能听得懂，又能记得住"？这里给大家介绍三点"诀窍"：

一、条块信息串联

语块或条块（chunking）的概念最先由心理学家米勒在20世纪50年代提出。他认为短期记忆中的信息可以以单项形式存在（例如某个单词或某个数字），也可以以条块形式存在，而创建信息条块可以建立孤立信息点之间的联系，在有限的短期记忆中保存更多信息。

口译中也是如此。口译的条块化类似创建副标题，也就是将一系列含义相似或相连的信息通过"命题"（theme）的方式进行整合。下面我们以上海旅游的介绍为例展示条块记忆的方法。

例5-1

Located on the East China Sea and the mouth of the Yangtze River, Shanghai is the largest city in China. Its skyline is filled with skyscrapers, while shiny shopping malls, luxurious hotels and prestigious art centers are rising alongside. The city nights in Shanghai are representative of the Western view of Chinese cities with bright neon signs, bustling streets and numerous businesses.

我们可以将这段话划分为三个条块（见图5-1），每个条块中可以通过记录关键词或符号的方式摘取核心信息点。这里要把握两个原则：第一，对听到的信息进行有意识的筛选，缩小记忆量；第二，记录最大暗示信息，即按照自己的记忆习惯，选择能够给予最大信息提示的关键词加以记忆。

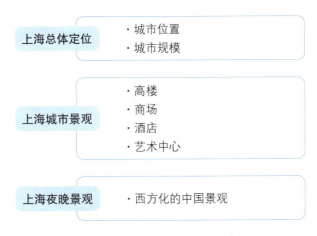

图5-1　条块信息串联练习示例

信息条块创建完成后，我们需要对源语意义进行分析和整合，实现条块之间的"串联"。这样一来，各组信息之间就不再是零散的信息单位，而会通过某种方式有机互联，回忆起其中任何一组便能够牵连出其他信息，从而达到"记忆扩容"。从图5-1中我们能够看出，三条信息条块并非简单并列，而是层层推进，这就是信息整合的结果。

整合的过程中同样要把握两个原则：第一，理清逻辑；第二，搭建架构。对此，吉利斯（Gillies, 2019: 43）总结了口译实践中常见的七种逻辑架构：

(1) past, present, future: the past situation, the current changed situation, the problems (or the solution) that arise as a result;

(2) for, against, conclusion: a logical argument explaining the "for" and "against" of an issue

and a conclusion arising from those arguments;

(3) beginning, middle, end: a narrative speech, explaining a series of events in chronological order;

(4) problem, causes, solution;

(5) tell them what you're going to say, say it, recap what you've said;

(6) introduction, development, conclusion;

(7) introduction, argument, counter-argument, conclusion.

这七种逻辑结构基本涵盖了我们在口译任务中常遇到的情景，包括按时间顺序（past-present-future）、分立场论述（for-against-conclusion）、按因果顺序（problem-causes-solution）等构建的讲者发言。在真实口译活动中，讲者还有可能通过排列或者嵌套的形式组合使用这七种逻辑。这就需要译者对这七种"元逻辑"足够熟悉，并在平时的口译实践中不断训练自己的逻辑分辨能力，以便在临场发挥时准确抓住讲话人的思路，甚至达到预测发言内容、逻辑走向的程度，更加从容地应对口译任务。

二、视觉图像构建

将文本信息与视觉图像联系起来是增强记忆的有效方式，也是将短期记忆转换为长期记忆的处理模式之一（Gillies, 2019: 39）。实践证明，当处理一段内容复杂的讲话时，如果能在脑海中构建相应的图画印象，这种多维复调的叙事模式能有效巩固我们对单纯文本内容的记忆，帮助形成"讲述者心态"。

譬如，还是以上述上海旅游介绍为例，我们曾将28名学生分为两组，每组14人：引导第一组学生单纯记忆核心字词；对第二组讲解关于视觉图像构建的技巧，引导学生在脑海中通过图文并用的方法进行记忆。结果表明，利用视觉图像辅助记忆的学生在复述的完整性、准确性和逻辑性方面均明显高于第一组学生，且译文更加流畅自然。

进行图像构建时也要掌握一定技巧。首先理顺文章逻辑，之后构建"环环相扣"的联想图式。以上海介绍为例，语段采用"zoom-in and -out"的介绍方式，首先鸟瞰上海在地图中的位置（位于长江入海口），然后镜头拉近至上海街道（摩天大楼、购物中心、豪华酒店和著名的艺术中心等），最后想象自己漫步在上海霓虹闪烁的夜晚，眼前是一派"西式"的中国城市景观。

三、讲述者心态构建

最后我们来谈谈"讲述者身份构建"。想象一下自己在向朋友描述周日遇到的逸闻趣事，我们可能一讲就是几个钟头。讲述过程中仿佛亲临其境，逻辑缜密且细节兼备。之所以能够拥有如此强大的记忆和复述能力，重要原因就在于"讲述者心态"。如果能把这种心态迁移至口译练习将有助于提高我们的记忆能力。讲述者心态包含两个层面的含义：其一表现在技术层面，其二表现在心理层面。

首先,一个故事通常由若干事件以某种逻辑关系进行串联,因此只要记住其中一个或几个环节,就能按照其提供的逻辑暗示,承上启下地牵连出一幅完整的画面。由此可见,讲述过程中的两个关键因素是逻辑和联想。

其次,保持轻松的心态也是圆满达成"讲述"任务的必备心理素质。口译任务通常"万众瞩目",对译员的临场发挥和控场能力形成巨大考验。如何在"高压"下保持轻松心态积极应对是译员的心理必修课。这一部分内容我们将在之后第十五章里具体讲解。

记忆能力是译员做好口译工作的核心"利器"。我们已经介绍了增强记忆的基本技巧和诀窍,但若想达到理想效果还需要大量训练。下一节我们将为大家介绍基础口译中的"小组传话"练习,这对于初级译员提高记忆、开展联络口译尤为有效。

第二节 "小组传话"练习

"小组传话"是联络口译的主要训练形式之一,可以翻译出来,也可以单纯考查记忆,不翻译成目的语。口译学习初期,学生通常难以对段落进行完整复述,而在真实的口译实践中绝对"充分"的复述也难以苛求。因此,"小组传话"的操练方式不仅能够模拟真实的联络口译情景,也能够缓解单纯复述练习造成的厌烦情绪,增加口译练习的趣味性。

"小组传话"训练应采用层级递进的设计方式:可以先以2人、3人或4人成组,然后递增到6—8人、10—12人,进而提升训练质量与效果。练习内容的选择上也遵循循序渐进的原则。建议初学时选择逻辑性较强的科普型段落或短文,训练逻辑分析能力,形成记忆框架,拓宽专业知识面。当传话水平达到一定程度后,可挑选逻辑性不那么强的叙述性文本来提高概括能力,模拟实战口译中的各种情形。

在课堂的小组传话中,出现信息谬误和偏离是常见现象。让我们来看下面这个例子:

例5-2

Xi'an was once the start of the Silk Road that made commerce between many countries in Eurasia possible. It was also the Imperial seat for no fewer than thirteen dynasties between 1000 BC and 1000 AD.

在这项关于中国历史的练习中,学生A一时口误,将"thirteen dynasties"传为"thirty dynasties",导致传话内容与原文发生较大偏差。当学生A将错误信息传递给学生B时,B根据历史常识对这一数字提出质疑,向A求证后发现信息错误,加以修正后准确还原了原文信息。

由此可见,无论是练习时还是在真实的联络口译情景中(例如商务谈判、法庭审讯、医疗服务等),由于情形复杂多样,交际双方信息悬殊,译员在完成本职工作的同时,还需发挥多样的人际功能，充当把关员、调解员、解说员和协调员的角色。当发现讲话者错误时，译员应敢于求证，保证内容符合讲话人的真实意图。此外，联络口译还需要译员具有丰富的专业知识背景，遵守道德行为准则，培养强烈的责任意识，这些都是一名优秀译员的必备素质。

参考文献

Ballester A, Jimenez C. Approaches to the Teaching of Interpreting: Mnemonic and Analytic Strategies[M] // Dollerup C, Loddegard A. Teaching Translation and Interpreting: Training, Talent and Experience. Amsterdam/Philadelphia: John Benjamins Publishing Company, 1992: 237-244.

Gillies A. Consecutive Interpreting: A Short Course[M]. London/New York: Routledge, 2019.

仲伟合，王斌华．基础口译［M］．北京：外语教学与研究出版社，2009．

专项练习

1. 句子传话练习

要求：以2—3人为小组，进行中英文传话练习。第一次可以只复述，不翻译成目的语。练习结束后与第一位同学对照，检查是否准确传达原文内容和逻辑，分析语义偏离之处和原因。之后可以根据准确的原文，各自再翻译一遍。

英文传话

(1) China, the gateway to East Asia, is a fascinating country. It is an ancient civilization that gave the world Peking Man, gunpowder and silk.

(2) Kunming is the economic, transportation, industrial and cultural centre of Southwest China, which is linked by rail through all of China's major cities.

(3) In addition to its own charms, Kunming serves as a base from which to explore the rainbow of ethnic minority in the area.

(4) Hangzhou is famous for its natural scenery. And its West Lake has been immortalized by countless poets and artists.

(5) Hangzhou's most famous site West Lake is a large lake separated by causeways and lined with ancient buildings and gardens designed for relaxation and self-cultivation.

(6) Yangshuo in South China was once a magnet for backpackers because of its cheap prices

in laid-back atmosphere, but today it draws all sorts of travellers to enjoy its beautiful scenery and karst mountains.

(7) For the trip back from Guilin to Yangshuo, many travellers choose to rent bicycles since the route is relatively flat and gives them the opportunity to view farmers toiling in their fields.

(8) Lhasa, famous for its Potala Palace on the Red Hill, is the most important city in Xizang and one of the highest elevated in the world at 11,500 feet.

(9) The Jiuzhaigou Valley has been described as a fairyland because of its many waterfalls, snow-covered karst mountains and 108 blue turquoise lakes that are so crystal clear that one can see the bottom.

(10) The Jiuzhaigou Valley is also the habitat of giant pandas, though the chances of seeing them are slim due to the park size and the number of tourists.

中文传话

（1）谈到中国美食，西方国家有时会陷入思维定势，认为中国美食只有炒菜、面条和饺子，实际不然。

（2）中国饮食文化绵延上万年，讲究色、香、味俱全。不同时代、地域和民族呈现出不同的菜式特色，构成异彩纷呈的中国美食。

（3）中国南北饮食差异巨大：北方气候寒冷，肉类和碳水摄入较多；南方沿海海产丰富，长江三角洲盛产鱼蟹。

（4）水稻种植需要大量水分，南方雨水充足，雨量大于北方，因此在南方，炒饭、米线和肠粉等以水稻为原材料的饮食很常见。

（5）小麦种植无需过多水分，北方气候干燥，因此面条和馒头等面食是北方餐桌上的常见主食。

（6）南方以粤菜为代表，其中点心是一种以蒸为主的小食，以木薯粉制成的肠粉和虾饺就是典型的广式点心。

（7）东部江浙地带水域宽广，素有"鱼米之乡"的美称，因此淡水鱼和虾蟹类是菜单上的主角，其中松鼠桂鱼就是苏帮菜的代表。

（8）北方美食中的绿叶菜较少，素食以土豆、茄子和白菜为主，肉类占主导，尤其是牛羊肉，是逢年过节的必购食材。

（9）烤鸭是享誉世界的北京菜式，起源于中国南北朝时期，在当时是宫廷食品，以色泽黄亮、外脆里嫩享誉全国。

（10）西南部植被茂盛，以亚热带气候、熊猫和辛辣食物出名。盛产的青辣椒口感又麻又辣，是菜肴中重要的调味品。

2. 段落传话练习

要求：以3—5人为小组，进行中英文传话练习。第一次可以只复述，不翻译成目的语。练习结束后与第一位同学对照，检查是否准确传达原文内容和逻辑，分析语义偏离之处和原因。之后可以根据准确的原文，各自再翻译一遍。

英文传话

(1) For centuries, people have kept large amounts of cash at home during difficult times. But these metal coins and paper bills can be a source of worry rather than hope. The fear is that these objects, possibly touched by thousands of people, could be a way for the virus to spread.

(2) In many areas, cash was already beginning to disappear due to the increased risk of robbery, the ease of internet ordering, and the ubiquity of cell phones. Sweden, Finland, Norway and others have slowly reduced cash use to the point where using it in large amounts seems unusual. And in China, cash use has dropped as electronic payment services increased in popularity over the past ten years.

(3) Hainan Airlines, China's fourth-largest carrier, launched a service in late March that helps passengers deliver their luggage home. The service is available at Beijing Capital International Airport and Haikou Meilan International Airport. By ordering the service online, passengers will be able to save the time of waiting for their checked luggage and they don't have to carry heavy suitcases by themselves.

(4) On the roof of the car, there is a glass dome that contains sensors of lasers, radars and cameras. These detect objects and their sizes in all directions at a range of 60 metres. Software then classifies objects based on their size, shape and movement pattern. The rounded shape of the car body and roof maximizes the field of view for the sensors on the roof — particularly for seeing objects very near the car.

(5) The car is designed for riding, not for driving. There is no steering wheel, pedals, gearstick, handbrake. The computer is housed under what would be the dashboard in a normal car. It's designed specifically for self-driving and assesses the speed of objects and adjusts the speed of the car accordingly.

中文传话

（1）作为风筝的发源地，山东省潍坊市有着悠久的风筝制作历史。潍坊风筝制作的历史可以追溯到2 000年前。起初，风筝用于军方通信，至明朝，风筝开始作为一种娱乐方式，在普通百姓中流行起来。

（2）56岁的杨红卫是潍坊风筝技艺的传承人。在杨家的风筝上，人们不仅可以看到常见的蝴蝶和燕子图案,还可以看到一些讲述中国神话、传说和历史的图案。

（3）北京冬奥会和冬残奥会上,许多优秀运动员参与了冰雪运动比赛,激发了中国人民对冬季运动的热情。实际上,中国自古以来就与冬季运动有着深厚的渊源,滑雪就起源于新疆维吾尔自治区。据考古学家估算,该区发现的先民滑雪的岩画距今可能有1万多年的历史。

（4）制作滑雪板一直是维吾尔族的一项传统手艺。手工制作的滑雪板附有一层马皮。马皮上的皮毛可以帮助滑雪者在滑下山坡时减少摩擦,也可以防止滑雪者在上山时摔倒。

（5）90后国潮设计师王平热衷于制作中国传统的凤冠。制作一顶凤冠通常需要一周至几个月的时间,用到30多种材料。王平还学会了制作古代服装,让头冠和服装能够搭配。他说,会坚持将中国传统文化与时尚元素相结合,制作更精美的头冠。

篇章练习

要求:将下列篇章分别口译成汉语或英语。本练习是手脑协调的训练,主要使用脑记,但允许用笔记录数字、专名和列举,尽力保留更多细节。

Text 1: Low levels of vitamin D and dementia

Preview:

Dementias（痴呆）are brain diseases that damage thinking and memory processes, what scientists call "cognitive abilities". Dementias are difficult to treat. Taking care of someone who has dementia is extremely demanding. And the disease is very frightening to sufferers. More than 47 million people around the world suffer from dementia. The World Health Organization reports that 60 percent of them live in low- and middle-income countries.

Now a new study in the United States shows a possible link between dementia and low levels of vitamin D.

Glossary:	
lentil: 扁豆	mackerel: 鲭鱼

Rutgers University：新泽西州立罗格斯大学（Rutgers, The State University of New Jersey），通称罗格斯大学（简称RU）

Health experts have long known that vitamin D is important for healthy bones and teeth. It may also help to protect the body against diseases such as diabetes and cancer. And now, researchers say vitamin D might help fight brain diseases called dementias. //

We get vitamin D from some foods like nuts, lentils and fatty fish like salmon and mackerel. We also get vitamin D from the sun. But that is not dependable. In some parts of the world, there is not enough sunlight to provide enough vitamin D. Also, sun block substances prevent the vitamin from entering the body. To add to the problem, the skin's ability to process vitamin D weakens as a person ages. As a result, low levels of vitamin D are common among older people. //

Researchers at Rutgers University in New Jersey are exploring the relationship between vitamin D and dementia. The team recently measured vitamin D levels and cognitive ability in older people. Nutritional sciences professor Joshua Miller led the team. He said cognitive abilities differed among the study subjects. He said tests showed that about 60 percent of the group was low in vitamin D. Those subjects who had low vitamin D levels showed more short-term memory loss. They were also less able to organize thoughts, order tasks by importance and make decisions. //

Text 2: Common ways to preserve food

Preview:

When you preserve food, you are taking action to stop it from breaking down, as it does naturally. You are killing or preventing the growth of microorganisms (微生物). Today, we will explore how you can preserve some of the fresh produce you buy or grow. By following a few easy steps, you can still eat those tasty fruits and vegetables when they are out of season. You can preserve late-summer fruits and vegetables in four basic ways. These include freezing, canning (罐装), pickling (腌制) and drying or dehydrating.

Glossary:	
freeze-grade bag：冷冻包装袋	microorganism：微生物
dehydrator：脱水机	

Freezing is the simplest way to save produce. It is important to freeze the produce as quickly as possible, and to do so in freeze-grade bags or other containers. One problem to avoid is freezer burn, which can affect the taste and feel of food. To prevent this, use plastic bags, wraps or containers designed for the freezer. //

There are two main ways to can produce: boiling hot water baths and pressure canning. A boiling water bath involves putting food in glass canning jars and then heating the jars in a pot of boiling water. The heat forces air from the glass jars and frees the food from bacteria and microorganisms. You can then seal the jars. Pressure canning food requires a pressure canner. Whichever method you use, always test the seal that keeps out fresh air. //

Pickling means preserving food in vinegar, salt brine or a similar mixture. You can pickle whole vegetables, like green beans or okra. //

A final way to preserve food is by drying it. Whatever food you are drying should be just ready to eat and not have bruises. Drying methods include air drying, oven drying and using a dehydrator. A dehydrator is probably the best choice. If you think you will be drying foods regularly, think about investing in an electric dehydrator. //

Text 3: 人工智能和就业问题

Glossary:	
条形码扫描仪：barcode scanner	自动柜员机：ATM (automated teller machine)
出纳：teller	自动驾驶：auto driving; auto pilot
疲劳驾驶：driver fatigue; tiredness while driving; driving when you are tired	

人工智能的兴起让人类面临危机。大家担心这会淘汰数以百万计的就业岗位，但是一份报告指出，我们没有必要如此悲观。实际上，普通员工的前景会更加乐观，因为人们可以不必从事机械劳动，而把时间用在更富创造性的工作上，从而提升工作满意度。//

历史上的技术革新对就业的负面影响并没有人们最初担心的那么大。我们可以举几个例子：在美国，条形码扫描仪并没有取代收银员的角色，在1980年至2013年间，零售业的就业岗位反而以每年2%的速度增长；自动柜员机的诞生让部分银行出纳转而向客户提供财务建议。//

人工智能简化了一些工作。卡车驾驶便是一个例子。有些人担心卡车司机会被自动驾驶所取代，但是在繁忙的街道上驾驶卡车要比在高速公路上困难得多，所以司机可以在行驶到郊外时切换到自动驾驶模式，抓紧时间休息一下，而到城里再改为人工驾驶。这一点和喷气式客机的原理类似：飞行员负责起飞和降落，但是在三万五千英尺处就打开巡航模式。从这种意义上来说，人工智能可以防止因疲劳驾驶引发的事故。//

Text 4: 口译工作与跨文化沟通

Preview:
　　口译工作是一项关键的语言服务,旨在实现跨文化交流和理解,使不同语言文化背景的人能够互相沟通。口译员需要具备出色的语言技能、文化敏感度和快速反应能力,通常在会议、研讨会、商务洽谈等场合中担任重要角色,将演讲和讨论内容以口头形式转译成目标语言。他们还需要具备解释和传达复杂概念的能力,确保信息准确传递,并在紧迫的时间限制下保持高质量的口译。口译工作对促进国际合作、文化交流和全球化具有重要意义,是一份兼具挑战性和成就感的工作。

Glossary:

跨文化交流: cross-cultural communication	一对一对话: one-on-one conversation
同声传译: simultaneous interpreting	交替传译: consecutive interpreting

　　口译员在打破语言障碍、推动跨文化交流方面发挥着至关重要的作用。口译员的主要任务是将一种口头或符号言语准确、流畅地转化为另一种语言,以实现交际的目的。
　　常见的口译类型主要有两种:同声传译和交替传译。本学期我们主要学习交替传译。交替传译是指口译员在讲话人停顿时进行翻译,将之前所说的内容以目标语言表达出来,适用于小型会议或一对一对话。
　　口译员的工作场所非常多样,包括但不限于国际会议、商业会谈、医疗机构等。他们可能需要熟练掌握两种或者更多语言,能够理解不同文化。口译员的工作不仅仅是字面的翻译,他们还需要理解背后的文化和语境,以传达确切的意涵和情境。
　　虽然口译员的工作压力大且需要非常严谨,但这个职业同时也非常有成就感。他们让世界变得更加互联,聆听并理解彼此的声音,并将其传递给更广大的听众。
　　因此,口译员的工作不仅对个体有重要意义,也对促进全球交流和理解具有深远的影响。他们的工作融合了挑战与机遇、技能与灵活性。对于那些寻求挑战、对语言和文化具有热情的人来说,成为口译员无疑是一个值得骄傲的职业选择。

第六章
学会记忆（Ⅱ）

第一节　短期记忆与长期记忆

在上一章节中我们已经对口译记忆进行了简单的入门介绍，阐述了调动大脑、进行有效记忆的基本方法。这一章节中，我们将深入挖掘大脑记忆的基本原理，解释口译活动中不同记忆类型的工作原理。

记忆是指人脑对信息（例如个人经历、知识、概念和情感等）的存取及加工（任文，2009：58）。著名英汉口译理论与教学专家赛顿和杜蕴德将记忆分为三种类型：回声记忆（echoic memory）、工作记忆（working memory，又称short-term memory，即短期记忆）和长期记忆（long-term memory）（Setton & Dawrant, 2016: 206）。这三种记忆之间的关系如图6-1所示：

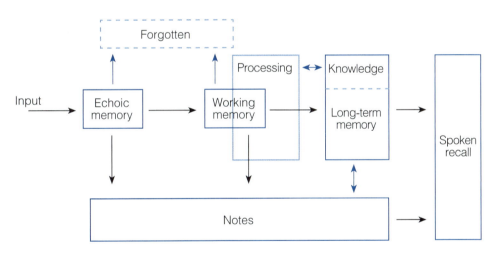

图6-1　短期记忆与长期记忆（Gillies, 2019: 33）

一、回声记忆

"回声记忆"，顾名思义，是指人脑接收到外界刺激信号时做出的即时反应。这种记忆的特点是反应快、时间短，文本、图像或声音信息在大脑中保留的时间仅几秒钟，在此过程中大脑不对信息做任何处理。回声记忆类似多重记忆模型中的"感官记忆"（sensory register）（Atkinson & Shiffrin, 1968），即人体五官（听觉、视觉、嗅觉、味觉、触觉）在接受外界信息源刺激时产生的信息记忆。口译活动中，译员主要通过视觉和听觉接受信息，之后将所得信息转入工作记忆进行处理。当然，如图6-1所示，在此转换过程中，部分信息难免被"舍弃"。这种舍弃可能是有意为之,也可能是无意的疏漏。因此在口译活动中,译员要保持精力高度集中,充分"捕捉"外界的信息输入,才能最大程度地将"有效信息"转入下一步处理。

二、短期记忆

"短期记忆"又称"工作记忆",意味着大脑启动工作模式,对接受到的信息进行处理整合。短期记忆的信息来源于两个方面:回声记忆和长期记忆。短期记忆运作时,译员一方面接收回声记忆的信息传输,另一方面结合自己在长期记忆库中的知识和经验对新信息进行理解和加工。之后,人们通过两种途径创建输出记忆:创建笔记或创建长期记忆。创建输出的过程主要受限于短期记忆的空间和时间,必须快速完成,这也是译员记忆的主要瓶颈。因此"短期记忆"通常是口译记忆练习的核心内容,下面我们将结合具体例子进行详细分析。

短期记忆只能保存5至9个信息单位,每个单位信息的容量可大可小,既可以单项形式存在(例如某个单词或某个数字),也可以条块形式存在(例如句子或段落)。最典型的例子是"开场白"口译,如下例所示:

例6-1

女士们,先生们,亲爱的朋友们:

首先,我谨代表中国政府和人民,对本次亚太经合组织人力资源开发部长级会议的召开表示热烈祝贺!对与会各位代表表示诚挚欢迎!对所有组织协调本次会议的工作人员表示衷心感谢!

开场口译通常遵循特定话术,也即我们所说的"客套话",可以概括为"首先,我谨代表……,对……表示热烈祝贺,对……表示诚挚欢迎,对……表示衷心感谢"(Firstly, on behalf of the ..., I would like to extend my warmest congratulations to ..., sincere welcome to ..., and heartfelt gratitude to ...)。对于有经验的译员来说,这一段内容可看作一个信息单元,只需要根据具体场合或会议更新信息即可。而对于不熟悉这种话术的译员来说,这段话意味着5个不同的信息单位(人称—代表—诚挚祝贺—诚挚欢迎—衷心感谢),导致其短期记忆基本满载,留给其他信息的空间非常有限,遗忘或缺漏的几率大大提高。因此,同学们在平常准备的时候应多积累类似的模式化表达、常用短语和句式,这种"台下功夫"能有效缓解"台上压力",为接收新信息挪出记忆空间。

短期记忆的持续时间很短,专家认为最长不超过30秒(Atkinson & Shiffrin, 1968)。这就要求译员能够对接受的信息进行快速处理、删繁就简,通过脑记或笔记关键词的方式记录下核心内容。有经验的译员在此过程中还会通过"关键词回放"的方式不断巩固记忆。

三、长期记忆

"长期记忆"是指长久储存的信息,能持续几天至几年不等。与"短期记忆"不同,长期记忆并不倚赖即时速记,而是通过长期积累或反复强化在记忆中形成的"知识库",也即译员"台下功夫"的体现。口译活动中,长期记忆与短期记忆相互支撑,互相转化:长期记忆为短期记忆中信息的理解和处理提供知识参考;而被处理过的部分短期记忆则进入长期记忆库,成为译员背景知识的一部分。

口译活动中,长期记忆按照信息内容的不同,可分为以下几种类型:

一是情景记忆。对个人亲身经历的、发生在特定时间和地点的某一情景的记忆。上下文语境的相关记忆能够有效提高情景记忆。

二是语义记忆。对抽象事实或一般性知识的记忆,例如单词含义。

三是程序记忆。对完成特定事件所需过程和步骤的记忆,例如如何开车、游泳或骑自行车。很多情况下,程序记忆无须刻意强记,而是在反复练习或使用中形成的自然记忆。

有经验的译员通常不会依赖一种记忆类型,而是懂得结合不同记忆类型,最大限度地调动自己的记忆能力,在有限时间内达到最佳记忆效果。

综上所述,一名出色的口译员不仅要技巧熟练,还应在平时多注意积累各领域的专业知识,不断丰富个人阅历、拓展知识边界和个人视野。这些背景信息能够在很大程度上缓解译员临场发挥时的焦虑情绪,有效提高"短期记忆"信息的提取和处理效率,甚至能够在讲话者出现口误等情况下,根据自己的知识积累对错误信息进行纠正,达到调解和交际的目的。

第二节 记忆强化的训练方法

对于口译初学者而言,记忆训练的主要内容是短期记忆。它是"记忆系统"中言语信息的"来料加工场",负责信息的选择、加工、存取等。可见,短时记忆是译员进行高强度脑力活动的关键环节,译员可利用这一时段将收到的信息迅速进行各种关联或复杂加工,而长期记忆主要是配合短时记忆,进行后台支持。在第四单元中,我们已经初步介绍过复述和主旨口译这两种听辨的训练方法,二者在强化短期记忆时同样适用,毕竟听懂才是记忆的基础,经过听辨加工的信息才需要动用记忆存储。本节中我们将通过具体的例子向同学们进一步介绍听辨与记忆相结合的训练方法。

一、复述训练

第一种训练方法是复述。我们可以先听英文原文,然后用英文自己组织语言说出原文的意思。

例6-2

原文:

The Internet began its life displaying nothing more exciting than white text on a black background. Flat images were added in the 1990s. Video came to dominate in the 2010s. On that reading, a move into three dimensions is a logical consequence of the steady growth in computing power.

学生复述：

The Internet first featured plain texts; then images in the 1990s. Video became dominant in the 2010s. As computers become more powerful, it is logical for the Internet to move into three dimensions.

我们仔细观察一下这段复述就会注意到，学生输出的语言与原文虽然有点出入，但关键信息几乎没有丢失，达意效果比较理想。与此同时，我们也注意到复述中的措辞会受到原文表达的影响，学生倾向于使用原词（尤其当原文中出现了自己非常熟悉且掌握自如的表达时，如：move into）、原词的其他形式（如：dominate 变成了 dominant；power 变成了 powerful），或使用近义词替换（如：nothing more exciting 变成了 plain）。这种练习迫使我们把精力从单音听辨调整到对连贯语意整体的捕捉。

相反，过多关注细节会导致舍本逐末，出现遗漏、编造或者逻辑不通等情况，比如下面这个例子。

例6-3

原文：

It's no overstatement that digital mediums have taken over every aspect of our lives. We check what our friends are doing on the glowing screens in our hands, read books on dedicated e-readers, and communicate with customers and clients primarily through email. Yet for all the benefits digital mediums have provided us, there has been a growing body of evidence over the past several years that the brain prefers physical mediums.

学生复述：

It's no overstatement that digital medium is important to our lives. We check glowing screens, read books and communicate with customers through email. But over the past several years our brain prefers physical mediums.

从复述的结果来看，学生大量保留了原文中的词汇（overstatement、digital medium、glowing screen、physical mediums），但画线处明显误解了原文的意思。根据该学生的反馈，她在音频的开头就因为 "no overstatement" 而乱了阵脚，导致没有听明白 "e-readers"，误解为读音相近的 "read"。在最后的部分，她也没能把握 "yet for all the benefits" 所提示的 "转折加让步" 的关系，导致逻辑上有所缺失。

二、主旨口译

主旨口译是指译员简明扼要地传达发言人意图的口译方式。译员在进行主旨口译时，通常使用阐释、梳理、总结等方式对原文大意进行概括，实现原文的交际功能，对发言细节往往进行删减和压缩。主旨口译因其简明达意的特点被广泛应用于陪同口译、会议口译等实战场景中。同时，这一形式也常用于课堂教学和口译比赛（如海峡两岸口译大赛），成为考查译员理解和记忆能力的重要方法。

例6-4

原文：

What keeps us chewing while we sit down in front of the television with a meal or snack after a long day? Television isn't so much an appetite stimulant as it is an appetite distraction. When we watch TV, we're engaged in the program, which means we're paying less attention to the neurological and gastronomical cues that tell us we're getting full. Instead of taking note of how we're eating, we're engaged in somewhat passive consumption.

学生译文：

为什么我们在看电视的时候会不停地吃东西？不是因为电视刺激了我们的食欲，而是因为电视干扰了我们的注意力。我们看电视入迷了，所以注意不到自己吃饱了，一直处于一种被动进食的状态。

这段译文是典型的"得意忘言"：一些原文的表达形式经过调整，省略了部分细节和生僻词（如："neurological and gastronomical cues"）。该生之后坦言自己两个生词都不认识，但把意思化入"注意不到自己吃饱了"一并带过了。综合来看，这段主旨口译基本成功。下面再举一个汉译英的例子。

例6-5

原文：

世界上有两种食物人是离不了的：一种是物质的，一种是精神的，吃的东西如果是垃圾，人会得病，精神消费的东西如果是垃圾，社会将会得病，人也不会健康。今天来参会的各位出版界的朋友都是这两种食物的消费者，更是精神食粮的制造者。

参考译文：

There are two types of food: one is material, the other is spiritual. One gets sick by consuming poisonous food. Likewise, the society gets sick if spiritual rubbish poisons people's mind. Dear friends, as professionals in the publishing industry, you consume both types of food, and more importantly, produce the latter.

这段译文对原文的细节信息进行了合理的删减(如:删减了"人是离不了的""人也不会健康"),用相对简洁的英文传递了原文的核心内容。

通过本章节的讲解,相信同学们对记忆机制和训练方法已经有了基本的认识,也已经跃跃欲试了,下面就让我们通过一些练习来巩固所学内容吧!

参考文献

Atkinson R C, Shiffrin R M. Human Memory: A Proposed System and Its Control Processes[M]// Spence K W, Spence J T. The Psychology of Learning and Motivation: Vol. 2. New York: Academic Press, 1968: 89−195.

Gillies A. Consecutive Interpreting: A Short Course[M]. London/New York: Routledge, 2019.

Setton R, Dawrant A. Conference Interpreting — A Complete Course[M]. Amsterdam/Philadelphia: John Benjamins Publishing Company, 2016.

任文. 交替传译[M]. 北京:外语教学与研究出版社,2009.

专项练习

1. 英语复述及英汉口译

要求:以2人为小组,首先进行英语源语复述练习。其中一人负责朗读语段,另外一人仔细听取信息,随后凭记忆复述听到的语段,全程不可使用笔记。复述后进行错漏信息分析。源语复述练习后再进行英汉口译练习,翻译后对错漏之处进行分析。

(1) Penguins have long captured the imagination and the hearts of people of the world over, but while popular culture depicts them as clumsy adorable birds with endlessly abundant populations, the truth is that penguins are exceedingly graceful, often grumpy and their populations are in rapid freefall.

(2) The real-life situation is far more precarious than people think. And if current trends do not change, it may not be long before penguins can only be found in movies. Current threats to penguins include the destruction of both marine and terrestrial habitats, introduced predators, entrapment in fishing nets, and pollution from plastics and chemicals.

(3) There have also been several large-scale oil spills over the past 50 years that have killed or impacted tens of thousands of penguins around the world. But the two major threats to penguins today are global warming and overfishing.

(4) Global warming impacts penguins in multiple ways, from interrupting the production

of krill that they feed on due to decreased sea ice formation in the Antarctic, to increasing the frequency and severity of storms that destroy nests, to shifting the cold-water currents carrying penguins' prey too far away from penguin breeding and foraging grounds.

(5) Even though humans may be the greatest threat to penguins, we are also their greatest hope. Many research and conservation projects are underway to protect penguin habitats and restore vulnerable populations. With a little help from us and some changes in the practices that impact our planet and oceans, there is hope that our tuxedo clad friends will still be around in the next century.

2. 汉语复述及汉英口译

要求：以2人为小组，首先进行汉语源语复述练习。其中一人负责朗读语段，另外一人仔细听取信息，随后凭记忆复述听到的语段，全程不可使用笔记。复述后进行错漏信息分析。源语复述练习后再进行汉英口译练习，之后对译文的错漏之处进行分析。

（1）信用卡是一种非现金交易付款的方式，持卡人能够通过记贷方式支付商品和服务费用。简单来说，就是银行把钱先借给你用，你不需要往信用卡里存钱就可以拿着信用卡去消费。

（2）比如某个银行给你批了一张一万元额度的信用卡，你就可以用这张卡消费一万元，请注意这钱是要还的，虽然没有那么快。用流行的话来讲，这叫超前消费，就是你先把下个月工资给花了。

（3）那银行为什么要发行信用卡给你呢？因为银行会在信用卡交易的过程中赚取手续费，这个手续费不是向你收，而是向商家收。比如今天你到酒吧嗨了一晚上，结账的时候用信用卡刷了一千元，酒吧老板只能收到九百多元，那这少了的一点钱，大部分就是被银行赚走的。

（4）你可能要问，那酒吧老板不是白白损失了手续费，他为什么要让你刷信用卡呢？你想呀，今天你可能没钱，他不让你刷信用卡可能连这笔生意都做不成，而且你刷信用卡消费时不会那么心疼，他肯定希望你刷越多越好啊，反正后面还不还钱跟他没关系，那是你跟银行的事。

（5）除了购买商品外，还有一些人利用信用卡取现。用信用卡来进行资金周转是当今社会成本最低、最方便的方式。

3. 英汉主旨口译

要求：以2人为小组，进行英译汉主旨口译练习。其中一人负责朗读语段，另外一人仔细听取信息，随后凭记忆翻译听到的语段，全程不可使用笔记。口译后对错漏之处进行分析。

(1) Every college has different rules on what you can bring. It is essential that you check the list of approved and prohibited items from your college before you move in. Rules vary from school to school, and you may want to hold off on buying that mini-fridge or microwave combo until you make sure you can have them in your dorm.

(2) You probably shouldn't take your whole closet. Dorm storage space is one thing that many incoming freshmen overestimate. Depending on the size of your wardrobe, it might be a good idea to consider leaving everything but the necessities at home. Besides, you might find you don't need as many clothes as you think — most college laundry facilities are easy, inexpensive, and located right in the residence hall.

(3) You might not like your roommate, and that's not the end of the world. For your first semester of college, odds are you'll have either a randomly picked roommate or a roommate who was selected based on your responses to a brief questionnaire. And while it's completely possible that you will be the best friends, it's also possible that you might not get along. This can be uncomfortable, but remember that with classes, clubs, and other campus events, you probably won't be in your room very much anyway. However, if your roommate is a bit more than you can handle, Residential Advisors and Residential Directors can often help.

(4) Know where you can get good food. Food is an important part of the campus experience. Most colleges have multiple dining options, and it's a good idea to try them all during your first semester. If you want to know the best place to eat, or if you need vegan, or gluten-free options, you can always check the college's website, or just ask your fellow students. Don't forget to try outside the college, too — college towns almost always have good, cheap food.

(5) There are tons of things to do in the college. The last thing anyone should be worried about is being bored on campus. Almost every college has a host of student clubs and organizations, frequent campus events, and other activities. They're not hard to find, either. There are often fliers and posters all around campus for things to do and clubs to join. Some clubs even have their own social media sites, which could help you not only learn about the clubs, but also contact current members.

(6) Plan out your academic career early, but don't be afraid to change it. In order to make sure you have all the credits you need to graduate on time, it's a good idea to plan out your courses early. But keep in mind that your plan won't be written in stone. College is supposed to be a time of discovery.

(7) You can get good grades and have fun. A common fear when starting college is that there will be time for either studying or having fun, but not both. The truth is that with good time management it is possible to get good grades in all your classes and still have time to be in clubs and go have fun. If you manage your schedule well, you may even get a decent amount of sleep, too.

4 英汉主旨口译

要求：以2人为小组，进行英译汉主旨口译练习。其中一人负责朗读语段，另外一人仔细听取信息，随后凭记忆翻译听到的语段，全程不可使用笔记。口译后对错漏之处进行分析。

(1) In an era where technology serves as the backbone of our daily lives, innovation has extended its roots deep into the realm of travel and culture, bringing a transformation like never before.

(2) Travel isn't merely about a change of geography; it's about the immersive experiences that fuel knowledge and understanding. As we travel, we unfold pages of cultures, traditions, and histories, creating a global narrative of human civilization. This exploration is now being enhanced with the incredible power of innovation, making travel more enriching and enlightening.

(3) The advent of augmented reality (AR) and virtual reality (VR) has reimagined the way we travel. Cultural heritage sites, museums, and art galleries are employing these technologies to facilitate detailed and immersive storytelling.

(4) For instance, VR headsets can transport us to historical eras, helping us visualize the splendor of past cultures in their prime. Meanwhile, AR can superimpose information, translations, and animations onto exhibits, providing engaging narratives about cultural artifacts.

(5) On the other hand, social media platforms have created a global stage where cultures can display their uniqueness, further promoting cultural exchange and understanding. With each sharing of experiences, posting of pictures, or writing of travel blogs, every traveler contributes to the global cultural narrative, making the world a smaller, more accessible place.

(6) In conclusion, innovation has opened new vistas in culture-focused travel, making it more immersive and personalized. It's a revolution that upturns how we experience, share and preserve our journeys.

篇章练习

Text 1: Why climate change is a threat to human rights (excerpt)

Preview:

Mary Robinson, born on 21 May, 1944, was the 7th president of Ireland, serving from December 1990 to September 1997, the first woman to hold this office. Following her time as president, Robinson became the United Nations High Commissioner for Human Rights from 1997 to 2002. She was also the former Chair of the International Institute for Environment and Development (IIED) and led the Mary Robinson Foundation — Climate Justice between 2010–2019, a centre for education and advocacy on sustainable and people-centred development in the world's poorest communities. Mary Robinson asks us to join the movement for worldwide climate justice: "We are the first generation to understand how serious the climate crisis is and the last generation to be able to do something about it."

Glossary:	
UN High Commissioner for Human Rights：联合国人权事务高级专员	the UN Convention on Climate Change：联合国气候变化公约
greenhouse gas emission：温室气体排放	metric ton：公吨
kerosene：煤油	zero carbon：零碳
Uganda：乌干达	Malawi：马拉维

I came to climate change not as a scientist or an environmental lawyer, and I wasn't really impressed by the images of polar bears or melting glaciers. It was because of the impact on people, and the impact on their rights — their rights to food and safe water, health, education and shelter. And I say this with humility, because I came late to the issue of climate change. When I served as UN High Commissioner for Human Rights from 1997 to 2002, climate change wasn't at the front of my mind. // I don't remember making a single speech on climate change. I knew that there was another part of the United Nations — the UN Convention on Climate Change — that was dealing with the issue of climate change. It was later when I started to work in African countries on issues of development and human rights. And I kept hearing this pervasive sentence: "Oh, but things are so much worse now, things are so much worse." And then I explored what was behind that; it was about changes in the climate — climate shocks, changes in the weather. //

I met Constance Okollet, who had formed a women's group in Eastern Uganda, and she told me that when she was growing up, she had a very normal life in her village and they didn't go hungry, they knew that the seasons would come as they were predicted to come, they knew when to sow and they knew when to harvest, and so they had enough food. // But, in recent years, at the time of this conversation, they had nothing but long periods of drought, and then flash flooding, and then more drought. The school had been destroyed; livelihoods had been destroyed; their harvest had been destroyed. She formed this women's group to try to keep her community together. And this was a reality that really struck me, because of course, Constance Okollet wasn't responsible for the greenhouse gas emissions that were causing this problem. //

Indeed, I was very struck about the situation in Malawi in January of this year. There was an unprecedented flooding in the country, it covered about a third of the country, over 300 people were killed, and hundreds of thousands lost their livelihoods. And the average person in Malawi emits about 80 kg of CO_2 a year. The average US citizen emits about 17.5 metric tons. // So those who are suffering disproportionately don't drive cars, don't have electricity, don't consume very significantly, and yet they are feeling more and more the impacts of the changes in the climate, the changes that are preventing them from knowing how to grow food properly, and knowing how to look after their future. I think it was really the importance of the injustice that really struck me very forcibly. //

Governments around the world agreed at the conference in Copenhagen, and have repeated it at every conference on climate, that we have to stay below two degrees Celsius of warming above pre-industrial standards. But we're on course for about four degrees. So we face an existential threat to the future of our planet. And that made me realize that climate change is the greatest threat to human rights in the 21st century. //

And that brought me then to climate justice. Climate justice responds to the moral argument — both sides of the moral argument — to address climate change. First of all, to be on the side of those who are suffering most and are most effected. And secondly, to make sure that they're not left behind again, when we start to move and start to address climate change with climate action, as we are doing. //

In our very unequal world today, it's very striking how many people are left behind. In our world of 7.2 billion people, about 3 billion are left behind. 1.3 billion don't have access to electricity, and they light their homes with kerosene and candles, both of which are dangerous. And in fact they spend a lot of their tiny income on that form of lighting. 2.6 billion people cook on open fires — on coal, wood and animal dung. And this causes about 4 million deaths a year from indoor smoke inhalation, and of course, most of those who die are women. // So we have a very unequal world, and we need to change from "business as usual". And we shouldn't underestimate the scale and the transformative nature of the change which will be needed, because we have to go to zero carbon emissions by about 2050, if we're going to stay below two degrees Celsius of warming. And that means we have to leave about two-thirds of the known resources of fossil fuels in the ground. //

It's a very big change, and it means that obviously, industrialized countries must cut their emissions, must become much more energy-efficient, and must move as quickly as possible to renewable energy. For developing countries and emerging economies, the problem and the challenge is to grow without emissions, because they must develop; they have very poor populations. So they must develop without emissions, and that is a different kind of problem. Indeed, no country in the world has actually grown without emissions. // All the countries have developed with fossil fuels, and then may be moving to renewable energy. So it is a very big challenge, and it requires the total support of the international community, with the necessary finance and technology, and systems and support, because no country can make itself safe from the dangers of climate change. This is an issue that requires complete human solidarity. Human solidarity, if you like, based on self-interest — because we are all in this together, and we have to work together to ensure that we reach zero carbon by 2050. //

Text 2: 中国丝绸

Preview:
中国丝绸以其独特的魅力在全球历史和文化中占据重要地位。丝绸历史源远流长，早在四五千年前，中国的嫘祖就发明了缫丝织绸的技艺。养蚕源自先民对生命和宇宙的思考，丝织是对机械和数学的探索。2009年，"中国传统桑蚕丝织技艺"入选联合国教科文组织非物质文化遗产名录。通过著名的"丝绸之路"，中国丝绸远播至世界各地，以其永恒的美感和传统的价值在世界各地广受追捧，成为推动中西文化交流和文明互鉴的重要纽带。

Glossary:	
质地，纹理: texture	蚕: silkworm
养蚕业: sericulture	蚕茧: cocoon
丝织: silk weaving	丝绸之路: Silk Road

中国丝绸,也称"东方丝绸",在全球历史和文化中占据特殊地位。这种闪光且质地顺滑的面料令人着迷。但是你了解这种雅致面料背后的奇妙故事吗? //

中国丝绸起源于中国古代文明。蚕丝的生产是一个复杂且耗费劳力的过程,从一个小小的生物——蚕开始。蚕丝生产,又称养蚕业,涉及蚕的精心培育。这种古老的习俗据传始于约5 000年前。//

蚕丝的发现归功于黄帝的元妃嫘祖。有一天,她注意到一个意外掉入茶水中的蚕茧,居然可以拉出一条闪亮的线。经过长时间的不懈试验,她终于探索出丝织的奥妙。//

通过著名的"丝绸之路",中国丝绸被运往世界各地。这条古老的商路将中国与亚洲、欧洲和非洲国家相连,推动文化交流,使丝绸成为了全球广受追捧的面料。这种豪华面料无论在过去还是现在,都是高贵和财富的象征。例如,中国皇帝曾经以穿丝绸长袍彰显其权力和地位。//

中国丝绸并非仅仅是一种面料或商品,这一条丝滑闪亮的丝线更蕴含着历史、文化、工艺和国际关系的丰富内涵。美丽的中国丝绸以其永恒美感和传统价值成为优雅的象征。//

第七章
逻辑分析

第一节 逻辑与记忆

大部分口译初学者害怕较长的段落,担心"脑容量不够"记不下来。而在两种翻译方向之间,同学们普遍更加畏惧英译汉,尽管理论上译出母语的难度更高。口译者的"脑容量"是不是有限的呢?长的段落是否一定比短的难记呢?英语材料的记忆难度是否一定高于汉语材料呢?要了解这些问题,我们不妨暂且抛开跨语际转换,直接看看记忆本身的难度何在。

日常生活中,我们都有丰富的转述经验,例如向朋友介绍刚看过的一部电影,或是讲述往事、转述新闻。大多数时候,我们可以分享主要内容和部分细节,并不需要刻意回忆,也不觉得有什么负担。但如果让我们重复几个简单的手机号码,却往往需要借助笔记,不然就有可能出错。为什么会这样呢?二者之间最大的区别就是逻辑:前者能够沿着一两条线索自然发展,一气呵成;而后者只是孤立的数字组成的无序组合,每一个位数都是一个独立的信息点。如果那个号码是一串有规律的数字,如:12345678、66668888;或是能够包含其他特殊含义,如某人的出生年月、吉祥话的谐音数字等,那么记忆的负担又会低很多。现在,我们再回过头来回答本章开头提出的几个问题:

第一,口译者的"脑容量"是不是有限的?答案是肯定的,这也是为什么除了陪同口译、旅游口译等少数场合,大部分同传和交传的译员都需要做笔记。美国心理学家米勒(Miller, 1956)提出,通常人们的记忆容量是 7 ± 2,即短时记忆一般可以处理7个无序信息,并在5至9个之间波动。但需要注意的是,这里针对的是"无序信息"。零散的信息点如同一颗颗散落的珍珠,而逻辑就像是串联珍珠的一根线。只要这根线足够长、足够结实,就可以串联起超长的一串项链。也就是说,如果不同的信息点能够组成有意义的连贯内容,或是干脆构成约定俗成的预制语块(prefabricated chunks),那么就能够被大脑整体储存和调取,即帮助大脑"扩容"了。

第二,长的段落是否一定比短的难记呢?这倒未必。即便是主题内容、语言难度相仿的段落,长的也未必难记。有时候发言人开口没说几句话就停下来,反而令译者不知所措,这是因为语段太短或者无实际意义的套语过多,导致还不足以形成一个完整的信息点。译员无法根据上下文进行合理推测,只好非常概略地翻译一下。接着发言人切入正题,虽然有大段的介绍,但论点清晰、叙述有条理,就能够在听者的大脑中建立一条通路。这为译者提供了足够的语境，翻译起来反而容易了。当然，在无笔记的条件下，译者的短期记忆也是有限度的。如果信息点过于密集，或者并列的信息点过多，那么即便是富有逻辑的语段也会令人不堪重负。

第三，英语材料的记忆难度是否一定高于汉语材料呢？其实，由于两种语言不同的风格特征，有时候中文语段会比较抽象，不易把握。笔者曾在课堂上提过这样一个问题：在不涉及数字和专有名词的前提下，复述一二百字的中文语篇难吗？大家几乎都认为理解和记忆这类母语语段易如反掌，可是接下来的练习结果却出乎意料。

例 7-1

我国秉持共商共建共享的全球治理观，倡导国际关系民主化，坚持国家不分大小、强弱、贫富，一律平等，支持联合国发挥积极作用，支持扩大发展中国家在国际事务中的代表性和发言权。加大对发展中国家特别是最不发达国家援助的力度，促进缩小南北发展差距。

同学们听完普遍反映罗列项目和修饰性词句较多，脑子里一团糟，这是因为语段的语域较高，专业性较强，离我们日常生活的语言比较远。而且这段话还包含了大量名词性短语和固定搭配，语言更凝练，也就意味着同样时长里的信息点更密集，即使原文是汉语，看似没有听力理解的问题，翻译起来也很不容易。

相对汉语的重意合（parataxis），英语的行文则重形合（hypotaxis），含有较多关联词来指示逻辑关系，例如表转折的就有 but、yet、although、however、despite、nevertheless 等。如果能把握住这些"路标"，便能理顺思路。汉语的讲话有时句段之间的关系是内蕴的，是语言深层次上的连接。译者作为第一手的听众，首先需要根据语境和知识储备对信息进行初加工，整合出一套较为显化的逻辑并传译给听众。那么，为什么许多口译学习者仍然觉得英译汉更加"记不住"呢？这里的难点主要在于英语的听力理解，而非内容记忆。记忆的基础是理解，由于外语听力的局限性，英语学习者在捕捉英文信息、理顺逻辑方面会薄弱得多。听译的英文段落用于视译，学生们就会觉得容易很多；而同一篇汉译英材料在两种翻译模式下，学生却反馈难度差不多。由此可见，英译汉的难点主要在于"听不懂"，而不是"记不下来"。

第二节 口译中的逻辑分析

听辨是逻辑分析的基础，同时逻辑分析又能帮助译者听辨，二者相辅相成。如果能在提高语言基本功的同时，加强逻辑思维的训练，就能协助学生译员听懂、记忆和预测，也可以提高翻译产出的衔接性与连贯性，减轻听众的认知负担，改善跨语际传播的效果。正因为逻辑的重要性，有笔记交传中不能只记录具体的语义信息点，也要记录下相对抽象的逻辑线索。那些线条、箭头和其他符号可以提示信息的整合方式与走向，而这些内容都是逻辑分析后的产物,体现出译员对原材料的全面把握。

一、语篇类型与逻辑分析

要在口译中熟练地进行逻辑分析,首先需要熟悉发言中常见的语篇类型。口译素材按照语篇类型可以分为叙述型、说明型、议论型等。

说明型的语篇常常是描述性的,按照空间线索来描述,如从上到下、从西到东、由远及近、由内而外等。可以关注有关地点、方向的指示词,并且按照相关的顺序来预测、听辨,尝试视觉化记忆。例如:

例7-2

Now I'm going to give you a plan of the site and I'd just like to point out where everything is and then you can take a look at everything for yourself.

I've already pointed out the river which is on the left. And of course, running along the bottom is Woodside Road, got it? OK. Now we're standing at the entrance, see it at the bottom, and immediately to our right is the Ticket Office. You won't need that because you've got your group booking, but just past it are the toilets — always good to know where they are. In front of us is the car park, as you can see, and to the left, by the entry gate is the Gift Shop. That's where you can get copies of the guide, like this one here.

Now, beyond the car park, all the buildings are arranged in a half circle with a yard in the middle. The big, stone building at the top is the main Workshop. That's where the furnace is and where all the metal was smelted and the tools were cast, as you'll be able to see. Now, in the top right-hand corner, that building with bigger windows is the Showroom, where samples of all the tools that were made through the ages are on display. In the top left corner is the Grinding Shop, where the tools were sharpened and finished. And on one side of that, you can see the Engine Room and on the other is the Café, which isn't an antique, you'll be pleased to know, though they do serve very nice old-fashioned teas.

The row of buildings you can see on the left are the cottages. These were built for the workers towards the end of the eighteenth century and they're still furnished from that period so you can get a good idea of ordinary people's living conditions. Across the yard from them, you can see the stables where the horses were kept for transporting the products. And the separate building in front of them is the Works Office and that still has some of the old accounts on display.

Right, if anyone wants a guided tour then I'm starting at the Engine Room. If you'd like to come along, this way please, ladies and gentlemen.

这原本是剑桥雅思听力第四册第一套中的地图题（见图7-1），用于填空并不难。如果单纯去听并做笔记，那么就需要有较好的方位感并展开想象，例如大小、多少、形状、材质等（见画线部分），这样理解和梳理起来才会更容易。

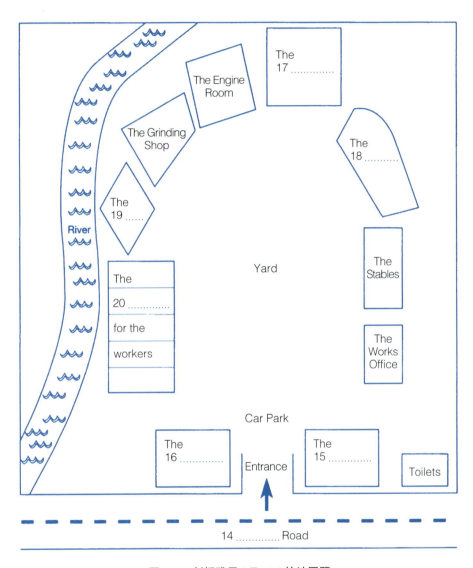

图7-1 剑桥雅思4 Test 1的地图题

议论型的语篇注重言之有理，论证严谨，环环相扣，其中关联词能够将内蕴的逻辑显化，提示口译初学者语篇发展的脉络，尤其是因果、转折、对比这几类。例如：

例7-3

Many college students have given up taking class notes by hand. Instead, they type on computers. But scientists say that method is less helpful.

If you need to remember something, write it. Writing notes by hand is much better for long-term memory of ideas. So, turn off your computer if you want to remember something.

Students who type notes on a keyboard often write down what the teacher says word-for-word. They may write without really thinking about what they are writing. These electronic notes contained more words. But scientists say it leads to "mindless transcription." Transcription means to write down something exactly as you hear it.

However, students taking notes by writing them, need to first process the information they hear. Then they record just the main parts. They use fewer words. This is because people usually write slower than they type. This process of summarizing information leads to a deeper understanding, say the researchers.

这则材料来自于VOA慢速英语,介绍了手记笔记和用电脑记笔记的效果区别,其中包含了大量的对比关系和因果关系(见画线部分)。本篇的内容对于理解和记忆也特别有启示意义:与其不加思索地记录下孤立的文字,不如边听边分析,厘清逻辑。

不过大多数材料是两种或三种类型的混合体,其逻辑关系也未必都有关联词和状语来提示。除此之外,一些语篇的逻辑本来就不太清晰,例如某些仪式致辞、寒暄问候等,信息点多而杂,思路也可能比较跳跃,对译者的考验更大。

二、思维导图与复述练习

口译中的逻辑分析如同在头脑中画一幅思维导图,协助译者进行结构化的思考,将大大小小的信息点归入不同模块、序列和层次。学者们将口译中的逻辑分析分为纵向分析和横向分析。纵向分析较为宏观和立体,重在理清语篇的整体结构,分清信息点的主次和层次,其可视化效果就像一棵树(见图7-2)。

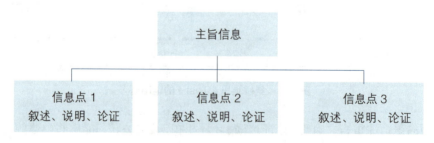

图7-2 纵向逻辑分析的可视化效果

横向分析是微观的、平面的,是将同一个层次上的信息点联系起来(connecting the dots)。它们之间的逻辑关系主要包括:因果(cause and effect)、转折(adversative)、递进(additional and progressive)、对照(comparison and contrast)、提出问题—解决问题(problem and solution)、排序(sequencing and procedural)和分类(classification)等。横向分析时如果

抓住关联词和其他彰显逻辑关系的语段，可以帮助译者减轻认知和记忆的负荷。例如：

例7-4

In the study, students listened to a teacher and then took a test. Some took notes by typing on a computer. The others took notes by writing them down. Both groups performed about the same in remembering facts. But students who typed their notes did much worse on conceptual questions. These questions required them to understand an idea.

Those who typed also could not stop transcribing even after they were told to try to avoid it. So even if you want to stop typing what you hear word-for-word, you might not be able to.

Also, researchers found that those who wrote their notes remembered conceptual information better a week later. Researchers believe that the students who wrote notes long-hand had a deeper understanding of ideas and concepts.

Scientists know that students probably will still use their laptops and tablets in class. But they suggest using some of the available technologies for writing notes by hand on computer screens. They say this might be a good compromise between old school and new school.

这段话里存在多处显化的转折关系，以"Some .... The others ..." "but"串联，提示译者下文的情况和前文相反。不管是脑记还是笔记，负担都相当于减半了。除此之外，语篇中还隐含着因果关系，只不过没有用"because"等关联词明示出来："Also scientists found that those who wrote their notes remembered conceptual information better a week later. Scientists believe that the students who took notes by writing them had a deeper understanding of ideas."正是由于手写笔记的学生理解更加深入，所以他们在一周后对概念信息的印象更为深刻。

同样，口译中的逻辑分析也是一种信息加工，目的是帮助译员留下深刻的印象。要锻炼集中注意力捕捉逻辑的能力，复述是很有效的方法，因为它强调信息的主干，而非具体用词。早在二十世纪六七十年代，巴黎释意派（the interpretative approach of the Paris School）的学者们就指出，口译者常常基于自身的认知，通过译入语的语言符号对原文进行一种解释，而不是追求语言单位的对等，所谓"得意忘言"便是复述训练的精髓。

复述练习的材料很容易搜集，速度适中的讲话或论述都可以，普通的听力材料也可抛却那些选择、填空题，以新的方式利用起来。这项训练能够培养边听边分析的好习惯，将音频转化为有层次、相关联的信息点和信息块，同时提高译文的流畅度和条理性。无笔记的复述练习对初学者尤为适用，它提倡依靠短期记忆来承载经过分析处理的信息，以免过度依赖笔记。进行源语复述时，我们也鼓励学生脱离原文的外壳，用不同的表达方式来重现内化了的信息和情感，这样就不会拘泥于个别复杂的句式和抽象的词汇，避免"只见树木不见森林"。

根据不同的情况和需求，复述有时可以源语进行，有时则可译述为外语；有时只需要抓住梗概（gist），有时候则需要提供更多的细节。口译初学者可以从概述入手，逐步要求自己尽可能多地译出主要细节。

参考文献

Miller G A. The Magical Number Seven, Plus or Minus Two: Some Limits on Our Capacity for Processing Information[J]. Psychological Review, 1956, 63(2): 81-97.

专项练习

1. 源语概述

要求：根据听到的内容，用源语概述主要内容，注意信息点之间的层次。

中文概述：社交媒体

随着通信技术的发展和智能手机的普及，互联网以前所未有的规模融入人们的生活，社交媒体成了人们交流信息、获取新闻的主要渠道。但社交媒体的双刃剑效应也逐渐凸显，社交媒体用好了会造福国家和人民，用不好就可能带来难以预见的危害。面对网络信息鱼龙混杂的乱象，我国已经初步建立了完善的网络监管制度体系及法律法规，并对包括社交媒体公司在内的互联网公司的自我管理、主体责任提出了更高要求。但由于网络传播本身的复杂性，突发事件仍然层出不穷，网络治理面临难题。

首先，社交媒体时代，互联网"真相叙事"更加复杂，不再由传统媒体或权威机构"一锤定音"。由于信息传播技术降低了信息发布的门槛，更多普通人根据自己的立场、情感及信念等，在网上快速、实时地对信息进行生产、传播、消费和改造，加剧了信息的碎片化，增加了公共话语中的真相叙事版本，导致真相建构结果具有不确定性。实际上，社会学意义的真相就是真相提供者和公众共建的结果，是一种社会共识，与信任密切相关，仅反映事实是不够的，还要让受众理解、接受。因此，传统新闻、专家视点等面临信任危机，而网上社区"人际圈"传播的信息得到更多信任。尤其是以"短视频"为代表的可视化内容呈现更是表现突出，其传播威力甚至远超文字叙述，应当引起高度重视。

其次，社交媒体的群聚效应激化了社会分歧，导致观点极化。一方面，社交媒体的特性使情绪化、简单化的表达更容易得到传播，放大社会负面情绪；另一方面，网络群聚效应引发"回音室""过滤气泡"等现象，让大多数人固执己见，加上"算法"等网络新技术带来的信息精准推送,使得观点不同的人之间很难进行交流并达成共识。一旦有引爆网络的事件出现,网民的情绪发泄甚于理性参与,使得真相在情绪的裹挟中进一步沉陷。

再次,"后真相"现象不完全等同于谣言和假新闻,其特殊之处在于它既不完全客观也不完全虚构,而是一种似是而非、真假难辨的状态。现实中由于正常的表达渠道受阻,弱势群体的利益表达常以非制度化方式呈现,其中不乏虚假、夸大和情绪化内容。但社交媒体毕竟为社会公众表达诉求提供了一个便捷、廉价的平台,所反映的人们的立场、情感与信念是真实的。

英文概述: How interpreters juggle two languages at once

For most of history, interpretation was mainly done consecutively, with speakers and interpreters making pauses to allow each other to speak. But after the advent of radio technology, a new simultaneous interpretation system was developed in the wake of World War II. In the simultaneous mode, interpreters instantaneously translate a speaker's words into a microphone while he speaks without pauses. Those in the audience can choose the language in which they want to follow. On the surface, it all looks seamless. But behind the scenes, human interpreters work incessantly to ensure every idea gets across as intended. And that is no easy task. It takes about two years of training for already fluent bilingual professionals to expand their vocabulary and master the skills necessary to become a conference interpreter.

To get used to the unnatural task of speaking while they listen, students shadow speakers and repeat their every word exactly as heard in the same language. In time, they begin to paraphrase what is said, making stylistic adjustments as they go. At some point, a second language is introduced. Practicing in this way creates new neural pathways in an interpreter's brain. And a constant effort of reformulation gradually becomes second nature. Over time and through much hard work, the interpreter masters a vast array of tricks to keep up with speed, deal with challenging terminology, and handle a multitude of foreign accents. They may resort to acronyms to shorten long names, choose generic terms over specific, or refer to slides and other visual aids. They can even leave a term in the original language while they search for the most accurate equivalent.

Interpreters are also skilled at keeping aplomb in the face of chaos. Remember: they have no control over who is going to say what or how articulate the speaker will sound. A curve ball can be thrown at any time. Also, they often perform to thousands of people and in very intimidating settings like the UN General Assembly. To keep their emotions in check, they carefully prepare for an assignment — building glossaries in advance, reading voraciously about the subject matter, and reviewing previous talks on the topic.

Finally, interpreters work in pairs. While one colleague is busy translating incoming speeches in real time, the other gives support by locating documents, looking up words and tracking down pertinent information. Because simultaneous interpretation requires intense concentration, every thirty minutes, the pairs switch roles. Success is heavily dependent on skillful collaboration.

Language is complex. And when abstract or nuanced concepts get lost in translation, the consequences may be catastrophic. As Margaret Atwood famously noted, "war is what happens when language fails." Conference interpreters of all people are aware of that, and work diligently behind the scenes to make sure it never does.

2. 复述

要求：请用源语复述听到的内容。在把握主题信息完整的前提下，尽可能保留细节，注意信息点之间的逻辑关系。

中文复述：青少年心理

在社会高速发展的今天，我们的孩子们再也不是我们那个年代的学习态度，再也不是我们那个年代的学习模式了。很多初中生早上六点多就要起床，晚上晚自习后回家，在学校呆十个小时，很多孩子拖着疲倦的身体回到家。对于父母来说，问问孩子的学习、关心孩子的身体，这些太正常不过了。而对于孩子来说，自己的疲惫没有被看见，自己的情绪没有被看见，何况还有那么多作业没做完。很自然的，亲子之间的冲突就会爆发。父母们还需要了解青少年的心理变化，以促进亲子沟通，促进孩子身心健康成长。

青少年的心理具有四大特点。

第一是过渡性。他们的身心发展既具有儿童期的特点，又具有成熟期的特点，处于半幼稚、半成熟状态，各种心理特征逐渐接近成人。

第二是闭锁性。人的心理活动具有某种含蓄、内隐的特点，中学生开始有了自己的秘密，自己的许多事情有意回避父母与师长，有了自己的心事，但不轻易告诉别人。

第三是社会性。由于社会地位的变化，青少年活动的社会性增强，对社会生活越来越关注。同时，他们与社会环境的接触越来越多，社会环境对青少年社会化的影响也越来越明显。他们已不再像儿童时期那样更多地受家庭、学校的影响，而是随着交往领域的扩大、活动范围的增加，更多地受同辈群体以及社会风气的影响，他们的心理带有很大的社会性。

第四是动荡性。中学生的思想比较敏感，容易偏激，容易摇摆。他们往往把坚定与执拗，勇敢与蛮干、冒险混同起来。他们精力充沛，能力也在发展，但性格未最后定型。

英文复述：Hunger

People do go hungry because the world does not produce enough food for everyone. According to the World Hunger Education Service, over the past three decades, significant growth in food production, along with improved access to food, helped reduce the percentage of chronically undernourished people in developing countries from 34 percent to 15 percent. The principal problem is that many people in the world still do not have resources to purchase or grow enough food.

Indeed, hunger is a consequence of poverty, and also one of its causes. Hunger exists because many countries lack social safety nets; because in many countries women, although they do most of the farming, do not have as much access as men to training, credit or land.

Conflict, governance systems that do not encourage investment in agriculture, poor management of land and natural resources, lack of educational opportunity, displacement of small farmers by natural disasters, and financial and economic crises that eliminate jobs at the lowest levels, all contribute toward creating conditions that push the poorest into hunger.

3. 无笔记口译

要求：请将听到的内容翻译成目标语，在把握主题信息完整的前提下，尽可能保留多的细节，注意信息点之间的逻辑关系。

无笔记汉译英：保护动物

以前原始文明打猎时，动物还有逃生的机会，现在的动物则不那么幸运。现在人类的技术十分先进，比如电鱼工具。任由这样的技术去危害生态文明，将会使得社会无以为继。

保护动物其实也是在保护人的核心利益。比如个人有抽烟的自由，但会影响其他人的健康权；若有人猎杀、买卖和食用动物，那也是侵犯人类与其他生命的生存权。

根据联合国2019年5月份的报告，近几十年内会有近百万物种灭绝。而一百万个物种面临灭绝，其实是在毁灭人类自身的前途。因此，我们要全力以赴去保护那些鸟类和其他动植物。否则，到时极有可能到处都是冰冷高耸的建筑和满地的塑料。

人类现在面临各种挑战，我们要从根本上去改变生活方式、生产方式和行为方式，并且去适应、迎接生态文明的挑战。

例如，我们一直呼吁不要强制学生们包塑料书皮。这些塑料书皮从生产、运输到废弃环节都对生态造成极大的破坏，尤其是对海洋生物。很多海洋生物的胃里都是大量的塑料垃圾，导致其死亡或身体畸形。

无笔记英译汉: Mass vaccination of dogs can eliminate rabies

Glossary:	
rabies: 狂犬病	rabid: 患狂犬病的
central nervous system: 中枢神经系统	domino effect: 多米诺效应
the School for Global Animal Health: 全球动物健康学院	Washington State University: 华盛顿州立大学

In the United States, we often say, "Dogs are man's best friend." While it is true that dogs are popular pets, it is also true that in some parts of the world, a dog bite can lead to a painful death.

In fact, about 70,000 people worldwide die every year of rabies. Rabies is a viral infection that people get mainly through dog bites. Rabies is uncommon in the West. But in India, and other parts of Asia and sub-Saharan Africa, dogs that have not received anti-rabies vaccine continue to threaten public health.

A rabies death is a painful process. After a rabid dog bites someone, the virus invades the person's central nervous system. Victims develop a severe and irrational fear of water. They shake violently. Then they go into a coma and almost always die.

However, the rabies virus is not immediately active in the human body. It is usually inactive for at least 10 days after a bite. Sometimes it remains silent for months. This is called an incubation period. During incubation, vaccination can still prevent infection.

Scientists say vaccinating dogs can effectively get rid of rabies outbreaks in dog populations. And this will have a domino effect — vaccinating dogs with rabies means fewer humans with rabies. Animal scientists are calling for mass vaccination of dogs as a way to get rid of human rabies.

One example of where this worked very well is in the African country of Tanzania. Public health officials there set up dog vaccination centers in 180 villages. Before the vaccination centers were set up, there were, on average, 50 rabies deaths every year in Tanzania. After the centers began working, that number dropped to nearly zero.

Guy Palmer is director of the School for Global Animal Health at Washington State University. He co-authored the study in Tanzania. Mr. Palmer says researchers found that immunizing 70 percent of dogs will wipe out rabies as a human threat. He said: "This is not something that requires 10 to 20 years of basic research to develop a vaccine. We have a vaccine that works perfectly. It's really an implementation strategy, and a desire to do so. And an implementation strategy like this strengthens those infrastructures within the most vulnerable communities and countries."

篇章练习

要求：分段收听音频，并将听到的内容翻译成目标语，只可以记录有关逻辑关系、专名、数字的内容。

Text 1: Handedness in sports

My topic is handedness — whether in different sports it is better to be left- or right-sided or whether a more balanced approach is more successful. I'm left-handed myself and I actually didn't see any relevance to my own life when I happened to start reading an article by a sports psychologist called Peter Matthews.

I think Matthews' findings will be beneficial, not so much in helping sportspeople to work on their weaker side, but more that they can help them identify the most suitable strategies to use in a given game. Although most trainers know how important handedness is, at present they are rather reluctant to make use of the insights scientists like Matthews can give, which I think is rather short-sighted because focusing on individual flexibility is only part of the story. //

Anyway, back to the article.

Matthews started researching several different sports and found different types of handedness in each. By the way, he uses 'handedness' to refer to the dominant side for feet and eyes as well as hands. Anyway, his team measured the hands, feet and eyes of 2,611 players and found that there were really three main types of laterality: mixed — you work equally well on both sides — both hands and eyes; single — you tend to favor one side but both hands and eyes favor the same side; and cross-laterality — a player's hands and eyes favor only one side but they are opposite sides. //

Let's start with hockey. Matthews found that it was best to be mixed-handed — this is because a hockey stick must be deployed in two directions — it would be a drawback to have hands or eyes favoring one side. An interesting finding is that mixed-handed hockey players were significantly more confident than their single-handed counterparts.

Things are slightly different in racket sports like tennis. Here the important thing is to have the dominant hand and eye on the one side. This means that there is a bigger area of vision on the side where most of the action occurs. If a player is cross lateral the racket is invisible from the dominant eye for much of the swing. It means that they can only make corrections much later ...

and often the damage has been done by then.

And moving to a rather different type of sport which involves large but precise movements — gymnastics. It's been found that cross hand-eye favoring is best. The predominant reason for this is because it aids balance — which is of course absolutely central to performance in this sport. //

Text 2: "双减"政策

Glossary:	
双减：double reduction	立德树人：moral education
家庭教育支出：household expenditure for education	核心素养：core competence
教育情怀、职业道德和研究能力：devotion, professional ethics, and research capacity	

> 请查阅有关"双减"和素质教育的中英文资料并做译前准备。

"双减"的本质不只是为学生和家长减负，还在于如何落实立德树人的教育方针，如何提升教育质量和教育水平，办好人民群众满意的教育。截至目前，"双减"政策实施已经取得阶段性成果。如今，数据显示，线下培训机构已剧减92.14%，线上培训机构已剧减87.07%。//

实际上，"双减"并不代表降低学习质量。在减轻学生负担的同时，教育部也在推动"双增"，即增加学生参加户外活动、体育锻炼、艺术活动、劳动活动的时间和机会。学校应当利用场地、师资等条件，为学生提供优质丰富有特色的活动，对学有余力的孩子更进一步拓展学习空间，开展丰富多彩的活动，比如选修课、兴趣小组活动、体育社团等。//

随着"双减"政策的落地，虽然学生学业负担、家庭教育支出有所减轻，但如何在"双减"的背景下不减学生的核心素养，还有很多工作要做。一方面，要加强教师教育情怀、职业道德和研究能力的培养；另一方面，需要在历史、政治、社会学、心理学等方面提供更优质的课程，以增强学生的人文社科素养，提升学生整体素质。//

Text 3: Fad diet

Glossary:	
New Nordic Diet：新北欧饮食	Scandinavia：斯堪的纳维亚半岛
canola/rapeseed oil：菜籽油	

In the United States, fad diets come and go. It is sometimes hard to keep track of them all. However, one diet that always makes the list of healthiest is the Mediterranean Diet. Well, now it has competition from the New Nordic Diet. The New Nordic Diet comes from the part of Northern Europe that includes Finland, Norway, Iceland, Sweden and Denmark. This area is sometimes called Scandinavia. //

Diet experts at Health.com explain that the New Nordic and the Mediterranean diets are quite similar. In fact, they were compared in a 2015 study. The study found that the New Nordic Diet reduced inflammation within fat tissue. This type of inflammation is linked to obesity-related health risks. Both diets include lots of vegetables and fruits, whole grains, nuts and seeds, and more seafood than meat. //

However, one big difference between the two is the choice of oil. The Mediterranean Diet uses olive oil. Olives are not grown in Scandinavia. So, canola, or rapeseed, oil is more common there. And that leads us to the heart of the New Nordic Diet. It considers the environment and food preparation.

It is rich in food that is local and seasonal. As much as is possible, the New Nordic centers on fresh foods that are grown, raised or caught where you live. What you can find in the forests — wild mushrooms, berries and herbs — are all important to this diet. Also found in this diet are lots of root vegetables such as parsnips, carrots and beets. //

The New Nordic centers around home cooked meals. Restaurant meals can be higher in fat and calories.

Eating better quality food but less of it is also part of this diet. It avoids processed foods — generally mass-produced foods that come already cooked and packaged. It stresses eating organic foods whenever possible and creating less waste as we cook and eat. //

The New Nordic is also an eco-friendly diet. It is more of a lifestyle — a way of living and eating — rather than a list of foods one can or cannot eat. Because it centers around local foods, it should not be surprising that fish is a main part of the New Nordic Diet.

Health experts on the Berkeley Wellness website say that people who eat fish "tend to live longer and enjoy lower risks of cardiovascular disease". They add that eating fish may even boost a person's brain health. Fish, they say, "contains vitamins, minerals, and other fats that may work with the omega-3s to protect the heart and overall health." //

But these experts also warn that it is important to eat the right kind of fish. Some are high in mercury. So, they advise eating smaller fish. They are "lower on the food chain". And if you catch the fish yourself, make sure and check with local experts to make sure the water quality is healthy. //

Text 4: 全民健身

Preview:
"十三五"计划以来,我国全民健身运动蓬勃发展,越来越多的人加入到健身的队伍之中,而体育产业也随之发展,各类运动App应运而生。

请查阅有关全民健身和运动软件的中英文资料并做译前准备。

Glossary:	
运动损伤: sports injury	北京体育大学: Beijing Sport University
直播平台: live streaming platform	国家体育总局: General Administration of Sport of China
健身步道: fitness trail	

由于缺乏对健身知识的了解,一些人容易陷入误区:一类是健身时动力不足,无效锻炼很多;另一类是过度健身,即健身时运动的方法和强度不当,导致超负荷运动甚至运动损伤。北京体育大学的教授鲍明晓表示,我们需要做好科学健身的宣传工作,要让更多人了解无效健身和过度健身的伤害。//

如今,体育产业将目光转向线上。不少知名健身品牌纷纷推出直播平台以及手机App,开展了诸多线上课程。方便和个性化是许多人热衷利用App健身的理由。专家表示:"健身App打破了时空的限制,为人们的健身活动提供了便利条件。但坏处是使用者无法与教练直接互动来及时纠正不规范的动作,也相对难以保持运动习惯。" //

要想让全民健身更好地服务于全民健康,健身设施的全面建设必不可少。国家体育总局的官员表示:"社区是人民生活的基本单元,我们要让健身设施走进社区,为老百姓营造就近健身的良好环境。我们不能只建大型体育馆,还要建设更多的体育公园和健身步道,充分满足并刺激公众的健身需求。" //

第八章

口译笔记（I）

第一节 "脑记"与"笔记"

通过上一章的学习，我们已经了解了口译员在处理信息时的大脑活动，即对信息进行逻辑分析。译员在完成口译任务时主要依赖于短时记忆，尤其是在信息的输入阶段。为了强化短时记忆，我们就需要借助逻辑分析将看似零散的、碎片化的信息尽量变得清晰、完整，从而建立更加持久的记忆框架，即我们所说的"脑记"。这里的"记"是"记忆"的"记"，即动脑。面对讲话人所传达的转瞬即逝的口头信息，除了充分调动大脑的认知能力对信息进行逻辑化处理，还需要通过口译笔记来辅助我们记录一些短时记忆负荷之外的内容，即我们所说的"笔记"。这里的记主要指记录的"记"，即动手。对初学者而言，在口译信息输入阶段，需要人为地对脑记和笔记的内容加以区分，让"脑记"和"笔记"既有分工，又有合作，共同为下一阶段信息的输出做好准备。

那么，"脑记"应该记些什么？"笔记"又需要记些什么呢？两者是否为完全区分开来的流水线工作？在我们的印象当中，口译员总是一边倾听讲话人说话，一边不停地在纸上做着笔记，而我们不禁要问，他们大脑中的"黑匣子"（black box）和手头那支神奇的笔究竟是如何分工合作的呢？

这要从口译员的工作模式谈起。有人将口译员的工作模式比喻为"导游"。导游需要记住并向游客介绍一个地方的文化、历史、风俗、游览路线等内容。在这些冗杂的信息中，抽象信息诸如文化、历史等内容是需要大脑去记住的；一些有逻辑脉络可捕捉的内容，如游览路线等也是可以通过脑记来实现的。而一张完整的地图、一些具体风俗的名字、游览路线中的车次和历史事件发生的具体年份则是需要借助笔记来记录的。换言之，对于口译员而言，能够通过理解来进行记忆的篇章主题是需要脑记的，信息片段或篇章的逻辑也可以通过脑记来完成，而一些无法通过短时记忆记住的数字、专有名词，或是讲话人罗列的内容、事例，则是需要笔记来辅助完成的。这是口译中脑记和笔记的分工，两者并不是完全割裂的。那些通过大脑所建立的信息逻辑，一方面需要用大脑记住，另一方面也需要体现在笔记之中，让口译笔记具有灵魂，而不至于沦为刚记完就无法识别的鬼画符，做了无用功。

下面我们来看看例子。

例8-1：人工智能对大学生成长的影响

Glossary:	
学术成就：academic achievement	自然语言处理：natural language processing
职业规划：career planning	数据挖掘：data mining
社会责任感：sense of social responsibility	公益活动：public welfare activities
认知习惯：cognitive habit	

译前准备阅读材料：

人工智能时代的到来正在潜移默化中影响和改变着现代人的生活节奏与方式，新时代的大学生也呈现出独具特色的社会心态与规律。对于高校教育教学工作而言，要进一步提升教育教学的效果和质量，就必须对新时代大学生成长规律进行深入分析和精准把控，及时发现和总结大学生所表现出的普遍特征和心理规律，进而为制定和优化教育教学与管理方案提供重要参考依据。

人工智能是一种快速发展的技术，正逐渐改变我们的生活和工作方式，人工智能进入高等教育领域，正在产生越来越大的功能和作用。在大学生成长的过程中，人工智能可以对学生的学术成就、职业规划、社会责任感和创造力等方面产生积极的影响。//

人工智能可以提高学生的学术成就。人工智能技术可以对学生的学习行为和学习方式进行跟踪和分析，深入了解学生学习的认知和行为习惯，并为学生提供更加个性化的教学支持和反馈。通过人工智能技术的辅助，大学生可以自主掌握学科知识，更好地利用学校提供的教育资源，从而获得更加优秀的学术成绩。//

人工智能可以协助学生做好职业规划。通过自然语言处理、数据挖掘等技术，人工智能可以为学生提供更加准确的职业规划和就业信息，帮助学生更好地了解市场动态和职业发展方向。人工智能还可以为学生提供更加个性化的培训和指导，从而提高学生的就业竞争力和职业发展能力。//

人工智能可以培养学生的社会责任感和创造力。现在的人工智能技术越来越注重引导学生参与社会服务和公益活动，鼓励他们投身社会事业、发起创新创意和公益项目，培养他们的社会责任感和创造力。人工智能还可以模拟真实的工作场景，为学生提供更加真实的职业体验和模拟实践，帮助他们逐渐适应未来的工作环境。//

以段落为单位，该语段的逻辑主要分为三个部分：

第一部分：人工智能可以提高学生的学术成就。
第二部分：人工智能可以协助学生做好职业规划。
第三部分：人工智能可以培养学生的社会责任感和创造力。

若以段落为单位，译员需要脑记的内容大致包括以下几点：

（1）人工智能如何提高学生的学术成就。
（2）人工智能如何协助学生做好职业规划。
（3）人工智能如何培养学生的社会责任感和创造力。

上述主要逻辑框架和各句的主要意义就是我们在口译时需要通过大脑分析和记忆的内容，这些内容构成了译文的基本框架，能够帮助译员通过理解对信息进行分析和记忆，也为下一步的转换做好准备。一方面我们需要对这些信息进行"脑记"，另一方面，也需要将这些信息之间的逻辑体现在笔记当中。

在明确了脑记的任务之后，我们再来看看哪些应该落实到笔记当中，即人工智能对学术成就、职业规划、社会责任感和创造力的具体影响。

（1）对学术成就的影响：学习行为和学习方式、学习的认知和行为习惯、人工智能技术的辅助。
（2）对职业规划的影响：自然语言处理、数据挖掘等技术提供职业规划和就业信息，提供个性化的培训和指导。
（3）对社会责任感和创造力的影响：引导学生参与社会服务和公益活动；提供真实的职业体验和模拟实践。

图 8-1 和图 8-2 为笔记示范，扫描图片右/左侧二维码可查看笔记大图。

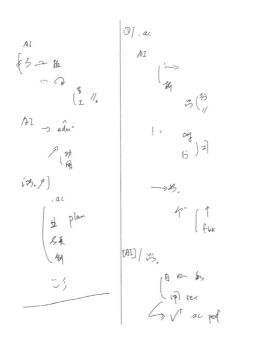

图 8-1　例 8-1 笔记示范 1

图 8-2

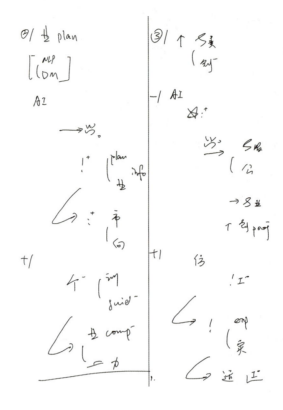

图 8-2　例 8-1 笔记示范 2

例 8-2：International Culture Festival

Preview:

北京大学于 2023 年举办了第 20 届国际文化节，主题是"在北大遇见世界"。本次文化节为后续的主题活动揭开了帷幕，来自世界上 100 多个国家和地区的学生和校友齐聚一堂，共同参与这次文化交流盛会。

Glossary:	
International Culture Festival：国际文化节	showcase：展示
carnival：嘉年华/狂欢节	Global Engagement Year：全球影响力年
flourish：蓬勃发展	

The 2023 Peking University 20th International Culture Festival was a spectacular showcase of unity and cross-cultural communication, weaving a vibrant tapestry of diverse cultures. Students and alumni from over 100 countries and regions had gathered to celebrate the university's 20th International Culture Festival (ICF), with the theme of "Meeting the World at PKU". //

This year's ICF showcased a series of themed events around the campus, including the International Culture Carnival, the Global Youth Forum, and the Top 10 International Students Singing Competition. The International Culture Carnival, for instance, featured an array of experiences, ranging from card games and language lessons to creative activities. Each booth that had been set up served as a gateway to another culture. //

The year 2023 marks the PKU Global Engagement Year. During this year, the world witnessed the school's dedicated efforts to foster global inclusion on campus and promote understanding between Chinese youth and their overseas peers. The grandeur of the ICF not only aptly marked its 20th anniversary but also reflected the growing international student population at the university. Let's hope that PKU's engagement with the world and China's engagement with the world will continue to flourish. //

上述语篇大致可以分为三个部分：第一部分介绍2023年国际文化节的基本情况，包括：主办方、参与者、主题；第二部分介绍与国际文化节相关的其他活动：国际文化嘉年华、全球青年论坛、国际学生校园十大歌手比赛；第三部分指出2023年国际文化节反映了北大的全球影响力。

其中，第一部分可以细分为对2023年北大国际文化节的简要介绍，对参与者背景的具体描述和对主题的介绍。第二部分可以细分为相关庆祝活动介绍，以及对其中一项"国际文化嘉年华"的说明。第三部分则分为2023年庆祝活动对北大国际影响力的意义，以及国际文化节本身的意义。最后是对北大世界影响力的祝福。

上述大意和逻辑都是需要通过大脑对信息进行分析来记忆的，即"脑记"，但同时也需要体现在笔记之中。根据之前的讲解，在各段中需要记录在笔记中的内容如下：第一段，国际文化节的基本情况：主办方（PKU）、参与者（students and alumni）和主题（Meet the World at PKU）。第二段，其他相关活动：国际文化嘉年华（Carnival）、全球青年论坛（Forum）、国际学生校园十大歌手比赛（Top 10 International Students Singing Competition）以及举例。第三段，北大的全球影响力年（Global Engagement Year）和ICF的影响力（not only marked ... but also reflected ...），以及对北大的祝福（flourish）。以上内容为该篇章的逻辑框架和主干信息，通过脑记和笔记的有效配合，译员能够掌握本篇的大意，并借助笔记顺利完成翻译练习。

图8-3为笔记示范,扫描图片左侧二维码可查看笔记大图。

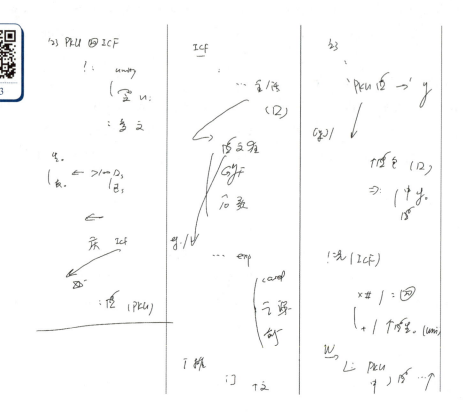

图8-3 例8-2笔记示范

第二节 口译笔记与精力分配

要充分认识口译笔记的特点,养成脑记与笔记配合的习惯,就应完整了解译员在进行口译工作时究竟需要调动哪些认知机能,以及这些认知工作机能是如何分工合作的。在口译过程中,我们主要完成的是理解意义(understanding sense)、脱离语言外壳(de-verbalization)、回归到另一种语言的表述或信息重构(reformulation/restoration)。具体认知任务可以分解为:听力理解(listening comprehension)、短时记忆(short-term memory)、笔记(note-taking)、信息的传达(delivery/production)以及各项认知任务之间的协同(coordination)。

Gile(1995)对译员的认知任务进行了深入剖析,建立了"认知负荷模型"。该模型可以帮助初学者更加直观、全面地了解口译的工作机制,了解译员的精力都需要耗费在哪些工作中,以及笔记在其中所扮演的角色。以交替传译为例,在交替传译中,我们所完成的认知任务可大致划分为两个阶段:

$$第一阶段 = L + N + M + C$$

$$\text{第二阶段} = \text{Rem} + \text{Read} + \text{P}$$

其中，第一阶段的L指listening and analysis，即听取和分析。N指note-taking，即笔记。M代表short-term memory operation，即短时记忆。最后，C指代coordination，即各项认知任务之间的协作。第二阶段的Rem代表remembering，即回忆第一阶段所听取的信息大意和逻辑，将其组合为完整的、有意义的内容。Read指代的是read notes，即对笔记进行辨识和整理，根据听取的信息和笔记的提示，使所记录的信息更加准确化、逻辑化。

在第一阶段，译员需要充分调动各项机能，完成对信息的输入、加工、记忆和记录等多项复杂任务。在这个过程中，笔记扮演着路标的角色，但真正重要的是听和分析，以及在短时记忆中储存下来，这就是各项认知功能之间的协作。可以设想一下，要是译员在第一阶段忙于在纸上记录，忽略了主旨理解和逻辑加工，虽然看似写了很多内容，把零散的信息都"记"下来了，但在下一阶段却会面临无法识别笔记和串联意义的窘境。

综上所述，口译笔记是信息输入和记录的重要环节，但不等于盲目在纸上写下所听到的只言片语。在信息输入阶段，口译笔记的作用在于帮助译员完成对信息的逻辑化处理，记录一些难以通过理解来串联的信息，或是短时记忆无法容纳的"死"内容。而在信息输出阶段，笔记则扮演着提示作用，帮助译员唤起信息大意，弥补短时记忆的缺漏。简言之，面对复杂的口译认知任务，译员应当以"脑记"为主，以"笔记"为辅，利用笔记的提示作用，而不是盲目速记，让笔记成为羁绊。初学者应该充分认识到这一点，并且从一开始就养成"脑记"为主的习惯，摆脱对口译笔记的依赖，正确判断该不该记、该如何记，让笔记成为工作利器而非用以炫技的"鸡肋"。

参考文献

Gile D. Basic Concepts and Models in Interpreter and Translator Training[M]. Amsterdam/Philadelphia: John Benjamins Publishing Company, 1995.

专项练习

要求：听下面的段落，进行段落总结练习（summary writing）。听第一遍，对其主题、逻辑进行简要记录，然后根据笔记内容完成一篇30—50字的总结。中文段落用中文进行总结，英文段落则用英文完成。在练习过程中，注意培养以脑记为主、笔记为辅的习惯，关注段落的主题、大意和逻辑。以笔记为辅，简要记录段落逻辑、关键名词、数字等信息。听第二遍，完成段落口译。

中文段落1：新质生产力形成新吸引力（节选）

Preview:

　　中国加大对传统产业的升级，以摆脱对外国技术的依赖，进而培育发展新质生产力的新动能。发展新质生产力并不意味着忽视或放弃传统产业，而是推动传统产业向高精尖、智能化、环保化转型。这种转型对于提升生产力和竞争力至关重要，也将惠及合作方和伙伴国的发展。当前全球正在重新定义工业供应链，强调互利共赢的中国方案值得借鉴。

　　中国具有吸引外资的显著优势。从产业结构来看，随着电子技术、新能源、半导体、智能技术的持续发展，这些前沿领域正在催生新质生产力，能够成为中国吸引外资的新增长点。//从产业基础和内需潜力来看，中国是全世界唯一拥有联合国产业分类当中全部工业门类的国家，强大的产业支撑和整合能力以及高素质的人员队伍将为外国企业在华发展提供有力支撑。//近年来，中国相关部门不断完善政策，鼓励外商发展，促进外商投资的高质量发展，确保符合条件的外商投资项目充分享受中国政府的优惠政策。//中国关于发展新质生产力的政策是基于统一的市场标准设立的，涉及财产保护、市场准入、公平竞争、社会信用等方面，中国政府已经出台了一系列"高水平对外开放"的政策，对外商形成新的吸引力。//

中文段落2：中国的农村发展

Preview:

　　农村发展受到了全球经济衰退及极端天气的严重影响，但中国8亿农民的生活已经出现了稳步的改善，这要归功于中央政府的政策。现在就让我们来了解一下这些政策。

Glossary:

"家电下乡"："bringing home appliances to the countryside"	白色家电[①]：white goods

---

[①] 人们通常把家电分为4类：白色家电、黑色家电、米色家电和新兴的绿色家电。白色家电指可以替代人们进行家务劳动的产品，包括洗衣机、冰箱等，或者是为人们提供更高生活环境质量的产品，像空调、电暖器；黑色家电是指可提供娱乐的产品，如DVD播放机、彩电、音响、游戏机、摄像机、照相机、电视游戏机、家庭影院、电话、电话应答机等；米色家电指电脑信息产品；绿色家电，指在质量合格的前提下可以高效使用且节约能源的产品，在使用过程中不对人体和周围环境造成伤害，报废后还可以回收利用。

农民的平均年收入去年超过了5 000元，相当于700美元。听起来这也许算不了什么，但如果我们对数字进行仔细分析，就会发现它比一年前提高了6%，比5年前提高了35%。收入的提高要归功于政府提高了农产品的收购价格。//

为了改善农民生活，政府还启动了"家电下乡"项目。如果农户购买政府补贴的家电套装，包括电视机、电冰箱、洗衣机及手机，它就能节省1 000元，相当于150美元。该项目旨在为农村家庭提供必需的家电产品。//

预计在今后4年里，政府将以优惠价向农村人口销售4.8亿台白色家电。资金由当地政府补贴。该项目受到了广大农民的欢迎，但也有人说希望家电的品种能够更加多样化，以扩大选择余地。//

全球金融危机的一个负面影响就是许多在沿海工厂打工的农民工失去了工作。为了帮助他们，中国政府的经济刺激一揽子计划中有很大一部分资金被用在农村地区基础设施建设上，并为中小型乡镇企业提供资金支持。//

政府另外还启动了一个10亿元的项目，为农民工提供教育和培训，帮助他们获取新技能、新技术。地方政府还对一些公司提出要求，不到万不得已尽量不要解雇农民工。//

英文段落1：How to harvest your potatoes (excerpt)

Preview:
　　下文节选自主题为"土豆如何收获"的一篇文章，本选段主要介绍如何判断土豆何时成熟并适合采收。

Glossary:

Associated Press：美联社，全称为美国联合通讯社

Many gardeners who grow potatoes are not sure when to dig them up. Because potatoes grow underground, we cannot see their size, feel how solid they are or smell them to know when they are ready to eat. If we dig potatoes up too early, they may be too small. This could stress the plant and its root system. So how do we know exactly when to harvest? //

Jessica Damiano writes about gardening for the Associated Press. She said the best time to start digging up potatoes is when half the plant's leaves have turned yellow. This will happen between 60 and 120 days from planting, depending on the weather and the kind of potato that is planted. You can stop watering the plants around this time. //

To help the potatoes mature, especially in wetter climates, you should cut the plants at soil level. This step is not necessary, however. If the plants are not cut, they will just die back on their own. After two weeks, the potatoes are ready to harvest. //

If you are still not sure about when to harvest, dig up a small test potato. Carefully dig into the soil near a tester plant, and take a potato from the outer part of the roots. The skin of a mature potato will stick to the potato if you run your fingers over it. If the skin rubs off, fill the hole back up and check again in about a week. //

英文段落2: Quick ways to say long expressions (excerpt)

Preview:
下文节选自主题为"美国人常用的缩略表达"的文章,本选段主要介绍派对中BYOB(自带酒水)和商务场景中ASAP(尽快回复)等表达的用法。

Americans often try to say things as quickly as possible. So, for some expressions, we use the first letters of the words instead of saying each word. //

Many common expressions or long names are shortened this way. B-Y-O-B is a short way of saying, "Bring Your Own Bottle." The letters BYOB are often found at the bottom of a written invitation to a simple social event or gathering of friends. // For example, let's say I had a New Year's Eve party. I might include on the invitation, "Please come to my party and BYOB." The bottle each person brings is what the person wants to drink at the party or wants to share. However, an invitation to a special event — such as a wedding — would never say BYOB. //

Another expression usually used for business and not parties is A-S-A-P. So, a colleague might say she needs something done ASAP. It means as soon as possible. She might also need something done by C-O-B. That means she wants to finish it by "Close of Business" or the end of the work day. //

▇ 篇章练习

要求:请听下面的篇章内容:听第一遍,对其主题、逻辑进行简要记录,然后根据笔记内容和提示完成大纲填空练习(outline writing)。在练习过程中,巩固以脑记为主、笔记为辅的习惯,熟悉篇章主题、大意和逻辑,并通过笔记辅助记录时间、人物、事件等具体信息。在听记之前,无需提前阅读大纲内容。听第二遍,完成篇章口译。

Text 1: 习近平在亚太经合组织工商领导人峰会上的书面演讲(节选)

Preview:
据央视网报道,当地时间2022年11月17日上午,2022年度亚太经合组织工商领导人峰会在泰国首都曼谷正式开幕。会议围绕"全球经济与亚太经合组织的未来""创新——下一个前沿""亚太地区贸易和投资的未来"以及"推动亚太经合组织成员经济体的成长与发展"等议题展开对话和讨论。

各位工商界代表,
女士们,先生们,朋友们:
很高兴来到美丽的曼谷,参加亚太经合组织工商领导人峰会。
世界又一次站到十字路口。世界向何处去?亚太怎么办?我们必须给出答案。
21世纪是亚太世纪。亚太地区占世界人口三分之一,占世界经济总量逾六成、贸易总量近一半,是全球经济最具活力的增长带。…… //
当前,亚太地区局势总体稳定,区域合作不断取得进展,和平发展、合作共赢是主流。同时,世界进入新的动荡变革期,地缘政治紧张与经济格局演变叠加,冲击亚太地区发展环境和合作架构。…… //
我们要走和平发展之路。……历史昭示我们,阵营对抗解决不了问题,偏见只会带来灾难。……
我们要走开放包容之路。……
我们要走和衷共济之路。……在合作中形成共同体意识,成为实现不断发展的深厚根基。…… //
新形势下,我们要汲取历史经验和教训,因应时代挑战,坚定推进亚太区域经济一体化,共同开拓发展新局面,构建亚太命运共同体。
第一,筑牢和平发展的根基。……
第二,坚持以人民为中心的发展理念。……
第三,打造更高水平的开放格局。……
第四,实现更高层次的互联互通。……
第五,打造稳定畅通的产业链供应链。……
第六,推进经济优化升级。…… //

大纲：
1. 亚太地区在当前世界形势下的定位、目标和优势：

2. 亚太地区要走什么样的发展道路：

3. 亚太地区应采取何种措施构建人类命运共同体：

Text 2：近代上海餐饮业的发展

Preview:
  上海自开埠以后，迅速成为中外贸易的全国集散中心。各地人士因为不同原因来到上海，都从他们出发的地方带来了独特的饮食习惯和风味。随着历史的沿革，那些几乎截然不同的习惯和风味在这座城市中不断碰撞、偶尔融合，频发新奇。

Glossary:	
姑苏船菜：Suzhou-style cuisine from boats	开埠：opened the ports
北伐革命：the North Expedition	本帮菜：Shanghai cuisine
西菜馆：Western restaurant	

  上海的苏菜馆以姑苏船菜为招牌。因为陈设雅洁，上下两层有几十个包间，中间为正厅，两旁分别为书房和厢房，四处挂满书画。上海的天津菜馆，从19世纪70年代开始兴旺，差不多一直延续到20世纪初。上海自开埠以来，不断有大量宁波移民，宁波菜馆也很早就出现了。//
  上海最早的徽菜馆是盐商来沪开设的。到了19世纪90年代，徽菜馆渐渐为人所了解，一度独霸沪上餐饮业。20世纪30年代以后，粤菜馆略见兴盛，猜想起来，这其中部分原因很可能是北伐革命的副产品。这些粤菜馆都设施豪华，菜肴精美昂贵。//

随后在20世纪40年代兴旺的是川菜馆。上海的川菜馆在20世纪30年代起步,有名的川菜馆有锦江川菜馆,由董竹君于1935年创办。上海的中菜馆还有闽菜、豫菜、杭州菜等。当然还有本帮菜,本帮菜原先比较下层,也是到20世纪30年代后才发展成高级菜馆。//

除以上中菜馆外,早在清末,沪上就出现了西菜馆。不过彼时很多西菜馆都是专门做中国人生意的,做法是西式,但味道实际上更接近于中餐。真正面向外国人的那种西餐厅倒是不会有中国人去吃。//

大纲:

1. 上海各类菜馆的发展历史及主要特点:

    苏菜馆:

    天津菜馆:

    宁波菜馆:

    徽菜馆:

    ……

2. 除此之外,上海当时还有其他的一些中菜馆:

3. 西菜馆的发展情况:

Text 3: Acupuncture

Preview:

针灸是一项古老的中国医疗技术,已经存在了数千年。本篇简单介绍了古代中国人如何缓解疼痛和针灸治疗的几种具体操作方式。

Glossary:	
acupuncture:针灸	relieve:缓解
treatment:治疗方法	holistic treatment:全面治疗
needle insertion:扎针	cupping:拔罐
scraping:刮痧	

Acupuncture, an ancient Chinese medical practice, has been the remedy for countless patients for thousands of years. Before modern medicine came to life, ancient Chinese used stone tools to relieve pain. Over time, this instinctual practice evolved into a comprehensive and profound medical system and shaped the root of acupuncture. //

Acupuncture is a treatment that aims to promote the body's self-regulating functions. Its therapeutic principles are in line with the philosophical concepts of traditional Chinese medicine, which emphasizes holistic treatment, meridian adjustment, balance of bodily functions and overall physiological well-being. //

Practices can vary in forms, including needle insertion, cupping and scraping. Needle insertion, the most common method, is carried out by inserting hair-thin needles into meridians, or specific points on the body that channel vital energy (the *qi*). Practitioners lift, twirl and rotate needles to unblock the flow of energy; restore yin and yang balance; and stimulate the body's innate potential to heal itself. //

Looking beyond China, acupuncture has become a global therapy. Over the years, acupuncture has seen many advancements in scientific research and modern medicine. It is now a mainstream alternative and complementary treatment for a variety of ailments. As an ancient Chinese medical practice with a rich history and deep cultural significance, acupuncture is an embodiment of profound cultural heritage and a holistic path to healing. //

Outline:

1. The origin of acupuncture:

2. The holistic treatment of acupuncture:

3. Various forms of practice such as needle insertion, cupping and scraping:

4. The influence of acupuncture both home and abroad:

Text 4: Why can parrots talk?

Preview:

本篇探讨为什么鹦鹉可以模仿人类讲话，介绍多种不同的鹦鹉种类，并通过生动的案例分析鹦鹉为何能够发出与其他动物不同的声音，甚至模仿人类的声音。

Glossary:	
songbird：鸣禽	jaw joint：下颌关节
mating：求偶	profanity：脏话
larynx：喉咙	vocalization：发出的声音
windpipe：气管	syrinx：鸟类的鸣管
vibrating membrane：振动膜	split and fuse：分散和聚合
airway：气道	beak：鸟喙

In 2010, a parrot that spoke with the same British accent as his owner went missing. They were reunited four years later, but the intervening time left a conspicuous mark: the parrot had lost its British accent and was instead chattering away in Spanish. Parrots and several other birds are the only animals that produce human speech. And some parrots do it almost uncannily well. How is this possible? //

Most wild parrots are highly social. They use vocalizations for mating and territorial displays and to coordinate group movements. Some species have flocks that continuously split and fuse, meaning individual parrots must be able to communicate with many others. Parrots use contact calls to interact and stay in touch when others are out of sight. But how exactly they use these calls depends on the species and the size of their flocks. //

So, how does a parrot actually declare that "Polly wants a cracker"? A person would string these sounds together using their larynx, the organ at the top of their windpipe. It consists of rings of muscles and a vibrating membrane that controls airflow. They'd finely shape the vocalization into enunciated words using their tongue and lips. For a parrot, however, the sound would originate in its syrinx, located at the base of its windpipe. Many other birds have two vibrating membranes within this organ. But parrots, like us, have just one. //

As sounds leave the airway, parrots shape them using their tongues and beaks. They can do this because they have especially flexible, powerful tongues that help them manipulate seeds and nuts. And while parrots' beaks are rigid, they have very flexible jaw joints, giving them a lot of control over how wide and how quickly they open their beaks. //

Like other animals with learned vocalizations, parrot brains contain interconnected regions that allow them to hear, remember, modify, and produce complex sounds. But while songbirds have just one song system in their brains, almost all parrots seem to have an additional circuit. Scientists think that this might give them extra flexibility when it comes to learning the calls of their own species — and ours. With this specialized anatomy, parrots can bark, scream, curse, and recite factoids. One intrepid lost parrot managed to get back home after repeating his full name and address to helpful strangers. //

But these impressive abilities raise another question: do parrots actually understand what they're saying? When most captive parrots talk, they're likely attempting to form social bonds in the absence of their own species. Many probably have associations with words and may be drawn to ones that elicit certain responses — hence their capacity for profanity. But, especially after training, parrots have been observed to say things in the appropriate contexts and assign meaning to words — saying "goodnight" at the end of the day, asking for certain treats, or counting and picking objects. One extensively trained African grey parrot named Alex became the first non-human animal to pose an existential question when he asked what color he was. //

Outline:
1. How is it possible that parrots could produce human speech?
2. Most wild parrots use vocalizations for mating and territorial displays and to coordinate group movements, but _____
3. Parrots could produce human speech because:
   a. _____
   b. _____
   c. _____
4. Do parrots actually understand what they're saying?
   _____
5. To truly understand parrots, we need to preserve and study them in the wild.

第九章

口译笔记（Ⅱ）

第一节　口译笔记的特点

通过前几章的学习，我们了解了译员在完成口译任务过程中所运用的认知资源，包括听力理解、逻辑梳理、短时记忆、口译笔记的记录和辨认等。我们还对大家所熟知的"脑记"和"笔记"进行了区分，帮助初学者在练习的过程中充分认识到"脑记"的重要性，明确两者的主次关系，并且注意它们之间的协调。

口译是不断挑战认知极限的过程。译员好像在钢丝上"戴着脚镣跳舞"，稍有不慎便前功尽弃。在完成一段连续的口译任务时，译员除了充分理解原文大意和逻辑，将其储存在短时记忆之中，还需借助笔记记下原文的逻辑，以及其中出现的人名、数字或罗列的细节，这在长篇大论和你来我往的发言中尤其重要。这里我们有必要重申：笔记只是起到辅助、提示的作用，并不是所有的口译任务都需要借助笔记才能完成。对初学者而言，建立正确认识是学好笔记的第一步，而这要从口译任务的特点说起。

首先，口译任务中的发言具有"即时性"的特点。译员在正式或非正式场合需要快速、连续地将讲话人所述内容在两种语言之间进行转换。译员所面临的挑战在于：一方面，如果只依赖脑记，面对不断输入的信息，很可能会顾此失彼、手忙脚乱。另一方面，由于讲话人所说的话转瞬即逝，译员最好在讲话人结束本轮发言的两秒内开口，整理思路和语言的时间十分有限。因此，口译员不得不一边听一边进行记录，并且速度要非常快。这就要求笔记必须简洁，这和速记（shorthand）完全不同，口译笔记不是听到什么就记什么，尽量以一个字、一个简写单词，或是箭头、线条、图形等符号指代一个意群。

其次，口译任务中，译员趋于"隐身"，主要目的是为讲话人服务。特别是在记者招待会这样较为正式的场合，译员个人的存在感较弱。在信息输入的过程中，译员像讲话人的影子，同时完成"听"和"记"。迫于短时记忆容量的压力，译员不可能在听完所有内容后再补记笔记，因此口译笔记具有"同步性"的特点，即与接收原文的过程同步发生。这里的"同步"还有另一层要求：由于笔记与听力理解同步发生，除了记录零散的字符，还要注意在笔记中体现"脑记"所解析的信息逻辑，确保所记内容有迹可循。这样在回看笔记进行翻译的时候，笔记能够有效地提示原文内容，而不会成为"一纸天书"。因此，我们鼓励同学们多用线条、箭头、圈框等标记来联系前文提到过的内容，将逻辑关系显化在纸面上。

第三，译员的任务是在不同的语言之间进行转换，因此，口译笔记不是速记源语，而是从

A语转换到B语的中间步骤。换言之,记笔记的目的是为了更好地理解、记忆原文,从而更加充分、顺畅地将其转换为另一种语言。口译笔记承载了一部分"deverbalization"的功能,即"脱离语言外壳",攫取语段含义,这样等到口述阶段,译员就不必抱着笔记重新"解码"。

第四,由于每个人理解和处理信息的方式不同,口译笔记具有"个性化"的特点。笔记与听力理解、短时记忆同步,而后者发生在译员大脑这个看不见、摸不着的"黑匣子"里,如何记笔记取决于每一位译员如何理解原文,如何利用笔记减少语言转换的认知负荷,以及如何处理所听到的每一个信息单位。不过,它也有一些范式。一般来说,口译笔记纵向排列(verticality),要"瘦身",忌讳横着记,这样可以在每一行清晰呈现出一个意群,也可以避免看串行。而对于一整句话,各行之间可逐级缩进(indentation),体现主从关系,下一句时再顶头重新逐级缩进(如图9-1)。

图9-1　口译笔记的缩进制

对于列举的项目,就更加要纵向排列,然后用尖括号括起来,体现出并列关系(superposition),在口译时逐一列出(如图9-2)。

$$\begin{cases} A \\ B \\ C \end{cases}$$

图9-2　列举项的叠加

在口译笔记方面,林超伦主编的《实战口译》(2004)提供了大量笔记示范,可供大家对比学习。当然,许多职业译员的笔记并不是严格遵照这些格式的,例如有的人习惯在每句话结束时划斜杠隔开,有的人则只会在一段讲话结束后才用斜线或横线分隔新旧内容,有的译员笔记中的缩进制也不明显。有的译员在听中文的时候,所有的笔记都是中文,而有的译员则用不同的语言夹杂着记。有的译员习惯使用特殊的符号指代一个意群或信息单位,例如用"箭头"(→)指代数据的变化趋势或时间的延续。而有的译员会根据每一个会议主题临时拟定一些适用于本场口译任务的笔记符号或缩写,例如,以经济为主题的会议用字母E指代所有"经济"相关词汇,以生态环保为主题的会议则用"eco"指代生态环境。

下面我们来看一下不同译员的口译笔记:

例9-1: Water crisis threatens Indonesia's Bali

Bali, Indonesia, is facing a worsening water crisis from tourism development, population growth and water mismanagement. Shortages already are affecting UNESCO World Heritage structure, food production and Balinese culture. // Experts warn the situation will worsen if existing water control policies are not enforced across the island. // It is no longer possible to work in the fields as a farmer, said farmer I Ketut Jata. He said the land is too dry to grow rice which he sells to provide for his family. // Bali is in the center of Indonesia's group of islands. Bali gets its water from three main sources: lakes, rivers and groundwater. A traditional irrigation system, called the "subak", sends water through a network of waterways, dams and tunnels. //

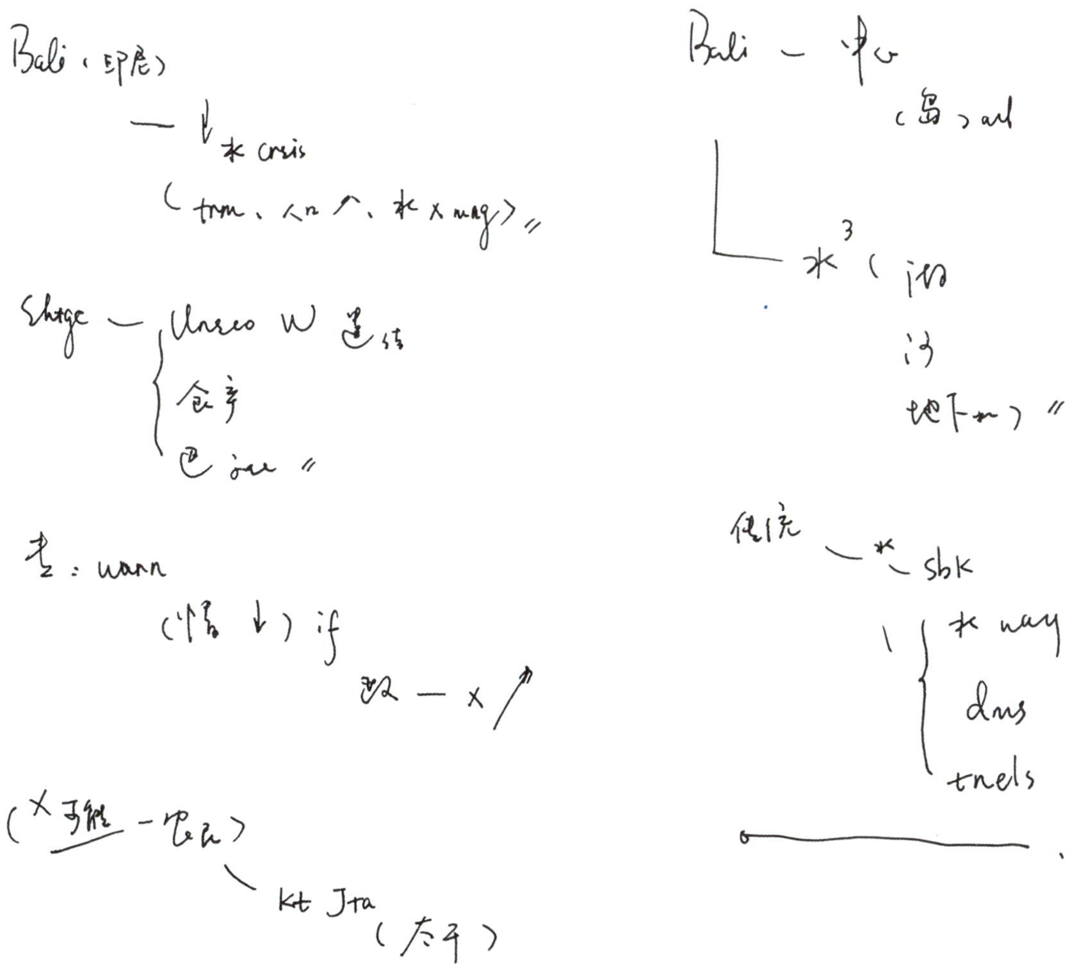

图9-3 译员1的英汉笔记

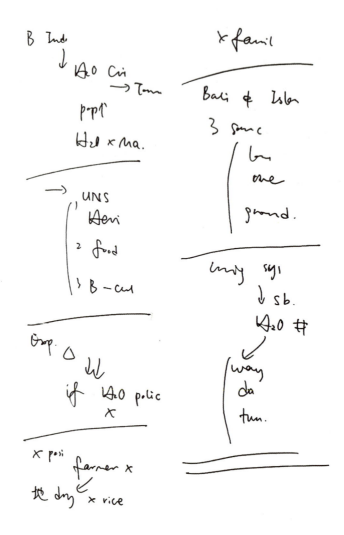

图9-4 译员2的英汉笔记

例9-2：重新吸引外资：中国还能成为热土吗？

改革开放以来，中国打开国门，积极拥抱国外资本，成为全球吸引外资的热土。//受到中国经济高速增长的鼓舞，以及中国廉价劳动力和庞大消费市场等方面的吸引，大量外国资本纷纷涌入中国。中国成为仅次于美国的第二大外国直接投资（FDI）接受国，并且在个别年份成为当年最大的FDI接受国。//不过，作为曾经的全球外资热土，中国在最近几年对外资的吸引力有所下降，由于劳动力成本提高，加上国际供应链在全球范围内重新配置等原因，部分外资开始向东南亚和非洲等地转移，外资对中国的投资规模出现萎缩。//如何稳定外国投资，增加国内外资本对中国经济的信心，已经成为当前亟须解决的重要问题。

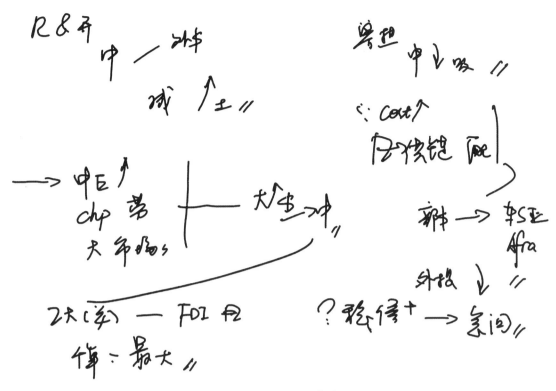

图9-5 译员1的汉英笔记

图9-6 译员2的汉英笔记

综上所述，口译笔记要简短、快速，注意与听力理解和短时记忆配合，同时还具有一定的个性化特征。编者对从业十年以上的口译员进行了简单的采访，其中一位译员对笔记的概括十分精辟：口译笔记就是记"容易忘的"和"最重要的"。而在对学习口译两年左右的学习者的随机采访中，大部分人都强调笔记应当辅助逻辑分析和记忆。有的学习者指出："从内容上而言，口译笔记应该是译员大脑处理加工后的产物，记录的是听懂并经过分析的逻辑和意群。"有的学习者结合自身经验指出："口译笔记的作用就是辅助译者输出，其符号和记法不需要参考范本，译者个人能够解读即可。笔记中容易忽视的是逻辑关系、数字的单位和长难句的理解性记忆。"

第二节　口译笔记的形式与内容

在明确口译笔记的特点之后，我们就来回答"如何记"这个问题。在信息化时代，网上海量的学习资料为我们提供了无数的口译笔记法，但是很多初学者仍感到无从下手。这里需要牢记三点。第一，明确"脑记"为主，笔记为辅。第二，笔记需要体现句子或意群之间的逻辑关系。第三，擅用缩写、符号提高笔记效率。

初学者往往将大量精力用于琢磨第三点，学习和发明各种符号，这就忽视了口译笔记的初衷。而且，网上各类关于笔记符号的帖子大多数是由普通网友提供的，并不一定经过长期实践的检验，对于自己也未必适用——毕竟口译笔记是个性化的。即便这些符号本身很有效，"知道"和"记住"并不代表能够熟练运用于实践。如果平时练习得太少，临场遇到可以简写的意群仍然会不自觉地逐字听写（taking notes by verbatim）。

"脑记"既包含听力理解，也包含逻辑分析，可以通过源语复述、无笔记交传进行训练，培养对段落大意和逻辑结构的敏感度，通过训练逐渐做到第一时间就能建立起语言转换的基本框架，即句子结构。

那么如何在笔记中体现逻辑关系呢？这包括两个层面：一是整体逻辑，即段落或句子间逻辑；二是句内逻辑。具体操作时，首先，在信息输入的过程中，我们应当以意群或短句为单位从上往下写。其次，可以借助括号"（　）"或短横线"–"这样的符号表明逻辑关系，用括号将次要信息、插入语、修饰语、从属关系等括起来，用短横线连接一个句子里不同的意群。再次，灵活运用数学符号，例如因为"∵"和所以"∴"，或者向上或向下的箭头。最后，在一个翻译片段结束之后，用双斜线"//"或长横线"——"等符号明确表明结束，区分不同的口译段落。

战略上明确了笔记的作用后，战术层面还需要对缩写、简写以及符号多加积累。常用的缩写或简写方式如下：

第一，仅保留部分英文单词或去掉部分元音字母，但是首字母为元音的单词需要保留首字母。如用"eff"指代"efficient"，用"hospt"指代"hospital"，用"mkt"代表"market"，或用"brn-s"指代"brain-storming"，用"schl"指代"school"。

第二，用部首代替整个汉字，或用单字指代词语。如用病字头指代"疾病"，用提手旁指代"打",或用"医"指代"医院"。

第三,用部分符号作为固定的"偏旁部首",套用于其他文字和符号之上。常见的角度符号"。"备注在文字右上角时,可以表示这是在形容人类。例如,"忙。"就是"忙碌的人","pro。"是"专业人士","学。"是"学生",等等。右半框"⌐"将文字或时间框起来时,代表"自从某个时间/事件之后"。

第四,用符号、缩写指代中英文中的常用词。如用方框"囗"指代"国家",再在方框中穿插向左或向右的箭头分别指代"国内/进口"或"国际/出口"。用三角形"△"或五角星"☆"指代"重要"一词,用"∽"指代"之间/互相/转换"等表示双方关系的意思,用笑脸符号":)"指代"问候、高兴、满意、出色"等积极情绪。

第五,对于国家、国际组织、政府机构等专有名词,它们一般有自己固定的缩写,可以提前熟悉并背诵,训练时巩固加强。我们在课堂上曾对学生说,不妨看一场奥运会的开幕式,留意每个国家出场时屏幕底部的文字,就能掌握大量国家名的缩写。当然,汉字简写有些时候更方便,但是要尽量避免混淆,比如"巴"可能是"巴西"也可能是"巴基斯坦","印"可能是"印度"也可能是"印度尼西亚",这些情况需要标识清楚,或是形成自己的惯用体系。

除此之外,还应注意以下几点:

第一,在笔记中应尽量用单个的字或符号指代一个意群。例如用"人"加上感叹号指代原文中提到的"人民当家作主"这一整个意群,用eco加上向上的箭头指代"the economy improved greatly after the long-term depression"。需要注意的是,使用这一方法对记忆的要求较高,译员需要在脑海中记住所指代的所有信息。

第二,笔记以输出为导向,可以适当用目的语记录。在听中文的时候,可以在笔记中快速处理一些关键词或逻辑关系,直接用英文进行记录。例如听到"所以"的时候,可以用"so"或"∴"记下来。同理,在听英文的时候,也可以直接用中文记录。例如听到"we are now faced with the changes unseen in a centenary",可以直接记录"大变局"。

第三,不要苛求笔记的完整和工整。这里主要针对平时习惯于将句子写完整或对书写要求比较高的同学。记笔记的时间十分有限,所以需要摆脱一笔一划书写的习惯,尽量快速、连续书写。平时可以多加练习,形成固定的书写模式。

此外,每次口译的现场译者也可能临时"发明"一些符号、简笔画和缩写,可能是一次性的,也可能后续会内化到个人的符号体系中。例如,有同学在某次训练中临时画了个钟表符号来指代时间,画了个眼镜符号代表眼镜(见图9-7),之后就固定了下来。

图9-7 口译者创造的简笔画符号

下面我们以中、英两个段落为例展示口译笔记的特点，说明如何运用符号来表明逻辑关系。

例9-3：Fig trees can survive cold weather

One popular method for burying trees for their protection is called "the Minnesota tip". It involves digging a narrow, shallow area where the tree can be laid. The space should be about 30 centimeters deep, 60 centimeters wide and as long as the tree is tall. // To prepare the tree, gather its branches and tie them together with soft rope. Next, push a shovel into the soil about a half-meter from the trunk on the side opposite the hole. Lift that side of the tree's root ball out of the ground. Then, gently push the tree toward the hole. When it is lying flat, cover the tree with plastic. // Pack soil around the exposed side of the roots, and around the length of the tree. Load soil over the tree. Make it at least 30 centimeters deep. You will need more soil than you removed from digging. //

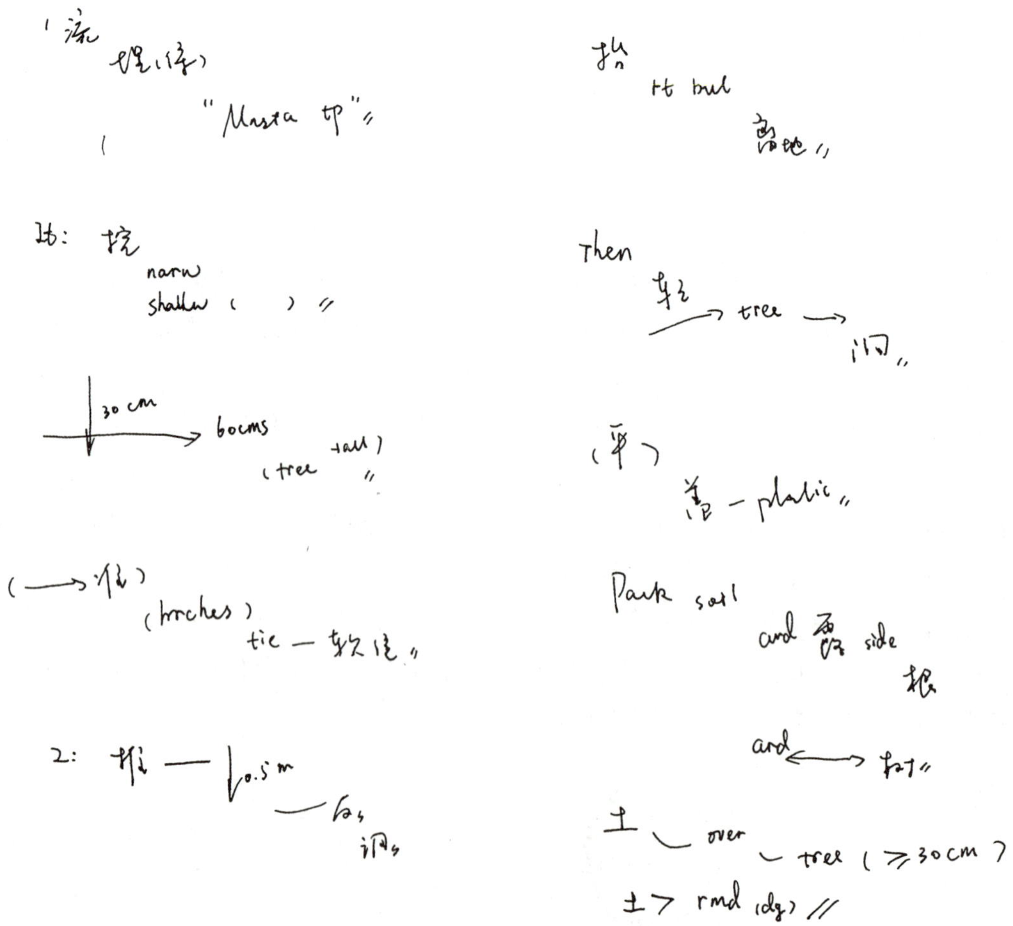

图9-8　例9-3口译笔记

例9-4：外交部亚洲司司长刘劲松在中日邦交正常化50周年民间纪念活动开幕式上的致辞

很高兴代表吴江浩部长助理出席中日邦交正常化50周年民间纪念活动开幕式。// 再过几天，我们将迎来中日邦交正常化50周年纪念日。值此重要节点，我们在此共同回顾中日友好交流历程，重温历史经验启示，展望两国关系未来，恰合时宜，意义深远。// 借此机会，谨向日中邦交正常化50周年纪念活动在华执行委员会、中国公共外交协会等主办单位表示祝贺，向所有支持、推动和参与中日友好事业的朋友们表示敬意和感谢。//

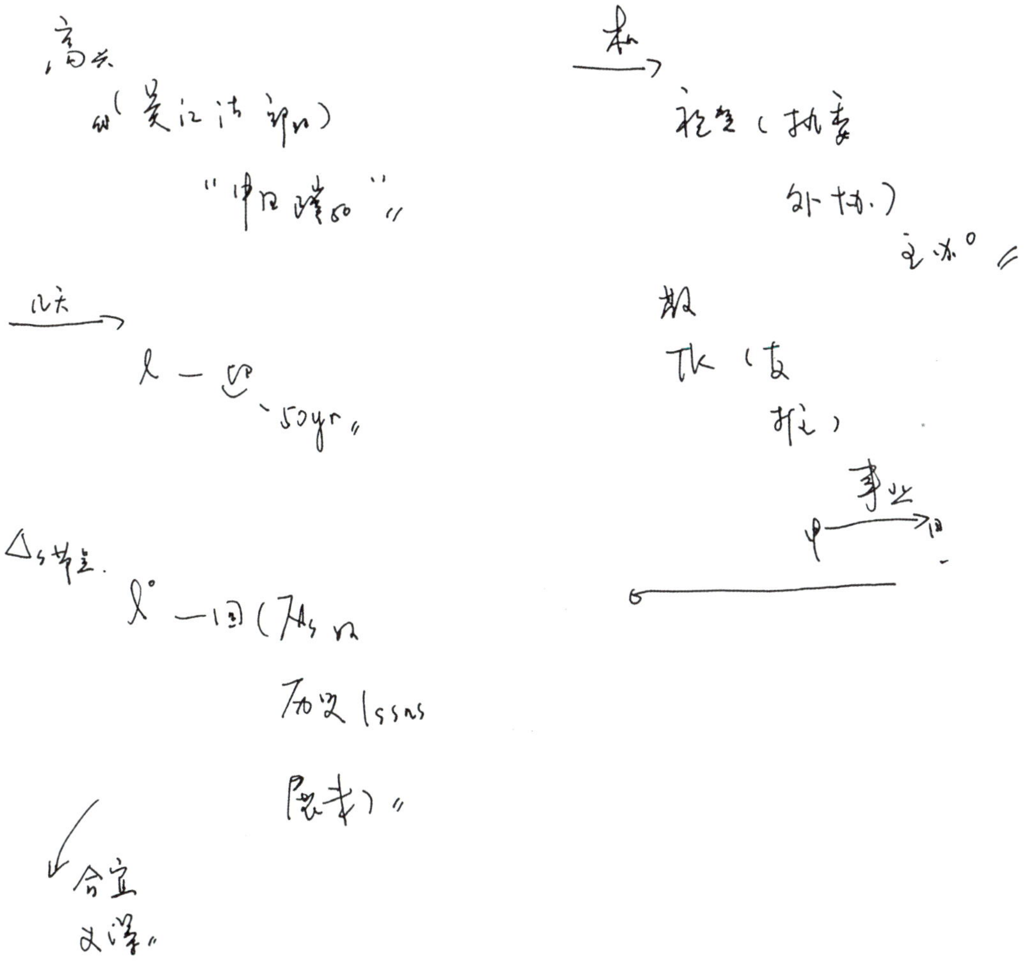

图9-9　例9-4口译笔记

总而言之，口译笔记的初衷是辅助记忆，为语言转换进行提示。口译笔记的具体操作方法有很多，需要不断地琢磨、反思，最终才能形成一套属于自己的笔记方法。随着我们口译技能的提高、脑记容量的扩展，口译笔记可能还会变得越来越简化。此外，英汉口译和汉英口译的笔记特征也有可能不同：英译汉的时候由于原文是外语，听辨占用的工作记忆较多，逻辑梳理完毕后才做记录,笔记可能较为精简,呈现出"以点带面"的特征;而汉译英时,由于听力理解的障碍相对较低,记录的信息能更全一些。最终要牢记的一点是,评判笔记效率的标准是它对口译是否有帮助,即说出来的译文是否准确清楚,而不是笔记自身多完整、多具体、多整洁。

参考文献

林超伦.实战口译[M].北京:外语教学与研究出版社,2004.

专项练习

要求:本阶段的练习可先从边看边记开始,即一边看原文一边模拟口译场景做记录。建议先从中文段落入手进行练习,逐步过渡到英文段落。无须翻译。

第一遍练习时建议先将原文的每个分段逐个转换成笔记,然后用红笔圈出笔记中冗余、模糊之处,并将一些完整的字、单词替换为简写或符号。对照笔记复述原文。

第二遍练习时用听觉输入代替视觉输入,听原文做口译笔记。注意"脑记"为主,"笔记"为辅。

汉英段落1: 兔种起源

Glossary:	
啮齿类: rodent	门齿: incisor

在古人口中,兔作为十二生肖之一是与月同辉的瑞兽,而在今人眼里,兔也是聪明、可爱的代名词。//从演化到驯化,兔如何跨越六千多万年的时光,走进我们的生活?//兔与鼠都曾经被归类为啮齿类动物,而兔比鼠多出来一对小门齿,让人们重新开始讨论它们究竟是否存在亲缘关系。//研究证实,在6 200万年前,鼠与兔的祖先曾一起生活在这里,既是好邻居,又是相亲相爱的"姐妹俩"。//根据以上研究,我国科学家李传夔于1980年正式提出"鼠兔同源",而现代生物学的证据也支持了这一观点,这场持续300年的"亲缘大战"终于落下帷幕。//

汉英段落2: 汽车与环境

Glossary:	
乙醇: ethanol	内燃机: combustion engine

汽车无疑是有史以来最重要的发明之一。它使大众交通更加便利，我们的日常生活大多离不开它。但目前的汽车在不远的将来会面临一些巨大的挑战。// 首先是汽车所需的能源问题。汽油是石油产品，而石油是一种不可再生的资源。终将有一天它会耗尽，无法满足人类需求。虽然关于这一天何时会到来存在不同的观点，但很可能会在我的有生之年内发生。// 即使汽油被可再生资源乙醇所替代，但仍然存在内燃机排放的问题，也就是二氧化碳。二氧化碳是最常见的温室气体。美国32%的二氧化碳来自交通领域。因此，尽管汽车非常实用，但它并不可持续，几乎贡献了三分之一的二氧化碳排放，而这种气体会破坏气候稳定。我们必须有更好的解决方案。//

英汉段落1: US reopens visa, consular services in Cuba

> **Glossary:**
>
> visa and consular services：签证和领事服务

The United States Embassy in Cuba is reopening visa and consular services on Wednesday. The embassy says it will prioritize immigration permits to help Cubans join their families in the US. // The move comes during one of the largest waves ever of Cuban migration to the US. Economic and political problems on the island are among reasons Cubans are leaving. // The embassy expects to give out at least 20,000 visas a year. But that is just a small part of the total number of Cubans migrating towards the US. // In late December, US officials reported stopping Cubans 34,675 times along the Mexico border in November, up 21 percent from 28,848 times in October. // That number has slowly risen each month. Cubans are now the second-largest nationality after Mexicans appearing on the border, US Customs and Border Protection data shows. //

英汉段落2: Concerns grow over sports betting in Africa

In at least five African countries, many people consider sports gambling as a way to get regular income. Some consider sports gambling a way out of poverty. But critics warn that sports betting in Africa is increasing while poverty, unemployment and a lack of industry rules remain big problems. // In one example, a Ugandan health official was so sure Argentina would win its World Cup soccer game against Saudi Arabia that he bet $1,800. The money was loaned to him by officials from an amount meant to go to 243 people who had taken part in a polio vaccine campaign. // Argentina lost the game, and the official lost the money. Later he was chased by an angry crowd and locked himself indoors for days. His supervisor said he could lose his job. // In Uganda, the official's loss was a lot of money. Yearly income per person in the country was $840 in 2020. Sports gamblers include students, politicians, workers and government officials. //

篇章练习

说明：建议每个篇章练习两遍。第一遍为听记加口译。第二遍中，结合本章所讲解的笔记要点对笔记进行反思和修改。首先，查看笔记中各片段末是否有明显的结束符号。其次，查看笔记是否为纵向记录。第三，查看各个意群之间的逻辑关系是否在笔记中清楚呈现。最后，删除笔记中多余的字符。

Text 1: 古丝绸之路

Glossary:	
"一带一路"倡议：The Belt and Road Initiative	使节：envoy
21世纪海上丝绸之路：21st Century Maritime Silk Road	汉武帝：Emperor Wu of the Han Dynasty
商队：caravan	盟友：ally
丝绸之路经济带：Silk Road Economic Belt	联盟：alliance

"一带一路"是"丝绸之路经济带"和"21世纪海上丝绸之路"的简称。谈及"丝绸之路"，人们便会想到过去遥远的古丝绸之路，它在中国历史上占有重要地位。//

至于丝绸之路的相关人物，大多数人首先想到的是汉朝张骞，因为古丝绸之路正是由他开辟出来的。从此，路上出现了络绎不绝的使节、商队，为沿途各国贸易带来了生机。//

张骞受汉武帝委托出使西域，其主要目标是启动丝绸之路上的跨大陆贸易，并建立政治盟友关系。丝绸之路的中亚部分主要是由他在公元前114年左右出使西域拓展而成的。//

张骞的经历由司马迁于公元前1世纪编入史书。今天，他被推崇为中国的民族英雄，因他为中国争取到了更广泛的商业贸易和对外联盟的机会。我们还能确定的一件事，就是他有极强的冒险精神。因为只有敢冒险的人，才会接受这样的任务。//

Text 2：数字人民币

Preview:

  数字货币并不是一种新的货币，它属于央行管控的数字形式上的法定货币，其实就是电子版货币，英文全称digital currency（数字货币）/ electronic payment（电子支付），简称DC/EP。它和纸钞、硬币等价。电子支付的工作环境基于一个开放的系统平台（即互联网），把支付信息通过信息网络安全地传送到银行或相应的处理机构，用来实现货币支付或资金流转的行为。电子支付包含了移动支付业务类型，其类型按照电子支付指令发起方式分为网上支付、电话支付、移动支付等。

  移动支付指的是使用手机完成支付，而不是用现金、银行卡或者支票支付，其通过移动终端对所购买的产品进行结算支付。移动支付的主要表现形式为手机支付，用户可以用手机随时随地进行支付活动，并对个人账户进行查询、转账、缴费、充值等功能的管理，了解自己的消费信息，不受时间和空间的限制。

Glossary:	
移动支付：mobile payment	中国互联网络信息中心：China Internet Network Information Centre
中央银行：China's Central Bank	数字人民币：digital RMB（或者e-CNY）
电子支付：electronic payment	防伪技术：anti-counterfeiting technology
不可追溯性：untraceable	区块链技术：blockchain technology
跨国结算：international settlement	跨国汇款：transnational remittance

  我国的移动支付系统全球领先，覆盖了社会生活的方方面面，不仅助推了我国经济的发展，也方便了人们的生活。中国互联网络信息中心的最新统计数据显示，如今已有64.7%的智能手机用户习惯使用移动支付进行交易。//

  近几年以来，央行开始大力推广数字人民币，并在深圳、苏州等多个城市试点运行。截至2020年8月底，使用数字人民币进行的交易超过312万笔，交易金额超过11亿元。然而，我们现在都已经习惯了用微信和支付宝付款，国家为什么还要推行数字人民币呢？我认为主要有四点。//

  最基本的原因是保障国家电子支付体系的安全。截至2021年年底，阿里巴巴的支付宝和腾讯的微信支付在中国移动支付的市场占有率达90%以上。中国中小企业的平均寿命不到3年，大一点的企业平均寿命是7到8年，世界五百强的平均寿命大约是40年。虽然这两

家企业规模很大,目前的经营状况也很好,但是市场经济的浪潮瞬息万变。//

第二个原因是降低成本。国家需要为印制纸币、研发防伪技术、运输与存储纸币等各个环节付出大量的人力财力。相比之下,数字人民币的成本几乎为零。

第三个原因是打击犯罪。纸币具有不可追溯性,所以成为贩毒、行贿等各种犯罪行为的首选交易方式。如果未来彻底废除纸币,全面推行数字人民币,那么所有交易过程国家都了如指掌,大多数违法交易行为将无所遁形。//

第四个原因是方便国际交易。数字人民币采用区块链技术,可以将现有的跨国结算时间由几天缩减为几秒,大幅提高交易效率,提高资金流动性。比如,从A国到B国跨国汇款,中间要经过五个机构,按照传统支付方式,汇款手续只能按顺序一个机构一个机构地走,但如果我们采用数字人民币结算,汇款信息会被五个机构同时看到、同时确认。//

Text 3: Humans significantly alter Earth

Glossary:	
geological:地质学的	consumption:(能量、食物或材料的)消耗
fossil fuel:化石燃料	glaciers:冰川
biosphere:生物圈	ice core:冰芯
permafrost:永冻层	

Human activities significantly change the rates of many of Earth's surface processes. To understand the workings of earth's systems, we need to understand the role of humans in those systems. To do this, we can think of humankind as a geological agent, one that we need to consider along with Earth's natural processes. //

The effect of humans on earth's systems increases with our population and with our per capita consumption of natural resources. Earth scientists use the geologic record to distinguish between natural and human influences on Earth's systems. They find evidence for natural and human influences on Earth's processes in a number of places. These include ice cores and soils, as well as sediments from lakes and oceans. //

Humans cause global climate change through fossil fuel combustion, land use changes, agricultural practices, and industrial processes. The consequences of global climate change include melting glaciers and permafrost, rising sea levels, shifting patterns of precipitation, increased forest fires, more extreme weather, and the disruption of ecosystems worldwide. Humans affect the quality, availability and distribution of earth's water, through the modification of streams, lakes, and ground water. //

The distribution of water and sediment can be changed by such structures as canals, dams and levees. Water quality can be reduced by pollution from sewage runoff, agricultural practices, and industrial processes. Overusing water for electrical power generation and agriculture reduces the amount of available drinking water. //

Human activities alter the natural land surface. Humans use more than one third of the land surface that is not covered with ice to raise or grow their food. Large areas of land are transformed by human land development. This includes such delicate ecosystems as these wetlands. These land surface changes affect many processes such as groundwater replenishment and weather patterns. //

Human activities accelerate land erosion. Right now, the rate of global land erosion caused by human activities is very high. It exceeds all natural processes by a factor of 10. These activities include urban paving, removing vegetation, surface mining, diverting streams, and increasing rain acidity. //

Human activities significantly alter the biosphere. Because of human activities, Earth is experiencing a worldwide decline in biodiversity, a modern mass extinction. This is due to loss of habitat area and high rates of changes to the environment. The rates of extinctions now compare to the rates of mass extinctions in Earth's geologic past. //

Many of these human impacts on Earth's systems are not reversible over human lifetimes. Through cooperation among humans, their impacts on future generations can be lessened and even reversed. An Earth science literate public, informed by current and accurate scientific understanding of Earth, is critical to the promotion of good stewardship, sound policy, and international cooperation. Earth science education is important for individuals of all ages, backgrounds, and nationalities. //

Text 4: A smart loan for people with no credit history

Preview:

Trust: How do you earn it? Banks use credit scores to determine if you're trustworthy, but there are about 2.5 billion people around the world who don't have one to begin with — and who can't get a loan to start a business, buy a home or otherwise improve their lives. Hear how TED Fellow Shivani Siroya is unlocking untapped purchasing power in the developing world with InVenture, a start-up that uses mobile data to create a financial identity. She is going to share a story of Jenipher, a 65-year-old small-business owner in Nairobi, Kenya, who benefited from the program. "With something as simple as a credit score," says Siroya, "we're giving people the power to build their own futures."

Glossary:	
aggregation：聚合	small-business owner：小企业主（缩写为sbo）
loan shark：高利贷	chama, a savings group：一种地方性的储蓄小组,可称为"互助会"

Banks, credit card companies and other financial institutions don't know us on a personal level, but they do have a way of trusting us, and that's through our credit scores. Our credit scores have been created through an aggregation and analysis of our public consumer credit data. And because of them, we have pretty much easy access to all of the goods and services that we need, from getting electricity to buying a home, or taking a risk and starting a business. But ... there are 2.5 billion people around the world that don't have a credit score. //

That's a third of the world's population. They don't have a score because there are no formal public records on them — no bank accounts, no credit histories and no social security numbers. And because they don't have a score, they don't have access to the credit or financial products that can improve their lives. They are not trusted. So we wanted to find a way to build trust and to open up financial access for these 2.5 billion. So we created a mobile application that builds credit scores for them using mobile data. //

There are currently over one billion smartphones in emerging markets. And people are using them the same way that we do. They're texting their friends, they're looking up directions, they're browsing the Internet and they're even making financial transactions. Over time, this data is getting captured on our phones, and it provides a really rich picture of a person's life. //

Our customers give us access to this data and we capture it through our mobile application. It helps us understand the creditworthiness of people like Jenipher, a small-business owner in Nairobi, Kenya. Jenipher is 65 years old, and for decades has been running a food stall in the central business district. She has three sons who she put through vocational school, and she's also the leader of her local chama, or savings group. //

Jenipher's food stall does well. She makes just enough every day to cover her expenses. But she's not financially secure. Any emergency could force her into debt. And she has no discretionary income to improve her family's way of living, for emergencies, or for investing into growing her business. If Jenipher wants credit, her options are limited. She could get a microloan, but she'd have to form a group that could help vouch for her credibility. And even then, the loan sizes would be way too small to really have an impact on her business, averaging around 150 dollars. Loan sharks are always an option, but with interest rates that are well above 300 percent, they're financially risky. //

And because Jenipher doesn't have collateral or a credit history, she can't walk into a bank and ask for a business loan. But one day, Jenipher's son convinced her to download our application and apply for a loan. Jenipher answered a few questions on her phone and she gave us access to a few key data points on her device. And here's what we saw. So, bad news first. Jenipher had a low savings balance and no previous loan history. These are factors that would have thrown up a red flag to a traditional bank. //

But there were other points in her history that showed us a much richer picture of her potential. So for one, we saw that she made regular phone calls to her family in Uganda. Well, it turns out that the data shows a four percent increase in repayment among people who consistently communicate with a few close contacts. We could also see that though she traveled around a lot throughout the day, she actually had pretty regular travel patterns, and she was either at home or at her food stall. And the data shows a six percent increase in repayment among customers who are consistent with where they spend most of their time. We could also see that she communicated a lot with many different people throughout the day and that she had a strong support network. Our data shows that people who communicate with more than 58 different contacts tend to be more likely to be good borrowers. In Jenipher's case, she communicated with 89 different individuals, which showed a nine percent increase in her repayment. //

These are just some of the thousands of different data points that we look at to understand a person's creditworthiness. And after analyzing all of these different data points, we took the first risk and gave Jenipher a loan. This is data that would not be found on a paper trail or in any formal financial record. But it proves trust. By looking beyond income, we can see that people in emerging markets that may seem risky and unpredictable on the surface are actually willing and have the capacity to repay. //

第十章
数字口译

第一节 数字口译的特征与类型

数字是政府报告、项目展示、商务洽谈等场合中的重要信息，也是口译听辨、听记的难点之一。即便只是听母语记数字，在信息密集、语速快的情况下也容易出错，更不用说听外语记数字并准确地翻译出来了，这是因为数字口译时承受的信息压力比一般性的政治演讲口译高出约20倍（鲍刚，2011：186）。

数字口译说难不难，因为它是为数不多的具有明确对等项的内容，即所谓的"说一不二"。数字口译大致可分为以下几个部分：单纯数字、数字的修饰成分、单位、数字所指涉的概念。

单纯数字存在小数、分数、百分比、序数、时间等不同形式，但万变不离其宗的还是那十个最熟悉的阿拉伯数字。只要能够听辨清楚、准确记录，一般稍加思考总能翻译对，只是熟练度和流畅度的问题。因此，克服畏难心理、反复练习、形成"肌肉记忆"，对于攻克数字口译的难关来说十分关键。根据我们的课堂教学实践，除了涉及中英文位数转换的大数字、精确到个位的复杂数字之外，分数、负数、序数也是出错率较高的类型，因为学生平时较少接触这些形式的数字。

不过，实际生活中我们使用的许多数字并不是精确的，因此就需要数字的修饰成分。常见的包括表示"超过"的over、more than、above和表示"不足"的almost、nearly、no more than。需要进一步修饰时也可以用well below、significantly beyond、far below等表达。学生基本掌握单纯数字的读数和口译后，一开始往往会忽略或误译数字的修饰成分，但经过训练后可以按含义将它们大致分成几类，并借助相应的笔记符号完善数据的准确性。

数字口译说易不易，因为数字属于无序信息，基本无法预测，仅依靠脑记存储对工作记忆的要求较高。我们的短期记忆是有限的，而"好钢要用在刀刃上"。在无笔记口译阶段，我们一般不要求大家记住和复述数字，除非是特别简单的那些。

数字口译的难点还在于它背后的信息，包括其单位和所指涉的概念。这些内容往往比数字本身更重要，因为如果只是数字本身记录不全，尚可以用约数法翻译个大概，但是如果不知道它指的是什么东西，或者弄错了单位，那么数值本身再准确也没有意义，严重时可能导致整段译文语义缺失。过度紧张于单纯数字，追求精确到个位，反而容易拣了芝麻丢了西瓜。下面这例在课堂练习中就给许多同学造成了困扰。

例 10-1

原文：

By 2002, China has accumulatively approved 378,000 foreign funded enterprises with a contractual value of USD 717.01 billion, of which USD 372.83 billion has been actually paid in.

参考译文：

到2002年，中国累计批准设立外商投资企业37.8万家，合同外资金额为7 170.1亿美元，实际使用外资金额为3 728.3亿美元。

后两个数字误译率很高，主要的错误类型包括数位错误（将372.83 billion译成了37.283亿、372.83亿）和数字错误（将717.01 billion译成717.1亿）。更遗憾的是，不少学生读对了数字，却将单位译成了"元"，笔者询问后发现他们都只记录了数字，没有记下单位。而正好篇章讨论的是中国问题，就想当然地译成了"元"。同样道理，当音频中出现HKD、Canadian Dollar等货币单位时，若是只记下了美元符号$，翻译时出错也就在所难免了。

例10-1中，"contractual value"和"actually paid in"又是两个失分点。部分同学没有完成口译任务，虽然他们记下了数字和单位，但对常用的经贸概念不熟悉，不知道它们代表什么金额，无从下口。有时即使数字本身很简单，但还是容易犯类似的错误，以下这句话就被译得五花八门。

例 10-2

原文：

Between 1990 and 2012, the country reported a 67 percent drop in the number of children dying before the age of five.

参考译文：

报道称，从1990到2012年，该国五岁以下儿童的死亡率下降了67%。

核对口译笔记发现，大多数同学记下的信息点为：1990—2012, 67%, <5儿，结果有的误译成"五岁以下儿童的平均死亡率为67%"。译文纵使读数正确，也与原意大相径庭，因为他们忽略了数字背后的信息"drop"（↓）。

译员的短期记忆是有限的，数字口译的信息量又大，因此成为口译笔记的重点之一。记忆和记录时应包括三部分：数字、单位和指涉概念，缺一不可，而且后两者的重要性甚至超过数字本身。例如翻译例10-1中的"USD 717.01 billion"时，一些学生虽未记全数字，但懂得变通，采取"四舍五入"或保留"下位"的应对策略，译成"约7 000亿美元"或"超过7 100亿美元",尚能勉强过关。如果反过来,数字译准确了,不知道其单位和指涉概念,那么整段话都毫无意义了。

我们曾经做过一项调研,考查学生译员在英汉交替传译中数字口译的情况,通过分析课堂表现和相关问卷,归纳了一些常见的错误。调查和实验选取的材料包括单纯数字,也包括数字的修饰成分、单位和数字所指涉的概念三部分,结果显示:

(1)单纯数字的英汉口译中,万以上的数值错误率最高。从错误类型来看,错译(占43.9%)和漏译(占39.1%)最为常见。单纯数字部分出错的原因主要在于,学生译员对于大数字和位数级不够熟悉。

(2)学生译员在数值的修饰成分、单位和指涉的概念三部分的口译中,错误率高于对单纯数字的口译。一方面,此类错误是由于译员不熟悉部分术语或表达而造成的;另一方面,这反映出译员的翻译策略不合理,过于关注单纯数字部分,导致其他信息出现错漏。

基于对学生译员的数字口译实验和问卷调查,我们认为训练数字口译时应将单纯数字、含有数字的句子、含有数字的篇章结合起来,以期达到最佳练习效果。这样既可以锻炼数字口译基本功,又能运用数字口译的不同策略,积累一些应对技巧来处理困难、减少错误,从而提高英汉交传中的数字口译能力。

第二节　数字口译的训练方法

一、读数练习

数字是口译中的一个困难诱因(problem trigger)(Gile, 1995)。它出现频率高、预测性低、信息量大,对准确性的要求又高,常见于经贸、人口、科技类的讲话。如果译员对数字不敏感,那么就极容易出错,甚至因此而丧失信心,直接放弃整个翻译任务。

译员对所听到的数字愈是熟悉,翻译难度就愈低。但是英文中的数字三位一进(three-digit),分别有thousand、million、billion、trillion等常见单位,而中文里的数字是四位一进(four-digit),以万、亿来进位,这就导致我们对英语数字的读法不那么熟练,敏感度低。这方面可以通过强化训练来提高,比如试着分别用中英文朗读下面这个大数字:

　　　　176 099 038
　　　　中文:1/7 609/9 038
　　　　一亿七千六百零九万九千零三十八
　　　　英文:176,099,038
　　　　One hundred and seventy-six million ninety-nine thousand and thirty-eight

如果读数存在困难,或者读法不标准,那么在听到正确的英文读数时就会措手不及。有的同学在英文读数时会漏掉中间的"and",记笔记的时候便容易漏掉数字中间的"0",导致数字错位或数量级发生改变。例如,读数不熟练的译者可能将上面的数字误记成如下:

17 609 938

17 699 038

1 769 938

数字虽然相对比较有定数，但同样的数字也可能有不同的读法，例如"a thousand million"其实就是"one billion"。有同学已经将"billion=十亿"记得滚瓜烂熟，但是听到"a thousand million"时却反应不过来，因为我们平时比较习惯直接使用"billion"。类似的情况还有"nineteen hundred"，这和我们平时惯用的"one thousand and nine hundred"其实是同一个数字。除了常规的正整数，特殊数字的读法也会对译员构成障碍。例如有的同学平时没有碰到过"negative 2"（-2），听到时很难及时反应过来并记录下来。

二、数字笔记

数字口译一般依赖于笔记，因为人的短时记忆通常只能容纳7±2个信息组块（Miller，1956），而大部分数字本身就是彼此毫无联系的数字和符号，稍微复杂点的单个大数字就可能让译者的记忆超负荷了。这就是为什么日常生活手机验证码一般是四位或者六位，不然的话人们就容易记错或者需要反复翻看。

我们在口译课上曾播放过音频《美国的人口》（"Population in the United States"），其中开篇有一句是："According to the most recent government census, the population is 281,421,906"结果大部分学生译员都出现了疏漏，甚至闹出"美国人口超过中国"的笑话。

由于中英两种语言的进位法则不同，做笔记时不妨采取"逗点法"，即每三位打一个逗号。例如，"281,421,906"就要比"281421906"容易识读，花一点点时间打个逗号可以避免读数错误，可谓事半功倍。逗点法的使用还有一个好处，那就是不容易因为遗漏数字中间的"0"而发生数量级的位移。以下面的数字为例：

one million forty-seven thousand and sixty-two

建议大家听到"million"和"thousand"时都顺势在数字后写下逗号，这样即使由于没有留意"and"而误记成了"1,47,62"，也能根据"三位一进"的原则将"0"补上，还原为"1,047,062"。

学生译员必须熟悉中英文数字读法之间的转化，可以自己写一组八位以上的数字，分别用英语和中文读出；或请同学用一种语言读数，自己用另一种语言译出。一般通过两三周的密集练习就能够逐渐掌握常用的变换法，例如："100 million"为"一亿"，"1 billion"为"十亿"，"一千万"为"10 million"，"trillion"为"万亿"（"trillion"也可译为"兆"，但除了科技类篇章外，这种译法较少使用），直到汉译英和英译汉时都能转换自如。

第三节 积累核心概念词

数字还经常涉及有关增加、减少、占比等信息，译对难度不大，但是如果想译好，那么就需要注意辨析词义，丰富表达，增加语言的多样性。笔者教授汉译英口译课程，发现在翻译表示

"增加/减少"的概念时，绝大部分同学都一直沿用"increase/decrease"的表达。这固然是正确的，但是我们不应满足于此，因为地道的英文里有几十种不同的表示"增加/减少"的表达，彼此之间还有微妙的差异。

杨承淑（2005：21）曾对概念词做了总结，包括表意和描述两类，前者表达说话者的立场，后者用于描述客观事物（见表10-1）。

表10-1 两类概念词枚举

表意类概念词	观点：建议、劝告、意图、看法、决断、态度、主张 情感：喜怒哀乐、谢意 征询：询问、请求 意向：重视、强调、反对、同意
描述类概念词	增减：增加、减少、变化 形体：几何图形、体积、大小 位置：东西南北、高低、内外 数量：年龄、数量词、度量衡、货币单位、日期、比率、倍数、约数

以其中与数字口译关联最密切的"增减"为例，我们曾帮助学生列表总结了相关的核心概念词（见表10-2）：

表10-2 关于"增减"的核心概念词表

提高、增长、 发展、扩展等	advance, aggrandize, aggravate, amplify, augment, boost, broaden, build, build up, deepen, develop, dilate, double, enhance, enlarge, escalate, exaggerate, expand, extend, further, gain in, go up, grow, heighten, increase, inflate, intensify, lengthen, magnify, mark up, mount, mount up, multiply, progress, proliferate, prolong, protract, raise, redouble, reinforce, rise, sharpen, snowball, spread, step up, strengthen, supplement, swarm, swell, teem, thicken, triple, widen, skyrocket, soar, etc.
下降、减弱、 减少、退化等	abate, calm down, check, contract, crumble, curb, curtail, cut down, decay, decline, decrease, degenerate, depreciate, deteriorate, devaluate, die down, diminish, droop, drop, drop off, dry up, dwindle, ease, ebb, evaporate, fade, fall, fall off, go/come down, lessen, lighten, lose edge, lower, narrow down, plunge, reduce, restrain, run low, shrink, shrivel, sink, slacken, slack off, slash, slow down, slump, soften, subside, tail off, wane, weaken, wear away, wear down, wither, etc.
比率	account for, be composed of, comprise, constitute, make/take up, occupy, represent, etc.

这样做看似很花功夫，毕竟同一个意思掌握一种说法似乎也可以应付翻译任务，但其实核心概念词数量虽然有限，出现频率却比较高，尽早掌握可以说是磨刀不误砍柴工。积累

核心概念词可以增加英文的接受性词汇（receptive vocabulary），在听和读的时候容易抓住关键。同时，这样的练习也能促使译员主动积累产出性词汇（productive vocabulary），使其英文语言更丰富。这一点对于汉译英来说十分关键，因为英文的风格讲求变化，一般来说会尽量避免重复用词，除非是为了达到某种修辞效果（连淑能，1993：173）。在之后的训练中，我们不妨多积累表10-2中词汇的多样化英文表述，并且在汉译英时有意识地避免使用最普通、最宽泛、最容易想到的那些词，让自己的语言更加准确和生动。

参考文献

Gile D. Basic Concepts and Models in Interpreter and Translator Training [M]. Amsterdam/Philadelphia: John Benjamins Publishing Company, 1995.

Miller G A. The Magical Number Seven, Plus or Minus Two: Some Limits on Our Capacity for Processing Information [J]. Psychological Review, 1956, 63(2): 81-97.

连淑能. 英汉对比研究 [M]. 北京：高等教育出版社，1993.

杨承淑. 口译教学研究：理论与实践 [M]. 北京：中国对外翻译出版公司，2005.

鲍刚. 口译理论概述 [M]. 北京：中国对外翻译出版有限公司，2011.

专项练习

1. 读数练习

要求：用英语朗读下列数字，再对照音频检查自己的读数是否正确。

(1) 2,408,732
(2) 37.75%
(3) 47,090
(4) 16,300,050
(5) 824,050,000
(6) 3/4
(7) 0.067
(8) 170,030
(9) 798
(10) 7,901,000
(11) 6,300
(12) －4.5
(13) 2021年
(14) 1905年
(15) 公元前4世纪
(16) 20世纪80年代
(17) 2/3
(18) 0.7%
(19) 两倍
(20) 12th
(21) 八又四分之一
(22) 一亿三千七百万

2. 数字口译

要求：用以下材料做有笔记口译练习并录音，对照文本复听自己的口译音频，检查准确性并总结错误的原因。英文材料做跟读练习。

(1) 32,050
(2) around 50 billion
(3) 84,635,550
(4) nearly 700,000
(5) 6,001
(6) 7 billion and 32 thousand
(7) 8.3 million
(8) 0.4%
(9) 7.4 trillion
(10) two hundred and forty thousand million
(11) over 57 thousand
(12) 405 million
(13) a quarter of a million
(14) the 30th
(15) 500,090,000
(16) -670
(17) 72,050,000
(18) a dozen of
(19) no more than 600
(20) 56.1 million
(21) 八百二十七万
(22) 五千三百二十七
(23) 一亿两千万
(24) 近八成
(25) 五个百分点
(26) 大年初一
(27) 四万亿
(28) 十二点三刻
(29) 三十万零二十
(30) 不足八分之一

3. 带单位的数字

(1) hundreds of millions of people
(2) 30 degrees Fahrenheit
(3) 50,000 pounds
(4) 45 inches
(5) 400 gigabytes
(6) the 15th century
(7) 609 billion RMB
(8) half a million pairs of shoes
(9) basement first floor
(10) 105 million HK$
(11) tens of thousands of miles
(12) 7 billion tons
(13) the second quarter of the year
(14) dozens of boxes
(15) nought/naught point eight kilos
(16) 70英尺
(17) 970盎司
(18) 零下十度
(19) 近四分之一个世纪
(20) 零点五欧元
(21) 十点一刻
(22) 50尺

(23）一斤
(24）两周左右
(25）8英寸
(26）960万平方公里
(27）7 800立方米
(28）《海底两万里》
(29）1 024兆字节

4. 带数字的段落

Glossary:	
market capitalization：市值	Sustainable Development Goals (SDGs)：可持续发展目标
China Construction Bank：中国建设银行	the Museum of the Qin Terracotta Warriors and Horses：秦始皇兵马俑博物馆
"十三五"计划：the 13th Five-Year Plan	2022年冬奥会：2022 Winter Olympics
国家统计局：the National Bureau of Statistics	天猫：Tmall
（大气环境中的）细颗粒物：fine particulate matter	微克/立方米：microgram per cubic meter
流域：basin	

(1) At present, Asia has already formed a rather sophisticated financial market system consisting of multiple financial centers, including Hong Kong, Shanghai and Singapore. In 2014, the total market capitalization of Asia-based listed companies stood at U.S. $20.67 trillion, accounting for 32.1 percent of the world's total.

(2) The United Nations has 17 Sustainable Development Goals. Number one on the list is eradicating extreme poverty by 2030. Between 2015 and 2018, global poverty continued its historical decline, with the poverty rate falling from 10.1 percent in 2015 to 8.6 percent in 2018.

(3) The report predicts that 87 million African children will be born into poverty each year in the 2020s. An estimated 40 percent of Africans still live on less than one dollar 90 cents a day. A child born into poverty faces greater risks of illiteracy, greater risks of mortality before the age of five.

(4) Buying children a house and paying for their wedding are the top priorities for Hong Kong's middle class. The China Construction Bank surveyed 2,500 Hongkongers in January on their savings and wealth management habits. Twenty-two percent of respondents said they were saving to buy their children property, while 12 percent said they were saving for their children's weddings.

(5) There are 2,200 museums in China, including 625 non-governmental museums. With a total collection surpassing 20 million items, these museums hold more than 8,000 exhibitions a year. Museums based on cultural relics, like the Museum of the Qin Terracotta Warriors and

Horses in Xi'an, have become a fixture on tourists' schedules.

（6）"十三五"计划以来，我国全民健身运动蓬勃发展，越来越多的人加入到健身的队伍中。我国经常参加体育锻炼的人数比例达到37.2%。人们的健身环境更加舒适，健身的热情日益高涨。

（7）在申办2022年冬奥会过程中，中国曾向国际社会作出"带动3亿人参与冰雪运动"的承诺。最近的数据显示，中国已经实现了这个目标。国家统计局的数据显示，自2015年北京获得冬奥会主办权以来，截至今年1月份已有逾3.46亿人参与了冰雪运动。

（8）11月11日，天猫销售额达到创纪录的2 684亿元人民币，同比增长约25.7%。今年有超过5亿消费者在天猫购物，比上一年增加了约1亿。其中，95后消费者约占30%，而50岁以上的消费者增长率最高，同比增长42%。全球超过20万个品牌加入了天猫购物节，在销售额超过1亿元的299个品牌中，有几十个是新入驻的商家。

（9）2021年，北京市大气环境中的细颗粒物（PM2.5）年均浓度降至33微克/立方米，较2013年降幅达到63.1%，平均每年下降7.9%，远超发达国家城市同期下降幅度。全国城市优良天数比率为87.5%，同比上升0.5个百分点。

（10）密西西比河是北美大陆上最长的河流，也是世界上第四长的河流。它发源于明尼苏达州北部，向南流232英里，注入墨西哥湾。其流域面积322万平方公里，占美国面积的41%。1900年以前，这条河每年输送的沙子、石头、泥土等约合4亿吨。而过去20年中，这个数字仅为每年1.45亿吨。

5. 核心概念词拓展练习

要求：按照表10-2的示范展开头脑风暴，将下表的核心概念词翻译成英语，表述形式越丰富越好。

建议、劝告、决断、主张、意图、看法	e.g. advice, advocate, argue, assert, believe, contend, decide, hold, intend, maintain, prefer, propose, propound, put forward, recommend, request, state, suggest, urge, etc.
询问、请求	
重视、强调	
反对	
同意	

比率	
倍数	
约数	

篇章练习

Text 1: Population in America

Preview:

World War Two ended finally in the summer of 1945. Life in the United States began to return to normal. Soldiers began to come home and find peacetime jobs. Industry stopped producing war equipment and began to produce goods that made peacetime life pleasant. The American economy was stronger than ever. Some major changes began to take place in the American population. Many Americans were not satisfied with their old ways of life. They wanted something better. And many people were earning enough money to look for a better life. Millions of them moved out of cities and small towns to buy newly-built homes in the suburbs.

Our program today will look at the growth of suburbs and other changes in the American population in the years after World War Two.

Glossary:	
congressman: 国会议员。美国国会是美国最高立法机构,由参、众两院组成。两院议员由各州选民直接选举产生。参议员每州2名,共100名,任期6年,每两年改选1/3。众议员按各州的人口比例分配名额选出,共435名,任期两年,期满全部改选。两院议员均可连任,任期不限。	Baltimore: 巴尔的摩
	Cleveland: 克利夫兰
	life expectancy: 预期寿命

The United States has always counted its population every 10 years. The government needed to know how many people lived in each state so it would know how many congressmen each state should have.

The first count was made 200 years ago. At that time, the country had about 4 million persons. One hundred years later, the population had increased to about 63 million persons. By 1950, there were more than 150 million persons in the United States.

In the early years of America, the average mother had 8 to 10 children. Living conditions were hard. Many children died at an early age. Families needed a lot of help on the farm. So it was good to have many children. //

This changed immediately after World War Two. Suddenly, it seemed, every family started having babies. Parents were hopeful about the future. There were lots of jobs. And people everywhere felt the need for a family and security after the long, difficult years of the war. So the birth rate increased suddenly.

The number of children between the ages of 5 and 14 increased by more than 10 million between 1950 and 1960. //

Many of the new parents moved to homes in the new suburbs. The word "suburb" comes from the word "urban", or having to do with cities. A suburb was sub, or something less than, a city.

It usually was created on an empty piece of land just outside a city. A businessman would buy the land and build houses on it. Young families would buy the houses with money that they borrowed from local banks.

Life was different in the suburbs. There were all sorts of group activities. //

Parents did everything they could to make life good for their children. The number of boys playing on Little League Baseball teams increased from less than 1 million to almost 6 million between 1950 and 1960. During the same period, the number of Girl Scouts increased by two million. And twice as many bicycles were sold.

Parents also tried to improve their children's education. In 1960, parents bought almost three times more educational books for children than 10 years earlier.

Parents also bought millions of dollars' worth of pianos, violins, and other musical instruments for their children. Families in the suburbs wanted a new life, a good life, for their children. //

It was true that the average number of children per family was increasing. But the total population of the United States did not increase as much during this period as one might have expected.

The reason for this was that fewer immigrants were coming from foreign countries. In fact, the number of immigrants to the United States had been dropping for many years. In 1910, 11 immigrants were coming to America for every thousand Americans already living here. By 1950, just 1.5 immigrants were coming for every thousand Americans.

The kinds of immigrants were changing, too. In the past, most came from northern and western Europe. But now, growing numbers of people came to the United States from Latin America, Asia, and southern and eastern European countries. //

Many Americans moved to different parts of the country in the 1950s.

Most Americans continued to live in the eastern, central, and southern parts of the country. But growing numbers moved to the western states. The population of the western states increased by almost 40 percent during the 1950s.

America's biggest city in 1950 was New York, with almost 8 million persons. Second was Chicago, with more than 3.5 million. Then came Philadelphia, Los Angeles, Detroit, Baltimore, Cleveland, and Saint Louis. //

Another population change was in life expectancy. In the early 1900s, the average newborn American could only expect to live about forty-seven years. But by the 1950s, most American babies could expect to live well past their 60th birthday.

This increase in life expectancy was due to improvements in living conditions and medical care. And it would continue to increase steadily in the years that followed. //

Text 2: 留守儿童

Glossary:	
农村剩余劳动力: rural surplus laborer	落实随迁子女就地入学: enable the children of migrant workers to go to school in cities where their parents work
乡村振兴战略: the strategy of rural vitalization	

留守儿童指的是由于父母外出打工而被留在家乡或寄宿在亲戚家中,长期与父母分开生活的儿童。由于现代化的发展,大批农村剩余劳动力向城市转移,他们往往无法担负过高的城市生活成本而不能接孩子进城。留守儿童的现象一般只发生在中国,也是中国近年出现的一个严重社会现象。//

过去十几年的调查显示,留守儿童普遍学习动机不强,学习兴趣不高;孤独、焦虑、抑郁,甚至敌对情绪是他们常见的情绪状态,主观幸福感和生活满意度等积极情绪偏低;自尊较低,有严重的自卑感;攻击等违纪行为较多,社会适应不良问题较突出。//

留守儿童问题不仅关乎家庭,更关乎发展,关乎未来。近年来,在乡村振兴战略引领下,党和政府大力推动务工人员返乡创业就业、落实随迁子女就地入学等工作,为从源头减少留守现象提供了有力支持。2020年农村留守儿童规模为1 289.7万人,相较2019年减少94.7万人。//

与此同时,技术进步也为留守儿童的生活状况带来可喜变化。视频通话在一定程度上打破了时空分离,让亲情沟通更便捷高效;短视频平台记录和展现留守儿童生活日常,也为社会提供更广阔的关注视角。幼吾幼以及人之幼,是中华民族的传统美德。有了制度和技术的帮助,留守儿童将不会是"被遗忘的花朵",而将健康成长,迎接美好的明天。//

Text 3: Student loan forgiveness

Preview:

The U.S. Department of Education will forgive $10,000 in a person's outstanding federal student loans and up to $20,000 for those people who received needs-based Pell Grants. Both of these targeted actions are for families who need it the most — working and middle-class people making under $125,000 a year. Danielle Douglas-Gabriel, national higher-education reporter for *The Washington Post*, is talking about the targeting groups of student loan forgiveness; how exactly this is going to work; and what this means for the economy and people's lives.

Glossary:	
Pell Grants:佩尔助学金;联邦佩尔助学金计划	adjusted gross income:调整后总收入(AGI),是指一年中的收入,包括工资、红利、投资收入减去某些调整费用,如个人退休金、商业费用、交通费用、生活费用等。
loan forgiveness/relief:债务减免	

As for the ones who may benefit from the plan, it's pretty broad eligibility here. Here we're talking parents. We're talking graduate students, undergraduate students, anyone with those direct loans, anyone with parent loans, grad loans, all of that. So, roughly about 43 million of the 45 million people who have federal student loans will be eligible for this relief. //

The student loan relief starts off at $10,000. But if you ever received a Pell Grant, which is a form of federal financial aid for people whose families typically make under $60,000 a year, you're eligible for an additional $10,000. Now, of the pool of people who have federal loans, 60 percent of them had Pell Grants at some point in their college career. So, the vast majority of folks are getting this $20,000 worth of loan forgiveness, which was very unexpected. //

Of course, there is income eligibility requirements for the student-loan forgiveness. Key to this plan is that for individuals, you have to be making $125,000 or less, and this was in the 2021 or 2022 tax year. And this is your adjusted gross income. And for couples who are married, filing jointly, you'd have to be making $250,000 or less. //

The amounts that the White House is proposing or planning to do would really wipe out the debt completely for about 20 million borrowers and cut it in half for very many more. A lot of the distribution of the relief, I think, goes to people who typically earn $75,000 or less. I think they said about 90 percent of the relief is going to them. //

Text 4: 职业教育

Glossary:	
国民教育体系: national education system	人力资源开发: human resources development
产教融合、校企合作: the integration between industry and education and the cooperation between schools and enterprises	高素质技术技能人才: skilled/technical professionals/talents/workers
"职教高考"制度: vocational college entrance exam system	职业规划: career planning

职业教育是国民教育体系和人力资源开发的重要组成部分,是广大青年打开通往成功成才大门的重要途径。我国经济持续快速发展,职业教育功不可没,已为各行各业累计培养输送2亿多高素质劳动者。//

当前,我国有1.13万所职业院校、3 088万名在校生,在现代制造业和现代服务业等领域,一线新增从业人员70%以上来自职业院校。随着各地深化产教融合、校企合作,更多高素质技术技能人才、能工巧匠、大国工匠将从职业院校中走出来。//

然而,高技能人才依旧紧缺,许多企业反映面临的最大问题是招工难。这是因为一方面,优质职业教育资源供给不足;另一方面,传统观念认为职业教育没有前途。因此我们一方面要加快建立"职教高考"制度。另外,还要从根源上提高技能人才的工资待遇与社会地位。//

让一部分学生接受职业教育,不但为社会提供充足的劳动力,也充分考虑到学生的自身发展,有助于学生做好职业规划,促进未来就业。只有发展高质量的职业教育,让成为技能型人才也纳入年轻人的自主选择范围,才能有力缓解当前社会的教育焦虑。//

第十一章
公共演说

大多数的口译工作,特别是正式场合的会议口译,都要求译员具备良好的公共演说能力,能够在"大庭广众"之下克服紧张情绪和心理焦虑,充分运用自己的专业能力,做好语言服务。

第一节 口译与公共演说的共性与区别

《易传·系辞传上》有言"鼓天下之动者存乎辞",出色的演讲能力在很多情况下能够有效实现沟通、交际甚至宣传的目的,达到事半功倍的效果。口译和公众演说既有共性,又存在差异,主要表现在以下几个方面。

一、讲话内容方面

公众演说的内容由讲者自行拟定,口译则是对讲者所说内容的"转述"。口译中,译员受制于源语内容的约束,无法脱离原文自由发表自己的观点,但却可以在逻辑组织、层次结构和词语选择上发挥主动性,调动自己全部的语言和知识资源,对讲话者提供的信息进行二次加工,构建自己的篇章框架,更好地传达信息要点。这种"二度创作"的过程同演讲如出一辙,为译者表达自己、发挥其主体性保留空间。

二、服务对象方面

公众演说主要面向听众,讲话力求符合多数听众的语言和认知能力;而口译则需同时兼顾讲者和听众两个方面,力求在准确理解讲者发言的前提下,以听众能够理解的语言和逻辑传达发言内容。也正因如此,口译工作也常被称为"两面三方"的交流。

同演讲一样,口译工作开展前也需仔细分析讲话的服务对象,这包含两方面。首先是讲话人分析。实际工作中,讲话人通常是译员的"直接客户",其满意度直接决定了译员的服务质量和职业口碑。因此,译员在开展业务前,最好先同讲话人进行沟通,了解讲者的身份背景、交际目的、个人立场和讲话习惯,提前适应其口音特点。如讲者之前从未有过使用口译服务的经验,应提醒讲者适时停顿,为口译留出时间。对于讲话中可能出现的专业术语和修辞信息(如隐喻、幽默等),最好事先做好沟通,以期达到最佳预期效果。

其次是听众分析。口译服务的最终目的是让听众理解讲者所说的内容,所以事先了解听众信息也很重要。这些信息包括听众的身份、专业、文化和语言背景,他们的兴趣、立场和期待，尤其应注意了解特定群体的文化、宗教和政治禁忌，这样才能在口译中选择合适的语言，准确恰当地再现原文信息和意图。

三、表达方式方面

口译的译入语表达阶段和公众演说的有声表达阶段非常相似，译员的语音素质、语言组织、表情仪态和面对观众压力之下的心理素质都直接影响译入语产出的效果。例如，呆板平淡的机械传译会让听众感到厌倦，拿腔拿调的夸张表演则会喧宾夺主；语速过慢会让听众丧失兴趣，语速过快则会影响听众理解。专业的译员应是一名出色的讲者，与讲者共享舞台的同时，懂得充分运用声音、语调和肢体动作，引发听众共鸣，最终实现理想的交际目的。

由此可见，口译同公众演说一样，是一门全方位的艺术，不仅考验语言功底（包括措辞使用、语言组织、逻辑结构、内容连贯），还涉及诸多非语言因素（包括声音控制、语速调节、语音语调、肢体动作和眼神交流、心理素质等）。在实战口译中，这些非语言因素往往对译者的临场表现起到举足轻重的作用。本章中我们将着重为大家介绍口译工作对译员声音、仪态和心理素质方面的要求，帮助大家熟悉并运用公众演说技巧，以便在日后的实战口译中沉着应对、稳定发挥。

第二节 声音与仪态

在口译的有声表达阶段，声音和仪态是保证信息有效发布的核心环节。美国加州大学洛杉矶分校对影响听众印象的因素进行的调查显示，演讲者的声音（音质、声调、语气、音量、语速）占比高达38%，其他非语言交际因素（面部表情、手势动作等肢体仪态）占比5%（Mehrabian & Williams, 1969）。

一名专业的口译员需要懂得如何运用声音技巧充分调动听众的参与度和专注度，举止得体，落落大方，与听众保持一定的眼神交流。

一、声音

声音方面，译员在平常训练中应着重留意语音、语调、语速和音量四个方面。

1. 语音

对于语音大家时常会有一定的认识误区，认为只有标准的美式或英式发音才是"完美语音"。实际上英语作为一种全球化的通用语言，其基本功能是实现跨文化交际。而作为亚洲英语学习者的我们，口音中保留一定的"亚洲韵味"也未尝不可，也许更能够凸显出我们的身份特征。但需要注意的是，"亚洲韵味"不等同于"中式英语"（Chinglish），尤其要注意三点：第一，用语正确，遣词造句需符合使用规范。第二，发音清晰且正确，不要增加没有的音节，例如将"need"发成"neede"；或将咬舌音/θ/或/ð/发成/s/或/z/。第三，避免频繁使用"um""uh""well"等口头禅和填充词，这些短音经话筒放大会显得尤其刺耳，与其如此，不如适当停顿略作思考。

2. 语调

语调这里不仅指单词发音的语调,也是对整体节奏的把控和调节。不同的翻译场合、不同的交际功能往往需要译员根据讲者的现场情绪对翻译的语调进行调整。例如,在翻译领导贺词和一般会议时通常采取不同的语调,前者慷慨激昂,后者相对客观平缓。但无论在哪种场合,译员都需要拿捏尺度,一方面需避免"平淡无味",另一方面也需警惕"用力过猛",显得浮夸。

3. 语速

合适的语速不仅能够给听众带来愉悦的心理感受,也是展现译员自信沉着的重要指标。对于口译初学者而言,很容易因忽快忽慢的语速"露馅":当遇到自己熟悉的内容时,表达如行云流水,滔滔不绝;而遇到信息断片时,就会突然卡壳,多次重复已经说过的内容或插入大量口头禅,以期弥补冷场的尴尬。实际上,真正的"行家里手"更懂得克制的艺术,尽量保持语速在每分钟120—150单词左右,匀速适当的语流能给大脑留出更多思考的空间,避免出现"断片"的尴尬。

4. 音量

无论在何种场合进行口译服务,译员都应保持声音清晰,保证在场所有听众均能接收到信息。如果是线下口译,建议译员提前进行实地考察,或在活动前二十分钟到场,查看是否配备麦克风,调试话筒音量,保证坐在房间最后一排的听众也能够听清讲话。对于口译初学者而言,切忌因信心不足、情绪紧张等原因导致音量不足,或因对部分内容不熟悉而突然降低音量,以期"蒙混过关"。假如真的遇到信息疏漏,与其含糊其辞,不如联系上下文合理推测、平滑过渡,将注意力转移至主要信息点。

二、仪态

除声音外,译员的仪态举止能够辅助信息传递,也是反映职业素养的重要方面。译员应注意个人仪表、眼神交流和肢体动作三个方面。

1. 个人仪表

译员需根据不同服务场合选择合适着装,但干净整洁、大方得体是职业译员着装的基本要求。如果是商务交传或陪同口译,可选择商务休闲着装,而如果是正式会议口译,建议选择较为正式的西装套装。男士西装建议选择深色,搭配领带,可给人一种沉稳专业的感觉。女士可选择西装或商务裙装,但切忌裙子过短。另外需注意发型和首饰应简洁利落,切勿遮挡视线或因佩戴夸张首饰造成听众分心。

2. 眼神交流

包括同讲者和听众两方面的眼神交流。译员需将主要精力用于听力、记忆和笔记,眼神交流频次适当为宜。当讲者说话时间过长时，译员可通过眼神示意其停顿。口译过程中，译员也可不时将目光从笔记上转移到听众身上，表示尊重的同时，也可收集听众反馈，并基于此做出适当调整。

3. 肢体动作

肢体动作包括译员的站姿、坐姿及口译过程中的肢体语言。译员以站姿或坐姿进行口译时，应尽量保持身体竖直，展现良好的精神面貌。口译过程中根据情景需要，可适当增加手势，例如陪同口译中用手势指示景点或引路。但在正式的会议场合，过多运用手势反而会显得牵强刻意，通常以眼神交流代替手势即可。

第三节 心理素质

口译工作不仅是对译员职业素质的考验，更是高压情况下对心理素质的考验。很多人也正是因为无法承受临场口译中的巨大压力，而最终未能在口译这条路上长久地走下去。然而，无论将来从事哪种工作，学会与恐惧并存、化压力为动力，都是我们人生的"必修课"。

译员的主要心理问题就是"怯场"，指的是面对大庭广众，心跳加速、手心出汗、喉咙发紧、张口结舌、不知所措等现象（翁显雄，1998）。这是一种常见的心理应激反应，广泛出现在公共演说、舞台表演、会议发言等各种需要直面大量观众的场合。想要克服怯场情绪，首先我们需要了解其深层的成因，才能"见招拆招，逐一破解"。

常见的怯场原因可分为外部因素和内部因素。

外部因素是指客观环境对译员心理的影响，可能包括听众人数过多、听众面孔陌生、现场出现临时变故，或讲者临时调整讲稿等。一般而言，我们都愿意在"小范围"内讲话，而面对大量观众时则会出现天然的紧张情绪，这种情绪主要源于担心"丢人丢大了"的心理预设。众目睽睽之下，似乎任何细小的错误都会被放大。尤其是面对我们不熟悉的场地和陌生的面庞，难以判断听众"是敌是友"。这种心理暗示下难免出现心慌手抖、思维断片等问题。

内部因素是指译员因评价忧虑、消极暗示或译前准备不足而产生的紧张、焦虑情绪，这也是造成怯场的主要原因。口译活动的评价往往是单向的，也即由听众"裁判"译者的翻译水平，很难得到即时的积极反馈，容易加重译者的心理压力，使其不知不觉陷入消极的自我暗示：担心准备不充分而无法理解讲者发言，担心漏译或错译而当众出丑，或担心翻译得不够流利而显得专业能力不足等。这些负面的情绪会占据大量工作记忆，导致因"内耗"而无法集中精力。

了解了怯场的根本原因，我们究竟该如何应对呢？多数情况下，当我们面对演讲或口译带来的恐惧、焦虑和紧张情绪时，总是本能地希望"克制"或"消解"，这是一个很大的误区。实际上，与其否定它，我们更需要勇敢承认，学会与之"共存"。这里给大家提出几点建议，希望大家能够与紧张情绪"化敌为友"。

一、认识到紧张心态人皆有之

即便是久经沙场的口译行家,在每次口译任务中也难免紧张。但与新手不同的是,他们能够从容处理自己的紧张情绪,即使内心波涛翻涌,表面依然镇定自若。如果下次你感到紧张,请在内心对自己说:"我明白我正经历紧张和恐惧,那又怎样呢?我只需要继续往下做就好,完成比完美更重要。"

二、专注做好眼前的事,不要与别人比较

口译初学者通常会对经验丰富的职业译员产生崇拜,但也不要因短期内达不到同等水平而否定自己,产生自卑情绪。多数情况下的焦虑都源于害怕自己的翻译达不到观众预期,或受到同行负面评价。实际上,这些担忧很多是自己臆想出来的,即便真实存在,也无须过多关注。与其在乎别人的评价,不如专注于"做事",抱着学习和增长经验的心态对待每一次口译。

三、充分做好译前准备

被誉为"卓越演讲家"的美国前总统林肯曾说:"即使是有实力的人,若缺乏周全的准备,也无法做到系统、有条理地演说。"译员对主题了解得越充分,就越容易理解源语语篇的内涵,越能够轻松组织译语。因此准备工作务必到位,包括通过多方途径了解会议议程、讲话主题及内容、主题背景和相关术语等。充分的译前准备也能带来积极的心理暗示:"我就是此领域的专家,没有人会比我更加了解这一主题。"带着这种自信去翻译,能有效缓解怯场情绪。

四、巧用肢体暗示

除了我们上面介绍的心理暗示之外,肢体暗示也是行之有效的缓解紧张、建立自信的方法,可惜这一点经常被大家忽略。有研究表明,开放的身体姿态能够增加自信,例如张开双臂、伸展腰肢、挺直脊柱;反之,蜷缩的身体姿态则会加剧自卑和焦虑。在开始口译任务前,我们不妨昂头挺胸,伸展肩颈和手臂,呈现出最佳状态迎接任务。另外,我们还可以采用肌肉紧松法来释放压力。这种方法类似瑜伽动作,首先尽量握紧双手或紧绷双臂,之后慢慢放松,如此反复直至紧张的肌肉变得松弛。

五、听众并非"假想敌",他们也希望译员成功

之前我们曾讲过,造成怯场的原因之一就是我们总认为自己受到听众的"裁判"。实际上,多数听众很宽容,理解临场口译的难度,明白在高压情况下说错个别单词或漏掉某个句子都在情理之中。译员不妨把听众当作朋友,将口译当作一次"两面三方"的交谈。可以试着在人群中寻找一些热情、积极的面孔,增加同他们的目光交流。他们的微笑能够给予你正面反馈,鼓励你从容地完成口译任务。

克服怯场情绪最重要的是去除对完美自我的执念,简而言之就是不要怕丢脸。英国剧作家肖伯纳口才出众,但年轻的时候却十分腼腆。谈及自己的成功经验时他坦言:"没有人

比我更能明白恐惧、怯懦的滋味，连我自己都常常难堪得无地自容。我学演讲就像学滑冰，唯一的办法就是不断出丑，让自己显得像个傻瓜，直到习惯为止。"只有当我们真正破除了对自我形象的执念，才能把精力集中于口译的内容和表达上，达到"不管风吹浪打，胜似闲庭信步"的沉着心态（仲伟合，2006：206）。

参考文献

Mehrabian A, Williams M. Nonverbal Concomitants of Perceived and Intended Persuasiveness[J]. Journal of Personality and Social psychology, 1969, 13(1): 37-58.

翁显雄. 试论英语演说的技巧[J]. 中山大学学报, 1998, (2): 68-72.

仲伟合. 英语口译教程（上）[M]. 北京：高等教育出版社, 2006.

专项练习

1. 演讲及英汉口译练习

要求：两人为一个小组，分别扮演演讲者和译员，在全班面前进行公众演讲和交替口译。注意语言组织、声音控制及仪态表现。

英汉段落1: Message for the International Day for the Elimination of Sexual Violence in Conflict

(1) Sexual violence in conflict is a cruel tactic of war, torture, terror and repression. It reverberates down generations and threatens both human and international security.

(2) In places affected by conflict, the turmoil caused by the war has made it even more difficult to hold perpetrators of sexual violence to account. At the same time, survivors face new obstacles to reporting crimes and accessing support services.

(3) Even as we respond to the severe and complex situation, we must investigate every case, and maintain essential services for every survivor. We cannot allow this already underreported crime to slip further into the shadows.

(4) Perpetrators must be punished. Investment in recovery from the current situation must tackle the root causes of sexual and gender-based violence.

(5) On this International Day for the Elimination of Sexual Violence in Conflict, let's resolve to uphold the rights and meet the needs of all survivors, as we work to prevent and end these horrific crimes.

英汉段落 2: Message for World Day to Combat Desertification, Drought

(1) Humanity is waging a relentless, self-destructive war on nature. Biodiversity is declining, greenhouse gas concentrations are rising, and our pollution can be found from the remotest islands to the highest peaks.

(2) We must make peace with nature. The land can be our greatest ally. But the land is suffering.

(3) Land degradation from climate change and the expansion of agriculture, cities and infrastructure undermines the well-being of 3.2 billion people. It harms biodiversity and enables the emergence of infectious diseases.

(4) Restoring degraded land would remove carbon from the atmosphere. It would help vulnerable communities adapt to climate change. And it could generate an extra $1.4 trillion dollars in agricultural production each year.

(5) The best part is that land restoration is simple, inexpensive and accessible to all. It is one of the most democratic and pro-poor ways of accelerating progress towards the Sustainable Development Goals.

(6) This year marks the start of the UN Decade on Ecosystem Restoration. On this International Day, let us make healthy land central to all our planning.

2. 演讲及汉英口译练习

要求：两人为一个小组，分别扮演演讲者和译员，在全班面前进行公众演讲和交替口译。注意公众演讲中的语言组织、声音控制及仪态表现。

汉英段落 1: 习近平在北京冬奥会、冬残奥会总结表彰大会上的讲话（节选）

（1）同志们，朋友们：

历经7年艰辛努力，北京冬奥会、冬残奥会胜利举办，举国关注，举世瞩目。

（2）中国人民同各国人民一道，克服各种困难挑战，再一次共创了一场载入史册的奥运盛会，再一次共享奥林匹克的荣光。

（3）事实再次证明，中国人民有意愿、有决心为促进奥林匹克运动发展、促进世界人民团结友谊作出贡献，而且有能力、有热情继续作出新的更大的贡献！

（4）北京冬奥会、冬残奥会的成功举办，凝结着各条战线人们的辛勤付出和智慧汗水。……广大冬奥建设者、工作者、志愿者牢记党和人民的重托，满怀为国争光的壮志，在各自岗位上真诚奉献、默默耕耘，涌现出一大批作出突出贡献的先进集体和先进个人。

（5）今天，我们在这里隆重集会，总结北京冬奥会、冬残奥会的经验，表彰突出贡献的集体和个人,弘扬北京冬奥会、冬残奥会筹办举办过程中培育的崇高精神,激励全党全国各族人民为实现第二个百年奋斗目标、实现中华民族伟大复兴的中国梦而努力奋斗!

汉英段落2:世界海洋日致辞(节选)

Glossary:	
《第二次世界海洋评估》: The Second World Ocean Assessment	海沟: ocean trench
环礁: atolls	酸化: acidification

(1)在喜迎今年的世界海洋日之际,全世界也正在竭力应对气候危机,消除海洋和海洋资源遭受的持续人为侵害。

(2)最近发布的《第二次世界海洋评估》指出,在全球海洋为人类提供的诸多资源中,许多正因我们自己的所作所为而遭到损害。

(3)我们的海洋充斥着塑料垃圾,从最偏远的环礁到最深处的海沟,这些垃圾无处不在。

(4)过度捕捞每年造成近900亿美元的净效益损失,这使得妇女们更加脆弱,而她们对小规模捕鱼企业的生存至关重要。

(5)碳排放不断加剧海洋变暖和酸化,破坏生物多样性,导致海平面上升,对人口稠密的沿海地区构成威胁。

(6)今年庆祝活动的主题是"海洋:生活与生计",着重强调海洋对世界各地社区的文化生活和经济生存的重要性。超过30亿人靠海为生,其中绝大多数在发展中国家。

▣ 篇章练习

Text 1: What makes a good life? (excerpt)

Preview:
 What keeps us happy and healthy as we go through life? If you think it's fame and money, you're not alone — but, according to psychiatrist Robert Waldinger, you're mistaken. As the director of a 75-year-old study on adult development, Waldinger has unprecedented access to data on true happiness and satisfaction. In this talk, he shares three important lessons learned from the study as well as some practical, old-as-the-hills wisdom on how to build a fulfilling, long life.

Glossary:	
octogenarian: 八旬老人；80至89岁的人	cholesterol: 胆固醇
bicker: (为小事)斗嘴，发生口角	millennial: 千禧一代
feud: 长期不和，世仇	

The Harvard Study of Adult Development may be the longest study of adult life that's ever been done. For 75 years, we've tracked the lives of 724 men, year after year, asking about their work, their home lives, their health, and of course asking all along the way without knowing how their life stories were going to turn out.

So what have we learned? What are the lessons that come from the tens of thousands of pages of information that we've generated on these lives? Well, the lessons aren't about wealth or fame or working harder and harder. The clearest message that we get from this 75-year study is this: Good relationships keep us happier and healthier. Period. //

We've learned three big lessons about relationships. The first is that social connections are really good for us, and that loneliness kills. It turns out that people who are more socially connected to family, to friends, to community, are happier, they're physically healthier, and they live longer than people who are less well connected. And the experience of loneliness turns out to be toxic. People who are more isolated than they want to be from others find that they are less happy, their health declines earlier in midlife, their brain functioning declines sooner and they live shorter lives than people who are not lonely. And the sad fact is that at any given time, more than one in five Americans will report that they're lonely. //

And we know that you can be lonely in a crowd and you can be lonely in a marriage, so the second big lesson that we learned is that it's not just the number of friends you have, and it's not whether or not you're in a committed relationship, but it's the quality of your close relationships that matters. It turns out that living in the midst of conflict is really bad for our health. High-conflict marriages, for example, without much affection, turn out to be very bad for our health, perhaps worse than getting divorced. And living in the midst of good, warm relationships is protective. //

Once we had followed our men all the way into their 80s, we wanted to look back at them at midlife and to see if we could predict who was going to grow into a happy, healthy octogenarian and who wasn't. And when we gathered together everything we knew about them at age 50, it wasn't their middle age cholesterol levels that predicted how they were going to grow old. It was how satisfied they were in their relationships. The people who were the most satisfied in their relationships at age 50 were the healthiest at age 80. And good, close relationships seem to buffer us from some of the slings and arrows of getting old. Our most happily partnered men and women reported, in their 80s, that on the days when they had more physical pain, their mood stayed just as happy. But the people who were in unhappy relationships reported, on the days when they had more physical pain, it was magnified by more emotional pain. //

And the third big lesson that we learned about relationships and our health is that good relationships don't just protect our bodies, they protect our brains. It turns out that being in a securely attached relationship to another person in your 80s is protective, that the people who are in relationships where they really feel they can count on the other person in times of need, those people's memories stay sharper and longer. And the people in relationships where they feel they really can't count on the other one, those are the people who experience earlier memory decline. And those good relationships, they don't have to be smooth all the time. Some of our octogenarian couples could bicker with each other day in and day out, but as long as they felt that they could really count on the other when the going got tough, those arguments didn't take a toll on their memories. //

So this message, that good, close relationships are good for our health and well-being, this is wisdom that's as old as the hills. Why is this so hard to get and so easy to ignore? Well, we're human. What we'd really like is a quick fix, something we can get that'll make our lives good and keep them that way. Relationships are messy and they're complicated and the hard work of tending to family and friends, it's not sexy or glamorous. It's also lifelong. It never ends. The people in our 75-year study who were the happiest in retirement were the people who had actively worked to replace workmates with new playmates. Just like the millennials in that recent survey, many of our men when they were starting out as young adults really believed that fame and wealth and high achievement were what they needed to go after to have a good life. But over and over, over these 75 years, our study has shown that the people who fared the best were the people who leaned in to relationships, with family, with friends, with community. //

So what about you? Let's say you're 25, or you're 40, or you're 60. What might leaning in to relationships even look like?

Well, the possibilities are practically endless. It might be something as simple as replacing screen time with people time or livening up a stale relationship by doing something new together, long walks or date nights, or reaching out to that family member who you haven't spoken to in years, because those all-too-common family feuds take a terrible toll on the people who hold the grudges.

I'd like to close with a quote from Mark Twain. More than a century ago, he was looking back on his life, and he wrote this: "There isn't time, so brief is life, for bickerings, apologies, heartburnings, callings to account. There is only time for loving, and but an instant, so to speak, for that."

The good life is built with good relationships.

Thank you. //

Text 2: 联合国人权理事会第49届会议高级别会议讲话（节选）

Preview:
　　2022年2月28日，国务委员兼外长王毅在北京以视频方式出席联合国人权理事会第49届会议高级别会议，并发表题为《坚持公平正义推动全球人权事业健康发展》的讲话。王毅表示，人人充分享有人权，是人类社会的不懈追求。促进和保护人权是各国的共同事业。鉴于此，中方提出四点主张：一是做保护人权的真正践行者；二是做人民利益的忠实守护者；三是做共同发展的积极贡献者；四是做公平正义的坚定维护者。本文节选自王毅讲话。

Glossary:	
联合国人权理事会: United Nations Human Rights Council	《世界人权宣言》: the Universal Declaration of Human Rights
全球发展倡议: Global Development Initiative (GDI)	政治对抗: political confrontation
不懈追求: unremitting pursuit	

主席先生，各位同事：

　　很高兴代表中国政府向联合国人权理事会第49届会议致辞。

　　人人充分享有人权，是人类社会的不懈追求。当前，世界发展日新月异，人权意识深入人心，我们前所未有地具备了促进和保护人权的能力与条件。同时，由于日益加剧的贫困和不平等问题，全球人权事业发展又面临严峻挑战。//

　　促进和保护人权是各国的共同事业。鉴此，中方主张：

　　第一，做保护人权的真正践行者。《联合国宪章》《世界人权宣言》树立了全球人权事业的崇高目标，如何有效实现这一目标，需要各国不断探索前行。人权是历史的、具体的、现实的，人权事业发展必须立足本国国情和人民需求，协调增进全体人民的经济、政治、社会、文

化、环境权利,促进和实现人的全面发展。//

第二,做人民利益的忠实守护者。人民过上幸福生活是最大的人权。一国人权状况好不好,根本上要看人民对美好生活的向往是否得到满足,人民的所需所急所盼是否得到解决,人民的获得感、幸福感、安全感是否得到增强。要坚持以人民为中心,推动国家治理和发展成果更多更公平惠及全体人民,不让任何人掉队。//

第三,做共同发展的积极贡献者。没有发展,一切人权都无从谈起,也难以持续。习近平主席提出全球发展倡议,致力于同联合国及各国一起,加快落实2030年可持续发展议程,这是中国为促进国际人权事业贡献的又一公共产品,已获得联合国和近百个国家的响应支持。//

第四,做公平正义的坚定维护者。评价一个国家是否有人权,不能以别的国家标准来衡量,更不能搞双重标准,甚至把人权当作干涉别国事务的政治工具。要坚定不移推动国际关系民主化和法治化,践行真正的多边主义,推动全球人权治理朝着更加公平合理包容的方向发展。人权理事会应当秉持非选择性和非政治化原则,不能沦为大搞政治对抗的舞台。

……

预祝本届人权理事会取得积极成果!

谢谢大家。//

Text 3: To eliminate waste, we need to rediscover thrift (excerpt)

Preview:

There's no such thing as throwing something away, says Andrew Dent — when you toss a used food container, broken toy or old pair of socks into the trash, those things inevitably end up in ever-growing landfills. But we can get smarter about the way we make, and remake, our products. Andrew Dent shares exciting examples of thrift — the idea of using and reusing what you need so you don't have to purchase anything new — as well as advances in material science, like electronics made of nanocellulose and enzymes that can help make plastic infinitely recyclable.

Glossary:	
thrift: 节约,节俭	disassemble: 拆卸,拆开
geotagging: 地理定位,地理标记	

Let's talk about thrift. Thrift is a concept where you reduce, reuse and recycle, but yet with an economic aspect. I think it has a real potential for change. My grandmother, she knew about thrift. This is her string jar. She never bought any string. Basically, she would collect string. It would come from the butcher's; it would come from presents. She would put it in the jar and then use it when it was needed. When it was finished, whether it was tying up the roses or a part of my bike, once finished with that, it'd go back into the jar. This is a perfect idea of thrift; you use what you need, you don't actually purchase anything, so you save money. Kids also inherently know this idea. When you want to throw out a cardboard box, the average kid will say, "Don't! I want to use it for a robot head or for a canoe to paddle down a river." They understand the value of the second life of products. //

So, I think thrift is a perfect counterpoint to the current age which we live in. All of our current products are replaceable. When we get that bright, new, shiny toy, it's because, basically, we got rid of the old one. The idea of that is, of course, it's great in the moment, but the challenge is, as we keep doing this, we're going to cause a problem. That problem is that there is really no way: when you throw something away, it typically goes into a landfill.

Now, a landfill is basically something which is not going to go away, and it's increasing. Currently, at the moment, we have about 1.3 billion tons of material every year going into landfills. By 2100, it's going to be about four billion tons. See, instead, I'd prefer if we started thrifting. //

What that means is, we consider materials when they go into products and also when they get used, and, at the end of their life: When can they be used again? It's the idea of completely changing the way we think about waste, so waste is no longer a dirty word — we almost remove the word "waste" completely. All we're looking to is resources. Resource goes into a product and then can basically go into another product.

The industry that's not doing so well is the architecture industry. One of the challenges with architecture has always been when we build up, we don't think about taking down. We don't dismantle, we don't disassemble, we demolish. That's a challenge, because it ends up that about a third of all landfill waste in the US is architecture. We need to think differently about this. There are programs that can actually reduce some of this material. //

A good example is this. These are actually bricks that are made from old demolition waste, which includes the glass, the rubble, the concrete. You put up a grinder, put it all together, heat it up and make these bricks we can basically build more buildings from. But it's only a fraction of what we need.

My hope is that with big data and geotagging, we can actually change that, and be more thrifty when it comes to buildings. If there's a building down the block which is being demolished, are there materials there that the new building being built here can use? Can we use that, the ability to understand that all the materials available in that building are still usable? Can we then basically put them into a new building, without actually losing any value in the process? //

So now let's think about other industries. What are other industries doing to create thrift? Well, it turns out that there are plenty of industries that are also thinking about their own waste and what we can do with it. A simple example is the waste that they basically belch out as part of industrial processes.

Most metal smelters give off an awful lot of carbon dioxide. Turns out, there's a company called Land Detector that's actually working in China and also soon in South Africa, that's able to take that waste gas — about 700,000 tons per smelter — and then turn it into about 400,000 tons of ethanol, which is equivalent to basically powering 250,000, or quarter of a million, cars for a year. That's a very effective use of waste. //

Text 4: 联合国粮农组织总干事致世界环境日的公开信(节选)

Preview:

  6月5日是一年一度的世界环境日。2022年的主题是"只有一个地球",呼吁"践行可持续生活,与自然和谐共生",通过发出"和谐共生"的号召,警醒世人,地球属于全人类,不分男女老幼,也没有城乡之别。唯有承认每个人的作用,尊重每个人的权利,做到兼容并蓄,实现人人切实参与和投入,才能实现"和谐"的发展目标。本文节选自联合国粮农组织总干事屈冬玉博士在世界环境日发表的公开信。

Glossary:	
生态系统退化: ecosystem degradation	营养不良: malnutrition
水资源短缺: water scarcity	一线: frontline
主人翁: stakeholder	联合国粮食及农业组织: Food and Agriculture Organization (FAO)
催生变革的生力军: catalyst for change	农业粮食体系: agri-food system

  全球人口中很大一部分是青年,其中不乏专业人才。面对地球遭遇的重重危机,如气候变化、生态系统退化、生物多样性丧失、饥饿和营养不良、水资源短缺、能源获取和普及健康

等问题,青年长期深受影响。再不投袂而起,青年的未来只会一片渺茫。//

青年一向积极呼吁采取行动,今后必须继续为自己的未来大声疾呼。青年有担当、有激情,深入基层一线拼搏奋战,拼尽全力发挥创意,为地球可持续发展贡献力量。青年积极倡导完善政策,努力唤起人们对重大环境问题的意识,并踊跃动员公众采取行动,克服当前一些最紧迫的环境挑战。青年积极推进保护和恢复工作,而且往往在幕后作出了巨大贡献。全世界都要倾听青年的心声,听取青年对如何构建和支撑可持续发展未来的看法,并与青年携手共进,赋予青年地球主人翁、守护者和未来领军者的重任。//

前不久,韩国政府和联合国粮食及农业组织在首尔主办了第十五届世界林业大会,认真倾听了青年的声音。在全球林业系统商讨如何共建绿色、健康且有韧性的林业未来之际,600余名青年代表积极参与相关磋商,以其独有的朝气、拼劲和远见,推动大会达成一项建设性成果,最终发布题为"你我同行——青年行动呼吁"的青年宣言。// 这项呼吁敦促有关各方深化合作、鼎力支持,围绕教育和能力建设机遇、体面工作和就业、性别平等主流化、融资以及各级政策和战略决策参与问题,完善标准并拓宽获取渠道。这都是提升和加强林业部门青年及青年专业人才贡献、合作和参与的重要着力点,有助于实现国际商定的全球目标,推动落实2030年可持续发展议程。//

青年是催生变革的生力军,激发奋进潜力,推动农业粮食体系朝着更高效、更包容、更有韧性且更透明的方向转型。放眼世界,青年始终引领变革,积极推动实现更好生产、更好营养、更好环境和更好生活,不让任何人掉队。我们必须确保青年发挥主动性,掌握自己的未来。//

第十二章
跨文化意识

口译作为一种跨语言的交际活动，具有很强的多元文化属性。一名合格的口译员不仅应熟知语言之间的差异，更应扮演跨文化沟通的角色，甚至在文化冲突时肩负调解的使命。英汉双向口译中造成文化障碍的主要问题包括口音与听辨，习语、俚语、谚语，以及文化习俗与禁忌三个方面。下面我们就主要从这几个方面逐一破解，为大家提供相应的解决思路。

第一节 口音与听辨

在之前的章节中我们已经讲过，源语听辨是口译中的基础环节，而口音则是源语输入的变量之一。来自不同文化背景的讲话者口音存在巨大差异。许多同学在进行训练时，常以英美国家标准口音为蓝本，忽略口音在实战中的影响。实际上，标准口音只是口译的"理想状态"，而五花八门的口音才是口译工作的"常态"。根据国际会议口译员协会（AIIC, 2002）的调查，86%的会议口译员认为复杂的口音会阻碍他们的听辨理解，62%的译员认为口音是口译压力的主要来源之一。

对口音的听辨主要可分为英语母语国家和非英语母语国家两类。在口译训练中，需尤其注意不同文化中英语发音的差异，熟悉其各自的特点，以提高适应能力和理解准确率。

即便在英语母语国家，不同地区的人们说话方式也各有特色。下面我们将以英国、美国、加拿大和澳大利亚为例，分别剖析其发音特色。

以英国为例，本土就存在五大口音，包括英国标准口音（Received Pronunciation）、考克尼口音（Cockney Accent）、苏格兰口音（Scottish Accent）、爱尔兰口音（Irish Accent）和威尔士口音（Welsh Accent）。口音之间的差异主要表现在对个别字母的发音上，如t、r、h等。英国标准口音即我们常说的"女王音"，通常被视作中上层阶级的身份象征，也是BBC新闻的官方播报口音，相当于中文的标准普通话。其发音特点主要体现在r的发音上，例如，mother这个字的发音听起来会像是muh-thuh。除此之外，有些单词如chance、bath和dance的a的发音较长，给人一种正式庄严的感觉。

考克尼口音也即我们常说的"伦敦腔"。"Cockney"一词意为"伦敦东区的人或口音"，因此这一口音常与英国伦敦的工人阶层或中产阶级相联系。其发音特点是字母t的发音强度较小，单独夹在两个元音之间时则会以清齿龈塞音发出，有时甚至被完全省略，在语音学上称为喉停。例如，later读起来更像lah-uh。一些单词开头的字母也会被省略发音，比如headache开头的h，这样听起来会更像edache。此外，复合元音（diphthong）变异也比较明显，例如：

/eɪ/ 发为 [æɪ]: bait　[beɪt]→[bæɪt]

/əʊ/ 发为 [æʉ]: coat　[kəʊt]→[kʰæɪt]

/aɪ/ 发为 [ɑɪ]: bite　[baɪt]→[bɑɪt]

/aʊ/ 可发为 [æə]: town　[taʊn]→[tʰæən]

相比于英国口音，美国口音最大的区别在于卷舌，例如fire在英音中为['faɪə]，而在美音中则为['faɪər]。标准美国腔英语（General American）使用者通常是受过高等教育的美国人，或是来自美国中部和西部地区的美国人。此外，纽约口音和南方口音也略有不同。纽约口音倾向于拉长元音，尤其是对a和o的发音，例如将coffee发为caw-fee，talk发为tawk。南方口音则因语速较慢，显露出一种悠闲随意的姿态，又称为"南方慢腔"，词语之间连读明显，例如gonna（going to）和lemme（let me）。

其他英语母语国家在英国英语和美国英语的基础上，结合本民族特点，发展出不同的发音规律。加拿大式英语最大的特点在于倾向将[aʊ]发为[əʊ]，例如将out、about、house读作oat、a boat、hose。澳大利亚英语在词汇、口音、发音、语域、语法和拼写等各方面与其他种类的英语也不同。澳洲英语的最大特色是使用很多当地的口语化表达，例如用arvo替代afternoon、用brekkie替代breakfast等。澳洲英语词汇多样，很多是外来语，这同其独特的文化历史关系密切。18世纪50年代，第一次澳大利亚淘金热引起了移民潮，爱尔兰移民为澳洲注入了新的表达，例如人们常说的"tuck for the native food, tuck in"，其实就是"吃吧"。一些澳大利亚土著语言和托雷斯海峡岛屿语言也被澳大利亚英语吸收，包括一些地名，如Canberra（堪培拉）在当地语言中意为"开会的地方"；此外还有动植物名，如dingo（澳洲野狗）、kangaroo（袋鼠）等。

在全球化背景下，"世界英语"（World Englishes）的概念逐渐兴起。它指的是英语的本地化变体，相关研究聚焦于全球不同社会语言环境中使用的各种英语，分析社会语言历史、多元文化背景及环境对不同地区英语使用的影响。由此可见，标准的英音或美音早已不是统一的衡量标准，口音已经成为各民族讲话者文化身份的标记。这一现象在日本、韩国、印度等非英语母语国家尤为明显。日语的特征是音节短小，没有类似于sp、sk等的复辅音，单词容量很小（只有五个元音），发音少。因此，日本人会把母语的特点加入英语中，对复合元音的发音有时把握不准。韩语中单词连读情况较多，倾向于拖长最后一个音节，这种情况也迁移到韩国人的英文发音中。此外，很多韩国讲者无法分辨l和r，也无法发出th的音。印度人说英语口音重、语速快，经常将标准英语中本应该咬舌送气的音th简化为t，在t的发音上又接近d。因此印度人经常拿自己这个发音特点开玩笑，例如将"我30岁了（I am thirty）"说成

"我有点脏（I am dirty）"。此外，印度英语中还经常将p和b、k和g、r和l读音混淆，在口译中应该尤加注意。

同日韩和印度的英语学习者一样，中国人说英语也有独特的发音和语调特点，但这并不妨碍我们与世界交流。反之，当我们使用带有"中国味道"的英文发音进行讲述时，也能显示出本民族的身份特色，促进中国异质文化符号在世界文化中的传播，讲好中国故事。因此无论是在语言学习还是与人交流的过程中，我们都不应带着有色眼镜进行沟通，更不该因某种口音不符合标准英国或美国口音而产生"口音歧视"，不妨主动了解口音背后的文化渊源，怀着一颗包容之心增进彼此的了解。

在口译训练中，教师可按照从轻到重、循序渐进的原则开展口音适应性训练，选择不同口音的听力材料作为教学资源。在日常训练中不宜选取口音过重的语料，而应尽量选取中度口音语料，培养学生对口音的熟悉度和翻译信心，逐步提升源语感知和理解水平。

第二节　习语、俚语、谚语的处理

习语、俚语、谚语通常具有很深的文化根基，在日常交流时能够有效增加讲话的丰富性和生动性，因此频繁出现在交际场合。然而在要求快速反应的即时任务中，这几类词语常令译员头疼。一方面，译员需要对源语文化有足够深入的了解，才能够准确把握此类词语的引申义；另一方面，很多习语、俚语和谚语在译入语中并无直接对应项或可套用的现成范式，对译员临场应变能力是一大挑战，处理不好容易闹出笑话。

对于习语、俚语、谚语这三类表达，很多同学都会产生混淆。要想准确翻译，首先应精确把握其各自的形式和特点。下面请同学们对比这三类语汇的定义：

（1）习语(idiom)：An expression that cannot be understood from the meanings of its separate words but that has a separate meaning of its own.

（2）俚语(slang)：An informal nonstandard vocabulary composed typically of coinages, arbitrarily changed words, and extravagant, forced, or facetious figures of speech.

（3）谚语(proverb)：A brief popular epigram or maxim.

从定义中可以看出，习语的特点在于其"隐喻"性，其含义不止于表面意思，通常以事喻理，通过具体事件来阐释深刻道理。隐喻构成的深层逻辑通常扎根于源语文化典故之中。例如，在下面两个句子中出现的Troy、Trojan词项就来源于希腊神话。

例12-1

原文：

It is unfair that the historians always attribute the fall of kingdoms to Helen of Troy.

参考译文：

历史学家总是把王国的灭亡归咎于红颜祸水，这是不公平的。

例 12-2

原文：

They claim he is a Trojan horse being used by the party bosses attempting to steal the nomination.

参考译文：

他们声称他是一名内奸，被党魁利用以窃获选举提名。

如果同学们熟悉特洛伊战争的话，那么在口译时就能够理解这两句话的"弦外之音"。"Helen of Troy"是希腊神话中宙斯与勒达之女海伦，其美貌冠绝希腊，被称为"世上最美的女人"。她和特洛伊王子帕里斯私奔，引发了特洛伊战争。例12-1中的"Helen of Troy"如果直译为"特洛伊的海伦"，对于不熟悉希腊神话的听者来说不易理解，而且这一表述在句子中并非特指，而是一种泛称。译者不妨结合上下文语境解释为"红颜祸水"，以实现原文信息的有效传达。例12-2中的"Trojan horse"来源于"木马屠城"中希腊士兵的攻城计谋，在这个语境中有"内奸"之含义。鉴于"特洛伊木马"在译入语文化中比较普及，这里可以意译处理为"内奸"，也可直译为"特洛伊木马"。诚然，意译导致了源语中一些文化隐喻和文学色彩的流失，但在大部分联络口译的场合中，无法"形神兼顾"时，译者会优先实现口译的交际功能，适当"舍形取意"。

相比于习语，俚语在大众的日常交流中经常出现，较为通俗易懂。俚语通常来源于当地民间习俗或认知习惯，其最显著的特点是非正式性和口语性。下面请看几组口译中易混淆的俚语（见表12-1）：

表12-1　易混淆的英语俚语及其翻译

俚　　语	错　误　翻　译	正　确　翻　译
baby kisser	亲小孩的人；妈妈	为竞选而到处笼络人心的政客
dead president	死去的总统	美钞
backseat driver	后座司机	因瞎指挥而坏事的人
road apple	撒在路上的苹果	马粪
Dutch courage	荷兰勇气	酒后之勇
Dutch treat	荷兰招待	各自付钱的聚餐

从上述示例可以看出，俚语虽然不像习语有那么强的隐喻性，但如果一知半解很容易闹出笑话。因此我们在日常训练时可以加强积累，而临场时如果对讲者所说的某一表述存

在疑问,一定要及时求证,避免因想当然闹出将"dead president"译为"死去的总统"这样的笑话。

谚语是人们在劳动、生活和社会活动的体验与观察中所总结出来的名言警句。它在形式上与习语和俚语存在较大差异,其结构是固定的,一般以句子形式出现,表述一个完整的思想和观点,常使用修辞,例如比喻、拟人、对偶、押韵等。

处理谚语时,对于那些在译入语中有对应翻译的表述,应优先采取套译法(见表12-2)。

表12-2 套译法翻译英语谚语

谚 语	参 考 译 文
Justice has long arms.	天网恢恢,疏而不漏。
A book is the same today as it always was and never changes.	好书千载常如新。
Joy puts heart into a man.	人逢喜事精神爽。
Man proposes, God disposes.	谋事在人,成事在天。

对于在译入语中无对应翻译的谚语,可根据句意采取直译或意译。但处理时应尽量保持原文的隐喻、拟人等修辞风格,或在翻译时增加引述语,例如"常言道""俗话说""英语/中文里有句谚语"等,让听众能够感知到原文的谚语形式(见表12-3)。

表12-3 直译法或意译法翻译英语谚语

谚 语	参 考 译 文
Every day of thy life is a leaf in thy history.	每天的生活都是构成历史的一页。
Moderation in all things.	凡事要适可而止。
Wisdom is to the mind what health is to the body.	知识之于思想,犹如健康之于身体。
A child's back must be bent while it is young.	修树须趁早,育人要趁小。

习语、俚语和谚语的翻译是对译员的一大挑战,但如果广泛阅读、勤加积累,就能够在其中收获语言和文化探幽的乐趣。译员在平常训练时不仅应了解英语国家文化,也要熟知本民族文化,知己知彼才能在讲者引经据典时从容应对。

第三节 文化专有项

在英汉口译实践中,最让译员"头疼"的一类词汇就是文化专有项,又称文化负载词。这类词汇扎根于语言背后最深层的文化认知,同生态文化、社会文化、宗教文化等各个方面息息相关，带有鲜明的民族特色。文化专有项常常导致译员临场陷入"文化不可译"的难题。那么这些文化元素到底是否可译？如何处理才能准确恰当地实现双方交际的目的？下面我们就来一起探索这其中的诀窍！

要想破解文化专有项翻译，首先我们需要对口译中常见的文化词汇进行分类，对症下药。根据源语和译入语文化的差异程度，文化相关表述可大致归纳为三类：文化相似项、文化差异项和文化缺失项。

文化相似项是指那些在源语和译入语文化中具有相似内涵的文化符号，也即认知语境差异相对较小的词汇，对于这类词汇应优先寻找译入语中的对应翻译。例如，汉语中的"裸婚"一词，是指在结婚时因财力不足导致无房无车，不举办婚礼或蜜月的情况。英美国家文化中也同样存在所谓"裸婚"，是指双方不举办盛大仪式的结婚形式，对应英文是"no frills wedding"，夫妻双方只需要进行法定注册（即"No Frills" Statutory Registration）即可结为夫妻。因此中文的"裸婚"译入英文时可采取同化翻译方法，译为"no frills wedding"，不可按照字面意思译为"naked wedding"。而对于那些在译入语中有相似认知语境，但无明确对应词条的文化专有项，则可采取"意象保留+阐释"的方式进行处理。

例 12-3

原文：

去年面对罕见的巨大冲击，我们及时果断采取措施，但也保持定力，没有搞"大水漫灌"。

参考译文：

In the face of unprecedented severe shocks last year, we acted in a prompt, decisive and focused manner. We did not flood China's economy with massive liquidity.

"大水漫灌"原意是指农业生产中的灌溉方式，这里用"没有搞'大水漫灌'"来喻指政府关注制约经济发展的重要领域和关键环节，执行针对性经济政策，而非如大水漫灌一样不抓重点。这里如果直译为"did not use flooding irrigation"会很突兀，似乎话题由经济领域突然转至农业生产领域，让人不知所云。因此建议通过追加文内阐释，显化"大水漫灌"和经济发展之间的关系，处理为"did not flood China's economy with massive liquidity"，这样既能保留原文的生动性和画面感，又能调动中西文化中关于"liquidity"的相似认知，准确传达隐喻内涵。

文化差异项通常是指那些在源语和译入语中均存在的文化意象，但内涵却大相径庭。相比于文化共有项，文化差异项更容易引发语义混淆，是尤其值得警惕的一类表述。

例 12-4

原文：

America is littered with white elephants such as airports which cost hundreds of millions of dollars but serve only a handful of passengers.

参考译文：

美国有很多造价昂贵的设施成了摆设，比如斥巨资盖了机场但乘客寥寥无几。

此句中的"white elephants"是指造价昂贵但用处不大的东西。相传一位古代的泰国国王遇到不喜欢的人，就会送给他一头白象。白象很珍贵，又象征着皇室，但是饲养起来非常耗财力，相当于是对领赏之人的惩罚。如果译员不理解其文化内涵，很容易将"white elephants"直译为"白色的大象"，令听众不知所云。处理此类中英差异较大的文化专有项时，如果时间有限，意译是最简单的处理方法（如例12-4的参考译文）。此外，也可采用"直译+阐释"的方法进行说明，这种方法尤其适合纠正现场过失。在上述例子中，译员如意识到将"white elephants"直译为"白色的大象"不妥，可继续补充说明"白色的大象，也就是说，一些造价昂贵但沦为摆设的设施"。这样一来不仅避免了临时改口造成的尴尬，也能准确传达引申含义。

文化缺失项是指那些仅存在于源语文化中，在译入语中无对应文化符号的专有项。这类词汇作为文化特色词汇，在口译中通常采用"音译/直译+阐释"的方式进行处理。例如在翻译"孟婆汤"时，可以先译为"drink of forgetfulness by Meng Po"来提示这一表达的核心信息（即"forgetfulness"），再进一步用追加句子的方式解释"孟婆"的文化含义——"a Chinese mythological figure whose task is to ensure souls ready to be reincarnated do not remember their previous life"。这种追加文化阐释的方式能够最大限度地还原源语文化内涵，达到文化传播的目的，在旅游翻译中较为常见。然而，时间紧张时，译员也需具备提炼核心文化意象的能力，简洁重现原文内涵。

例12-5

原文：

有人说官员要"爱惜羽毛"，也就是所谓"声誉"。

参考译文：

Some say that officials need to "cherish their reputation".

"爱惜羽毛"是一个具有中国特色的历史成语，典出西汉·刘向《说苑·杂言》"夫君子爱口，孔雀爱羽，虎豹爱爪，此皆所以治身法也"，用来比喻珍重爱惜自己的声誉。而英语文化中，"feather"使人联想到拥有洁白羽翼的天使，因此常用来传达神的佑护。由此可见，汉英文化在对"羽毛"的象征内涵上差别迥异，如果将原文直译为"cherish one's feather"可能令目标读者感到迷惑甚至产生误解，因此这里建议采取省译，只翻译核心意涵，译为"cherish one's reputation"。

第四节 习俗与禁忌

作为跨文化交流的使者，译员经常同来自世界各地、不同肤色和文化的人们打交道。因此，熟悉对方的文化习俗，尤其是文化偏好和禁忌对于圆满完成口译任务非常重要。对于同一事物，不同文化背景的人们可能会产生截然不同的评价和认知。例如在亚洲，打断对方谈话会被认为是不礼貌的行为，因此讲者通常会主动停顿，译员也会等到讲者完全结束讲话后再进行翻译。而在西班牙，听众可能随时插话，这会被认为是积极参与的表现，而讲者主动停顿的意识则不强。如果讲者一直滔滔不绝，译员应果断暗示或打断，为自己争取翻译时间。根据泰勒和威廉姆斯编纂的《世界各地的礼仪与禁忌：社会科学的地理百科全书》（Taylor & Williams, 2017），我们总结了各国文化中的禁忌项，供同学们参考：

（1）美国：在美国切记不可把黑人称作"Negro"，"Negro"主要是指从非洲贩卖到美国为奴的黑人，有贬义色彩，可使用"black"一词，以避免种族歧视之嫌。社交礼仪方面，美国人忌讳询问个人收入和财产情况，忌讳问年龄、婚姻状况以及服饰价格等私事。

（2）英国：英国人在情感表达上较为含蓄，尤其是公共场合不会轻易表态。家庭成员之间也经常使用"请""对不起""谢谢"等礼貌用语。在对英国人的称呼上应尤其注意，不可按照汉语习惯称其为"English"，因为"English"是对英格兰人的称呼，不适宜用于称呼苏格兰人、威尔士人或北爱尔兰人，使用"British"更为恰当。

（3）加拿大：受欧洲移民的影响，加拿大人的礼貌、礼节和英法两国相似。握手被认为是一种友好的表示，握手的同时也可进行简单自我介绍以示尊重。加拿大人不习惯在公共场合谈论关于政治、性、宗教及私生活话题，除非出于工作要求。由于加拿大重视文化包容性和多元发展，相比于其他国家，更忌讳公开讨论种族，尤其是少数族裔话题。

（4）澳大利亚：澳大利亚人时间观念强，因此如果客户是澳大利亚人，译员应尤其注意准时赴约。澳大利亚文化注重谦逊平等，不宜过分强调或夸大头衔和身份，交谈中避免自夸或抱怨，否则容易被认为是装腔作势和不礼貌。在澳大利亚推荐使用标准英语，无需为体现融入而刻意使用当地俚语。当使用V字手势时，应避免掌心向内，其含义相当于"竖起中指"，是十分不礼貌的动作。

（5）法国：法国是世界上最早公开行贴面亲吻礼的国家，但通常在家人或朋友之间使用，初次见面以握手行礼也符合规范。亚洲的译员如果不习惯亲吻礼，无需贴面，保持一定距离在脸颊两侧示意即可。公共场所落座时应避免双腿分开，可交叉或并拢膝盖坐好。应避免在公共场所打哈欠、抓挠身体或打喷嚏，如有需要尽量在房间外无人处进行。如被邀请去法国人家中做客，可送鲜花作为礼物，但避免赠送菊花，它被视为葬礼用花。在没得到主人邀请时不要擅自参观房屋或进入厨房等私人空间，饭桌上避免将肘部放在台面上。晚餐是法国人享受美食、社交和放松的时间，避免讨论工作问题。

（6）德国：德国人注重秩序、隐私和守时。初次见面进行自我介绍时使用姓名即可，无需突出头衔，同时应注意不要将手插在口袋中，否则会被视为有失尊重。不要直呼德国人的名字，应使用其头衔和姓氏以示尊重。在德国，康乃馨、黄菊花通常用于悼亡或葬礼，避免用于礼物赠送。服饰和其他商品包装上尤其忌用纳粹或相似标志。

（7）俄罗斯：俄罗斯人初次见面通常行握手礼，且一般由年龄较长者或资历较高者先伸手。不要在门口或门槛上握手，因为当地民间文化认为这样做将招致厄运。在正式活动中，客人应等到主人开始用餐后才开始用餐，等到贵宾离开后才可离席。俄罗斯酒桌文化丰富，宾客每人至少敬一杯酒，第一杯通常由主人来敬。俄罗斯人对自己的文化感到非常自豪，宴间可适当与客户谈论其音乐、艺术、文学和舞蹈，将有助于拉近彼此关系。

除上述国别文化的禁忌项外，译员还须注意讲话场合对音量的要求。例如在日本和一些非洲国家，吃饭时忌高谈阔论。如果此时需要进行口译任务，可尽量压低音量，保证能听清即可。同时，译员也要避免在一些被认为是神圣或肃静的地方高声讲话，例如欧洲的教堂和泰国的庙宇等。

参考文献

AIIC. Interpreter Workload Study — Full Report [EB/OL]. [2023-07-10] http://aiic.net/page/657, 2002.

Taylor K, Williams V R. Etiquette and Taboos around the World: A Geographic Encyclopedia of Social and Cultural Customs [M]. Manhattan: Bloomsbury Publishing, 2017.

专项练习

1. 习语口译练习

要求：翻译下列句子，注意画线部分的翻译。找出习语相关文化典故和出处，对译文进行小组讨论。

英译汉

(1) Sarah has been feeling under the weather and decided to stay home from work.

(2) Mathematics may be his heel of Achilles.

(3) The union has launched an eleventh-hour decision to call off the strike.

(4) I'm at my wits' end. I don't know how to help him.

(5) I'm afraid you're casting pearls before swine with your good advice — he won't listen.

(6) In view of the subject of the motion, none of us is expert. It is a case of the blind leading

the blind.

(7) He escaped from the secret police by the skin of his teeth.

(8) When those idols are found to have feet of clay, the pain of disenchantment can be profound.

(9) The mortgage on his house had become a millstone around his neck.

(10) The threat of a cut in funding is hanging over the Opera House like a sword of Damocles.

汉译英

（1）很多名人都不是天赋型选手，只是凭借着日复一日的努力实现量变到质变的跨越。这就是我们常说的"笨鸟先飞"的精神。

（2）周一的考试对于大家未来的升学至关重要，在这里我预祝大家能够取得满意的成绩，祝愿各位马到成功！

（3）大家不要着急上火，和气生财，我们坐下来慢慢商议。

（4）对于这个问题我一直沿用之前的陈旧思维，您刚刚的一番话让我茅塞顿开，解决思路顿时清晰明确了。

（5）这家厂商因为出售过期食品而遭消费者抵制，并被相关主管单位移送监察办，真是赔了夫人又折兵。

（6）处于劣势中的军队，只有破釜沉舟，拼死一战，才能死里逃生。

（7）在外交方面，激进盲动给中国带来的灾难余痛犹存，韬光养晦的告诫言犹在耳。

（8）家长望子成龙的心情是可以理解的，但不要过分加重孩子的学习负担。

（9）为了应付伊拉克的动乱，美国不得不拆东墙补西墙，从阿富汗战场上调兵。

（10）老师应该注意学生的个别差异，每个小孩都有不同的特质。如何激发学习动机、对学生因材施教，这是教育者应该思考的首要问题。

2. 俚语口译练习

要求：翻译以下对话，尤其注意画线部分的俚语翻译。

英译汉

(1) — Nathan was already working two jobs. Now he's taken a third. He's definitely bitten off more than he can chew.

— Definitely, he should learn to be kinder to himself.

(2) — How's it going with your study this semester?

— Without meaning to blow my own trumpet, I came top of the class.

(3) — What are you going to buy Sally for her birthday?

— I don't know. I don't have much money.

— Maybe we can all pitch in and buy her something great.

(4) — I can't understand why I failed math.

— You know you didn't study hard, so you're going to have to face the music and take the class again next semester if you really want to graduate when you do.

(5) — You've met my friend Amy, right?

— Hmmm, I'm not sure, but that name rings a bell. Was she the one who went to Paris last year?

汉译英

（1）——大家好，时间不多了，我就开门见山。最近我们办公室遇到了一些重大问题。

——没关系，您尽管直说，我们全力配合。

（2）——她下单时一定是头脑发热，赚的这么少，怎么买得起这么贵的奢侈品！

——谁说不是呢？这下又要省吃俭用好几个月了。

（3）——约翰含着金汤匙出生。父母对他有求必应，送他去最好的私立学校。

——这真令人羡慕！

（4）——简拥有点石成金的能力。她运营的每一项业务都非常成功。

——这背后一定少不了辛勤的汗水，毕竟头脑和勤奋缺一不可。

（5）——你今晚什么打算？

——我想到市里吃饭，但是不知道堵不堵车，咱们到时候随机应变吧！

3. 谚语口译练习

要求：请将下列谚语翻译成汉语或英语。

英译汉

(1) The pot calls the kettle black.

(2) If there were no clouds, we should not enjoy the sun.

(3) Blessed are the pure in heart.

(4) An ounce of mirth is worth a pound of sorrow.

(5) There are as good fish in the sea as ever came out of it.

(6) There is no royal road to learning.

(7) A man becomes learned by asking questions.

(8) Never put off till tomorrow what you can do today.

(9) Enough is as good as a feast.

汉译英

（1）君子之交淡如水。

（2）塞翁失马,焉知非福。

（3）世上无难事,只要肯攀登。

（4）人之初,性本善。

（5）有钱能使鬼推磨。

（6）冤家宜解不宜结。

（7）一言既出,驷马难追。

（8）知己知彼,百战不殆。

（9）虚心使人进步,骄傲使人落后。

（10）实践是检验真理的唯一标准。

篇章练习

Text 1: Don't insist on English

Preview:

Patricia Ryan is a long-time English teacher who asks a provocative question: Is the world's focus on English preventing the spread of great ideas in other languages? In other words: What if Einstein had to pass the TOEFL? It's a passionate defense of translating and sharing ideas.

Glossary:	
Abu Dhabi：阿布扎比,阿拉伯联合酋长国的首都	British Council：英国文化教育协会
bandwagon：流行,时尚,潮流	Germanic languages：日耳曼语族
Romance languages：罗曼语族	Dark Ages of Europe：欧洲黑暗时代
dyslexic：诵读困难的	

I want to talk to you today about language loss and the globalization of English. I want to tell you about my friend who was teaching English to adults in Abu Dhabi. And one fine day, she decided to take them into the garden to teach them some nature vocabulary. But it was she who ended up learning all the Arabic words for the local plants, as well as their uses — medicinal uses, cosmetics, cooking, herbal. How did those students get all that knowledge? Of course, from their grandparents and even their great-grandparents. //

But sadly, today, languages are dying at an unprecedented rate. A language dies every 14 days. Now, at the same time, English is the undisputed global language. Could there be a connection? Well, I don't know. I was recruited by the British Council, along with about 25 other teachers. And we were the first non-Muslims to teach in the state schools there in Kuwait. We were brought to teach English because the government wanted to modernize the country and to empower the citizens through education. And of course, the UK benefited from some of that lovely oil wealth. //

Now this is the major change that I've seen — how teaching English has morphed from being a mutually beneficial practice to becoming a massive international business that it is today. No longer just a foreign language on the school curriculum, and no longer the sole domain of mother England, it has become a bandwagon for every English-speaking nation on the earth. And why not? After all, the best education — according to the latest World University Rankings — is to be found in the universities of the UK and the US. So everybody wants to have an English education, naturally. But if you're not a native speaker, you have to pass a test. //

Now can it be right to reject a student on linguistic ability alone? Perhaps you have a computer scientist who's a genius. Would he need the same language as a lawyer, for example? Well, I don't think so. We English teachers reject them all the time. We put a stop sign, and we stop them in their tracks. They can't pursue their dream any longer, till they get English. Now let me put it this way: If I met a monolingual Dutch speaker who had the cure for cancer, would I stop him from entering my British university? I don't think so. But indeed, that is exactly what we do. We English teachers are the gatekeepers. And you have to satisfy us first that your English is good enough. Now it can be dangerous to give too much power to a narrow segment of society. Maybe the barrier would be too universal. //

But I hear you say, "What about the research? It's all in English." So the books are in English, the journals are done in English, but that is a self-fulfilling prophecy. It feeds the English requirement. And so it goes on. I ask you, what happened to translation? If you think about the Islamic Golden Age, there was lots of translation then. They translated from Latin and Greek into Arabic, into Persian, and then it was translated on into the Germanic languages of Europe and the Romance languages. And so light shone upon the Dark Ages of Europe. // Now don't get me wrong; I am not against teaching English, all you English teachers out there. I love it that we have a global language. We need one today more than ever. But I am against using it as a barrier. Do we really want to end up with 600 languages and the main one being English, or Chinese? We need more than that. Where do we draw the line? This system equates intelligence with a knowledge of English, which is quite arbitrary. //

And I want to remind you that the giants upon whose shoulders today's intelligents stand did not have to have English, they didn't have to pass an English test. Case in point, Einstein. He, by the way, was considered remedial at school because he was, in fact, dyslexic. He did not have to pass an English test, because they didn't start until 1964 with TOEFL, the American test of English. Now it's exploded. There are lots and lots of tests of English. And millions and millions of students take these tests every year. Now you and me might think: "Those fees aren't bad, they're okay," but they are prohibitive to so many millions of poor people. So immediately, we're rejecting them. //

My daughter came to England from Kuwait. She had studied science and mathematics in Arabic. It's an Arabic-medium school. She had to translate it into English at her grammar school. And she was the best in the class at those subjects. This tells us that when students come to us from abroad, we may not be giving them enough credit for what they know, and they know it in their own language. When a language dies, we don't know what we lose with that language.

Let us not keep ourselves in the dark. Let us celebrate diversity. Mind your language. Use it to spread great ideas. //

Text 2: 春节传统

Glossary:	
祭祀祖先: offer sacrifices to ancestors	对联: red couplets
猜灯谜: to solve lantern riddles	放爆竹/烟花: set off firecrackers/fireworks
压岁钱: lucky money	

春节是中国的农历新年。它首先体现了中国人的家庭观念，人们回家祭祀祖先、探望父母、会聚亲人。除夕这天要吃团圆饭，春节期间还要走访亲友。人们通常会说一些吉祥的话，比如"身体健康""万事如意""恭喜发财"等。拜年的意义在于亲朋好友之间走访联络感情，表达对新一年生活的美好祝福。//

春节也是对中国传统文化艺术的传承。人们会贴上红色的对联，不仅增添喜庆的节日气氛，也展示了高超的书法和诗词功力。晚会和节庆活动汇聚了各地的民间艺术形式。正月十五的元宵节是春节的另一个高潮，人们悬挂彩灯和猜灯谜，充满了智慧和趣味。//

如今春节的传统也发生了一些变化。过去人们会放爆竹来庆祝新的一年，而如今为了减少空气污染和噪音污染、防止火灾，一些地方现在禁止燃放烟花爆竹。过去长辈们会给晚辈们压岁钱，因为钱一般是放在红纸袋里，所以也称之为"红包"；而现在许多人会通过微信来给亲人朋友发电子红包，这样即使不在一个城市也能够传达祝福。//

Text 3: The history of tea

Preview:

Tea and tea culture have been an intrinsic part of Chinese history and society for centuries, and act as an important and unique window into the evolution of Chinese culture. Many believed that Chinese tea was first discovered by Shennong, the inventor of Chinese agriculture, who accidentally chewed the tea leaves that fell down from a tea tree, which magically eliminated the poison in his stomach. In China, Tang and Song were the first dynasties to witness the thriving development of tea culture. Chinese tea was introduced into Europe in the early 1600s and became especially favored by British aristocrats. The British Empire spread its own interpretation of tea to its dominions and colonies, which facilitated the diversified development of tea culture in the world.

Glossary:	
the Great Pyramids of Giza：吉萨大金字塔	expanding colonial influence：扩大殖民影响
clipper ship：飞剪船（此类帆船因船首前端尖锐突出，在平静海面与倒影相映成剪型得名）	trading on unfavorable terms：不平等交易
British East India Company：英国东印度公司	Turkish Rize tea：土耳其红茶
Xizang butter tea：西藏酥油茶	Darjeeling：（印度）大吉岭

Shennong, the mythical Chinese inventor of agriculture, highlights tea's importance to ancient China. Archaeological evidence suggests tea was first cultivated there as early as 6,000 years ago, or 1,500 years before the pharaohs built the Great Pyramids of Giza. That original Chinese tea plant is the same type that's grown around the world today, yet it was originally consumed very differently. It was eaten as a vegetable or cooked with grain porridge. Tea only shifted from food to drink 1,500 years ago when people realized that a combination of heat and moisture could create a complex and varied taste out of the leafy green. // After hundreds of years of variations to the preparation method, the standard became to heat tea, pack it into portable cakes, grind it into powder, mix with hot water, and create a beverage called *muo cha*, or *matcha*. Matcha became so popular that a distinct Chinese tea culture emerged. Tea was the subject of books and poetry, the favorite drink of emperors, and a medium for artists. They would draw extravagant pictures in the foam of the tea, very much like the espresso art you might see in coffee shops today. //

In the 9th century during the Tang Dynasty, a Japanese monk brought the first tea plant to Japan. The Japanese eventually developed their own unique rituals around tea, leading to the creation of the Japanese tea ceremony. And in the 14th century during the Ming Dynasty, the Chinese emperor shifted the standard from tea pressed into cakes to loose leaf tea. At that point, China still held a virtual monopoly on the world's tea trees, making tea one of three essential Chinese export goods, along with porcelain and silk. This gave China a great deal of power and economic influence as tea drinking spread around the world. //

That spread began in earnest around the early 1600s when Dutch traders brought tea to Europe in large quantities. Many credit Queen Catherine of Braganza, a Portuguese noble woman, for making tea popular with the English aristocracy when she married King Charles II in 1661. At the time, Great Britain was in the midst of expanding its colonial influence and becoming the new dominant world power. And as Great Britain grew, interest in tea spread around the world. By 1700, tea in Europe sold for ten times the price of coffee and the plant was still only grown in China. The tea trade was so lucrative that the world's fastest sailboat, the clipper ship, was born out of intense competition between Western trading companies. All were racing to bring their tea back to Europe first to maximize their profits. //

At first, Britain paid for all this Chinese tea with silver. When that proved too expensive, they suggested trading tea for another substance, opium. This triggered a public health problem within China as people became addicted to the drug. Then in 1839, a Chinese official ordered his men to destroy massive British shipments of opium as a statement against Britain's influence over China. This act triggered the First Opium War between the two nations. //

The British East India Company also wanted to be able to grow tea themselves and further control the market. So they commissioned botanist Robert Fortune to steal tea from China in a covert operation. He disguised himself and took a perilous journey through China's mountainous tea regions, eventually smuggling tea trees and experienced tea workers into Darjeeling, India. From there, the plant spread further still, helping drive tea's rapid growth as an everyday commodity. Today, tea is the second most consumed beverage in the world after water, and from sugary Turkish Rize tea, to salty Xizang butter tea, there are almost as many ways of preparing the beverage as there are cultures on the globe. //

Text 4:"中国神草" 青蒿素

Preview:

　　1972年是一个具有特殊意义的年份,当年屠呦呦课题组提纯得到抗疟有效单体青蒿素,这一发现标志着人类抗疟历史步入新纪元。青蒿素挽救了全球数百万人生命。凭借在青蒿素发现中的原创性贡献,屠呦呦成为第一位获得诺贝尔科学奖项的中国本土科学家。如今,耄耋之年,屠呦呦依然矢志研究青蒿素的深层机制。从抗疟到抗疫,应对传染病,中医药彰显出独特优势。有识之士希望继屠呦呦之后,中医药人才能薪火相传,群峰竞起,发掘出更多的"青蒿素",挽救更多人的生命。

Glossary:	
疟疾: malaria	青蒿素: artemisinin
艾草: sweet wormwood	世界卫生组织: World Health Organization (WHO)
一线药物: first-line treatment	诺贝尔生理学或医学奖: Nobel Prize in Physiology or Medicine

　　疟疾自古以来就是人类的致命问题。通常,人们遭到携带病毒的蚊子叮咬就会感染疟疾,无数人因此丧命。值得庆幸的是,中国科学家屠呦呦发现了一种叫作青蒿素的药物,能够有效对抗疟疾。//

　　1969年,屠呦呦成为国家抗疟药物研发项目的负责人。屠呦呦团队采取了一种独特的方法,研究有关中医的书籍。在阅读了2 000多种古老疗法后,屠呦呦率团队采集了600多种植物,列出了约380种有可能治疗疟疾的疗法。//

　　其中一种疗法使用艾草进行治疗,至今已经有1 600年历史。屠呦呦发现这种疗法有效,便试图以此提取青蒿素来制造药物。起初提取失败了,于是她又转头研究古籍,终于找到了一个方法。屠呦呦用低温法提取青蒿素,并最终于1972年取得成功。//

　　在屠呦呦团队证明了青蒿素可以治疗小白鼠和猴子的疟疾后,屠呦呦和两名同事主动充当志愿者试服药物,而后才在患者身上测试。结果表明青蒿素是安全的,所有接受测试的患者都康复了。青蒿素逐渐成为世界卫生组织推荐的一线抗疟药物,挽救了全世界数百万人的生命。//

　　2015年,屠呦呦被授予诺贝尔生理学或医学奖,她没有独揽所有的荣誉,反而盛赞自己的同事和中医药。屠呦呦曾经说过:"每个科学家都梦想能做一些可以帮助这个世界的事情。"//

第十三章
临场应对

维也纳大学翻译研究中心教授弗兰兹·波赫克（Pöchhacker, 2004: 11）将口译定义为"一种在源语只说一遍的情况下，即时用另一种语言说出来的形式，且初译即为终译（a form of translation in which a first and final rendition in another language is produced on the basis of a one-time presentation of an utterance in a source language）"。我们从这一定义可以看出，口译过程难以预测且充满变数，译员要做到听懂"只说一遍"的原文并且准确输出"初译即为终译"的译文，必须具备很强的临场应变能力。本章将从材料、讲者、译者以及环境这四个方面入手，为大家介绍口译各个环节中译员可能面临的挑战和突发状况，并分享相应的应对策略。

第一节 材料问题

一、专业性强

译员首先需要做好译前准备，充分熟悉主办方提供的会议议程、嘉宾介绍、主旨发言摘要、往届会议或同类会议的内容，额外收集、查阅相关资料，准备好词汇表（glossary）。但可惜的是，译员无论准备多么充分，都有可能遇见自己不熟悉、专业性又很强的材料。

某些场合下，译员可以通过重复原文或者向现场专家求助来应对。例如，在一场面向医学生的病人心理讲座上，讲者说道："A common reaction is to assume that what they have is not serious or will go away quickly. Most people with serious diseases react this way, including those with cancer and CHD." 译员如果没有一定的医学知识，译前准备又不足，恐怕无法译出"CHD"（冠心病）。这时与其省略或停下来询问，不妨直接重复字母缩略语，因为听众都是医学院的学生，对此缩略语应当非常熟悉。再举一例，"bump in" 特指在奥运会前把相关的家具、固定装置和技术设备等运进场馆的阶段，为奥组委内部术语，通常译为"物资移入期"。该说法无法在公开资料中查到，译员初次听到时多半会感到困惑，需要向会议现场的专家、同事请教确切的含义，或者直接进行源语重复。

保留源语或缩略语看似是权宜之计，有的时候反而是最符合双方语言习惯的做法。在一些组织机构的例会上，参会人员会反复使用内部交流的缩略语以便提高效率。译员也应迅速适应并融入其中。请看下面这个例子：

例 13-1

原文:

We are seeking confirmation that these vehicles can access the arrival terminal at PEK.

参考译文:

我们需要你方确认这些车可以进入 PEK 的抵达航站楼。

这里的"PEK"指的是北京首都国际机场。一位译员在一次会议期间注意到中方人员之间内部沟通时也都直接使用"PEK"而非其中文名称,因此在之后的口译时也都统一使用字母缩写。

译者遇到专业术语还可以根据上下文合理推测,选用近义或上义词来解释说明。

例 13-2

原文:

Energy-efficient light bulbs are a low-cost, high-reward upgrade that can lead to saving both energy and money. Unlike other energy-efficiency upgrades, replacing incandescent bulbs with high-efficiency ones requires no infrastructure or electrical tweaks.

参考译文:

节能灯泡是一种低成本、高回报的升级方式,既能节约能源又能省钱。和其他能效升级不同,用节能灯泡取代白炽灯不需要基建或电路改造。

变通译文:

节能灯泡是一种低成本、高回报的升级方式,既能节约能源又能省钱。与其他能效升级不同,用节能灯泡取代传统灯泡不需要基建或电路改造。

这里的"incandescent bulbs"有一定的专业性,但是前面提到的"energy-efficient light bulbs"却可以根据字面很容易译出。既然是用节能灯来替换,那么被替换的势必是传统的、高能耗的灯泡。

二、信息密集

除了专业性强,材料信息密集也会给译员的理解、记忆、笔记带来很大的压力。一般而言,面对密集的信息,译员需要抓大放小、厘清逻辑、适度省略,才能在有限的时间里快速输出可接受的译文。例 13-3 就是典型的一例。

例 13-3

原文:

Cognitive load features in anything we might do as a learner, from reading a text, to watching and replicating a series of dance moves, following a presentation with slides, to doing a math problem, and more. Thinking about the types and amount of cognitive load in a learning experience can help us design well. It allows us to be more sensitive to the complex demands that tasks and experiences can make on an individual's working memory, which has limited capacity.

简化译文：

认知负载存在于任何学习中，无论是阅读、学跳舞、听报告还是做数学题。了解学习中的认知负载可以帮助我们更好地设计学习方式，更加敏锐地意识到各类学习任务对于人类有限的工作记忆的复杂要求。

这段材料细节信息十分密集，且逻辑关系较为复杂。译员在处理的时候可以将细枝末节的内容适当简化，比如"watching and replicating a series of dance moves"可以简化为"学跳舞"，"following a presentation with slides"可以简化为"听报告"，"types and amount"可以省略，"tasks and experiences"可以模糊处理为"学习任务"。这样便能快速把握主干信息，较为从容地完成口译。

信息密集程度和信息量还和讲者的语速有关。同样的语段用1.2倍的速度来说，译者的工作记忆面临的挑战更大，即便内容是其比较熟悉的。这方面我们将在下一节"讲者问题"中具体介绍。

第二节 讲者问题

一、语言习惯

当讲者持续语速过快或停不下来时，译员要及时介入，主动沟通以寻求帮助。例如，译员可以在下一段开始翻译前提醒讲者语速的问题，或是在合适的句段间打断，直接说明："请让我先翻译一下。"讲者和译员之间虽然可能存在雇佣的关系，但目标一致，那就是完成跨语言和跨文化的沟通。从这种意义上来讲，译员其实是在帮助讲者实现目标，因此讲者一般来说也会充分谅解并积极配合。

在个别会谈中，一方讲者可能会忘记自己是在和另一方会谈，而把译员作为自己的交际对象。讲者连续说了三四分钟，其实只有不到一分钟的内容是说给对方的，其余的内容都是在和译员抒发自己的情绪或是解释自己的想法。译员只能翻译出一分钟的内容，那么另一方就可能会认为译员遗漏了大量内容，质疑译员的业务能力和职业素养。这种情况下，译员应当主动和另一方解释清楚避免误会，但同时也要注意不能泄露讲者明确不希望另一方知晓的信息和态度。

二、逻辑不明与表述冗余

理想的讲者思维清晰、逻辑缜密，但现实情况未必尽如人意。有的讲者（尤其在即兴演讲时)可能思维过于跳跃,想到哪儿说到哪儿。此时译员需要自行给原文"润色",服务听众。他们需要在很短的时间内理清原文的主干和不同层次,完善断句和衔接不当之处,省略重复、纠正语病,将指代不明的地方说清楚等。请大家试着分析并翻译下面这段话。

例13-4

原文:

各位女士、先生,各位同学,大家好。非常高兴来伦敦政经学院就中国的老龄化问题和大家进行一次汇报交流,不太理想的是,一个是时间压迫得很紧,到了我这儿时间就很有限了,这是不公平的。我们到了伦敦也讲公平嘛,是吧;第二个呢,刚刚沉浸在美好的中国传统文化的记忆中,甚至又进入一个过春节的状态,马上又转到了我们心情很沉重的一个话题:老龄化问题。这个安排不太科学,这个和我个人没有关系啦,不管怎么说,我们都要转换一下,尽管整个来一个一百八十度转弯,我们也要接受我这个课题。我的题目就是《老龄化形势与对策》,我没有做PPT,因为我想,我的感觉呢,是你看着我能给我一些灵感,你不要去看着那个PPT,我希望你更多地看我,我这个人有一种自恋的感觉,你看我,我有灵感,我会讲得更好。

参考译文:

Ladies and gentlemen, dear students, it is my pleasure to be here at LSE. Since we're already behind the schedule, I'll try to be brief and go without slides. My topic is "Aging Society in China", a rather grave one, especially when everyone is in the mood for the coming Spring Festival.

这段即兴演讲存在不少冗余和模糊之处。讲者正说着老龄化,突然转到中国传统文化和春节,旋即又回到老龄化问题,如此跳跃的思维让人摸不着头脑。该讲者是上午论坛的最后一名嘉宾,因为前面的发言人超时,轮到他时已临近午餐时间,所以他表示有点"不公平"。此外,上一位嘉宾的演讲话题是中华传统文化,因此他才即兴提到"刚刚沉浸在美好的中国传统文化的记忆中"试图呼应和过渡,不过效果并不理想。由此我们可以明白,讲者实际想表达的意思是"刚刚听了一个美好的关于中国传统文化的讲座,再加上春节即将来临,本来大家心情都很愉悦,但现在我却要说一个沉重的话题"。作为译员,不仅要理解字面的语意,还要联系会场语境快速反应,才能精准地传递出讲者真正想说的话。

参考译文不仅表达出了讲者的实际意图,符合礼仪,而且还删除了大量填补语(如"因为我想,我的感觉呢")和冗余的表达(如"你看着我能给我一些灵感""你看我,我有灵感")。这样可以为听众呈现干净利落的译文,也能缩短会程,让与会者早些用餐。

三、表达不得体

有时候讲者可能会因为缺乏外语的文化背景和思维方式,无意中使用一些在本国语境中无伤大雅但在其他文化中欠妥的表达。如果译员不加思考直接对译,很可能会引起外语听众的反感甚至冒犯到他们。如上一单元所说的,译员作为跨文化交际的专家应当具有较强的文化敏感度,选择合适的译文表达,避免误会。

译员在注意到讲者出错的时候,需要快速判定错误的类别:如果仅仅是口误,可以在译文中直接纠正;如果是与事实、常识相违背的错误,一般而言,译员应当按照事实来翻译。

例 13-5

原文:

我校是一个典型的精英式学校。学校规模在全国高校中是比较小的一个,小就意味着精,而且我们的培养目标也是精英式。

学生译文:

Our university is a typical school of elitism. The university is small; however, small means elitism, and therefore our target is elitist.

参考译文:

The university upholds excellence. Though small in size, it aims to excel and turn out the best talents.

在中文语境下,"精英式"的说法或许不会引起听众的反感,甚至会让被称作"精英"的群体感到自豪。但在当前英语世界社会政治环境中,"elitism"是一个广受诟病的概念:暗含着自私、势利、排他、高人一等、盛气凌人的含义,通常被用作贬义词。因此处理这一段内容时,需要灵活变通,将"精英"一词用中性甚至褒义的词语表达出来。

此外,讲者还可能因为情绪激动说了不得体的话。笔者曾经参加过一场中外合资企业的董事会例会,中外双方高层就人事任命问题发生了激烈争执。一方代表十分生气,骂了几句脏话。作为译员,面对脏话的通常做法是尽量降调处理或是略去不译,并且同时可以用"this is outrageous"或者"I am really upset"等相对中性的表达传递出讲者的态度。但少数情况下,译员也可能会被明确要求把脏话翻译出来。笔者曾经作为篮球队的随队翻译为一场央视直播的篮球比赛做现场翻译,因为教练认为存在"黑哨"现象,所以向裁判喊了脏话,而且大声要求译者把这些脏话翻译出来。在这种情况下,译员只能将詈骂语如实译出。但总体而言,降调处理是比较常见且稳妥的做法。

第三节 译 者 问 题

一、词汇量不足

除去专业术语,口译学习者也有可能遇见生词或者陌生的表达,尽管这些词原本是现阶段应该掌握的。一般而言,我们可以基于语篇的整体意思,利用省略、上义词、范畴词甚至添加句子阐释等方式来应对。

例 13-6

原文：

We have all heard plenty about the "college bubble" in recent years. Student loan debt is at an all-time high and tuition costs continue to rise at a rate far outpacing inflation, as they have for decades. Credential inflation is devaluing the college degree.

参考译文：

近些年我们听到了许多关于"大学泡沫"的讨论。助学贷款创历史新高，而学费花销继续上涨，比通货膨胀还快，几十年来都是如此。学历通货膨胀正在让大学学历贬值。

学生译员在听到这段材料时，有可能听不懂"credential"，因此将"credential inflation"直接翻译为"inflation"。联系上文的"college bubble"，我们很容易就能推断此处指的是"学历通货膨胀"。此外，还有学生译员把"credential inflation"全部省略了，直接将最后一句译为"大学学历贬值"，也能基本达意。

上面这个例子中，译员遇到的问题是外语的接受性词汇不足。还有一种情况下，译者能够听懂原文，就是不知道如何用外语表达。此时，译员不要花过多精力去纠结精准的译法，更不能中断口译停下来思考，而是应该凭借已掌握的近似表达进行阐释。

例 13-7

原文：

所以在那个时候，我们有一句话就是"即使是猪站在风口上也会飞起来"，因为那时候风大，所以大家都飞得非常高。

参考译文：

Back then, there was a saying, "At the wind tunnel, even a pig can fly." The "wind" was strong, so everyone could fly high.

变通译文：

Back then, there was a saying, "a strong wind can carry a pig high." The "wind" was strong, so everyone could fly high.

学生译员在处理这一段内容的时候，很可能会被"风口"一词难住。有的学生译员甚至停下来思考，语流就此被打断。如果我们将注意力放在整句的内容上，我们会发现关键信息其实落在"风大"而非"风口"上，因此"风口"一词完全可以被模糊处理而不影响大意。当然，此句也有学生译员意译为"Back then, people would say, 'with the right opportunities, even a pig can fly'. Opportunities were everywhere, so everyone could fly." 这种译法虽然将大意传递出来了，但是笔者建议译文尽量保留"风"的比喻，因为译员无法预料讲者是否会在下文中就"风"这个意象继续展开。如果下文中继续用"风"来玩文字游戏,那么采取阐释法的译员就会陷入被动。

二、漏译错译

译者在口译现场的压力下,可能会因为注意力分配不当而遗漏信息。此时需要快速判定遗漏信息的属性。如果是次要信息,不会对听众的整体理解构成影响,那么可以略去不译或是模糊处理;如果是重要信息,则需视场合采取不同的策略。若会议比较正式,建议先模糊处理,保持冷静,集中精力翻译后面的内容,因为讲者很有可能再次提及前文中译员遗漏的内容,甚至进一步阐释,译员或许有机会不动声色地补救。若现场较为轻松自由,那么译者可以直接向发言人或者现场专家请教,得到解答后再继续翻译。

例13-8

原文:

据权威机构发布的汽车网络安全报告显示,2020年全球已有 3.3亿辆汽车实现互联。联网汽车数量的快速提升也引起了汽车网络攻击事件的频发,自2016年以来,汽车网络安全事件数量增加了605%。

学生译文:

According to a report on car cybersecurity, over 300 million vehicles had got connected by 2020. The rapid increase in the number of connected vehicles has resulted in more frequent cyberattacks on vehicles. Since 2016, cyberattacks on cars had increased tremendously.

参考译文:

According to an authoritative report on automotive cybersecurity, by 2020 the world had seen 330 million vehicles connected. The rapid increase in the number of connected vehicles has invited more cyberattacks. Since 2016, the number of automotive cybersecurity incidents has increased by 605%.

上面这个例子中,有同学在做笔记时没有将数字记录下来,在第一处采取了约数法取下位,在第二处干脆直接模糊处理成了"大幅度增加"。这样的译法当然不够理想,但是对于保持镇定、改善语流、增强信心还是有一定帮助的。

同样道理,若译员意识到自己前面译错了,也需要分情况处理。如果是细枝末节的表述问题可以直接忽略,切忌反复改口(backtracking)。如果译错的是较为重要的信息,译员可以插入"what I really mean is""我的意思是"等话语,然后重述正确的内容。

三、注意力不集中

理想状态下译员需要全程保持注意力高度集中,但在现实中他们难免因现场环境嘈杂、疲惫等情况一时走神。此时,译员可以通过平行重组(parallel reformulation)来补充一些符合事实、基本切题、逻辑一致的语句。所谓的"平行重组",就是译员由于无法理解原文的部分内容,于是根据交际语境创造性地合理增译,以避免长时间沉默或者话只说一半。("The interpreter cannot understand elements of the original and decides to invent something that is different from the original but more or less plausible in the communicative context, so as to avoid long pauses or unfinished sentences.")(Li, 2015)。

例13-9

原文:

《北京城市总体规划(2016—2035)》明确提出,丽泽金融商务区重点发展互联网金融、数字金融、金融信息、金融中介、金融文化等新兴业态,主动承接金融街、北京商务中心区配套辐射。丽泽金融商务区是"国家级智慧城市试点""北京市绿色生态示范区"和"北京市服务贸易示范基地"。

参考译文:

The Beijing Urban Master Plan(2016—2035)clearly indicates that Beijing Lize Financial Business District will focus on the development of emerging business patterns, such as Internet finance, digital finance, financial information, financial intermediaries, and financial culture. It will absorb the spillover from the financial industry of the Financial Street and the CBD of Beijing. Lize is a "National Smart City Pilot", "Beijing Green Ecological Demonstration Zone", and "Beijing Service Trade Demonstration Base".

变通译文:

The Beijing Urban Master Plan(2016—2035)clearly indicates that Beijing Lize Financial Business District will focus on the development of digital finance and other emerging business patterns. It will absorb the spillover from the financial industry of the Financial Street and the CBD of Beijing. Lize is a pilot in multiple areas, such as high-tech, green development and the service industry.

口译学习者遇见密集的专有名词列举,如果译前准备未能覆盖到这些信息,或者讲者语速稍快,一般很难全部准确译出。但为了让口译顺畅进行,译员可以集中注意力听专有名词的核心内涵(比如类型关键词),将其提炼出来并进行描述和阐释(见变通译文的画线部分),从而把原文大意传递出来。

第四节 现场环境问题

译员需要留意现场安排及环境变化,首先须随时关注议程的调整。到达会场后,译员需要快速浏览现场获得的资料。例如,笔者参加过一个论坛,主办方主持人在开幕辞中提到

"论坛将主要采用1+3模式"。如果译员没有事先获得活动日程表,可能只好将这句话翻译成 "the Forum will be conducted in the 1+3 model",但这样字对字的翻译对于听众来说意义不明,帮助不大。好在笔者提前熟悉了会议流程,马上反应过来这里的 "1+3" 指的是 "上午一场开幕大会、下午三场分论坛",这样译文就能优化为 "the Forum will be conducted in the 1+3 model, namely the opening session with keynotes in the morning and three panel forums in the afternoon"。

另一种常见的突发状况是设备故障。过去我们谈到设备故障,大多认为是同传译员才会面对的问题,这是由于搭建同传箱所需的设备较为复杂,而交传译员只需确保话筒正常工作即可,在某些小会场或者联络口译中甚至可以不借助设备。但如今大量的国际交流活动由线下转为线上,会前各种线上会议软件的调试也成了交传的常态。网络连接不稳定会导致语流传输断断续续,因此译员在会议开始前一定要检查好网络连接与软件设置。如果突发连接中断或者信号干扰导致听不清,译员需要及时联系会议联络人员或技术人员进行调试,并且在通信恢复正常后告知发言人故障发生时的会议内容。

此外,由于线上会议使用的一些软件会优先呈现当前讲话人的屏幕,发言人可能会忘记译员的存在,连续说上五六分钟。遇到讲者发言时间过长,译员可以在聊天框里提醒,或是私下联系会议联络人提醒发言人。当然,译员也应夯实本领,努力锻炼长交传的能力。

陪同口译时,译员常常处于站立或行进中,无法记笔记,需要强化记忆能力。译员可以提前与讲者沟通,解释无笔记口译的困难,约定好缩短每一段的时间。此外,译员还可能会遇到笔的墨水用完的情况,因此需要准备一支备用。总体而言,各类困难都可积极应对,无论是自行补救或是现场求助,都应保持交流而不是冷场。

参考文献

Li Xiangdong. Putting Interpreting Strategies in Their Place: Justifications for Teaching Strategies in Interpreter Training [J]. Babel, 2015(2): 170−192.

Pöchhacker F. Introducing Interpreting Studies [M]. London/New York: Routledge, 2004.

专项练习

英汉段落1: Swearing

Like antibiotics, curse words can lose their power with overuse. Cable TV liberally douses American living rooms with as many "goddamns", "shits", and "motherfuckers". So, did those words make you cringe, or have you been watching too much TV?

It's hard to say whether the increase of cursing on TV reflected an increase in cursing among average Americans, or whether TV "corrupted" how Americans speak. Regardless, the result is the same: More Americans are becoming inoculated against these words — perhaps even to the point of immunity. Taboos change, and so swearing must too.

Some taboos disappear — "damn" doesn't carry the fire and brimstone heft of damnation that it once did — while social changes can bring about new taboos. Before the civil rights movement in the United States, derogatory epithets describing one's race, creed or sexual orientation were used by all sorts of regular folks who didn't consider for a second that they were being prejudiced. Today, these words are most certainly taboo.

英汉段落2：Name

It is time to question an accepted social practice that is in fact quite unacceptable, and in our time more than repellent. Why is a woman expected to change her name when she marries?

Historically, the use of a single name for most people became confusing with the growth of population, and so grew the practice of adding a last name. The last name was based on trade, such as Smith or Taylor; on location, the village or town one came from; and on lineage, the chosen family name. In the 9th century, English common law developed the doctrine of coverture, which became standard practice in the western world: a woman at birth is "covered" by her father and after marriage is "covered" by her husband. The latter meant her legal identity merged with her husband's. Perhaps "submerged" was the more appropriate term, because coverture implied that only the husband could vote, hold property or go to court.

This absurd legal fiction provides the basis for the widespread practice of a woman having to shed her name and take on the last name of her husband when she marries. The absurdity scales new heights now that women are marrying late and meanwhile acquiring academic degrees, professional qualifications and senior-level work experience in their own names. As the price of her wedded bliss, a woman must undergo the painful exercise of abandoning her identity, legally change all her licenses and certificates, and notify her employer, lawyer, doctor, and all other contacts. In an age of Google and LinkedIn, this represents a huge handicap and a staggering professional disadvantage.

汉英段落1：一起向未来

"一起向未来"是北京作为"双奥之城"，给奥林匹克精神和理念留下的又一中国印迹，在与2008年北京奥运会主题口号"同一个世界，同一个梦想"一脉相承的基础上，不仅体现了共享办奥、开放办奥的理念，还反映了世界各国渴望携手走向美好明天的共同心声。

"一起"体现了人类命运共同体面对困境时的坚强姿态，更指明了"团结"才是战胜困难、开创未来的成功之路。英文"together"与今年国际奥委会在奥林匹克格言"更快、更高、更强"后新加入的"更团结"相互映射和呼应，意在激励奥林匹克运动战胜暂时的困难，走向可持续发展。

汉英段落2：城市规划

自2000年开始，中国已经投资修建了世界最大的地铁系统。地铁线路管理有方、准时且可靠，几乎每一个城区居民都可以在15分钟内从家或者办公室到达地铁站。人们不必居住在拥挤且昂贵的核心城市，就可以享受到城市群的好处。此外，共享单车体系也解决了重要的交通问题。现在在中国大多数城市，不用开车也能到处游玩，这对未来建造更好的城市很重要。

与此同时，世界规模最大的高铁系统也已接近完成，连接起中国多数大城市。下一项大的基础设施投资将是把小城市与大的核心区连接起来的铁路系统。三个大的综合区域，即京津冀地区、长三角地区、珠三角地区，将成为全球最大的城市群。这将减少核心地区的压力，提升全国交通的效率。

篇章练习

Text 1: Proposal on "Resource and Environmental Effects in Global Karsts Dynamic Systems"

Glossary:	
Proposal on "Resource and Environmental Effects in Global Karsts Dynamic Systems"："全球岩溶动力系统资源环境效应"计划	Karst：岩溶，是水对可溶性岩石进行以化学溶蚀作用为主，流水的冲蚀、潜蚀和崩塌等机械作用为辅的地质作用，以及由这些作用所产生的现象的总称。由喀斯特作用所造成地貌，称喀斯特地貌（岩溶地貌）

Distinguished colleagues,
Ladies and gentlemen,

On the occasion of the opening ceremony of the announcement of the proposal on "Resource and Environmental Effects in Global Karsts Dynamic Systems", I am delighted to send you this message of encouragement.

Our planet is facing many challenges: climate change, population growth, access to fresh water, education for all, to name but a few. Sometimes, taken together, these problems can seem insurmountable. But I believe in the ability and innovativeness of humanity not only to rise to these challenges but to surmount them. //

Earth is home to many fragile environments, one of which is our precious areas of karst. Often the home of inspiring landscapes and mysterious caves and caverns that provide shelter to an enormous biological diversity, karst environments can however be very harsh places for local communities to make a living. Thin and often poor soils, the inability of the rock to hold surface water and quite often the remoteness of these areas are all challenges local people must face. I see that your proposal will research and help propose solutions for some of these issues. //

I am delighted that many of our UNESCO Global Geoparks and natural World Heritage Sites are in karst areas and are also working through the UN Sustainable Development Goals to address some of the same problems. I would like to express my support for the international scientific cooperation envisaged in this project. I believe this kind of collaboration is essential to overcome the problems we all face as a global society. I am sure the project will be a great success and I look forward to hearing about its progress and successes. //

Text 2: Privacy

Imagine having a master key for your life. A key or password that gives access to the front door to your home, your bedroom, your diary, your computer, your phone, your car, and your safe deposit. Would you go around making copies of that key and giving them out to strangers? Probably not the wisest idea — it would be only a matter of time before someone abused it, right? So why are you willing to give up your personal data to pretty much anyone who asks for it?

Privacy is the key that unlocks the aspects of yourself that are most intimate and personal, that make you most you, and most vulnerable: Your past, present and possible future diseases; your fears, your losses, your failures; the worst thing you have ever done, said and thought; your inadequacies, your mistakes, your traumas; the moment in which you have felt most ashamed; your most drunken night. //

When you give that key, your privacy, to someone who loves you, it will allow you to enjoy closeness, and they will use it to benefit you. Part of what it means to be close to someone is sharing what makes you vulnerable and trusting that person never to take advantage of the privileged position granted by intimacy. People who love you might use your date of birth to organize a surprise birthday party for you; they'll make a note of your tastes to find you the perfect gift; they'll take into account your darkest fears to keep you safe from the things that scare you. Not everyone will use access to your personal life in your interest, however. Fraudsters might use your date of birth to impersonate you while they commit a crime; companies might use your tastes to lure you into a bad deal; enemies might use your darkest fears to threaten and extort you. People who don't have your best interest at heart will exploit your data to further their own agenda. Privacy matters because the lack of it gives others power over you. //

You might think your privacy is safe because you are a nobody — nothing special, interesting or important to see here. Don't shortchange yourself. You have your attention, your presence of mind — everyone is fighting for it. They want to know more about you so they can know how best to distract you, even if that means luring you away from quality time with your loved ones or basic human needs such as sleep. You have money, even if it is not a lot — companies want you to spend your money on them. Hackers are eager to get hold of sensitive information or images so they can blackmail you. You can probably work; businesses want to know everything about whom they are hiring — including whether you might be someone who will want to fight for your rights. You have an identity — criminals can use it to commit crimes in your name and let you pay for the bill. You have personal connections. You are a node in a network. You are someone's offspring, someone's neighbor, someone's teacher or lawyer. Through you, they can get to other people. That's why apps ask you for access to your contacts. You have a voice — all sorts of agents would like to use you as their mouthpiece on social media and beyond. //

Text 3：互联网产业

企业是推动互联网产业发展的主力军，是科技创新主体和产业变革主体，支撑一国数字经济发展。各国互联网企业普遍积极拓展业务范围，快速布局科技新兴领域，不断孕育新技术、新业态、新模式、新服务。//

北美地区互联网产业发展遥遥领先于全球其他地区。美国拥有数量众多的互联网企业，并在全球居于领先地位，尤其是苹果、谷歌、微软、亚马逊等互联网巨头几乎主导着全球互联网的发展动向。拉美地区互联网产业发展迅速，为国外互联网企业提供了良好的环境。//

欧洲各国语言多样，各国平均人口较少，不利于大型互联网企业的孕育发展，目前全球市值前20名的互联网公司没有一家来自欧洲地区。亚洲地区的互联网产业发展水平极不平衡，其中，中国、印度、日本、韩国等互联网企业实力雄厚，尤其是中国的互联网初创企业发展迅速。//

Text 4：交流会致词

很荣幸受邀参加今天的在线交流会。首先，我谨代表北京冬奥组委，感谢孙大使和中国

驻印度使馆精心安排此次富有意义的活动。我也要感谢印度奥委会和青年领袖联合会对北京冬奥会的关注和支持。//

还有不到一个月，举世瞩目的北京冬奥会即将拉开大幕，各国人民将共襄全球最大规模的冬季综合性体育盛会。还有不到一个月，奥林匹克之火将再次在国家体育场"鸟巢"上空燃起，北京将成为全球第一座同时举办过夏季奥运会和冬季奥运会的城市。我们热忱欢迎各国（地区）奥运健儿参加北京冬奥会、冬残奥会！//

中国政府高度重视北京冬奥会、冬残奥会筹办工作。自2015年成功申办北京冬奥会以来，习近平主席先后5次赴冬奥赛区实地视察，作出了一系列重要指示批示，要求我们做好筹办工作。十一天前，习近平主席在2022年新年贺词中表示，我们将竭诚为世界奉献一届奥运盛会。// 世界期待中国，中国做好了准备。这是对全世界的庄严承诺，也是对北京冬奥组委的决战动员令。一周前，习近平主席再次莅临北京冬奥组委总部和部分场馆视察，展现我们成功办奥的信心与决心，令我们备受鼓舞。

六年多来，北京冬奥组委全面落实"绿色、共享、开放、廉洁"办奥理念，遵循"简约、安全、精彩"办赛要求，扎实推进各项筹办任务，取得重要成果。//

朋友们，伴随着今天倒计时24天的钟声，我们热切期盼北京冬奥会拉开帷幕，我们热烈欢迎印度在内的各国（地区）冰雪健儿前来参赛。据我了解，印度一名高山滑雪运动员已获得北京冬奥会参赛资格，衷心祝愿他勇于拼搏、赛出风格、赛出水平。我迄今曾经陪同多位印度青年体育部部长、副部长在中国各地考察体育工作，能感受到体育工作在印度受到的重视，印度青年对板球的热衷给我留下深刻印象。// 我也希望印度朋友们持续关注冬奥、支持冬奥。我们坚信，北京作为全球首座"双奥之城"，一定会给世界呈现一届"简约、安全、精彩"的奥运盛会。让我们谨记"更快、更高、更强、更团结"的奥林匹克格言，携手"一起向未来"，为弘扬奥林匹克精神、促进中印人民友谊、推动构建人类命运共同体作出新的贡献。谢谢大家！//

第十四章
模拟会议

在口译入门阶段,同学们的重点在于夯实语言基本功、掌握基本的口译技巧,课堂练习主要以"讲解——听译——反馈——复听——重译"的模式进行,并没有连续、不受干扰的口译实景。到了学期末,同学们已经经历过不少专项练习、对话口译练习和篇章口译练习,在口译技巧、公共演说和临场应对等方面都渐入佳境。这时候不妨安排一次模拟会议,检验一学期所学的成果,也让同学们能够体会到实战口译的现场感与种种挑战,获得更高的成就感。

为了提高课堂效率和会议口译的质量,不妨提前布置会议主题与明确分工,让同学们角色代入,提前做好准备。会议中途教师不对学生的表现和遇到的各种情况进行干预,模拟会议结束后统一复盘和讲评。

第一节 模拟会议的组织形式

根据班级的规模,模拟会议有不同的组织形式,可以是对话模式,也可以是主旨演讲模式。暂时不发言的同学可以扮演现场观众,向讲者提问,增加模拟会议的互动性和真实感。

在对话模式下,一般可设置不同主题的多场对谈。每场有一位主持人、一位中文讲者、一位中文译者、一位英译中的译员、一位中译英的译员(见图14-1)。一场对话会涉及五位参与者,如果有四至五场对话,那么基本就可以涵盖到英文小班授课的全体同学。

图14-1 对话型模拟会议

在主旨演讲模式下,可以有一位大会主持人,若干名中文或英文讲者,并配备相应数量的英译中和中译英的译者(见图14-2)。每个主旨演讲会涉及两位参与者,即一位讲者和一位译者,但由于一场大会一般有五至六位主旨发言人,因此总共可以有11至13位同学(含大会主持人)参与其中。两场大会可以设置两个不同的主题,以便容纳下全体同学。

图14-2 主旨演讲型模拟会议

模拟会议可以分为会前准备、课堂模拟和会后反思三个阶段。这一形式可以培养学生的译员身份，避免教师朗读段落或播放录音的机械操作。模拟会议时教师不妨扮演会务人员，做好基本场务和设备工作，并协调现场的突发状况。这样做可以调动课堂气氛，让学生有备而来，有知识、有目的地去译，充分了解译员工作的真实压力。

第二节 会前准备

说"会前准备"，而不是常用的"译前准备"，是因为讲者和译者都需要充分准备，而观众对话题也并非一无所知，这与真实会议是一致的。教师可以提前一两周给出大会的主题，例如：环境问题、教育问题、妇女权益、人口老龄化等。讲者们可以分头搜集资料和准备更为具体的话题：例如"环境"主题的对话内容可能围绕着联合国气候变化大会第27次缔约方会议（COP27）展开，"教育"主题的对话内容可能是在线教育。具体的话题由讲者团队商议，并提前一周给译者们提供对照语料、词汇表等，供其做译前准备。

讲者组的具体讲稿可以在准备周里编写和润色，如果是对话则可以简单彩排一下。我们希望如果时间充裕，且学生也有余力，学生的讲稿不是现成的某一篇或某一段稿子，而是根据主题查阅中英文资料自主编写的。其中的英文段落可以根据英文新闻、评论、视频等资料改编，不必完全自行撰写。这样既能降低任务难度、节省准备时间，还能保证语言的地道性和一定的复杂性。

为了给讲稿质量把关，教师最好让讲者们提前几天提交原文并亲自修订，以保证模拟会议的效率和效果。例如，有的初稿是根据新闻和社论改编的，语言过于书面化，不符合演讲和对话的风格；有的是基于真实演讲改编的，但是用词专业性和句式复杂度较高，超出了同学们现阶段的知识储备和口译水平。这些时候教师就需要介入，帮助修改或者指导同学们酌情简化，让讲稿更加自然和流畅，避免模拟会议的现场发生不必要的冷场。

扮演译员的学生收到讲者组提供的对照语料和词汇表后，便紧锣密鼓地开始准备，这一流程同学们应该都已经非常熟悉了。但是，如果只是阅读给定的材料并背诵词汇表，就大大削弱了模拟会议的教益。此时，同学们需要像职业译员一样在有限的时间内积极检索和学习背景知识，建立自己的语料库和词汇表。网上的信息很多，但译前准备贵在"精"，可以优先查看具有权威性、相似性和时效性的材料。例如，在获知具体主题是"气候变化大会"时，译者们可以检索最近一两届大会的主题和嘉宾发言,观看相关视频,阅读会议的新闻报道,并在这一过程中搜集人名、地名、会议、组织等专有名词,熟悉气候变化领域内的专业术语。他们也可以主动与讲者联系,争取获得议程和更多资料。当然,讲者可以选择提供或不提供,资料的详细程度也不作规定。如果某位同学扮演的是领导人、专家等知名人士,译者就可以查找其过往的发言,了解其基本观点和立场,熟悉其语言风格。就这样,译者的背景知识像滚雪球一样越来越多,逐渐能够应对专业性强的口译任务。

扮演观众的学生也需要在会前浏览材料,掌握主题信息和大部分术语,即便不能上升为产出性词汇(productive vocabulary),也至少要将其纳入接受性词汇(receptive vocabulary),做到能迅速听懂。只有带着兴趣、带着背景知识、带着问题去参会才有意义。

第三节 课 堂 模 拟

课堂上的模拟会议首先需要布场,例如教师可以提前架设好摄像设备以便全程录像。教室的大屏幕上可以根据主题放一页幻灯片作为会议背景图,列出讲者和译者姓名,营造现场氛围。由于筹备时间有限,我们一般不要求模拟会议的讲者制作演讲的幻灯片。

另一个问题是人员位置的安排。主旨演讲的站位比较清楚,台上一共两人,译者站在讲者的侧后方,手持有一定硬度的笔记本或文件夹来记笔记。对话访谈时的座位安排相对复杂。译员最好能够观察到双方讲者的举动和侧脸,以便更好地接受信息和及时沟通。在没有主持人的模拟对话中,座位可以做如下安排(见图14-3)。

图14-3 无主持人的模拟会议座位安排

一般来说,英文讲者的侧后方是英汉译者,而中文讲者的侧后方是汉英译者。在外交场合中,为了能把己方的意思准确传达,通常都是由自带的译员来翻译的。

模拟会议的翻译过程与一般课堂口译基本一致,但是更富有现场感。它强调声音质量、风度仪态、麦克风礼仪等非语言素质,这方面远胜于"听录音——被录音——放录音"的传统课堂训练。讲者和译员都要特别注意仪态和着装,也更加需要临场应变能力,遇到疑难要运用各种沟通方法和应对策略,也可以直接询问发言人。译者可以带上准备的资料和术语表以备不时之需,这就是所谓的口译员的"小抄(cheat sheet)"。

会议进程中,讲者和译者其实都面临挑战。讲者可以带稿子,但是不建议完全"埋头苦读";可以将其作为提示卡来使用,有需要的时候看一眼,大部分时候和观众或与会谈人保持眼神交流。如果讲者具备感染力,也能调动起译员的情绪。

讲者和译员之间也需要互相配合，这主要体现在停顿和衔接方面。课堂录音训练中，一段结束往往会有提示音，或者由教师口头提示"开始"；但会议中讲者会自然停顿、稍作等待，而译员需要迅速领会意图并尽快开始翻译，如果等候时间过长，现场气氛就会比较尴尬。译员如果看到讲者通过点头、眼神交流等方式示意，就可以开始翻译了。如果发现译员遇到困难没有准备好，有经验的讲者也会接着多说几句，给译员缓冲的时机和更丰富的语境，以便其整理思路和把握主旨。有的时候，讲者由于准备充分，演讲太过投入，可能停不下来，那么译员就需要通过恰当的方式来打断，以避免自己的认知负荷过重。在对话和访谈类模拟会议中，比较容易出现的一种情况是，中英文双方的讲者直接开始对话了，没有给予译员说话的机会。这一方面是由于对话稿是事先准备好的，讲者们都知道对方何时会停顿；另一方面是因为两位同学都是双语者，实际上并不需要译员就能展开对话，因此很容易忘记翻译的必要性。此时译员就需要及时介入，比如提醒"稍等，我先翻译一下"，或者直接开始翻译内容，稍加犹豫就会完全错过这轮翻译任务。

模拟会议的与会观众也并非无所事事。同学们可以选择像译员一样做笔记，与现场译文进行对比，并用不同颜色的笔标注出错误和问题；也可以选择像普通观众一样关注内容、保持思考，适度做笔记，准备会后提问。

模拟会议的气氛比真实会议还是要轻松不少，但上场人员仍然会感受到一定的焦虑。"焦虑其实就是口译译员的面子受到威胁时的心理反应。如果威胁过小，译员可能会松懈，如果威胁过大，译员可能会害怕，这些都是负面焦虑（debilitating anxiety）"（李游子，2007：70）。一般"听录音——被录音——放录音"的教学中，只有少数同学的录音会被播放和点评，抽中的概率低、随机性高，所以有的同学会心存侥幸，甚至可能不开口，这就是过度放松的表现。而一旦把自己定位成译员，就无法逃避口译任务，自然会产生焦虑。如果译前准备充分、心中有底，现场的压力就会降低，从而减少负面焦虑。

第四节　会后反思

模拟会议结束后，如果课堂尚余时间，可以邀请现场观众进行点评。如果没有专心听会、勤作比较，就很难提出有建设性的意见，往往只能非常笼统地说译者表现好或不太好，这样参会的收获也会非常有限。不过，一场会议的时长一般在15—20分钟，其间会出现大量的各式各样的问题，不可能一一罗列，也没有必要。点评者需要从内容、语流、公共演说等不同方面，提纲挈领地举出最有代表性的实例。这对学生来说要求比较高，因此在一两位同学点评之后，教师可以做总结。

模拟会议的现场架设了摄像机，讲者和译员回去之后需要复盘总结，可以发现许多现场根本没有注意到的东西，包括音量、语速、肢体语言、眼神交流、口误、口头禅等下意识的问题。如能在译后做复盘转写工作（见附录），就能更为客观翔实地总结自己的口译表现，找出常见问题并形成规律性的认识。

在模拟会议中，观众一般不愿直接指出译员过失，因此自评才是最重要的（Riccardi, 2002: 116-117）。录像为自评创造了机会，让译员从讲者意图和观众需求的角度重新分析原文内容，辨析自己译文的不足。例如，模拟会议的讲话原文并不是许多口译教材中的理想原文，存在许多重复、停顿、停顿填充词（pause filler, 如：那个、嗯、uh、I mean）、口误、用词不当、逻辑混乱等问题。译员不必逐一译出，可以根据交际需求适当压缩和改进原文，口译时间一般是原话长度的三分之二到四分之三（Jones, 1997: 40），否则会议冗长导致与会者疲劳，反而不利于信息传达。

组织模拟会议需要较多的时间和精力，如果课时量不允许，或者缺乏相应的软硬件条件，这一环节并不是必须的。课堂和小组练习中也可以采取有备口译的形式，只要选材难度适当、译前准备充分（见第二章），一定程度上也能起到模拟会议的效果。

参考文献

Jones R. Conference Interpreting Explained [M]. Manchester: St. Jerome Publishing, 1997.

Riccardi A. Evaluation in Interpretation: Macrocriteria and Microcriteria [M]//Hung E. Teaching Translation and Interpreting 4: Building Bridges. Amsterdam/Philadelphia: John Benjamins Publishing Company, 2002: 115-126.

李游子. 口译学习指标和测试评估[J]. 外语研究, 2007(2): 69-70.

专项练习

要求：根据大会主题和具体话题，分小组筹办一次模拟会议，完成会前准备、课堂模拟和会后反思这三个步骤。

1. 会议主题：线上教育

Glossary:	
得克萨斯州凯蒂市七湖中学：Seven Lakes High School in Katy, Texas	school board：校董事会
莱西·摩尔：Lacey Moore	online learning：线上教育
远程教育：distance learning/education	Canvas：美国知名K12远程教育平台
superintendent：校监	bell schedule：在校作息时间表，上下课铃声

A：大家好，今天很荣幸邀请到德克萨斯州凯蒂市七湖中学英语老师莱西·摩尔。随着互联网技术的发展，我们的教育系统已经转向远程教育，这在教育界是一个相当大的转变。大多数人在互联网搜索引擎上寻找有关远程教育的信息和咨询。那请问您是什么时候开始使用远程教育，在此之前做了哪些工作呢？

B：We began distance learning on Monday, March 23rd, 2020 in my district. Preparation for distance learning was a bit overwhelming and stressful in the ten or so days leading up to March 23rd. It consisted mostly of emails from everyone from the superintendent of the district, to the school board, parents of my students, and the students themselves. We, as teachers, had to quickly get ourselves acquainted with an online learning platform known as Canvas. But I had never used it to teach my course.

A：在一些情况下，由于时空的区隔，教师只能进行线上教学，而许多老师缺乏线上教学经验，对线上教学平台不熟悉，就会出现各种各样的问题和挑战。有些老师甚至认为线上授课比解决十道数学难题都要难。还有很多教师遇到了电脑与网络方面的问题。那么请问您在这方面遇到的最大困难是什么？

B：The biggest obstacle for me is not being there, in person, to help my students with special needs. The emails of panic from these students and their parents have been flooding in, because an online approach to learning does not necessarily meet specific needs that I would be able to address if they were sitting in my classroom. I have had Zoom video conferences with some of them to try to help accommodate and further specify instructions, which has seemed to help, but it has placed an added stress on the teachers and students.

A：虽然线上教育给老师带来了一些挑战，但它为我们提供了教育教学的新思路、新方法。此外，线上教育中教师和学生可以自己设定学习进度，而且还可以根据每个人的日程安排灵活地安排学习时间。那么在您看来，线上教育还有哪些优点呢？

B：I think a positive impact is that it has taught everyone the importance of patience and time management. Without a bell schedule prompting students from one class to the next, they have had to learn to manage their classes and responsibilities on their own, which can only benefit them in the future. It has also taught my students the value of physically being in a class with their peers and their teachers.

A：刚刚谈了这么多，但是我们都知道凡事有利就有弊，线上教育也不例外。而且许多人对此存有争议，认为线上教育缺乏监督，学生很容易被手机和其他电子设备转移注意力，这种教学方法不适用于缺乏自制力的学生。那您能说说线上教育有什么缺点吗？

B：I am also aware that there are going to be some negative impacts, as well. The biggest one being that students may not be fully prepared next year when they start the next level in their courses. Especially in a course like math, for instance, where they learn new skills and strategies daily that carry over into the next week, month, and even years. The students who didn't grasp the concepts being taught in distance learning are going to struggle to catch up in the years to come and their teachers are going to have to adapt and adjust accordingly.

A：好的，非常感谢莱西·摩尔老师和我们分享有关线上教育的经历。隔着屏幕，缺少了老师与学生之间的通畅的交流，缺少了重要的互动，缺少了言语的关注，缺少了教育的温度。

B：Indeed. Anyway, it does break the limit of time and space and has therefore redefined "school", which in turn shall promote education equity. We won't see it as a substitute of face-to-face education, but a complement.

2. 会议主题：垃圾分类

Glossary:	
垃圾分类：garbage/waste sorting/classification	表情包：memes
拾荒者：scavenger	waste to energy：转废为能
waste-free city：无废城市	Ministry of Housing and Urban-Rural Development of the People's Republic of China：中华人民共和国住房和城乡建设部
prefecture-level city：地级市	外卖餐盒：takeout containers and bags
押金，德国的空瓶回收押金：Pfand	

A："垃圾分类"这个词登上了几次新闻头条，在网络上掀起了一股表情包的浪潮。《经济学人》指出，上海每年的垃圾生产量达到了900万吨，超过了伦敦。在缺少有效回收机制的情况下，单靠原来的拾荒者捡垃圾和旧物回收站是无法承受如此庞大的垃圾生产量的。

B：China is building hundreds of "waste to energy" plants and establishing a "waste-free city" scheme. As far back as 2000, the Ministry of Housing and Urban-Rural Development of the People's Republic of China designated eight prefecture-level cities, including Shanghai, to pilot "garbage sorting" programs. Shanghai's new program is the most visible and extensive recycling initiative ever attempted in China. Importantly, the system in Shanghai is uniquely public and punitive.

A：但是，很多人都觉得在合适的时间把垃圾丢到它们该去的地方实在是太难了。微博有人发文称，有些人开始找人"代收垃圾"，帮他们解决这件事。喝不完的奶茶是湿垃圾，纸杯是干垃圾，吸管和包装是塑料……垃圾分类使我戒掉奶茶。

B: People find it counter-intuitive that fish bones belong to "kitchen waste", while ribs belong to "other waste". And corncob should go into "other waste" instead of "kitchen waste", because it doesn't decompose.

A: 让我们再来看看外卖行业的垃圾问题。在中国，外卖应用发展迅猛，外卖餐盒泛滥成灾。中国的回收系统却没有跟上脚步，整个系统并不完善。研究人员和回收人员表示，大部分塑料最终会被丢弃、掩埋或与其他垃圾一起焚烧。

B: Scientists estimate that the online takeout business in China was responsible for 1.6 million tons of packaging waste in 2017, a nine-fold jump from two years before. That includes 1.2 million tons of plastic containers, 175,000 tons of disposable chopsticks, 164,000 tons of plastic bags and 44,000 tons of plastic spoons.

A: 我们也可以向德国学习经验，德国是废弃物循环利用的领先者。德国的回收系统在世界排名第一，其废弃物分类十分细致。在德国，还有所谓的押金，占瓶装饮料价格的一定比例，如果将瓶子送回经过认证的商店，即可退还押金。

B: The garbage-sorting policy could bring down the cost of reusing domestic waste significantly, as consumers will separate off plastics from dirty kitchen waste and rinse off food containers before throwing them in the trash. The policy is a lesson to other developing countries that the first step in creating a modern waste management system is to educate the public and foster a sense that recycling is a civic responsibility.

3. 会议主题：基因编辑

Glossary:	
gene editing/genome editing：基因编辑	genetic mutation：基因突变
亨廷顿氏病：Huntington's disease/HD	CCR5基因：CCR5 gene
西尼罗河病毒：West Nile virus	

主持人: Gene editing was only a term several years back but now the technology is at full swing with more scientific research and experiments being done in various countries. Today we have with us two renowned experts from China and the US to share with us their thinking on this matter from technological, safety and ethical perspectives.

A: Inherent diseases pass on from parental genes to their offspring. With the usage of genetic engineering, scientists can prevent the flow of these diseases to the embryo. As we know, genetic mutation is being held responsible for many diseases and syndromes; gene editing could play a crucial role in completely eradicating some diseases. Getting rid of these diseases could be a huge milestone in the history of medical science.

B：但是，科学家们要想完全搞清楚与各种疾病相关的基因还有很长的路要走，即使基因编辑是一项安全高效的技术，而且所有人都选择使用这项技术，它还是无法消除遗传疾病。比如，即便是已经被研究得相当透彻的亨廷顿氏病，要攻克起来都没有那么容易，因为导致这种疾病的原因在于一段特定基因序列的重复；重复越多，症状就越严重，这种重复会随着代代相传而增加，因此，想要攻克这种疾病并不容易。理想是很美好的，但也就仅限如此了。

A: The future of a nation lies in the hands of its next generation. With genetic screening prior to birth, many children could be saved from the harsh realities of inborn diseases that continue to affect their life after birth. If it can be screened, it can also be cured at the earliest. This can also contribute towards making the future of the nation healthier and well developed. Some diseases that hamper the development of a child can also be cured if genetic engineering is allowed to be made a part of medical practice in our nation. Birth defects could be cured and perhaps one day no one will be born handicapped. Genetic engineering can be a real bliss if used in the correct way.

B：但是，改变基因不一定是在创造美好未来。无论我们能多么精确地编辑基因，有些东西也不是我们能一编了之的，更别提安全性了。很少有功能单一的基因。编辑数千种基因会让身体陷入难以预料的境地。比如说，删掉CCR5基因可以让人们免疫艾滋病病毒，但也让他们死于西尼罗河病毒的风险高上13倍。通过基因编辑剔除某种疾病有可能会增加另一种疾病的患病风险，从而产生适得其反的效果。

A: It is true that the use of gene editing techniques without any scruples may have unintended consequences. But if carefully studied and experimented, gene editing technology can be used to cure off cell borne diseases and disorders. It takes time but gene editing will get mature and widely applied.

B：即便基因编辑技术已完全成熟到风险可控，一旦这项技术被推广，那么就会带来严重的社会问题：想变漂亮的、变聪明的人，都能改变自己或者后代的基因，甚至像电影里演的那样，淘汰所谓弱势基因，实现基因定制。而这背后带来的社会问题将无法估量。我们的世界已经注定要被种族主义、种族差异、对另一人种的不宽容、对美的既定规则以及我们评判他人的一切所束缚。

第十五章
技术驱动下的口译学习与口译行业

2022年12月,由美国人工智能实验室OpenAI发布的对话式大型语言模型ChatGPT引起了国内外大量媒体的关注。仅仅几天时间,其用户数量突破百万,注册用户数量激增更是导致服务器一度过载。ChatGPT全名为"Chat Generative Pre-trained Transformer",是人工智能技术驱动的自然语言处理工具。它从问世到全球爆火的速度之快,业界甚至还没有找到合适的中文译名。据介绍,它能够通过学习和理解人类的语言来进行对话,还能根据聊天的上下文进行互动,真正像人类一样来聊天交流,甚至能完成撰写邮件、视频脚本、文案、写论文、翻译等任务。但是,人们在乐此不疲地与ChatGPT交流的同时,也不禁担忧:"人工智能真的会取代人类吗?"这也是翻译行业一直以来争论不休的话题。

随着各类语料库的建立和应用,以及AI技术和互联网技术的不断发展,翻译已不再囿于译员一人之智,翻译活动也不再局限于面对面的交流。面对不断发展的技术,与其纠结人类是否会被其取代,不如思考如何让技术成为人类的助力。对翻译行业而言,技术带来的便利数不胜数。借助各类现有的语料库和通过使用语料库技术建库,口译员可以更加全面、高效地整理行业词汇,更好地完成译前准备。语音识别、人工智能等技术红利也不断推动着口译行业的发展。依靠Zoom、Lark、Webex、Teams等各类远程会议软件,译员通过网络为与会者提供的远程口译服务,让来自世界各地、说着不同语言的行业精英可以实现真正的无缝交流。这一章,我们将从学习者的视角出发,对前沿的技术在翻译学习和翻译行业中的应用进行初步介绍。

第一节 借助语料库的译前准备

什么是语料库?语料库(Corpus),就是把日常对话的语句、文学作品、报刊杂志和学术文章上出现过的语句段落等语言材料整理在一起形成的一个集合,以便从事科学研究的时候能够从中取材或者得到数据佐证。而现代的语料库可以简单地理解为对真实出现过的口头或书面语言材料,甚至是多媒体材料的一种系统性整理。至于如何整理呢?首先,必须是以计算机为载体,即数据为数字形式。其次,材料须通过系统性的加工。语料库按用途可以分为通用语料库和专用语料库,按时效性可以分为共时语料库和历时语料库,按语体可以分为书面语料库和口语语料库,按语种可以分为单语语料库、双语语料库和多语种语料库,按是否母语可以分为母语语料库和外语学习者语料库,按是否标注可以分为生语语料库和熟语语料库。语料库建设者按一定的规模、领域、体裁、时代、语体和语种收集建立语料库,借助人工或机器对语料的词性、句法、语义等进行标注和编码,将加工后的语料用于词典编纂、机器翻译等领域。

在口译学习中,语料库的辅助功能不容忽视。它能够客观地揭示词汇、搭配、短语以及句型在语言实际使用中的频度。借助大型平行语料库或口译语料库,学生能够熟练掌握高频语言单位的翻译策略,为口译打好坚实的语言基础。其次,语料库对会议发言、法庭审判、商务洽谈、学术报告等口译场景中的语篇特征进行了汇总,有利于口译学习者做到有的放矢,迅速适应不同的翻译场景。著名翻译学府美国加州蒙特雷大学的陈瑞清教授(Wallace Chen)在多场讲座中专门介绍了如何利用语料库辅助口译工作。他指出,口译的前中后阶段皆涉及大量文字,因此很适合使用语料库作为辅助工具,随时为译者提供丰富的语料参考。从译前准备词汇及积累知识、译中动态查询,一直到译后的文字整理工作,语料库都扮演关键作用,对口译质量和提升译者灵活应变能力都至关重要。

下面,我们主要谈一谈语料库技术如何有助于提升译前准备的效率。徐然(2018)通过对国际口译员协会(AIIC)会员准备、使用及管理术语的情况进行了调查,发现大多数口译员认为专业性会议难度大,需要通篇阅读会议资料、人工标注、手工提取相关术语和表达,使用word文档来进行术语管理。如果组织方不提供任何材料,口译员就得全凭自行搜索、搜集相关资料,耗时耗力。相对这种传统模式,借助语料库可以更加高效地完成译前准备中较为重要的环节——术语表的生成。它包括两个关键步骤,即建库和检索。第一,建立语料库,提取专业术语,并通过工具和人工辅助的方式生成双语术语表。第二,通过搜索工具激活并建立针对某一场具体会议的术语表。这类方法主要借助的是以Sketch Engine为代表的具有网络"爬虫"功能、自动术语提取功能和语料检索功能的语料处理软件完成。其他一些常用的语料库建库软件还包括单语语料库分析研究工具AntConC(免费,可以直接在官网下载)、语料对齐工具Tmxmall、Abbyy Aligner和语料检索工具WordsSmith、CUC_ParaConc等,一些含有术语检索和整理的计算机辅助翻译软件如Trados也可以在译前准备过程中使用。

根据一些职业译员在使用过程中的反馈,语料库和术语管理能够大大提升译前准备的效率,但不可否认这种方式也存在弊端。例如,几秒之内抓取和生成的词汇表还需要人工后期整理,使用语料库技术也存在一定的技术门槛。但是作为口译学习者,我们需要了解的是,这种随着新技术应运而生的译前准备模式受到越来越多口译学习者和从业人员的关注,代表着一种适应当今信息时代发展的新模式,已成为当前讨论的热点话题之一。

第二节 远程口译

1976年,联合国教科文组织进行了首次实验证明远程口译在技术上的可行性。随着互联网技术的发展,尤其自2019年底以来,远程口译已逐渐成为口译行业中不可分割的一个部分。按口译借助的媒介划分,远程口译大致可以分为电话口译(OPI: Over the Phone Interpreting)和视频口译(VRI: Video Remote Interpreting)。以美国最大的远程口译服务公司为例,译员可以通过电话、视频的方式为客户提供医疗问诊、警局问询、心理干预、社区服务等场景下的口译服务,这类口译服务主要以交替传译的方式进行,可以理解为联络口译的一种。

远程口译在多语种国家的服务应用十分广泛。译员通过接收声音或视频等为身处不同区域或城市的客户提供口译服务。由于不受物理空间的限制,译员所接触的口译主题和内容差异较大。上一秒可能是在为病人解释如何进行阑尾切除手术,下一秒可能就是在帮助客户申请银行账户。由于不需要雇佣固定的职业译员,这类口译服务大大节约了使用者的成本,也使译员能够集中有限的时间和精力完成多项口译服务。

在2022年北京冬奥会和冬残奥会期间,北京冬奥组委将多语言呼叫中心设在北京外国语大学,依托北京多语言服务中心(见图15-1),为赛事提供第三方语言服务。据报道,该中心从2022年1月23日开始运行,为北京冬奥会提供英、法、俄等21个语种的三方通话翻译服务,其中,7个语种24小时值守,14个语种18小时值守。这是远程口译新型语言服务在冬奥会历史上的首次应用,提供的语言服务市场和语种也为历届冬奥会之最。冬奥会多语言呼叫中心在保障冬奥语言翻译需求的同时,还为110、120、12345和首都机场、大兴机场等公共服务热线提供英、法、德、俄、西、日、韩、阿等多语种服务工作,辅助冬奥期间城市基础设施顺畅运行。

图15-1　北京多语言服务中心[①]

---

① 图片来自《北外团委》公众号。

除了服务对象为个体的电话和视频口译,还有一种应用较为广泛的远程口译模式为远程同传(RSI: Remote Simultaneous Interpreting),或线上同传(On-line Simultaneous Interpreting),这类口译的服务对象为正式会议、论坛、研讨会等。远程交传所需要的技术支持较为简单,直接使用微信视频或腾讯会议等软件就能实现。而远程同传由于讲话人和译员需要同时说话,牵涉到音频、视频的同步传输问题,往往需要借助专业的远程口译服务平台。

目前口译市场上使用较多的平台还有Zoom、Kudo、Lark等。美国蒙特雷大学Barry Slaughter Olsen教授2020年受邀为香港浸会大学所作的演讲中提到,2019年时,他所供职的KUDO公司之前注册的译员约有3 000人,而如今已经涨到7 000人。每周组织的会议也从几十场增加到每周约500场。增长速度之快令人咋舌。中国翻译行业也于2018年推出了"译直播"远程口译平台。据该平台负责人叶鸿斌介绍,该公司所使用的远程同传系统基于互联网及云计算技术而开发。译员通过专属后台,远程观看现场直播或选择同传接力频道以实现远程同传,而观众亦可通过链接、扫码的方式同步收看现场直播,并根据需求选择对应语言频道。

远程同传也包含多种不同的具体模式。一种模式是不设线下会场,包括主办方、译员、讲话人、听众在内的所有人都使用线上平台进行沟通,这就要求参会人员尤其是翻译服务提供人员对软件操作十分熟练,听众也需要提前训练如何顺利地切换收音频道。还有一种模式是主办方设有线下会场,国内的讲话人和大部分听众在线下会场,而译员或部分无法到场的讲话人则通过远程会议口译软件与其他人保持沟通。这种模式对技术支持和网络条件的要求都很高,往往需要专业的翻译公司提前布置会场线路,进行网络测试。

近年来,编者就曾多次提供远程同传服务。会议设备均由专业翻译公司提供,由其提前设置好Zoom会议平台的译员传译界面(如图15-2),屏幕左侧是发言人展示的PPT内容,右

图15-2　Zoom会议平台的译员界面

侧为发言人的视频图像。译员主要留意屏幕右下方的"传译频道"是否为输出语种。由于会议日程较为紧凑（8:00—18:00）、发言人较多，主办方安排由三位译员共同配合完成口译，译员每20分钟左右轮换一次。该会议的主会场设在线下，由主持人、部分中方发言人和中方听众参与。

与其他线上线下融合的口译模式不同，该会场中的同传工作室是位于主会场斜对面的另一间会议室。因此，虽然译员和线下会场的物理距离不远，但其实仍然通过远程的方式进行传译。线下会场通过功放而不是耳机收听译员的中文译文，该会场的发言人通过Zoom会议软件进行发言。译员通过两台专用电脑轮流进行口译。在换手时，上一位译员会运用眼神或手势提示要接手的译员，并提醒对方注意输出语言的频道。

由于部分中方讲话人和全部外方讲话人、三位同传译员都不在线下会场，因此在会议开始之前，主办方专门利用两个半天的时间对网络和系统应用进行了测试。尽管如此，在会议过程中不可避免还是会出现译员偶尔忘记点击切换输出频道，讲话人由于对输入频道切换不熟练造成无法接收现场声音等小问题。比较有趣的是，在出现这些技术问题时，各方发言人开始进入了"自由发言"模式，译员也在"同传""交传"和"讲解"不同角色之间进行转换。这也是远程口译中非常常见的现象，对译员的临场应变能力有着巨大的考验。当线下会场的中方负责人用英文直接向发言人解释时，译员尤其不能大意，而是要时刻保持信息的输入和跟踪，做好准备在双方回到各自的语言频道进行交流时，将各方的对话进行翻译。此外，译员偶尔还要担任"临时技术顾问"的角色，用对方熟悉的语言耐心引导讲话人调整好设备，直到重新找回发言节奏。

对翻译行业而言，远程口译是一种较为便利的形式，为主办方节约了人力物力成本，也使译员不必浪费大量的时间和精力往返于各个会场之间。大多数译员甚至只要拥有一台能够使用互联网的电脑和安静的办公环境，就能在自己家里完成一整天的远程口译工作。但是远程口译中，译员也需要适应不同的会议平台，面临着网络问题导致发言断断续续、和搭档换手、沟通困难等问题。这都需要译员提前做好充分的准备，保障硬件条件，在会议开始前主动与主办方联系进行调试，并与搭档提前协商好信息沟通渠道和换手节奏。

第三节　语音识别、人工智能与口译行业

2023年年初，中国科幻电影《流浪地球2》刚上映就广受大众欢迎。影片中，来自俄罗斯的"诺夫"与来自中国的"王老师"通过翻译机实现面对面对话的场景相信让很多人印象深刻。在诺夫说着俄语的同时，翻译机将对应的中文说出，而王老师则根据听到的中文马上做出回应，翻译机再将其同步译为俄语。俩人你一言我一语，甚至互相调侃。

其实，这样的翻译技术在现实中早已出现。2018年4月8日，"博鳌亚洲论坛2018年年会"在海南博鳌开幕。与往届不同，科大讯飞作为科技企业的代表也应邀出席，并运用自身擅长的语音和人工智能技术"讯飞翻译机2.0"为会议提供了全方位的语言翻译服务。据

介绍,这款翻译机器支持中文到英、日、韩、法、西等20国语言的即时互译,也就是说,在博鳌论坛这样的国际性高端会议中,来自其他国家的与会代表可以借助这一技术与中国代表实现无缝交流。根据王华树、杨承淑(2019)的调查,同年7月在RISE科技峰会(亚洲最大的科技峰会)上,该类技术再次大展拳脚。2019年7月百度团队声明其研发的"度同传"(DuTongChuan)的汉译英准确率达到85.71%,英译汉准确率达到86.36%,可基本与经验丰富的人类同传译员媲美。

语音识别是一门涉及仿生学、语音学、语言学、信息理论、模式识别理论和神经生物学等的综合性学科。语音识别技术就是让机器通过识别和翻译把语音信号转变为相应的文本或指令的基础,并逐渐成为信息技术中人机交互的关键技术。国内外翻译技术厂商均将机器翻译作为AI技术的入口,推出形式各异的翻译机和App。借助语音识别和AI技术,许多科技公司都推出了自己主打的翻译软件和多模态人机互动终端,如腾讯公司开发的"腾讯翻译君"、科大讯飞公司推出的翻译机器等。以腾讯翻译君为例,用户首先选择互译语言为"中-英",再点击相应的语音输入按钮。当你用普通话说完:"早上好,欢迎来到北京",翻译软件马上就会将其译出"Good Morning, welcome to Beijing"。通过技术支持,这类软件或机器不仅能够翻译日常交流的语言,还能迅速将"有朋在远方来,不亦乐乎"等文言文翻译为"It's a pleasure to have friends coming from afar"。这主要是基于强大的语音转换、信息检索和信息提取功能。此外,如果你长期使用一款翻译软件,它还能通过AI技术学习你的语言习惯,将一些译文中的词汇调整为你常用的词汇,并不断改进句式。

无论是语音识别还是AI,其实都代表着一种技术发展的趋势,标志着一个新的翻译时代的到来。除了了解最新的技术,我们更应当深思技术变革对口译学习者、口译行业带来的影响。根据王华树、杨承淑(2019)的研究,技术的发展引发了口译服务模式的改变、提升了口译服务的效率,也对口译员的能力发展提出了新要求。技术的数字化和自动化发展正在创造新的工作模式。机器口译开辟了全新的口译模式和更多的口译场景。任文(2018)也指出,在口译技术的驱动下,出现了"同交传"或"交同传"的混合模式,讲话者的声音被识别后以文字形式同步显示在屏幕上,译员从"听译"为主变成"听译"与"视译"的融合。计算机辅助口译更是为译员提供了强有力的解决方案,利用各种搜索技术和工具,可以快速获取有效信息,直接提升口译效率。

在人工智能飞速发展的冲击下,社会上有一些关于外语和翻译学习必要性的担忧。实际上,日新月异的AI技术可能取代任何工种。如果语言只是被当作一项工具,可能会被机器代替,但它创造和表达思想的功能是无法替代的。我们不妨换个角度来看待技术对口译行业的影响。相比于其他形式的语言交流,口译本身对技术的要求就比较高,需要使用耳机、话筒、音像设备甚至是同传箱,因此技术的介入从来不是一个陌生的话题。技术为整个行业注入了强大的活力,也贯穿于口译的全过程,从借助语料库提升译前准备的效率,到通过远程口译实现跨地域的交流,再到译后的术语整理、将语音材料导入机器以促进机器自主学习。对学习者而言，口译能力不再只包括双语能力、口译技巧和行业知识，还应当包含口译技术能力。在日常的学习中，面对海量的语料，译者应当提升自己的"搜商"，即检索信息的能力，从而提高准备效率、提升口译质量。白阳明（2023）在谈到人工智能时代的翻译学习时提到，学生在翻译时应避免想当然，尤其是在汉译英时，不要基于"创造"，要学会首先找出目前已被广泛接受的译文，再结合语境优化个人翻译。这对于口译的译前准备工作同样适用。与其抗拒"机翻"，不如紧跟时代步伐，发挥好机器的辅助作用，让技术帮助我们更好地管理口译术语。不少学者也提出，在信息化时代，AI技术助力口译的模式已经形成互动融合与加速转换的趋势，影响将会越来越深远。口译学习者应居安思危，客观、理性地看待技术的发展，关注技术所带来的变革和挑战，抓住新的机遇，保持与时俱进。

参考文献

白阳明. 探索人工智能时代翻译技术赋能翻译教学策略［EB/OL］.（2023-01-06）. http://m.gmw.cn/baijia/2023-01/06/36284292.html.

任文. 新时代语境下翻译人才培养模式再探究：问题与出路［J］. 当代外语研究，2018(6)：92-98.

王华树，杨承淑. 人工时代的口译技术发展：概念、影响与趋势［J］. 中国翻译，2019(6)：69-79.

徐然. 基于语料库技术的口译译前准备模式构建［J］. 中国翻译，2018(3)：53-59.

专项练习

模拟会议口译练习：请以"2050双碳目标的实现策略"为主题，组织一场线上召开的国际研讨会。具体任务：

（1）明确角色和分工：小组成员分为中方讲话人（1—2人）、外方讲话人（1—2人）、译员（1—2人）、技术支持人员、主持人等角色。

（2）主持人组织其他成员设计会议流程，大致包含主旨发言（可设计多个）和问答两个环节，每个环节的具体持续时间可商量后决定。

（3）讲话人按主题准备讲话稿（可准备PPT），轮流进行发言，每人发言时长不超过10分钟。

（4）译员提前使用Sketch Engine等软件建立与会议主题相关的语料库，熟悉专业词汇。

（5）技术支持人员协助各方通过Zoom、腾讯会议等软件设置好在线会议平台，提前调试好设备和软件。

（6）译员（若多个译员可提前协商好分工）使用远程会议软件对讲话人的发言进行交传。会议期间技术人员做好数据的记录和收集，以便练习完成之后进行反思和评价。

参考答案

第一章

专项练习

英汉段落1：跳舞的健康益处

人们想要体验快乐的时候就会跳舞。世界各地的人听到音乐都会想跳舞。但人们最近才发现，跳舞不仅能让我们感到开心，还有益于健康。

和其他运动一样，跳舞刺激荷尔蒙分泌，比如多巴胺，它会让我们感到轻松快乐，减轻焦虑不安。

跳舞也是一种社交活动，这也是它让我们感到快乐的另一个原因。在一项研究中，实验对象被分成两组，一组在家里看视频跳舞，另一组则在工作室和一群人共舞。对比后发现，那些和他人一起跳舞的实验对象感到更加快乐。

英汉段落2：气候变化

证据无处不在：阿根廷的森林大火、孟加拉国的大洪水、西班牙的干旱。气候变化的影响已经显现，而且会越来越严重。根据一份历史性的联合国报告，这些影响不仅比以往所知的更严重，而且有些可能已经不可逆转。政府间气候变化专门委员会（可以源语重复，直接译成IPCC）今天的报告记录了人类的种种苦难，也是对气候变化领导不力的谴责。该报告以事实为依据，揭示了人类和地球如何受到气候变化的重创。来自60多个国家的200多名科学家组成了联合国小组，共同提出了这份报告。它强调地球变暖正以许多国家无法应对的速度和强度造成损害，而减少造成气候变化的污染的速度还不够快。

英汉段落3：热饮与癌症

下次你给自己沏一杯热茶或咖啡时，可能会等它凉一些再喝。研究人员表示，这可以帮助你避免某些癌症。

事实上，联合国癌症研究机构已将热饮、铅、汽油和废气列为"可能致癌的物质"。换句话说，它们都可能致癌。

国际癌症研究机构（可以源语重复，直接译成IARC）的研究人员发现，有证据表明，65度以上的饮料可能会导致食道癌。研究人员还考察了其他研究的结果。这些研究是在伊朗、中国和南美洲进行的，人们喝的茶和咖啡通常都在70摄氏度或以上。

不过，这一发现对喝咖啡的人来说是个好消息。1991年，世界卫生组织将咖啡列为"可能致癌的物质"。此后,世界卫生组织官员改变了观点,认为饮料的温度相比饮料本身是更大的风险因素。

汉英段落1: Benefits of cycling

Cycling is a very good sport, which exercises the body and brings enormous fun. First, as an aerobic exercise, it burns fat, makes you sweat, and trains the muscles of the whole body, including your legs, back and shoulders. Second, you feel happy and relaxed when you enjoy the scenery along the road. Stress leads to multiple diseases, such as anxiety, depression, diabetes, hypertension, digestive and cardiovascular diseases, etc. In addition, cycling improves your brain functions, for the rider needs to stay focused, which is also a kind of exercise for the brain.

汉英段落2: Artificial intelligence

Given the right data, machines are going to outperform humans. A teacher might read 10,000 essays over a 40-year career. An ophthalmologist might see 50,000 eyes. A machine can read millions of essays or see millions of eyes within minutes. We have no chance of competing against machines on frequent, high-volume tasks.

But there are things we can do that machines can't do. Where machines have made very little progress is in tackling novel situations. They can't handle things they haven't seen many times before. The fundamental limitations of machine learning is that it needs to learn from large volumes of past data. Humans don't. We have the ability to connect seemingly disparate threads to solve problems we've never seen before.

汉英段落3: Higher education and social mobility

In today's China, higher education is the basic premise for social mobility. In the information age in particular, knowledge is the main factor of individual development, which is highly relevant with higher education. Those who have received higher education have more opportunities to realize their own values and acquire abilities, thus moving up the social ladder. People from the lower class could work hard to pan out in fair selection and improve their social, economic and political status. There is no wonder that Chinese people yearn for quality education.

第二章

专项练习

Text 1: Establishing positions and setting conditions

P: 我们开始吧。我已阅读了您的提案,了解到您正在寻找各种风格的无品牌服装。

R: That's right.

P: 您主要看的是短袖T恤、背心、连帽衫、拉链衫和长袖T恤，对吧？

R: Correct.

P: 好的。那么第一个问题是：您想要订购多少？

R: Well, we're a reseller, so we rebrand the clothing and sell it to retailers. I suggest we start small and scale up later. We are thinking of starting with around 500 to 1500 units per SKU (stock keeping unit), with more in popular sizes and colors.

P: 那是每月，还是？

R: We'd prefer to keep things flexible to begin with.

P: 能再具体些吗？我不反对灵活性，但物流需要一定的前期规划。

R: Of course! Let me ask you something: what's the situation regarding production and delivery? How long does it take you to process orders?

P: 这不固定，但大约是两周左右。大额订单可能需要更长时间。

R: That's fine. So here's our situation: we don't have a lot of warehousing space. That means we can't commit to a fixed schedule for deliveries. Instead, we'll have to make orders once our stock level is low enough and we have the space.

P: 嗯……明白。但您要明确一件事：如果我们无法提前确定您的订货计划，将无法提供最低价格。

R: I understand.

P: 对于每个产品类别，例如短袖T恤，您需要多少种尺寸和颜色？

R: We need all the common sizes, from XS (extra small) to XXL (double XL), each in 16 colors. And if we're ordering around 100,000 units at one time, what kind of per-unit pricing can you offer?

P: 这取决于您是否可以承诺定期订货。假设您订期不确定，T恤和背心每件最低6美元，连帽衫和拉链衫最低15美元。

R: If we need higher volumes, would you be able to go lower?

P: 有可能，但定期货单对我们来说更重要。如果您可以保证每月的最低订购量，我们单价可降至5.5和14美元。

R: If we commit to a minimum volume over a six-month period, but with a flexible delivery schedule, could you offer us the same price?

P: 只要提前限定交付时间，应该是可以的。

Text 2: Resolving disagreements and setting the deal

R: Let's work out the details about delivery and scheduling.

P: 如果想要我们提供最低报价，就要保证每月交付，我们可以接受您根据货仓空间对订购数额进行一定程度的调整。

R: I think that's not going to work for us. Flexibility is essential for us; our whole model is based on just-in-time logistics, so there's no way around us.

P: 好吧，但在这种情况下我们将无法为您提供更低报价。灵活交付没有任何问题，但如果没有定期订购承诺，我们将无法提供最惠价格。

R: I'm sorry to be blunt, but this seems a little short-sighted on your part. We're considering ordering millions of units each year. Flexible delivery doesn't mean that we won't make orders regularly. It just means that we need to control the timing and quantities.

P: 我完全理解，但也请您理解我们也要处理物流问题。如果不能知道订单的确切时间和规模，就会给我们带来成本，这是我们不愿意承担的。如果您需要灵活交付，那么应该愿意为此买单。很抱歉，我必须明确界限，这对我们来说的确太冒险了。

R: It seems like we've reached a bit of an impasse. Shall we take a five-minute break?

P: 好主意。

（5分钟后）

P: 好的，我已经和几个人谈过了，我有一个建议，希望能实现双赢的局面。

R: Sounds good. What's your idea?

P: 我们的问题是，如果您无法保持一定的单月订量，我们降低报价可能造成亏损，这显然不行。

R: Sure.

P: 所以我的提议是：我们签订一份年度合同，允许灵活交付，但每个季度设置最低订购额度。若您在季末未能完成订量要求，这其中产生的差价需要您来支付。

R: I like the basic idea, but earlier I suggested a six-month contract, and that sounds like a much better deal for us.

P: 您看，我想促成这桩买卖，但至少要保证一整年的订单，我们才能降低价格。或者还有一个方案：T恤和背心5.75美元，连帽衫和拉链衫14.50美元。这样您可以签订半年合同，但保证单季度最低交易量。

R: That's a good offer, I need to call my team to confirm, but I think this should be feasible.

P: 太棒了！

Text 3: Visiting the Temple of Heaven

A: Hello Mr. Bennett, welcome to Beijing. My name is Ai Linlin, deputy general manager of China Arts and Entertainment Group Ltd. (CAEG). I will be responsible for your stay here in China.

B: 您好，艾小姐。很抱歉我的航班因暴风雨天气延误，只好乘坐凌晨的班机，给您的安排造成麻烦，实在抱歉！

A: No worries, a safe arrival is the greatest gift!

B: 谢谢！这是我们第一次到访北京，工作之余我们也很期待近距离了解一下这座文明古城。

A: No problem, it's all included in our agenda. Indeed, Beijing is a magnificent place where lots of great men and heroes have emerged, and it's rich in cultural and historical traditions. You must have heard of famous attractions such as the Great Wall and the Forbidden City.

B: 是啊！北京有这么多风景名胜，恐怕我们短暂的行程无法完全顾及，咱们可以走走停停，劳逸结合，保证留有足够的体力来讨论项目。来此之前我一直向往参观北京的天坛，不知能否安排？

A: Don't worry, we will arrange the itinerary reasonably to ensure the balance of work and rest. You can stay at the Hilton Wangfujing in the city centre, which is 15 minutes' drive to our company.

B: 很好，请问今晚有什么安排吗？

A: At 7 o'clock tonight, our general manager will hold a banquet of welcome at the company's restaurant, where you can taste the authentic Beijing fruit wood roast duck. I'm sure you will like it.

B: 没问题，我们今晚见！

（三天后）

A: I had a great time discussing with you last night. Today we can take a day off and have a visit to the Temple of Heaven in Beijing. Last night, I spent quite some time reading and researching to prepare myself for the visit, so hope I can give you an adequate introduction to the place.

B: 谢谢您的精心准备，看来您已经对天坛相当熟悉了，有您这位"活词典"我们太高兴了！

A: Haha, I'm much flattered then! Do in Rome as the Romans do, let's enter from South Gate and walk along the axis, then we can have a panoramic view of the Temple of Heaven.

B: 中国古代建筑真是设计巧妙，确实令人佩服！

A: It is the largest existing sacrificial building complex from ancient China. In 1961, the Temple of Heaven was listed as one of the first batch of national key cultural relics protection units, and was listed as a World Heritage site in 1998.

B: 看来我们来对地方了！

A: Of course! The whole temple complex is surrounded by two concentric walls, forming the Chinese character "回". Ancient Chinese believed that the earth was square-shaped and the heaven was a circle. Such philosophy is well represented in the design of the Temple.

B：有趣。

A：The inner wall extends more than 4,000 meters in circumference and has six gates. The main buildings are concentrated within the inner cordon, with the Circular Mound Altar and the Imperial Vault of Heaven in the south, and the Hall of Prayer for Good Harvests in the north. There is a wall in the middle, which constitutes the north-south axis of the inner temple.

B：中国建筑讲究对称构图，这一点和西方建筑美学有相似之处。

A：Right. The Circular Mound Altar is the place where the emperor offer sacrifices to Heaven. The numbers of balusters and steps here are either number nine or multiples of nine. Count them if you have any doubt.

B：那为什么它们都是9的倍数呢？这在中国文化中有什么寓意？

A：Good question. Since 9 is the largest digit, it was regarded as the most sacred number, also the greatest *Yang* number in ancient China. Many emperors in the ancient China loved the number 9 as a symbol of supreme power, longevity, and eternal prosperity of their empire.

B：哇！我还是第一次知道这些。

A：Right, that's why Chinese emperors wore Nine-dragon Imperial Robes and ordered to construct Nine-dragon Walls in the imperial palaces.

B：中国古人的智慧着实令人钦佩，能将建筑美学和数字科学如此完美融合在一起。看来我还要多来几次中国，才能够更加深入地了解中国文化的博大精深。

Text 4: Seeing the doctor

N：早上好，先生。请问有什么可以帮您？

P：Good morning. I had an appointment with the doctor at 9 AM.

N：您之前在我们这里注册过吗？

P：Yes.

N：请出示您的注册卡。或者我查一下您的手机号码。

P：OK. My mobile number is 178-××××-3728（如记录不下来，可以请对方重复一遍）.

N：好的，我找到了您的详细信息。您上次来是在2021年8月。

P：That's right.

N：您可以先在这里支付诊费。

P：Sure. Here is my card.

N：请坐，这里有水和报纸，您可以自取。

P：Thank you.

（一刻钟后，助理叫病人名字，病人进入医生诊室。）

P: Good morning doctor.

D: 早上好。今天感觉怎么样?

P: I'm feeling OK. Thank you.

D: 您哪里不舒服?

P: I've come for a regular checkup. I don't have any symptoms now, but a few years back a doctor advised me to undergo a precautionary checkup once a year.

D: 我看到您的视神经比正常人粗,所以可能是由于这个原因他要求您每年复查。您今天也可以做两个测试:视野分析和OCT检查(光学相干断层扫描)。报告结果出来后,下午就可以再做分析。

P: Thank you, doctor.

(两个小时后,病人带着报告再次拜访医生)

D: 测试过程还顺利吧?

P: Yes. And because I've taken these tests in the past, I knew what was coming.

D: 您的报告完全没问题。这些报告多年来结果都显示正常,所以我建议您以后可以每两年做一次检查,无需每年复查。

P: OK.

D: 为缓解眼部疲劳,我推荐一种眼药水,一日2—3次。长时间不眨眼地盯着电脑屏幕看,我们的眼睛会发干发涩,这是眼部疲劳的常见原因。这种眼药水可以起到润滑作用。您还有其他问题吗?

P: Yes. I see a few thin, black, wavy structures floating in front of my eyes and they don't disappear even when I close my eyes. What are they? Are they harmful?

D: 这叫飞蚊症,多数人随着年龄的增长会发展到不同程度。它们没什么害处。

P: Thank you, doctor. Thanks for your time.

D: 别客气。

第三章

专项练习

1. 复述练习

略

2. 主旨口译

英汉段落1: 养猫

中国近年来宠物数量逐渐增加,人们越来越倾向于选择养猫。尽管在全世界狗狗仍然是更常见的宠物,比如在英国和美国,但猫咪最近已成为欧盟国家最受欢迎的宠物。

在中国和其他地方,猫咪也变成了一种社会现象,它们成了表情包和短视频的主角。许多爱猫人士在网上还自称"猫奴"和"吸猫者",公开表达他们的喜爱。

研究人员将养猫人数激增归因于中国城市的生活方式,一些专家还指出,猫咪受欢迎与年轻一代追求个性有关。许多城市居民生活繁忙,住宿面积相对较小,因此猫成了理想的伴侣——养猫很简单,不像狗那样需要太多关注和户外活动。

英汉段落2:自动驾驶汽车

自动驾驶预计会比人工驾驶汽车更加安全。但即使第一批自动驾驶汽车已出现在马路上,大部分人至少还要过15到20年才会彻底放弃亲自驾驶。与此同时,自动汽车将逐渐在某些领域替代传统驾驶。

上世纪90年代以来,企业就一直在给汽车添加半自动的功能。不出几年,汽车也许可以预判事故并对车舱作出调整,包括移动座椅、关窗、收起方向盘。

英汉段落3:注意力残留

由于时间限制和纷至沓来的干扰,你经常不得不放下手头的事情,去处理更紧急或更重要的事务。

每一个未完成的任务都牵动着你的一小部分注意力,这就是"注意力残留"。当你出现注意力残留时,你的大脑正在超负荷运转,既要想着眼下的任务,又要考虑之前做了一半的任务。

如果不得不停下手头的活儿,你可以将它的待办细节写下来,以减少注意力残留。这样做有助于摒除大脑的杂念。

汉英段落1:Gap year

The "gap year" is a popular trend in the Western world, allowing young people to embark on a cultural journey or a completely different lifestyle before college years or before starting their career. The students explore new environments by traveling, taking odd jobs for extra money, or volunteering at public welfare organizations. In the meantime, they also know themselves better, discover their true interests, develop their potential, and ultimately become better citizens.

汉英段落2:Unemployment rate in the United States

In 2023, the US unemployment rate hit a new low due to strong demand in the service sector, including industries such as leisure, entertainment, and dining. Besides, the participation of elderly workers has been slow to recover, resulting in job vacancies. However, we believe that the US unemployment rate will still rebound, just not as early as previously expected. The risk of a hard landing for the US economy has significantly decreased, but it has not been completely eliminated.

汉英段落3: Information technology revolution

As the world undergoes a rebalancing of power, globalization has reached a new turning point. While it was once driven by international trade and later by finance, it is now propelled by data. Major economies are riding the new tides of information technology revolution and accelerating the development and use of the Internet to promote economic and social development, and to maintain their international competitiveness.

篇章练习

Text 1: 英国对含糖饮料征税与儿童拔牙住院人数下降相关（节选）

含糖饮料约占一至三岁儿童的饮食中添加糖的30%，占青春期后期青少年饮食中添加糖的一半以上。在英格兰，近90%的幼儿拔牙都是由于蛀牙，这每年会造成约60 000人次缺课。

世界卫生组织建议对含糖饮料征税来减少人们对糖的摄入，目前已有50多个国家实施了这一措施。2016年3月，英国政府宣布征收软饮料行业税或"糖税"，旨在通过鼓励饮料制造商重新配制产品来减少人们糖的摄入量。该税法于2018年4月实施。

虽然含糖饮料与蛀牙之间的关系已经得到证实，但还没有研究使用真实数据来研究糖税与牙齿健康之间的关系。

为了解这一情况，研究人员分析了2014年1月至2020年2月英格兰18岁及以下儿童因蛀牙而入院拔牙的数据。

总体而言，与不征收软饮料税时相比，18岁及以下儿童每月每10万人中因蛀牙入院的绝对人数减少了3.7人。这相当于相对减少了12%。

以2020年英格兰近1 300万儿童的人口数量为基础，研究人员估计，软饮料税使得5 638人免于因蛀牙而入院治疗。4岁以下儿童和5—9岁儿童的入院率降幅最大，绝对降幅分别为每10万人中6.5人和3.3人。

Text 2: What keeps you up at night?

What keeps you up at night? Pondering deep questions? Excitement about a big trip? Or is it stress about unfinished work, an upcoming test, or a dreaded family gathering? For many people, this stress is temporary, as its cause is quickly resolved. But what if the very thing keeping you awake is the stress about losing sleep? This seemingly unsolvable loop is at the heart of insomnia, the world's most common sleep disorder.

Almost anything can cause the occasional restless night — a snoring partner, physical pain, or emotional distress. And extreme sleep deprivation like jetlag can throw off your biological clock, wreaking havoc on your sleep schedule. But in most cases, sleep deprivation is short-term. Eventually, exhaustion catches up with all of us. However, some long-term conditions like respiratory disorders, gastrointestinal problems, and many others can overpower fatigue. And as sleepless nights pile up, the bedroom can start to carry associations of restless nights wracked with anxiety. Come bedtime, insomniacs are stressed. So stressed their brains hijack the stress response system, increasing heart rate and blood pressure, and jolting the body into hyperarousal. In this condition, the brain is hunting for potential threats, making it impossible to ignore any slight discomfort or night-time noise. And when insomniacs finally do fall asleep, the quality of their rest is compromised.

Fortunately, there are ways to break the cycle of sleeplessness. Managing the stress that leads to hyperarousal is one of our best-understood treatments for insomnia and good sleep practices can help rebuild your relationship with bedtime. Make sure your bedroom is dark and comfortably cool to minimize "threats" during hyperarousal. Only use your bed for sleeping and if you're restless, leave the room and tire yourself out with relaxing activities like reading, meditating, or journaling. Regulate your metabolism by setting consistent resting and waking times to help orient your body's biological clock. This clock is also sensitive to light, so avoid bright lights at night to help tell your body that it's time for sleep. Our sleeping and waking cycle is a delicate balance, and one that's vital to maintain for our physical and mental wellbeing. For all these reasons, it's worth putting in some time and effort to sustain a stable bedtime routine, but try not to lose any sleep over it.

第四章

专项练习

1. 复述练习

略

2. 主旨口译

英汉段落1：城市公园

许多美国城市居民与大自然的接触只限于市政公园系统。例如，一半的纽约人表示自己唯一亲近自然环境的机会就是在城市公园。美国有超过一百万亩城市公园，与荒野地区、海岸线和其他自然景观一样,它们很容易受到气候变化的影响。城市公园常被称为被遗忘的或是隐形的基础设施,这一说法恰如其分。

英汉段落2:苦乐参半

"苦乐参半"的心境意味着什么?它意味着人们意识到生命既有快乐也有悲伤,既有光明也有黑暗,你所爱的人、事、物总有一天会消逝。我最初经历这种心态就是在听伤感音乐的时候。我对伤感音乐一直都有这种奇妙的反应;这使我觉得自己与那些能够体会音乐家所表达之哀愁的人心意相通。最开始,我以为只有我是这样,但开始研究之后,我意识到许多音乐学家都在研究这个现象,因为很长时间以来许多人不止对音乐有这种感受,对人生体验中的其他方面也是如此。

汉英段落1: New quality productive force

China is now pursuing high-quality development as opposed to high-speed, quantitative growth. Its pursuit has been boosted by "new quality productive forces" and new innovations. This is not a bolt from the blue; instead, it has been conditioned by internal and external factors. Internally, China is pursuing high-quality, innovation-driven development. From the 1980s to the 2010s, China's GDP grew at an average rate of more than 9 percent per year, even in double digits for some years. While the development of China's agricultural and industrial sectors has reached higher levels, the development of the service sector has opened the door to grander achievements. Externally, global tensions have motivated China to focus on high-quality development, particularly to become self-reliant in key sectors and attain strategic sovereignty.

汉英段落2: E-commerce

As Internet Technology is widely applied across the globe, E-commerce, which characterizes this "Internet Economy" era, offers great opportunities for our country, especially China's western regions. The development of E-commerce in these regions, however, is still in its infancy with many problems unsolved and restraints to be removed. Generally speaking, compared with the eastern regions, the Western regions have fewer smartphone owners, fewer enterprises that use information technology, and relatively underdeveloped logistics of businesses.

篇章练习

Text 1: 纺织业

第一,如今纺织业价值近3万亿美元。目前为止,还没有任何一个亿万富翁或任何一个产业的价值接近这个数。正因纺织品如此广泛使用,纺织业与食品业和石油业一道成为世界最繁荣的行业,这也不足为奇。如今,全球服装纺织业每年生产服装800亿件,雇佣员工约7 500万名。

第二,到2023年,印度的纺织品市场总值预计将达到2 260亿美元。印度是世界上最大的纺织品生产国之一,高居世界第二,仅次于中国。其纺织品市场总值占印度国内生产总值的4%以上,占年度出口总值的14%以上。印度从事纺织业或与纺织业相关工作的人数达到1.05亿。印度一个明显的优势便是,生产天然纤维、合成纤维等各种纤维十分容易,如涤纶、尼龙。你猜怎么着?印度也是世界上最大的棉花生产国,2017年产量达到约600万公斤。

第三,美国是世界上最大的服装进口国。从哪里进口呢?没错,就是从中国。在美国销售的服装产品中,有高达50%的服装产品来自中国,其余则来自其他劳动力低廉的发展中国家,如孟加拉国或印度。实际上,在过去的二十年里,美国的纺织制造业已经下降了80%以上,之所以这样只是因为他国有更便宜的劳动力。美国是世界上出了名的时尚品消费国,美国人平均每年在服装上花大概1 700美元。

第四,技术才是纺织业未来的出路。技术现在应用于人类目前已知的每个行业。虽然进程缓慢,但毫无疑问,所有商品都由工厂里的机器和电脑生产制造。过去的100年里,我们已经取得了很大的进展,没有人打算停下脚步。纺织业也已经得到发展。如今,人们可以找到各种不同设计的纤维制品和纺织品,以适用于一些特定活动和不同体型。像运动服、舞服、跑步服、登山服、游泳衣、节日服装等都经过精心设计,也比以前更实用。如果想看看在这个行业里人类又取得了什么进展,看看众筹网站就一目了然。

第五,中国是世界上最大的纺织品生产国。总有一个国家为整个世界提供各种东西,像食品、服装、电子元件、自然资源等。纺织业内,中国是一个纺织强国,向世界出口大量不同的纺织品。印度紧随其后,在生产和出口方面都位列第二。中国最大的纺织业公司归国家所有,因此这些公司的成功有助于经济大幅增长。考虑到中国也是一个劳动力价格便宜的制造业大国,所以中国拥有世界上如此之大的经济体就不足为奇。

Text 2: Training for volunteers of the Beijing 2022 Winter Olympics

Dear volunteers. Hello. Welcome back to our general training session. I am from the Volunteer Department of the Beijing Organizing Committee for the 2022 Olympic and Paralympic Winter Games. Before we start our training, I would like to express our warmest welcome to you as a new member of the big family of volunteers. This will be a stage where you can shine in the spotlight. Dear friends, are you ready?

How many times in a lifetime can you, as a blessed generation, represent your own country? The Beijing 2022 Olympic and Paralympic Winter Games is a golden opportunity. But how can you deliver your service better?

Before we go into detail about our code of conduct we must first understand this concept. What is "code of conduct"? Simply put, it is a set of rules and regulations to which communities or individuals should adhere in public life. People's needs, likes and dislikes, and values have gradually shaped them. Members of a society should follow them in public life.

Volunteers for the Olympics are drawing the world's attention. In addition to showcasing volunteerism, we are also subject to the scrutiny of world. During the games, in our medal plazas and across almost all functional areas, volunteers may be captured by cameras and evaluated by the world. So you have to face the scrutiny of the whole world.

Like I said at the beginning, you are representing your country. Each of us must provide guests travelling to Beijing and Zhangjiakou with excellent service. This extends beyond the services we provide. It also concerns our speech and manners. Details matter, and we need to put code of conduct into everything we do.

第五章

专项练习

1. 句子传话练习

英文传话

（1）中国是东亚的门户，是一个迷人的国家。它拥有古老的文明，是北京猿人、火药和丝绸的发源地。

（2）昆明是中国西南地区的经济、交通、工业和文化中心。它通过铁路与中国主要城市联通。

（3）除了自身城市魅力之外，昆明还是探索少数民族多彩文化的重要基地。

（4）杭州以自然风光闻名，其西湖风景是无数诗人和艺术家笔下的不朽瑰宝。

（5）杭州最著名的景点西湖是一个大湖，由堤道隔开，两旁是古建筑和花园，怡情养性。

（6）华南阳朔曾因物美价廉、环境悠闲，成为背包客的圣地，如今吸引着各路游客前来欣赏美丽的风景和喀斯特山脉。

（7）从桂林返回阳朔的路途平坦，因此许多旅行者选择租自行车回程，这样就有机会看到农民在田间劳作的情景。

（8）拉萨以红山上的布达拉宫而闻名，是西藏最重要的城市，也是世界上海拔最高的城市之一，海拔11 500英尺。

（9）九寨沟素有仙境美誉，因为这里拥有众多瀑布、白雪覆盖的喀斯特山脉和108个蓝绿色的湖泊，清澈见底。

（10）九寨沟也是大熊猫的栖息地，但由于公园面积大、游客数量多，看到它们的机会很小。

中文传话

(1) When it comes to Chinese food, it's much more than just stir-fries, noodles and dumplings that Western countries might come up with.

(2) Chinese food culture has a history of more than ten thousand years, with combined criteria of color, aroma and taste. The types and characteristics of Chinese food may also vary in different times, regions and ethnic groups, forming a diversified picture of its food culture.

(3) There are huge differences in the diet between the North and the South of China: food in the North is heavy on meat and carbohydrate because of the cold climate, while the Southern seaboard is rich with seafood, and the regions around the Yangtze River Delta are teeming with river fish and shrimps.

(4) Rice cultivation requires a lot of water and the South gets plenty of it with more rain on average than the North. Therefore, in the South, you'll see a lot of rice-based diets such as stir-fried rice, rice noodles, and rice roll.

(5) The North specializes in wheat cultivation because it doesn't need all that much water. In the North, wheat-based foods such as noodle dishes and buns are the common staple food on the table.

(6) The Southern cuisine is represented by Cantonese cuisine. Dim sum is a type of small steamed brunch bite. Pink rice noodle rolls and delicate shrimp dumplings wrapped in tapioca flour are typical Cantonese dim sum.

(7) The eastern Jiangsu-Zhejiang region is known as the "land of fish and rice" due to abundant waterways. Freshwater fish and shrimps dominate the menu. The squirrel-shaped mandarin fish is a representative of Jiangsu cuisine.

(8) Leafy greens are less common in the North. Potatoes, eggplant, and cabbage are popular vegetables. Meat, especially beef and lamb, are must-buy ingredients during Chinese festivals.

(9) Beijing roast duck enjoys global reputation. It originated in the Northern and Southern Dynasties as court food in ancient China. It is famous for its bright yellow color, crispy skin and tender meat.

(10) The Southwest has a lush area known for its subtropical climate, pandas and spicy food. Green peppers are abundant here, and the spicy and numbing flavour makes them important

condiments in dishes.

2. 段落传话练习

英文传话

（1）几个世纪以来，人们习惯于在困难时期将大量现金存放在家中。但有些时候，这些金属硬币和纸币带来的可能是危险，而非希望。令人担忧的是，这些钱币可能被成千上万的人触摸过，由此成为病毒传播的一种方式。

（2）在许多地区，由于现金会增加抢劫风险，加之网上购物的便利和手机的普及，现金已经开始消失。瑞典、芬兰、挪威等国家正逐渐减少现金使用，以至于使用大额现金已经很罕见。在中国，随着近十年电子支付服务的普及，现金使用量也有所下降。

（3）国内第四大航空公司海南航空3月底在北京首都机场、海口美兰机场推出了"行李到家"服务。旅客只需线上下单，即可享受此服务，为旅客节约行李提取等待时间，免除大件行李搬运的劳累和不便。

（4）车顶上有一个玻璃罩，含有激光传感器、雷达和摄像头。它们可检测周围60米范围内各个方向的物体及其大小。然后，软件根据物体的大小、形状和运动模式对其进行分类。车身和车顶的圆形设计为车顶传感器提供了最大的视野，尤其是能监测到非常靠近车身的物体。

（5）这辆车是为乘坐而非驾驶设计的。它没有方向盘、踏板、变速杆或手刹。在普通汽车的仪表盘位置的下方，装有一台电脑。它是专门为自动驾驶而设计的，可以评估周围物体速度，并相应地调整汽车行驶速度。

中文传话

(1) Known as the birthplace of kites, Weifang in Shandong Province has a long history of making kites. Weifang kite-making can be traced back to 2,000 years ago. At first, they were often used by the military for communication purposes. During the Ming Dynasty, kites started to be popular among ordinary people as a form of entertainment.

(2) Yang Hongwei, 56, is an inheritor of the Weifang kite-making technique. On Yang's kites, people can see not only common patterns like butterflies and swallows, but also some prints telling Chinese myths, legends and history.

(3) The Beijing 2022 Winter Olympics and Paralympics saw many excellent athletes compete on ice and snow, prompting an enthusiasm for winter sports in China. In fact, the country has a long history of winter sports since ancient times, with skiing originating in Xinjiang Uygur Autonomous Region. Cave paintings of its people hunting on skis were discovered, which archaeologists estimated could be more than 10,000 years old.

(4) Making skis has been a traditional skill of the Uyghur people. The handmade skis have a layer of horse skin. The fur on the horse skin can help decrease friction when they slide down the hill, while the skis also prevent skiers from falling when they walk up.

(5) Wang Ping, a post-90s fashion designer, is obsessed with making traditional Chinese phoenix crowns. Making one crown often takes from one week to up to several months as it uses up to over 30 types of materials. Wang Ping also learned to make ancient clothing to match the crown. He said that he would insist on blending traditional Chinese culture and fashionable elements to craft more exquisite headdresses.

篇章练习

Text 1: 维生素D缺乏与痴呆

健康专家早就知道维生素D对骨骼和牙齿健康很重要，还可以预防糖尿病和癌症等疾病。不过现在研究人员表示，它可能还有助于对抗痴呆这种脑部疾病。

我们可以从食物中获得维生素D，如坚果、扁豆和富含脂肪的鱼类，如鲑鱼和鲭鱼。我们也从阳光中获取维生素D，但这一点并不可靠。一些地区光照不充足，而防晒物质也会阻止维生素D进入人体。此外，随着年龄的增长，皮肤处理维生素D的能力也会减弱。因此维生素D不足在老年人中很常见。

新泽西州罗格斯大学的研究人员正在探索维生素D与痴呆症之间的关系。该团队最近测量了老年人的维生素D水平及其认知能力。营养学教授乔舒亚·米勒主持这项研究。他说，研究对象的认知能力不同。测试表明，大约60%的被试体内维生素D含量偏低。这些人的短期记忆减损更严重，也不太善于组织思路、按重要性排序或做出决定。

Text 2: 保存食物的常见方法

冷冻是保存农产品最简单的方法。需要尽快冷冻农产品，并将其放在冷冻包装袋或其他容器中。需要避免冷冻室灼伤，因为这会影响食物的味道和口感，这就要使用冷冻专用塑料袋、包装纸或容器。

有两种罐装储存生鲜的方法：沸水浴和压力罐装。沸水浴是指将食物放入玻璃罐中，然后在沸水锅中加热罐子。热量迫使空气从玻璃罐中排出，使食物免受细菌和微生物的侵害，然后就可以密封罐子。压力罐装食品需要压力罐装机。无论使用哪种方法，都要测试密封件，以防止新鲜空气进入。

腌制法就是将食物保存在醋、盐水等混合物中。你可以腌制蔬菜，比如青豆或秋葵。

最后一种保存食物的方法是干燥法。食物要求是可以直接食用的，而且不能有碰伤。干燥的方法包括空气干燥、烘箱干燥和使用脱水器。脱水机可能是最好的选择。如果你认为你会定期干燥处理食物，不妨考虑购置一台电动脱水机。

Text 3: AI and employment

The rise of artificial intelligence, or AI, is haunting human being. Many fear that millions of jobs might be eliminated, but a report shows otherwise. In fact, the prospect of ordinary employees looks optimistic, because they shall be freed from mundane tasks for creative ones and thus increase the sense of achievement.

Previous technology innovation didn't impact employment as much as people had feared. A few examples may prove that. Barcode scanners did not replace cashiers in America. Actually, jobs in the retail industry grew at an annual rate of 2% between 1980 and 2013. The arrival of ATM shifted part of the bank tellers to offer customers financial advice.

AI has also made some jobs easier, and truck driving is an example in point. Some worry that truckdrivers would be replaced by auto-vehicles. But driving on busy streets is much more demanding than on the highway, so the driver could switch to auto mode to get a rest in the suburbs, and take over the wheel in the downtown. It works similar to jet plane pilots who take charge of the take-off and landing but turn to auto pilot at 35,000 feet in the air. In this sense, AI can prevent accidents due to driver fatigue.

Text 4: Interpreting and intercultural communication

Interpreters play a crucial role in breaking down language barriers and aiding cross-cultural communication. Interpreters' main job is to accurately and smoothly translate spoken or sign language into another language.

There are two main types of interpreting: simultaneous and consecutive. This semester, we will mainly study consecutive interpreting. This form of interpreting happens when the speaker pauses, and the interpreter then translates what was said into the target language. It's often used in small meetings or one-on-one conversations.

Interpreters work in many different places, such as international conferences, business meetings, hospitals, and more. They need to speak at least two languages fluently and understand different cultures very well. Being an interpreter is more than just translating words; they must also grasp the underlying culture and context to convey the precise intentions and situations.

Even though being an interpreter can be stressful and requires a lot of focus, it is also very rewarding. Interpreters help connect the world, allowing us to hear and understand each other better, and share those voices with a wider audience.

In conclusion, the work of interpreters is really important for individual understanding and for global communication. Their work is a combination of challenge and opportunity, skill and flexibility. For those who enjoy challenges and have a passion for languages and culture, becoming an interpreter is indeed a fulfilling career choice.

第六章

专项练习

1. 英语复述及英汉口译

（1）长期以来，企鹅一直引发全世界人类的想象，并深深地吸引着他们。流行文化中，企鹅被描述为一种笨拙、可爱并且数量庞大的鸟类。事实上企鹅十分优雅，时常脾气暴躁，同时它们的数量在急剧减少。

（2）它们所面临的危机远比我们所想的严重。如果现状无法改善，不久后我们就只能从电影中看到企鹅了。目前企鹅所面临的威胁包括海洋和陆地栖息地的破坏、捕食者的到来、渔网捕捞，以及塑料和化学污染问题。

（3）此外，许多大面积的漏油事件在过去的50年里扼杀或殃及了全世界数万只企鹅。然而企鹅当前面临的最大威胁是全球变暖和过度捕捞。

（4）全球变暖从不同方面影响着企鹅：南极海冰减少导致其食物磷虾的繁殖受阻；暴风雨的频率和强度加剧，导致企鹅巢穴受损；冷水流走向改变，使得企鹅的食物远离了它们繁衍和觅食的范围。

（5）人类或许是企鹅最大的威胁，同时也是它们最大的希望。很多研究和保护项目已经开始对企鹅栖息地进行保护，并逐步恢复珍贵的种群。只要我们献出一份力，改变生活中一些影响地球和海洋的行为，这些身着燕尾服的小伙伴们仍将伴随我们步入下一个世纪。

2. 汉语复述及汉英口译

(1) A credit card is a method of cashless transaction that enables cardholders to pay for goods and services based on their accrued debt. To put it simple, the bank lends you money first, and you can consume with the card without depositing money in it beforehand.

(2) For example, if a bank approves you a credit of 10,000 yuan, then you can consume with this card for 10,000. Please note that the money has to be repaid, though not immediately. In popular terms, this is called advanced consumption, meaning that you spend the next month's salary in advance.

(3) Then why does the bank issue a credit card to you? Because the bank will earn a commission during the credit card transaction, which is not charged to you, but to the merchant. Say, for example, today you had a good time in a bar where you spent 1,000 yuan with your credit

card, the bar owner could only receive a bit more than 900 yuan. The remaining part mostly went to the bank.

(4) You may ask: why would the bar owner allow you to use your credit card at the cost of losing his own commission? Think about it, as you don't have enough money today, he might not even be able to get the business done if he doesn't accept credit card. Moreover, using a credit card would release you from the guilt of splashing out, and the bar owner certainly wants you to spend as much as possible as he is not the one to deal with the debt. It's all between you and the bank.

(5) In addition to purchasing goods, some people use credit cards to get a cash advance, which is the cheapest and most convenient way for capital turnover in today's society.

3. 英汉主旨口译

（1）关于学生能携带的物品，每所大学都有各自的规定。在你搬进大学宿舍前，先查看学校准许和禁止携带的物品清单，这一点很重要。每个学校的规定各不相同，买迷你冰箱和微波炉之前最好先确认一下宿舍是不是允许。

（2）不要带太多衣服到学校。很多大学新生都高估了宿舍的存储空间。考虑到宿舍衣柜的尺寸，你还是只带一些必备衣服比较好。另外，你会发现自己需要的衣服没有想象的那么多，多数大学宿舍楼内都有便捷的洗衣设施，价格也不贵。

（3）你的室友可能不好相处，但也不要把问题想得太严重。进入大学的第一个学期你很可能会被随机分配室友，或者学校根据一份简短问卷给你安排室友。你和你的室友完全可能变成非常好的朋友，但也可能处不来。这会让人不爽，但是别忘了你还要上课、参加社团和其他校园活动，待在宿舍里的时间应该也不会太长。不过，如果你的室友实在让人受不了，你也可以求助于宿管人员。

（4）要知道哪里能吃到美食。饮食是校园生活的重要部分。大多数高校都有多家食堂，第一学期最好能把它们尝个遍。如果想知道哪里的饭菜最好吃，或者想吃素食或不含麸质的食物，你可以在校园网上查一下或者问问同学。别忘了尝试一下校外的美食，大学城里通常都有好吃又便宜的餐馆。

（5）大学里有很多事情可做，绝对不用担心自己会无聊，几乎每所大学都有大量的学生社团和丰富的校园活动。想要参加也很容易，校园里遍地都是社团和校园活动的传单和海报。一些社团甚至还有自己的社交媒体页面，可以帮助你了解社团和联系到现有成员。

（6）早早地规划好学业生涯，但也不要害怕做出改变。为了确保在毕业前修完全部学分，你最好早做课程规划。但也要记住，规划不是一成不变的。大学时光本来就是不断发现的过程。

（7）学习玩乐两不误。很多人担心上了大学后，时间要么用于学习，要么用于玩乐，但不能二者兼得。但其实只要你做好时间管理,不但所有课程都能取得好成绩,还能有时间参加社团和玩乐。如果你善于安排日程,甚至还能享有充足的睡眠时间。

4. 英汉主旨口译

(1) 在科技成为我们日常生活支柱的时代,创新已经深入到旅游和文化领域,带来了前所未有的变革。

(2) 旅行不仅仅是走出去,更是一场身临其境的体验,能够激发知识和理解。旅行时,我们可以翻开文化、传统和历史的篇章,创造人类文明的全球叙事。现在,不可思议的科技创新正为这一探索注入能量,使旅行更加丰富、更具启发性。

(3) 增强现实(AR)和虚拟现实(VR)技术的出现重塑了我们的旅行方式。文化遗产、博物馆和艺术画廊正在采用这些技术增强故事讲述的细节性和亲临感。

(4) 例如,戴上虚拟现实(VR)耳机可以帮我们重温历史,领略过去文化的辉煌。同时,增强现实(AR)技术可以将信息、翻译和动画叠加到展品上,使文物叙述更加引人入胜。

(5) 另一方面,社交媒体创造了一个全球性的舞台。在这里,文化得以展示其独特性,这将进一步促进文化交流和理解。通过分享经验、发布图片或撰写旅游博客,每一位旅行者都为全球文化叙事做出贡献,让世界变得更加紧密、触手可及。

(6) 总之,创新为文化旅行开辟了新的前景,使其具有亲临感和个性化。这是一场革命,颠覆了我们体验、分享和保存旅行经验的方式。

篇章练习

Text 1: 为什么气候变化对人权构成威胁(节选)

我关注气候变化,不是因为我是科学家或环境法律师,我对北极熊或冰川融化的景象也没有特别深刻的印象。我开始关注这一问题,是因为它对人类以及人类权利产生了影响。这些权利包括享有食物、安全用水、健康、教育和居所。说来惭愧,我开始关注气候变化问题的时间比较晚。1997至2002年间,我出任联合国人权事务高级专员,气候变化并非我首要考虑的问题,印象中也没有做过任何气候变化方面的演讲。当时我想,联合国有另外一个机构,即联合国气候变化大会,他们负责气候变化相关事宜。后来,当我开始在非洲国家从事国家发展和人权方面的工作,总是听到这样的话:"哦,但现在严重多了,情况严重多了。"自那之后,我就开始探索这背后意味着什么:这是关于气候变化的问题,包括气候剧变,以及天气的变化。

我结识了康斯坦斯·奥科莱特,她在乌干达东部建立了一个妇女组织。她告诉我,她小时候过着非常普通的乡村生活,人们不会挨饿,季节依时而至,知道何时播种,何时收获,所以大家有充足的食物。而近年来,就在我们谈话的当时,他们却因为久旱而颗粒未收,洪水接踵而至,之后则是更多的干旱天气。学校被摧毁,生计被摧毁,收成被摧毁。她建立这个妇女组织是为了让她的社区团结起来。这件事真的让我震惊,因为温室气体排放导致的问题并不应该由她来承担。

让我痛心的还有今年一月在马拉维发生的灾情。那里发生了前所未有的洪灾,大约三分之一的国土被淹没,超过300人遇难,成千上万的人失去生计。马拉维的人均二氧化碳年排放量是80千克,而美国的人均二氧化碳年排放量是17.5公吨。正在遭受苦难的那些人不开车,不用电,不过度消费,却首当其冲受到气候变化的影响。这些变化让他们不知所措,不知道该如何种植粮食,如何考虑未来。这种不公平使我备受冲击。

世界各国政府在哥本哈根世界气候大会上达成共识,并在每次气候大会上都重申:比起前工业时期的标准,全球变暖必须控制在2摄氏度以内,但是按照目前形势这一数字正逼近4摄氏度。我们星球的未来将面临生存威胁,这使我意识到在21世纪气候变化是对人权的最大威胁。

我因此开始关注气候正义。气候正义涉及道德论证,在应对气候变化的过程中应考虑各方的利益。首先,我们需要站在那些受苦难和影响最多的人们这边。其次,当我们开始应对气候变化时,要确保他们不被落下。

在如今这个不公平的世界中,掉队的人数之多令人震惊。全球人口总计72亿人,掉队群体竟高达30亿人。13亿人无法用电,他们用煤油和蜡烛照明,这非常危险。事实上,他们将微薄收入的大部分都用在了照明上。26亿人还在用煤、木头或动物粪便生成明火做饭,这导致每年400万人死于烟雾中毒,其中大部分是女性。可见这是一个多么不平等的世界,我们亟需改变。改变的规模和程度不可低估,因为我们必须在2050年之前实现零碳排放的目标,这样才能把全球变暖控制在2度以内。这就意味着需要将大约三分之二的已知化石燃料留在地下,不再使用。

这是一次巨变,意味着发达国家必须节能减排,尽快向可再生能源转型。对于发展中国家和新兴经济体,它们的问题和挑战是如何在零碳情况下寻求发展。对他们而言,发展是刚需,因为国家仍有大量贫困人口。他们必须在零碳基础上谋求发展,这是另外一个不同的问题。诚然,世界上没有任何一个国家可以真正实现零碳发展。所有国家的发展都曾使用化石燃料,之后可能再转向可再生能源。所以这是一个非常大的挑战,它需要国际社会全力支持,以提供必要的资金、技术和体制支持。气候变化带来的危险没有任何国家可以幸免。解决这个问题需要全人类团结起来。让我们团结起来,即便是为了自身利益也应如此。这是我们的共同课题,我们必须一起努力以确保在2050年前实现零碳排放。

Text 2: Chinese silk

Chinese silk, also referred to as "silk from the east", holds a special place in world history and culture. It is a splendid material famous for its shiny appearance and exceptionally smooth texture. But, do you know the fascinating story behind this elegant fabric?

Chinese silk has its origin in the ancient Chinese civilization. The production of silk is a complex and labor-intensive process that begins with a little creature, the silkworm. Silk production, known as sericulture, involves the careful nurturing of these silkworms. This age-old practice is believed to have begun around 5,000 years ago.

The discovery of silk production is attributed to the Chinese Empress Leizu. Legend has it that one day, she noticed that a cocoon, which accidentally dropped into her tea, produced a string of glossy thread. With time and experimentation, her discovery evolved into the craft of silk weaving.

Chinese silk, through the renowned "Silk Road", was transported to different parts of the world. This ancient network of trade routes connected China with countries in Asia, Europe, and Africa, sparking cultural exchange and making silk a sought-after commodity worldwide. This luxurious fabric has been and still is associated with royalty and wealth. Chinese Emperors, for instance, used to wear silk robes as a symbol of their power and prestige.

The story of Chinese silk is not just about a fabric or a trade commodity, but it imparts a rich narrative of history, culture, craft, and international relationships tied together. Its timeless beauty and traditional values indeed make Chinese silk an icon of elegance.

第七章

专项练习

1. 源语概述

中文概述：社交媒体

互联网时代，社交媒体成了人们交流信息、获取新闻的主要渠道。它是一把双刃剑，用好了造福国家和人民，用不好就可能带来难以预见的危害。我国已经初步建立了相关的制度、法律和法规，但由于网络传播本身的复杂性，网络治理仍然面临难题。

首先，社交媒体时代，信息发布的门槛降低，信息真实性不确定。由于社会学意义的真相需要公众参与建构，因此朋友圈传播的信息获得更多信任，尤其是短视频类的可视化内容。

其次，社交媒体的群聚效应激化了社会分歧，导致观点极化。一方面，社交媒体的特性使情绪化、简单化的表达更容易得到传播，放大社会负面情绪；另一方面，网络群聚效应让大多数人固执己见。

再次，"后真相"现象不完全等同于谣言和假新闻，其特殊之处在于它既不完全客观也不完全虚构。但社交媒体毕竟为社会公众表达诉求提供了一个便捷、廉价的平台，人们的立场、情感与信念是真实的。

英文概述: How interpreters juggle two languages at once

In the past, interpretating was mainly done consecutively. But with radio technology, simultaneous interpretating came into being after World War II. It seems easy, but takes professional training.

To listen and speak at the same time, students shadow speakers and repeat their every word exactly as heard in the same language. In time, they begin to paraphrase. Later, they will translate it into another language. Interpreters need to master a variety of skills and strategies.

Besides, interpreters need to have good stress management, public speaking skills and good preparation for tasks.

Finally, interpreters work in pairs and need skillful collaboration.

Language is complex and miscommunication may lead to conflicts and disasters. Conference interpreters work hard to make sure it never does.

2. 复述

中文复述: 青少年心理

在社会高速发展的今天,孩子们学习态度和学习模式发生了改变。很多初中生早出晚归,在学校呆十个小时,十分疲惫。对于父母来说,问问孩子的学习和身体再正常不过了;而对于孩子来说,作业压力大,自己的疲惫和情绪不受关注,这就会引发亲子矛盾。因此,父母还需要了解青少年的心理变化,以促进亲子沟通,促进孩子身心健康成长。

青少年的心理具有四大特点。第一是过渡性。他们的身心发展既具有儿童期的特点,又具有成熟期的特点,各种心理特征逐渐接近成人。第二是闭锁性。中学生开始有了自己的秘密,自己的许多事情有意回避父母与师长。第三是社会性。青少年与社会的接触越来越多,受到社会环境的影响也越来越明显。他们已不再像儿童时期那样更多地受家庭、学校的影响,而是更多地受同辈群体以及社会风气的影响。第四是动荡性。中学生的思想比较敏感,容易偏激,容易摇摆。他们精力充沛,能力也在发展,但性格未最后定型。

英文复述: Hunger

People do go hungry because the world does not produce enough food for everyone. The principal problem is that many people still do not have resources to purchase or grow enough food.

Hunger is both a consequence and a cause of poverty. It exists because many countries lack social safety nets, and women farmers are underprivileged in accessing to training, credit or land.

Besides, many other factors contribute to hunger among the impoverished, including conflicts, unfavorable government systems, poor management of land and resources, lack of educational opportunity, natural disasters, financial and economic crises, and unemployment.

3. 无笔记口译

无笔记汉译英：Animal protection

（括号中为可以省略的内容）

Unlike in primitive cultures, animals today do not have much chance to escape from modern hunting technologies (such as electric fishing tools). Unleashed technological development may endanger the ecology and social sustainability.

The protection of animals is in fact the core interests of human beings. (For example, individuals have the right to smoke, but it will also affect the health of others; If people kill, sell and eat animals, they are violating the right to life of people and other living beings).

(According to UN IPBES Global Assessment report in May 2019), millions of species will become extinct or near-extinct in recent decades (nearly one million species could become extinct in recent decades. And a million species are facing extinction). It actually endangers humanity's own future. Therefore, we should do our best to protect the animals and plants. Otherwise, the world may be crowded with tall buildings and plastic waste one day.

To meet the ecological challenges, we need to change our way of life and production.

For example, we've been calling that students should not to be forced to use plastic book covers. Their production, transportation and disposal have caused great damage to the ecological environment, especially the marine animals. (The large amounts of plastic waste in their stomachs lead to their death and deformities.)

无笔记英译汉：大规模给狗接种疫苗可消除狂犬病

（括号中为可以省略的内容）

在美国，我们常说："狗是人类最好的朋友"。虽然狗是很受欢迎的宠物，但在世界上的一些地方，被狗咬会导致痛苦的死亡。

全球每年有数万人（约有7万人）死于狂犬病。狂犬病在西方并不常见，但在亚洲和撒哈拉以南非洲，由于疫苗接种不利，它严重威胁着公众健康。

狂犬病死亡是一个痛苦的过程。病毒会侵入中枢神经系统，受害者对水产生严重恐惧，剧烈颤抖，陷入昏迷，最终死亡。

然而，狂犬病病毒不会立即在人体内发作。（它通常在被咬后有至少10天的潜伏期，有时长达几个月。）在潜伏期接种疫苗仍然可以预防感染。

科学家表示，给狗接种疫苗可以有效地消除狂犬病在狗群中的爆发，这将大大减少人感染狂犬病的数量。

坦桑尼亚就是一个很好的例子。那里的公共卫生官员（在180个村庄）建立了大量狗疫苗接种中心。（此前，坦桑尼亚每年平均有50人死于狂犬病。）此后每年死于狂犬病的人数几乎降为零。

盖伊·帕尔默是动物健康方面的专家（华盛顿州立大学全球动物健康学院的主任）。他参与了坦桑尼亚的这项研究。（研究发现，对70%的狗进行免疫可以消除狂犬病对人类的威胁。）他说："我们不需要10到20年的基础研究来研发疫苗，现在已经有现成的了。接种其实是一种战略，保护最脆弱社区和国家的基础设施。"

篇章练习

Text 1: 运动中的惯用手问题

我的话题是惯用手的问题。在不同的运动中，惯用左手、右手还是双管齐下会更加有效呢？我自己是左撇子，一直以来并没觉得这个问题对生活有任何影响，直到我偶然读了一位名叫彼得·马修斯的运动心理学家的文章。

我认为马修斯的研究结果的价值倒不在于帮助运动员加强弱势的一侧，而在于帮助他们确定在特定比赛中的惯用手策略。尽管大多数教练都知道这个问题很重要，但目前他们不太愿意将马修斯等科学家的研究结果用于实践。我认为这缺乏远见，因为关注个人用手的灵活性只是运动的一方面。

言归正传，回到这篇文章。

马修斯研究了几种不同的运动，并在每种运动中发现了不同类型的惯用手。需要指出的是，这里的"惯用手"指的是脚、眼睛和手的优势一侧。他的团队对2 611名球员进行了研究，发现确实有三种主要的类型：混合型，两边的手和眼睛使用均衡；单侧型，倾向于使用一侧，而惯用的手和眼睛处于同侧；以及交叉型，倾向于使用一侧的手和眼睛，但方向是相反的。//

第一项运动是曲棍球。马修斯发现混合型最具优势，这是因为曲棍球棍需要左右挥动，如果手或眼睛偏向一侧就会是个弱点。有趣的是，混合型的曲棍球运动员比单侧型的更有信心。

网球等挥拍类运动的情况则略有不同，最好有同侧的惯用手和主导眼。因为大部分动作发生在一侧，单侧型的运动员视野更好。如果球员是交叉型的，那么在挥拍的大部分时间里主导眼会看不到球拍，等看到就为时已晚了。

下面再来看看体操，这是一项很不同的运动，涉及许多精确的大动作。交叉型的选手最有优势，因为这有助于平衡，而平衡对体操的表现至关重要。

Text 2: "Double-reduction" policy

The "double-reduction" aims to not only alleviate the academic burden for both students and parents but also promote moral education, improve education quality and level, and run education to the satisfaction to people. The "double-reduction" policy has achieved initial results. Now, the number of offline tutoring institutions for primary and middle school students has been slashed by 92 percent and the number of online ones by 87 percent.

In fact, the "double reduction" policy will not diminish the education quality. The Ministry of Education not only intends to alleviate students' stress, but also promotes a "double increase" policy, which suggests that students have more time and opportunity to participate in outdoor activities, physical exercise, cultural events, and social practice. Schools should leverage their facilities and faculty to provide abundant high-quality and distinctive activities for students. Moreover, they should provide the overachievers with more learning opportunities and activities, such as setting up optional courses, hobby groups, and sports clubs.

Although students' stress and household expenditure for education have been cut down considerably due to the "double reduction" policy, much more work needs to be done to cultivate students' core competence. On the one hand, teachers should be trained in terms of devotion, professional ethics, and research capacity. On the other hand, to enhance students' overall competence, schools should increase students' attainment of humanistic quality, social and scientific literacy by providing better courses, including history, politics, sociology, and psychology.

Text 3: 流行的饮食模式

在美国，流行的饮食模式不断改变，很难一一列数。然而，地中海饮食一直是最健康的饮食之一，不过现在它的地位受到了新北欧饮食的挑战。新北欧饮食源自北欧地区，包括芬兰、挪威、冰岛、瑞典和丹麦。这个地区有时被称为斯堪的纳维亚半岛。

健康网的饮食专家解释说，新北欧饮食和地中海饮食非常相似。他们在2015年的一项对比研究中发现，新北欧饮食减少了脂肪组织内的炎症。这类炎症可导致与肥胖相关的健康风险。两种饮食模式都包括大量的蔬菜和水果、全谷物、坚果和种子，海鲜的摄入量比肉类多。

然而，两者之间的一大区别是对油的选择。地中海饮食使用橄榄油，而斯堪的纳维亚半岛不产橄榄，所以通常使用油菜籽。这就引出了新北欧饮食的核心，即顺应环境、就地取材。

新北欧饮食使用丰富的当地时令食材，尽可能选择当地种植、饲养或捕获的新鲜食材。森林的野生蘑菇、浆果和草本植物都是主要原料。这种饮食模式还大量使用根茎类蔬菜，如欧洲萝卜、胡萝卜和甜菜。

新北欧模式以家常菜为主，而在外就餐的脂肪和热量可能更高。

吃得好、吃得少也是这种饮食的特点。它避免加工食品，也就是那些批量生产的预制食品，强调尽可能吃有机食物，做饭和吃饭时减少浪费。

新北欧饮食也是一种环保饮食。它更多的是一种生活方式，而不是规定哪些食物可以吃、哪些不能吃。由于强调就地取材，所以鱼类是新北欧饮食的主要组成部分。

伯克利健康网站上的健康专家表示，吃鱼的人往往更长寿，患心血管疾病的风险更低。吃鱼甚至可能会促进大脑健康。鱼含有维生素、矿物质和其他脂肪，这些可能与欧米伽-3一起保护人的心脏和整体健康。

但这些专家也警告说，吃对鱼很重要，因为有些鱼含汞量高。他们建议吃小型鱼类，即那些"食物链下游"的鱼。如果是自己钓鱼，要和当地专家核实，以确保水质安全。

Text 4: The National Fitness Program

Some people tend to have misunderstandings about working out for lack of knowledge, leading to two kinds of result: one is ineffective exercising; the other is excessive exercising, featuring improper methods or intensity which leads to overexertion or even sports injuries. According to Bao Mingxiao, professor of Beijing University of Physical Education, we need to let the public know how to keep fit in a scientific way, and the harms to be caused by inadequate or over exercising.

The sports industry is turning online. Many famous fitness brands launched their live streaming platforms and apps to offer online courses. Many people are fond of these apps because they are convenient and personalized. Experts say that fitness apps are convenient by breaking time and space limit. However, due to the lack of face-to-face interaction with the coaches, users find it hard to correct their movements in time and keep their exercise habits.

It is essential to construct more fitness facilities to improve national health. An official from General Administration of Sport of China said, people spend most of their spare time in their nearby communities. We are supposed to construct fitness facilities in the communities so that everyone can do exercise nearby. Apart from big stadiums, we also need more sports parks and fitness trails, in order to meet and stimulate the public's demand for exercise.

第八章

专项练习

中文段落1: New productive forces create new attraction (excerpt)

China has a significant advantage in attracting foreign investment. From the perspective of industrial structure, with the continuous development of electronic technology, new energy, semiconductors and intelligent technology, these frontier fields are giving birth to new quality productive forces and can become new growth points for China to attract foreign investment. In terms of industrial base and domestic demand potential, China is the only country in the world with all the industrial categories in the United Nations industrial classification. Strong industrial support and integration capabilities as well as high-quality personnel will provide strong support for the development of foreign enterprises in China. In recent years, relevant Chinese departments have continuously improved their policies to encourage the development of foreign investors, promoted the high-quality development of foreign investment, and ensured that qualified foreign-invested projects fully enjoy the preferential policies of the Chinese government. China's policy on the development of new-quality productive forces is based on unified market standards, involving property protection, market access, fair competition, social credit, and so on. The Chinese government has issued a series of policies of "high-level opening to the outside world", forming a new attraction to foreign businessmen.

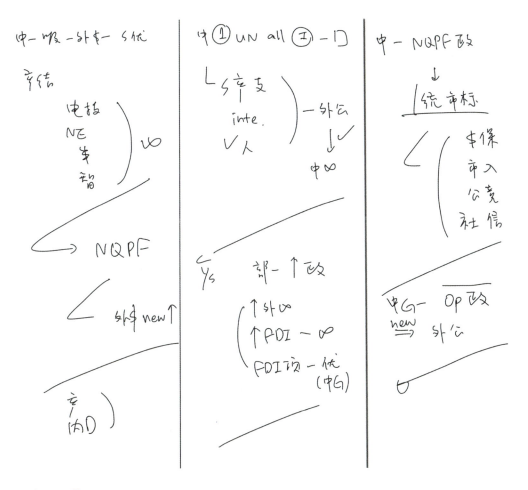

中文段落2: The development of China's rural areas

Farmers' average annual income last year exceeded 5000 yuan or 700 US dollars. This may not sound impressive, but if we put that figure into perspective, it is 6 percent more than what they earned a year earlier and 35 percent more than 5 years ago. The increase in income is attributable to higher government purchase price for agricultural products.

To make lives better, the government launched the project called "bringing home appliances to the countryside". If a family chooses to buy the government subsidized package including a TV set, refrigerator, washing machine and cell phone, it can save them 1000 yuan or 150 US dollars. The aim of the project is to provide rural families with essential home appliances.

The projection is within the next 4 years 480 million white goods would be sold to the rural population at a low price. The margin will be subsidized by local governments. The project has been generally well received by farmers although some say they would like a wider variety of home appliances to choose from.

One adverse impact of the global financial crisis is that millions of Chinese migrant workers lost their jobs in coastal Chinese factories. To assist them, a substantial amount of the Chinese governments' stimulus package went to building infrastructure in rural areas and financing small and medium enterprises in villages and townships across the country.

A one billion yuan project has been launched to educate and train the farmer-turned migrant workforce and equip them with new skills and knowhow. Local governments also asked certain companies not to lay off migrant workers until they absolutely had to.

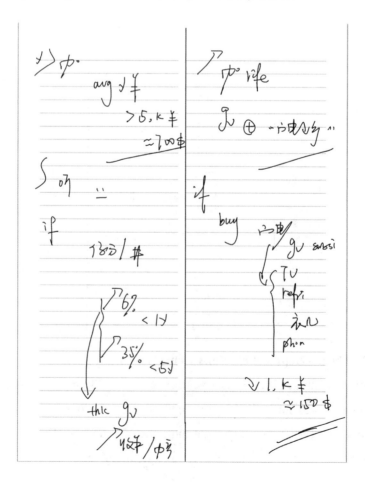

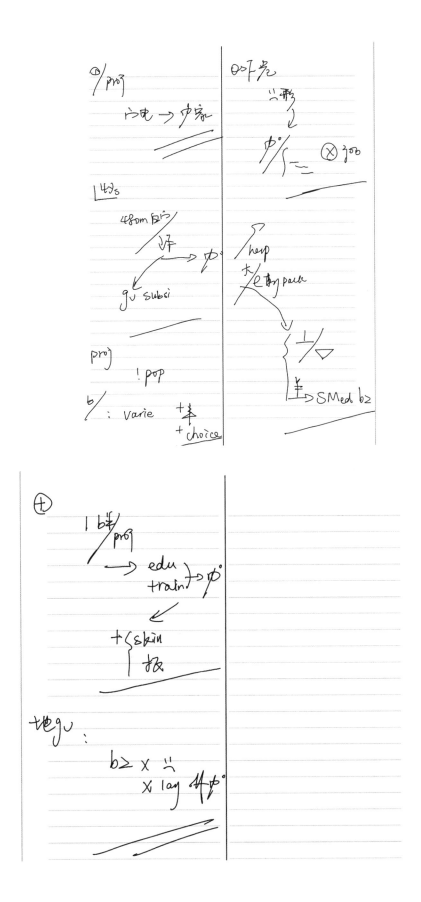

英文段落1：如何收获土豆

许多园艺爱好者种下了土豆却不知何时该将它们挖出来。因为土豆在地底下生长，我们看不见它们的大小，无法摸到它们的硬度，也无法通过气味判断它们是否已经成熟。如果挖早了，它们可能太小，而且还可能压迫到植株及其根茎体系。那么，我们到底应当如何判断何时收获呢？

杰西卡·达米安诺是为美联社撰写园艺专栏的作家。她写道，挖土豆的最佳时间是当一半的叶子已变黄的时候，也就是种下土豆约两到三个月之后。但具体还要取决于气候情况，以及所种植的土豆品种。不过差不多这时候就可以停止浇水。

为了帮助土豆成熟，尤其是在潮湿的气候条件下，你应该在土壤表面修剪植株。然而，这一步骤并非必要。如果不剪掉植株，它们自己会枯萎。两周后，土豆就可以收获了。

如果你还是拿不准应当何时收获的话，可以先挖一个小一点的土豆进行测试。小心地铲掉用于测试的植株附近的土壤，然后从根部的外层取下一颗土豆。若土豆成熟了，当你的手指摩挲它的外皮时，外皮会紧紧地贴在土豆上。若外皮剥落，那就得再把洞填上，等一周左右再来检查。

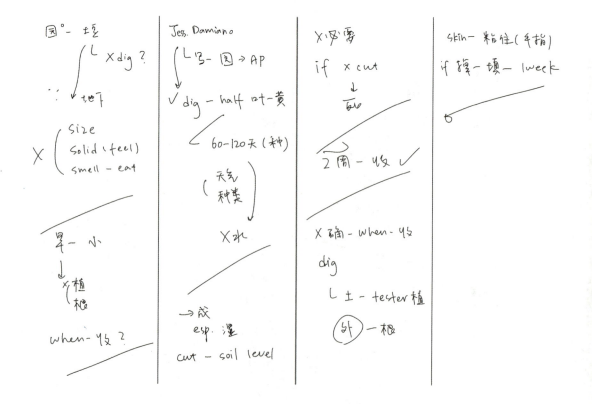

英文段落2：美国日常生活中的缩略表达（节选）

美国人通常尽可能快地表达自己的想法。所以，有的表达我们会用单词的首字母替代，而不是把每个单词说一遍。

很多常用的表达或长的名字是这样缩短的。比如，B-Y-O-B是"自带酒水"的简称。当你受邀参加一场普通的社交活动或与朋友聚会时，BYOB这四个字母通常会出现在邀请函的底部。比如，假设我将举办一个跨年派对。我可能在邀请函上写道，"欢迎参加我的派对，请自带酒水"。每个人带来的酒水就是他想在派对上自己喝或与他人分享的东西。但是，如果受邀参加一场特别的聚会，比如婚礼，那么是绝对不会让你自带酒水的。

另一个在商务场合而不是派对中使用的表达是A-S-A-P。所以，一位同事可能说她需要某事尽快办理。这四个字母指代的意思是尽可能快。她也可能说某件事需要在C-O-B之前完成，这个表达的意思是需要在"结束营业"或工作日结束之前完成。

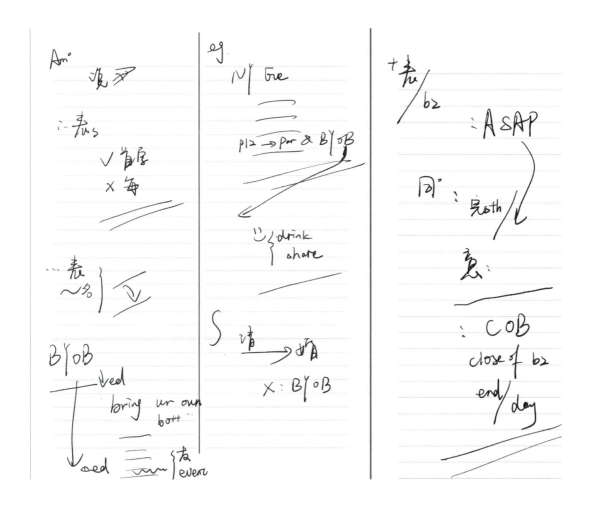

篇章练习

Text 1: Xi Jinping's written speech at APEC CEO Summit (excerpt)

大纲：
1. 亚太地区在当前世界形势下的定位、目标和优势：
作为全球经济最具活力增长带，未来发展何去何从？该地区具备人口、经济总量、贸易优势。
2. 亚太地区要走什么样的发展道路：
我们要走和平发展之路、和衷共济之路。
3. 亚太地区应采取何种措施构建人类命运共同体：
第一，筑牢和平发展的根基。
第二，坚持以人民为中心的发展理念。
第三，打造更高水平的开发格局。
第四，实现更高层次的互联互通。
第五，打造稳定畅通的产业链供应链。
第六，推进经济优化升级。

Representatives of the Business Community,

Ladies and Gentlemen, Friends,

It gives me great pleasure to come to the beautiful city of Bangkok for the APEC CEO Summit.

Our world has once again reached a crossroads. Where is it headed? What should we do here in the Asia-Pacific? These questions demand urgent answers.

The 21st century is the Asia-Pacific century. Our region, which accounts for one-third of the world's population, over 60 percent of the global economy and close to half of global trade, is the most dynamic growth belt in the world. ...

Currently, the Asia-Pacific enjoys overall stability. Cooperation in our region has been steadily advanced, and peace, development and win-win cooperation remain the underlying trend in this region. On the other hand, the world has entered a new period of fluidity and change. Both geopolitical tensions and the evolving economic dynamics have exerted negative impact on the development environment and cooperation structure of the Asia-Pacific ...

We should follow a path of peaceful development. ... History tells us that bloc confrontation cannot solve any problem and that bias will only lead to disaster. ...

We should follow a path of openness and inclusiveness. ...

We should follow a path of solidarity. ... Through cooperation, we have forged a sense of community, which has laid a solid foundation for steady progress.

Facing these new developments, we need to draw on past experiences and lessons, respond to the challenges of the times and steadfastly advance Asia-Pacific regional economic integration, so as to jointly break new ground in development and build an Asia-Pacific community with a shared future.

First, we should bolster the foundation for peaceful development. ...

Second, we should take a people-centered development approach. ...

Third, we should pursue higher-level opening-up. ...

Fourth, we should strive for higher-standard connectivity. ...

Fifth, we should build stable and unimpeded industrial and supply chains. ...

Sixth, we should promote economic upgrading. ...

Text 2: The development of the catering industry in modern Shanghai

大纲：

1. 上海各类菜馆的发展历史及主要特点：
   苏菜馆：招牌菜为姑苏船菜，店面陈设雅洁，有书画装饰。
   天津菜馆：1870年代兴起，发展到20世纪初。
   宁波菜馆：宁波移民使得宁波菜很早出现。
   徽菜馆：盐商来沪开设，一度独霸。
2. 除此之外，上海当时还有其他一些中菜馆：
   例如：粤菜馆，豪华精美；川菜馆，于1940年代兴旺；其他如闽菜、豫菜、杭州菜等。
3. 西菜馆的发展情况：
   早在清末就出现，做法西式，味道更接近中餐。

The most famous Suzhou-style cuisine in Shanghai is served from boats, which are usually decorated in a clean and tasteful manner. The restaurants typically have dozens of private rooms both on the ground floor and the second floor. The main dining room is centrally located, with study and guest rooms on either side, and the walls are adorned with drawings and calligraphy. In the 1870s, Tianjin-style restaurants began to rise and continued to flourish until the early 20th century. As more people migrated from Ningbo to Shanghai after the port was opened, Ningbo-style restaurants also emerged quite early in Shanghai.

The earliest Anhui-style restaurants in Shanghai were opened by salt merchants who came here for business. By the 1890s, they had gradually become well-known and were even the gem of Shanghai's fine dining. In the 1930s, Cantonese-style restaurants became quite popular, partly due to the victory of the North Expedition. They were extravagantly decorated and served delicate and expensive dishes.

In the 1940s, Sichuan-style restaurants had their time, and one of the most famous was Jinjiang Restaurant, founded by Dong Zhujun in 1935. Other Chinese restaurants in Shanghai included Fujian cuisine, Henan cuisine and Hangzhou cuisine. Additionally, Shanghai local cuisine, which was originally popular among the poor, developed into high-end restaurants in the 1930s.

Besides these Chinese restaurants, Western restaurants had already made their appearance in Shanghai as early as the late Qing Dynasty. However, many of them were targeted at Chinese clients, and even though the dishes were prepared in a western style, they still had a distinct Chinese flavor. As for those Western restaurants frequented by foreigners, Chinese people rarely visited them.

Text 3: 针灸

Outline:

1. The origin of acupuncture:

   Acupuncture evolved into a comprehensive and profound medical system.

2. The holistic treatment of acupuncture:

   It aims to promote the body's self-regulating functions in a comprehensive way.

3. Various forms of practice such as needle insertion, cupping and scraping:

   Needle insertion is carried out by inserting hair-thin needles into meridians.

4. The influence of acupuncture both home and abroad:

   Acupuncture, as an ancient Chinese medical practice with a rich history and deep cultural significance, has become a global therapy.

针灸是一种古老的中医实践,几千年来是无数患者的良方。在现代医学兴起之前,中国古人使用石器来缓解疼痛。随着时间的推移,这种本能的实践演变成了一套全面而精深的医学体系,并奠定了针灸的根基。

针灸是一种促进身体自我调节的治疗方法。其治病原则与传统中医的哲学概念一致,强调全面治疗、经络调整、身体机能平衡和整体生理健康。

针灸的操作形式多种多样,包括针刺、拔罐和刮痧等。其中,针刺是最常见的方法,在经络或身体特定穴位插入细如发丝的针。针灸师提起、扭动和旋转针来疏通能量流,恢复阴阳平衡,激发身体的自愈潜能。

针灸已走出国门,为世界广泛使用。多年来,针灸在科学研究和现代医学方面取得了许多进展,已成为多种疾病的主流替代和辅助治疗。作为一项拥有悠久历史和文化底蕴的古老中医实践,针灸是一项深厚的文化遗产,也是一条通往康复的整体化路径。

Text 4: 鹦鹉为何能模仿人的声音?

Outline:

1. How is it possible that parrots could produce human speech?
2. Most wild parrots use vocalizations for mating and territorial displays and to coordinate group movements, but how they use these calls depends on the species and the size of their flocks.
3. Parrots could produce human speech because:

    a. A parrot has a syrinx and only one vibrating membrane like human beings.

    b. Besides, a parrot could make good use of its tongue, beak and jaw.

    c. Also, a parrot's brain contains interconnected regions that allow it to do so.
4. Do parrots actually understand what they're saying?

    In most cases, no. But after training, some may understand.
5. To truly understand parrots, we need to preserve and study them in the wild.

2010年,一只与主人有着同样英国口音的鹦鹉走失了。四年后他们才得以重聚,但是这期间的经历在鹦鹉身上留下了明显的烙印:这只鹦鹉丢掉了它的英国口音,开始说西班牙语。鹦鹉和其他少数几种鸟类是仅有的能够发出人类声音的动物,而且一些鹦鹉说得尤其好。这是如何做到的呢?

大多数野生鹦鹉都具有很强的社会属性。它们通过发声来求偶、标记领土和协调群体行动。一些品种的鹦鹉群体不断经历分散再融合的过程，这意味着它们可能具有与很多不同鹦鹉交流的能力。鹦鹉通过交流信号来互动，也通过这种方式与视野之外的族群保持联系。但是它们具体如何使用这些交流信号取决于它们的品种以及族群的大小。

那么，鹦鹉是如何说出"波利想要一块饼干"的呢？人可以通过位于气管顶端的喉咙来发出这些声音。这包括使用一层层的肌肉以及控制气流的振动膜，然后通过舌头和嘴唇来控制声音，最终发出清楚的单词。鹦鹉的声音则从气管底部的鸣管发出。很多其他鸟类有两套振动膜，但鹦鹉与人类一样，只有一套振动膜。

当声音离开气道，鹦鹉通过舌头和鸟喙来控制声音。鹦鹉之所以能这样做是因为它们的舌头异常灵活有力，能够帮助鹦鹉控制诸如种子、坚果等物体。尽管鹦鹉的喙非常紧，但是它们的下颌关节很灵活，可以控制喙张开的宽度和速度。

与其他会发声的动物一样，鹦鹉大脑中各个区域相互连通，因此它们能够听见、记住、修正或发出复杂的声音。鸣禽大脑中只有一套鸣叫体系，而几乎所有的鹦鹉都有另一套体系。科学家认为这可能使它们在学习同族的叫声或人类的声音时更为灵活。借助这种特别的解剖结构，鹦鹉能够发出狗叫，能够尖叫、叫骂或者学脏话。一只大胆的鹦鹉曾经走失，而它通过不断向热心的陌生人重复它的名字和地址最终得以回家。

但这些让人惊叹的能力引发了另一个问题：鹦鹉是否理解它们自己在说什么？即使它们的同类不在场，大多数有这种能力的鹦鹉能够通过说话建立起社会关系。很多鹦鹉可能会与一些词汇建立联系，也可能将一些特定词汇与情境联系，做出固定的回答，这就是为什么它们能学会骂脏话。经过训练，鹦鹉还能根据语境说话并且赋予词汇语境意义，如在一天快结束的时候说"晚安"，向人索取吃的，或者数数、啄物品。一只名叫艾利克斯的非洲灰鹦鹉接受过大量的训练，所以它是除人类以外第一个能够提出存在性问题的动物——它曾问别人自己是什么颜色的。

第九章

📖 专项练习

汉英段落1: The origin of rabbits

In ancient times, the rabbit was considered a lucky animal (that basked in the moonlight) as one of the twelve zodiac animals, and today, it is also a symbol of intelligence and cuteness. How did rabbits survive over 60 million years, from evolution to domestication, and become part of our daily life? Rabbits and rats were once classified as rodents, but rabbits have an extra pair of small incisors, which prompted people to reconsider their kinship. Researches show that 62 million years ago, the ancestors of rats and rabbits lived together as good neighbors and loving "sisters".

Based on these researches, Li Chuankui, a Chinese scientist, officially proposed the "rodent-rabbit homology" in 1980, and modern biology also supports this view, bringing an end to the 300-year-old "kinship war".

汉英段落2: Cars and the environment

The car is unquestionably one of the most important inventions ever. It's made transportation available to the masses, and most of our daily lives aren't possible without one. But the car as we know it has some huge challenges looming over it in the not-so-distant future.

First, there's the problem of what goes into it. Gasoline is an oil product, and oil isn't renewable in any way. It's a resource that will one day be too scarce to meet demands, and while sources disagree on when that's going to be exactly, it's likely going to be within my lifetime.

Even if gasoline is replaced with ethanol from renewable sources, there's still the issue of what comes out of the internal combustion engine: carbon dioxide. CO_2 is the most common greenhouse gas and, in the US, 32% of that comes from transportation. So our cars, while useful, are not sustainable and are contributing almost a third of the CO_2 that's destabilizing out climate. There has to be a better way.

英汉段落1: 美国重新开放对古巴的签证和领事服务

美国驻古巴大使馆将于周三重新开放签证和领事服务。美国大使馆说，它将优先发放移民许可，以帮助古巴人在美国与家人团聚。这一举措的出台正值古巴人移民美国的一大浪潮之际。古巴的经济和政治问题是古巴人离开的原因之一。大使馆预计每年至少发放2万个签证，但向美国移民的古巴人远远超过这一数字。12月下旬，美国官员报告称，11月份在墨西哥边境拦截古巴人34 675次，比10月份的28 848人次增加了21%。这个数字每个月都在缓慢上升。美国海关和边境保护局的数据显示，古巴人现在是继墨西哥人之后出现在边境的第二大群体。

英汉段落 2: 对非洲体育博彩的担忧日益加剧

至少在五个非洲国家里，许多人认为体育赌博是一种获得固定收入的途径。一些人认为体育赌博是摆脱贫困的一种方式。但批评人士警告说，非洲的体育博彩正在蔓延，而贫困、失业和缺乏行业规则仍然是一个大问题。例如，一名乌干达卫生官员确信阿根廷会在世界杯足球赛中战胜沙特阿拉伯，于是下注了 1 800 美元。这笔钱其实是官员们借给他的，且原本将用于支付 243 人接种脊髓灰质炎疫苗接种的费用。阿根廷输了比赛，这名官员也输了钱。后来他被愤怒的人群追赶，把自己锁在屋里好几天。他的上司说他可能会丢掉工作。在乌干达，这位官员赌输的是一大笔钱。2020 年，这个国家的人均年收入仅为 840 美元。体育赌徒包括学生、政客、工人以及政府官员。

篇章练习

Text 1: The ancient Silk Road

"The Belt and Road Initiative" is an abbreviation for the "Silk Road Economic Belt" and the "21st Century Maritime Silk Road". When discussing the "Silk Road", people often evoke images of the ancient Silk Road, which occupies a crucial position in Chinese history.

As for prominent figures related to the Silk Road, Zhang Qian of the Han Dynasty is the foremost in most people's minds. It was through his efforts that the ancient Silk Road was opened, leading to a continuous influx of envoys and caravans that brought vitality to the trade of various countries along the route.

Zhang Qian's travel to the Western regions was commissioned by Emperor Wu of the Han Dynasty with the major goal of initiating transcontinental trade in the Silk Road, as well as securing political allies. The Central Asian parts of the Silk Road routes were expanded around 114 BC largely through his missions. Zhang's accounts were compiled by Sima Qian in the 1st century BC. Today, he is revered as a Chinese national hero for the key role he played in opening China to the wider opportunity of commercial trade and global alliances. Another thing we are sure of is Zhang Qian's adventurous spirit, as only someone willing to take risks would accept such a challenge.

Text 2: Digital RMB

China's mobile payment system has taken the lead in the world and covers every social sector. It not only makes our lives easier but also boosts economic development. According to the latest statistics released by China Internet Network Information Centre, 64.7 percent of smartphone users are using mobile payments as a regular method to make transactions.

In recent years, China's Central Bank has been promoting digital RMB and piloted it in cities like Shenzhen and Suzhou. By the end of August 2020, over 3.12 million transactions have been paid by digital RMB with a total value of more than 1.1 billion yuan. However, while we are already used to WeChat Pay and Alipay, why did the government bring in digital RMB? I think there are four reasons.

The primary reason is to safeguard the national electronic payment system. By the end of 2021, Alipay of Alibaba and WeChat of Tencent have accounted for more than 90 percent of China's mobile payment market. Small and medium-sized enterprises in China last for less than 3 years, while larger ones, 7–8 years, and the average life span of the world's top 500 enterprises is about 40 years. Despite the current stability and success of these two enterprises, their future remains unpredictable due to market volatility.

The second reason is to cut costs. Printing, transporting, and storing paper currency requires a significant amount of manpower and money, as well as developing anti-counterfeiting technology. By contrast, digital RMB costs almost nothing to produce.

The third reason is to combat crime. Since paper currency is untraceable, it is often used in illegal activities such as drug trafficking and bribery. By completely replacing paper currency with digital RMB, the government can trace all transactions and quickly identify any illegal activities.

The fourth reason is to simplify international transactions. Digital RMB utilizes blockchain technology, which can significantly reduce international settlement times from several days to just a few seconds. This improves transaction efficiency and financial liquidity. For example, with traditional payment methods, a transnational remittance from country A to B must go through five institutions one after another. However, using digital RMB instead allows all five institutions to see and confirm the remittance information simultaneously.

Text 3：人类活动极大地改变了地球

人类活动极大地改变了地球表面许多进程的速率。为了了解地球系统的运作，我们需要了解人类在这些系统中的角色。要做到这一点，我们可以把人类想象成一个地质因素，把人类与地球的自然进程综合考虑。

人类对地球系统的影响随着人口和我们对自然资源的人均消耗而增加。地球科学家使用地质记录来区分自然和人类对地球系统的影响。他们在许多地方找到了自然和人类影响地球进程的证据。这些物质包括冰芯和土壤，以及来自湖泊和海洋的沉积物。

人类燃烧化石燃料、利用土地、从事农业和工业生产都会导致全球气候变化。其后果包括冰川和永冻层融化、海平面上升、降水模式转变、森林火灾增加、极端天气的加剧以及全球生态系统的破坏。人类通过改变河流、湖泊和地下水来影响地球上水的质量、可及性及其分布。

河道、堤坝等构筑物可以改变水流和沉积物的分布。污水横流、农作实践和工业活动造成的污染会降低水质。发电和农业过度用水减少了饮用水的存量。

人类活动改变了自然地表。超过三分之一未被冰覆盖的陆地用于耕种，而人类开发改造了大片土地，包括像湿地这样脆弱的生态系统。这些地表变化影响了许多自然活动，如地下水补给和天气模式。

人类活动加速了土地侵蚀。目前，由人类活动造成的全球土地侵蚀率非常高。它超过了所有自然进程的10倍。这些活动包括城市铺路、移除植被、露天采矿、改道溪流和增加雨水酸度。

人类活动极大地改变了生物圈。人类活动导致全球范围内的生物多样性下降，这是发生在现代的大规模灭绝。栖息地面积缩水和环境的快速变化造成了这一切。现在生物灭绝的速度与地球过去地质时期的大规模灭绝速度不相上下。

人类对地球系统的许多影响在人类有生之年是不可逆的。但通过人类之间的合作，它们对子孙后代的影响可以减少甚至逆转。公众具备地球科学素养、了解当前准确的地球科学知识，对于完善管理、健全政策和国际合作至关重要。地球科学教育对所有年龄、背景和国籍的人来说都很重要。

Text 4：为没有信用记录的人提供智能贷款

银行、信用卡公司和其他金融机构并不了解我们的个人情况，但他们确实有办法信任我们,那就是通过我们的信用评分。信用评分是通过汇总和分析我们的公共消费者信用数据而创建的。凭借它们,我们可以很容易获得所需的商品和服务,从买电到买房,或者冒险创业。但是,全球有25亿人没有信用评分。

这是世界人口的三分之一。他们没有信用评分,因为他们没有正式的公共记录——没有银行账户,没有信用记录,也没有社保号码。因为没有评分,他们无法获得用于改善生活的信贷或金融产品。他们不受信任。因此,我们希望找到一种方法来建立信任,并为这25亿人打开金融渠道。我们创建了一个移动应用程序,使用移动数据为他们建立信用评分。

目前,新兴市场有超过10亿部智能手机,那里的人们使用手机的方式和我们一样。他们给朋友发短信、导航、浏览互联网,甚至进行金融交易。随着时间的推移,这些数据会被我们的手机捕捉到,它详细地描绘了一个人的生活图景。

客户允许我们访问这些数据,我们则通过移动应用程序捕获这些数据。它帮助我们了解像詹妮弗这样的人的信用度。詹妮弗是肯尼亚首都内罗毕的一个小摊贩,今年65岁,几十年来一直在中央商务区经营一个小吃摊。她有三个儿子,她供他们读完了职业学校,自己也是当地互助会的领导人。

詹妮弗的小吃摊经营得很好,每天挣的钱刚好够支付开支。但她的经济状况并不稳定,任何紧急情况都可能使她负债累累。她没有可自由支配的收入来改善生活、应对紧急情况,或投资发展自己的生意。如果詹妮弗想要信用贷款,选择极为有限。她可以获得小额贷款,但必须先组建一个小组帮她担保。即便如此贷款额度也很低,平均约为150美元,杯水车薪。高利贷也是一种选择,但利率远高于300%,存在财务风险。

由于詹妮弗没有抵押品,也没有信用记录,她不能向银行申请商业贷款。但有一天,她的儿子说服她下载了我们的应用程序并申请了贷款。詹妮弗在她的手机上回答了几个问题,让我们访问了她设备上的几个关键数据点。这就是我们所看到的:首先是坏消息,詹妮弗的储蓄很少,以前没有贷款记录。这些因素会向传统银行亮起危险信号。

但她的个人经历中还有其他一些方面向我们展示了潜力。首先,我们看到她经常给她在乌干达的家人打电话。数据显示,如果一个人经常与几个亲密联系人交流,他的还款率会提高4%。我们还可以看到,尽管她经常出行,但相当有规律,要么在家,要么在她的小吃摊。数据显示,如果客户每天行踪固定,其还款率会提高6%。我们还可以看到,她全天与许多不同的人进行了大量的交流,有一个强大的支持网络。数据显示,常用联系人超过58个的人往往更可信。詹妮弗经常与89个不同的人进行交流,这一结果使她的还款率提高了9%。

这些只是我们为了解一个人的信誉而查看的数千个数据点中的一部分。在分析了所有这些数据点后,我们承担了第一个风险,给了詹妮弗一笔贷款。这些数据不会出现在书面记录或任何正式的财务记录中,但这证明了信任。抛开收入我们可以看到,新兴市场的人们表面上看起来风险很大、难以预测,但实际上他们有意愿和能力偿还债务。

第十章

专项练习

1. 读数练习

(1) two million four hundred and eight thousand seven hundred and thirty-two

(2) thirty-seven point seventy-five percent

(3) forty-seven thousand and ninety

(4) sixteen million three hundred thousand and fifty

(5) eight hundred twenty-four million fifty thousand

(6) three quarters

(7) (zero) point zero six seven

(8) a hundred and seventy thousand and thirty

(9) seven hundred and ninety-eight

(10) seven million nine hundred and one thousand

(11) six thousand three hundred

(12) minus four point five

(13) two thousand and twenty-one/twenty twenty-one

(14) nineteen o five

(15) the fourth century BC

(16) the nineteen eighties

(17) two-thirds

(18) (zero) point seven percent

(19) twice/two times/double

(20) twelfth

(21) eight and a quarter

(22) one hundred and thirty-seven million

2. 数字口译

(1) 三万两千零五十

(2) 约五百亿

(3) 八千四百六十三万五千五百五十

(4) 近七十万

(5) 六千零一

(6) 七十亿零三万两千

(7) 八百三十万

(8) 百分之零点四

(9) 七点四万亿

(10) 两千四百亿

(11) 超过五万七千

(12) 四点零五亿

(13) 二十五万

(14) 第三十位/三十日

(15) 五亿零九万

(16) 负六百七十

(17) 七千两百零五万

(18) 十几个

(19) 不超过六百

(20) 五千六百一十万

(21) eight point two seven million

(22) five thousand three hundred and twenty-seven

(23) one hundred and twenty million

(24) nearly eighty percent
(25) five percentage points
(26) the first day of the Chinese New Year/the Chinese New Year's Day
(27) four trillion/four thousand billion
(28) a quarter to one/twelve forty-five
(29) three hundred thousand and twenty
(30) less than one-eighth

3. 带单位的数字

(1) 数亿人
(2) 三十华氏度
(3) 五万磅/英镑
(4) 四十五英寸
(5) 四百千兆字节
(6) 十五世纪
(7) 六千零九十亿人民币
(8) 五十万双鞋
(9) 地下一层（B1）
(10) 一点零五亿港元
(11) 数万英里
(12) 七十亿吨
(13) 第二季度
(14) 几十个箱子
(15) 零点八公斤
(16) seventy feet
(17) nine hundred and seventy ounces (oz)
(18) ten degrees below zero
(19) nearly a quarter of a century
(20) (zero) point five euros/half a euro
(21) ten fifteen/a quarter past ten
(22) fifty Chinese feet/fifty *chi*/about fifty feet
(23) a catty/one *jin*/half a kilo
(24) about a fortnight/about two weeks
(25) eight inches
(26) nine point six million square kilometers
(27) seven thousand eight hundred cubic meters
(28) *Twenty Thousand Leagues under the Sea*
(29) one thousand and twenty-four megabytes/one gigabyte

4. 带数字的段落

（1）目前，亚洲已经形成了由香港、上海和新加坡等多个金融中心组成的较为完善的金融市场体系。2014年，亚洲上市公司的总市值为20.67万亿美元，占全球总市值的32.1%。

（2）联合国有17项可持续发展目标。第一项就是到2030年消除极端贫困。2015年至2018年，全球贫困率持续呈现历史性下降，从2015年的10.1%降至2018年的8.6%。

（3）报告预测，到21世纪20年代，每年将有8 700万非洲儿童出生贫困。据估计，仍有40%的非洲人每天的生活费不到1美元90美分。一个出生在贫困中的孩子更有可能成为文盲，五岁前死亡的风险也更大。

（4）为孩子买房和支付婚礼费用是香港中产阶级的首要任务。中国建设银行1月份对2 500名香港人的储蓄和理财习惯进行了调查。22%的受访者表示他们正在攒钱给孩子买房，12%的人表示他们在为孩子的婚礼攒钱。

（5）中国有2 200家博物馆，其中包括625家非政府博物馆。这些博物馆的藏品总数超过2 000万件，每年举办8 000多场展览。以文物展品为依托的博物馆已经成为游客打卡的必选地，如西安的秦始皇兵马俑博物馆。

（6）Since the 13th Five-Year Plan, China's national fitness campaign has been developing vigorously, with more and more people engaged in physical activities. 37.2 percent of the Chinese people take part in regular exercises. As the environment for working out becomes more pleasant and public-friendly, enthusiasm in doing sports continues to grow.

（7）During its bid for the Beijing 2022 Winter Olympics, China made a commitment to the international community to "engage 300 million people in ice and snow activities", and recent statistics showed that the country has realized this goal. According to the National Bureau of Statistics, since Beijing won the bid to host the Beijing 2022 Winter Olympics in 2015, over 346 million people have participated in ice and snow sports by January this year.

（8）Tmall's sales on Nov. 11 reached a record of 268.4 billion *yuan*, marking a year-on-year growth of about 25.7%. Over 500 million consumers shopped on Tmall this year, increasing by some 100 million over one year ago. Those born after 1995 accounted for about 30 percent, while those above 50 years old reported the highest growth rate, rising 42 percent year-on-year. Over 200,000 brands worldwide joined the shopping festival on Tmall. And among the 299 brands with sales exceeding 100 million *yuan* that day, dozens were fresh players.

（9）In 2021, Beijing's average annual concentration of fine particulate matter (PM2.5) dropped to 33 micrograms per cubic meter, down by 63.1 percent compared with 2013. This means an average annual drop of 7.9 percent, far better than the rate of cities in developed countries over the same period. The days with good air quality in cities nationwide reached 87.5 percent, up 0.5 percentage point year on year.

（10）The Mississippi River is the longest river on the North American continent and the fourth-longest river in the world. It rises in Northern Minnesota and flows south for 232 miles into the Gulf of Mexico. Its basin covers an area of 3.22 million square kilometers, accounting for 41 percent of the size of the United States. Before 1900, every year the river transported an estimated 400 million tons of sand, stones, mud, etc. Yet during the last two decades, this number was only 145 million tons per year.

5. 核心概念词拓展

建议、劝告、意图、看法、决断、主张	e.g. advice, advocate, argue, assert, believe, contend, decide, hold, intend, maintain, prefer, propose, propound, put forward, recommend, request, state, suggest, urge, etc.

询问、请求	ask, ask (for/about), call for, claim, expect, inquire, insist on, order, request, require, seek, etc.
重视、强调	accentuate, attach importance to, draw attention to, emphasize, highlight, lay stress on, make a point of, prioritize, stress, underscore, etc.
反对	contradict, deny, differ, disagree, disapprove, dispute, dissent, refute, rebut, retract, etc.
同意	accept, agree, approve, assent, be of the same mind, be of the same opinion, consent, go for, see eye to eye, etc.
比率	account for, comprise, constitute, contribute to, make up, represent, etc.
倍数	double, triple, quadruple, (three/four/...)fold, (three/four/...) times, multiple, etc.
约数	about, approximately, around, close to, (a little) more than, nearly, over, roughly, etc.

篇章练习

Text 1: 美国的人口

一直以来，美国每10年统计一次人口。政府需要知道每个州有多少人，这样才能知道每个州应该有多少国会议员。第一次统计是在200年前。当时，该国约有400万人口。100年后，人口增加到约6 300万人。到1950年，美国有超过1.5亿人。

美国建国早期，平均每个母亲生过8到10个孩子。生活条件艰苦，许多孩子在很小的时候就夭折了。家庭农场需要帮手，所以有很多孩子是件好事。

这一情况在第二次世界大战后发生了改变：似乎每个家庭都开始生孩子了，父母对未来充满希望，国内有大量的就业机会。在经历了漫长而艰难的战争之后，世界各地的人们都感到需要一个家庭和安全感，因此出生率激增。1950年到1960年间，5岁到14岁的儿童数量增加了1 000多万。

许多新父母搬到了新郊区的家里。"郊区"（suburb）一词来自"城市"（urban）一词。郊区是城市的次一级，也就是英文的"sub"。它通常建在城市外围的一块空地上。商人会购买土地并在其上建造房屋。年轻夫妇会从当地银行贷款并用以买房。郊区的生活与城市不同，有各种各样的团体活动。

父母尽一切努力让孩子过上好日子。1950年至1960年间，参加少年棒球联盟球队的男孩人数从不足100万增加到近600万，同期女童子军的人数增加了200万。自行车销量翻倍，父母也试图为孩子创造更好的教育条件。1960年，美国父母为孩子购买的教育用书几乎是10年前的3倍。父母还为孩子购买了价值数百万美元的钢琴、小提琴和其他乐器。郊区的家庭希望孩子过上美好的新生活。

每个家庭的平均儿童数量在增加，但在此期间，美国总人口的增长并没有人们预期的那么多，原因是外国移民越来越少。事实上，移民来美国的人数多年来一直在下降。1910年，每1 000名美国人中就有11名移民。到1950年，这一数字下降到1.5。

移民的来源地也在改变。过去，大多数人来自北欧和西欧，但现在越来越多的人是从拉丁美洲、亚洲以及南欧和东欧国家来的。

20世纪50年代，美国国内发生了大规模的人口迁移。大多数人继续生活在东部、中部和南部地区，但越来越多的人迁至西部各州。20世纪50年代，西部各州的人口增长了近40%。

1950年，美国最大的城市是纽约，人口近800万。其次是芝加哥，超过350万人。接下来是费城、洛杉矶、底特律、巴尔的摩、克利夫兰和圣路易斯。

另一个人口方面的变化是预期寿命。20世纪初，美国新生儿的预期寿命只有47岁，但是到了50年代，大多数美国婴儿都能活到60岁。预期寿命的增加是由于生活条件和医疗保健的改善，未来将继续稳步增长。

Text 2: Left-behind children

Left-behind children refer to those who are left back in their hometown or live with relatives for most time of the year because their parents migrate elsewhere for work. Modernization has driven many rural surplus laborers to the cities, but the high cost of living forbids them from taking their children with them. Left-behind children are almost exclusively found in China and are becoming more alarming in recent years.

Surveys over the past decade show that left-behind children generally lack motivation and interests in learning; they often feel lonely, anxious, depressed, or even hostile and have low positive emotions such as subjective well-being and life satisfaction; they have low self-esteem and a severe sense of inferiority; they are more likely to attack people or violate rules in other ways, and more prominently, they are hard to fit in the society.

The issue of left-behind children not only concerns the family but also the development and the future of the nation. In recent years, guided by the strategy of rural vitalization, the Communist Party of China and the government have vigorously encouraged the migrant workers to return to their hometowns to start business or seek jobs. Arrangements have been made to let the children go to school in cities where their parents work. These measures get down to the fundamentals of the issue. In 2020, the number of left-behind children was 12.897 million, a decrease of 947,000 compared with 2019.

At the same time, technological advances also bring positive changes to the living conditions of left-behind children. The video calls get rid of the restrictions of time and space to some extent, and make the family communication more convenient and efficient. The short video platforms present the daily life of left-behind children which arouses social awareness of this special group. It is a traditional Chinese virtue to "care for others' children as one cares for one's own". With the help of policies and technology, these children won't be left untended, but will grow up healthily and have a bright future.

Text 3: 学生豁免贷款

这项计划的受惠人群相当广泛，覆及学生家长、研究生、本科生，不管是申请了直接贷款，还是家长贷款或研究生贷款，都包括在内。因此，在4 500万申请联邦学生贷款的人中，大约有4 300万人将有资格获得减免。

学生贷款减免的起始额为1万美元，但如果你曾经获得过佩尔助学金，你就有资格再额外豁免1万美元。佩尔助学金是一种联邦财政援助形式，申请者的家庭年收入通常低于6万美元。当前在拥有联邦贷款的人群中，60%的人在大学期间曾获佩尔助学金。因此，绝大多数人都将获得2万美元的贷款减免，这是非常出乎意料的。

当然，学生贷款减免对收入也有要求。这个计划的关键是，个人在2021或2022税收年度的年收入不能超过12.5万美元，这是你的调整后总收入。对于已婚夫妇联合申报的，家庭年收入必须在25万美元以下。

白宫提出或计划实施的债务减免将清除大约2 000万借款人的负债，还有更多的人债务将减半。我认为，大多数获减免的人群年收入在7.5万美元以下，据说大约90%的减免是面向这些人的。

Text 4: Vocational education

Vocational education is an important component of the national education system and human resources development. As a major path to success for young people, it contributes greatly to the sustained and rapid development of Chinese economy by training over 200 million qualified workers in all sectors.

Currently, there are 30.88 million students in 11.3 thousand vocational schools in China. In modern manufacturing and services sectors, more than 70 percent of the new employees come from vocational schools. With the integration between industry and education and the cooperation between schools and enterprises, more and more technical professionals and great craftsmen graduate from vocational schools.

However, hiring technical workers remains difficult mainly for two reasons. One is the lack of high-quality resources in vocational education, and the other is the stereotypical mindset that vocational students are less competitive. Therefore, we should accelerate the establishment of the vocational college entrance exam system. Besides, we should also ensure that skilled workers are better paid and respected.

Channeling part of the students to vocational education not only increases labor supply, but also benefits students' individual development by helping them with career planning and employment. With high-quality vocational education, young people will consider skilled workers as a good career choice, and hopefully it would relieve the public anxiety over education over time.

第十一章

专项练习

1. 演讲及英汉口译练习

英汉段落1：在消除冲突中性暴力行为国际日的致辞

（1）冲突中的性暴力是一种残酷的战争、酷刑、恐怖和镇压手段。其影响波及数代人，对人类安全和国际安全构成威胁。

（2）在受冲突影响的地方，战争引起的动荡使性暴力犯罪问责更加困难。与此同时，性暴力幸存者在报案及获得援助上也面临新的阻碍。

（3）即便当前形势严峻复杂，我们也必须彻查每一起案件，维持对每一位幸存者的基本服务。这种罪行的举报率本来就低下，我们绝不允许其隐藏更深。

（4）犯罪人必须受到惩处。努力改善现状的同时，也必须从根源上解决性暴力和性别暴力。

（5）值此消除冲突中性暴力行为国际日，让我们下定决心，在努力预防和制止这些可怕罪行的同时，维护所有幸存者的权利，满足他们的需要。

英汉段落2：在防治荒漠化和干旱世界日的致辞

（1）人类正在对自然发动一场毁灭自我的战争：生物多样性日益减少，温室气体浓度不断上升，从偏远岛屿到高耸山峰，人为污染随处可见。

（2）我们必须与自然和平相处。土地本可成为我们最有力的盟友，而此时却在蒙受灾难。

（3）气候变化、农业、城市和基建用地的不断扩张导致土地退化，不仅损害32亿民众的福祉，危害生物多样性，还为传染病的肆虐提供温床。

（4）整治退化土地不仅将消除大气中的碳含量，有利于弱势社群适应气候变化，还可使农业每年增收1.4万亿美元。

（5）所幸，土地恢复操作简单、成本低廉、人人可做，是实现可持续发展目标最民主、益贫的方法之一。

（6）今年是"联合国生态系统恢复十年"倡议的开局之年。值此世界日，让我们努力实现土地健康,将其作为所有计划的工作重心。

2. 演讲及汉英口译练习

汉英段落1: Xi Jinping's Speech at the Beijing 2022 Winter Olympics and Paralympics review and awards ceremony

(1) Comrades and friends,

After seven years of arduous efforts, we have successfully hosted the Beijing 2022 Winter Olympics and Paralympics, drawing wide attention both at home and from abroad.

(2) By overcoming various difficulties, the Chinese people, along with people from around the world, have once again presented the Games that will go down in history and together shared the glory of Olympics.

(3) Facts have proved again that the Chinese people not only have the willingness and determination to make contributions to advancing the Olympic movement and promoting solidarity and friendship among peoples across the world, but also have the ability and enthusiasm to make even greater contributions.

(4) The success in hosting the Games is a result of the efforts and wisdom of people working in different fronts for the preparation and organization of the events. ... All the builders, workers and volunteers, bearing in mind the trust of the Party and the people and driven by the aspirations to win glory for the country, worked tirelessly and dedicatedly in their respective posts, and many outstanding groups and individuals have stood out among them.

(5) Today, we gather here to review the experience of the Beijing 2022 Winter Olympics and Paralympics, and honor those who have made exceptional contributions to the Games, with a view to carrying forward the lofty spirit fostered during the preparation and hosting of the Games and inspiring the entire Party and all the Chinese people to strive for the second centenary goal and the Chinese Dream of national rejuvenation.

汉英段落2: Remark on World Oceans Day

(1) This year's observance of World Oceans Day falls as the world wrestles with the climate crisis, and mitigates the ongoing human impact on oceans and marine resources.

(2) The recently issued Second World Ocean Assessment confirmed that many of the benefits that the global ocean provides to humankind are being undermined by our own actions.

(3) Our seas are choking with plastic waste, which can be found from the remotest atolls to the deepest ocean trenches.

(4) Overfishing is causing an annual loss of almost $90 billion in net benefits — which

also heightens the vulnerability of women, who are vital to the survival of small-scale fishing businesses.

(5) Carbon emissions are driving ocean warming and acidification, destroying biodiversity and causing sea level rise that threatens heavily inhabited coastlines.

(6) The theme of this year's observance, "The Ocean: Life and Livelihoods", underscores the importance of oceans for the cultural life and economic survival of communities around the world. More than three billion people rely on the ocean for their livelihoods, the vast majority in developing countries.

篇章练习

Text 1: 什么造就了美好生活？（节选）

哈佛大学这项关于成人发展的研究可能是同类研究中耗时最长的。在75年时间里，我们跟踪了724个人的一生，年复一年，了解他们的工作、家庭、健康状况。当然，在这一过程中，我们完全不知道他们的人生将走向何方。

那么我们得到了什么结论呢？那长达几万页的数据记录了他们的生活。我们从这些记录中到底学到了什么？不是关于财富、名望或努力工作。在75年的研究中，我们得到的最明确的结论是：良好的人际关系能让人更加快乐和健康。就是这么简单。

关于人际关系，我们得到三大结论。第一，社会关系对我们是有益的，而孤独寂寞有害健康。我们发现，那些跟家庭成员更亲近的人，更爱与朋友、与邻居交往的人，会比那些不善交际、离群索居的人更快乐、更健康、更长寿。孤独寂寞是有害健康的。那些"被孤立"的人跟合群的人相比往往更加不快乐。等他们人到中年时，健康状况和大脑功能下降得更快，也没那么长寿。可惜的是，长久以来，每5个美国人中就至少有1个认为自己是孤独的。

而且即便你身处闹市之中，或者已婚，你仍可能感到孤独，因此我们得出的第二大结论是：孤独不取决于你有多少朋友或是否拥有伴侣，而取决于亲密关系的质量。研究表明，争吵冲突有害健康。例如，成天吵架、无爱的婚姻对健康的负面影响甚至大于离婚；而关系和睦融洽则有益健康。

当研究对象步入80岁时，我们会回顾他们的中年生活，以检验能否预测哪些人会在八九十岁时过得快乐健康，哪些人不会。我们将他们50岁时的所有信息进行汇总分析，发现决定其衰老速度的并非是中年时的胆固醇水平，而是对婚姻生活的满意度。那些50岁时满意度最高的人，到80岁时也是最健康的。另外，良好和亲密的婚姻关系能减缓衰老带来的痛苦。参与者中那些最幸福的夫妻告诉我们，在他们80多岁时，哪怕身体出现各种毛病，他们依旧觉得生活很幸福。而那些婚姻不幸福的人身体出现不适时，情绪痛楚将会放大身体上的痛苦。

关于婚姻和健康的关系，我们得到的第三大结论是：幸福的婚姻不单能保护我们的身体，还能保护我们的大脑。研究发现,如果80多岁时,你的婚姻生活还温暖和睦,对伴侣依然信任有加,知道对方在关键时刻值得依靠,那么你的记忆力就不容易衰退。而反之,那些无法信任伴侣的人记忆力更早表现出衰退。幸福的婚姻并不意味着一帆风顺。有些夫妻八九十岁了还天天拌嘴,但只要他们坚信,在关键时刻对方能靠得住,那这些争吵就不会影响记忆力。

所以请记住,幸福和睦的婚姻对健康有利,这是永恒的真理。但为什么我们总是办不到呢?因为我们是人类,总喜欢找捷径,总想一劳永逸。人际关系麻烦又复杂,与家人、朋友相处需要努力付出,一点也不"高大上"。这种努力需要一辈子投入,无穷无尽。在我们长达75年的研究中,那些最享受退休生活的人,是那些主动寻求新的玩伴来替代同事的人。和近期调研中的"千禧一代"一样,我们很多人年轻时也坚信名望、财富和成就是幸福生活的保障,但在75年的时间里,我们的研究一次次证明,最幸福的人群是那些主动与家人、朋友或者邻居建立良好关系的人们。

那么你们呢?也许你现在25岁、40岁或60岁。怎样才算主动与人建立良好关系呢?

方法有很多。最简单的是放下手机、电脑,去和真人交往,或者一起尝试些新事物,激活彼此的关系。例如,一起散个步,晚上约个会,或者给多年不往来的亲戚打个电话,因为这种寻常的家族矛盾对那些喜欢生闷气的人来说负面影响很大。

我想引用马克·吐温的一段话来作为结束。一个多世纪前,他回首自己的人生,写下这样一段话:"时光荏苒,生命短暂,别将时间浪费在争吵、道歉、伤心和责备上。用时间去爱吧,哪怕只有一瞬间,也不要辜负。"

美好人生,从良好的人际关系开始。

谢谢大家。

Text 2: Remarks at the High-level Segment of the 49th Session of the United Nations Human Rights Council (excerpt)

Mr. President,

Dear Colleagues,

It gives me great pleasure to speak on behalf of the Chinese government at the 49th session of the United Nations Human Rights Council.

To ensure full enjoyment of human rights by all is an unremitting pursuit of humanity. In a world of rapid development where human rights awareness has taken hold, we are more able and better positioned than ever before to promote and protect human rights. Meanwhile, due to exacerbating poverty and inequality, the global human rights cause is facing further grave challenges.

Promoting and protecting human rights is the shared cause of all countries. As such, China believes we should act as:

First, true champions of human rights. The UN Charter and the Universal Declaration of Human Rights have set a lofty goal for the global human rights cause. It falls on every country to keep exploring an effective way to achieve this goal. Human rights have historical, specific and practical contexts, and the human rights cause can only be advanced in light of each country's reality and its people's needs. The economic, political, social, cultural and environmental rights of all should be advanced in a coordinated manner to promote and achieve well-rounded human development.

Second, staunch guardians of people's interests. A happy life for all is the biggest human right. A country's human rights are essentially gauged by whether its people's aspirations for a better life are satisfied; whether their needs, concerns and expectations are addressed; and whether they enjoy a growing sense of fulfillment, happiness and security. It is essential to put the people front and center and deliver more benefits of national governance and development to all people more fairly, making sure that no one is left behind.

Third, positive contributors to common development. Without development, there would be no human rights to speak of, nor could the rights enjoyed by the people be sustainable. President Xi Jinping has put forth the Global Development Initiative (GDI), committing China to working with the UN and all countries to accelerate the implementation of the 2030 Agenda for Sustainable Development. The GDI is yet another public good China provides for the development of the global human rights cause. It has been endorsed and supported by the UN and up to 100 countries.

Fourth, firm defenders of equity and justice. In judging whether human rights are upheld in a country, one cannot use other countries' standards, still less apply double standards or use human rights as a political tool to interfere in the affairs of other countries. We need to steadfastly promote greater democracy and rule of law in international relations, follow true multilateralism, and steer global human rights governance toward greater fairness, equity and inclusiveness. The Human Rights Council needs to uphold the principles of non-selectiveness and non-politicization. It must not be reduced to a stage for political confrontation.

...

I wish this session of the Human Rights Council positive outcomes.

Thank you.

Text 3: 为了消除浪费，我们需要重新提供节俭（节选）

让我们谈谈节俭。节俭指的是减少使用、重复使用和回收利用，而它其实还有经济价值。在我看来这一概念极具潜力，能够给人们的生活带来改变。我的祖母很节俭。这是她装绳子的罐子。她从来没有买过任何绳子，这些绳子都是她收集来的，有的是买肉得来的，有的来自礼品包装。她会把它们放在罐子里，需要的时候拿来用。无论是用来捆扎玫瑰还是自行车部件，用完后她都会把绳子放回罐子。这是一个完美的节俭观念：不需要购买，你就能使用所需要的东西，钱就这么省下来了。这一观念是与生俱来的。当你想扔掉一个纸板箱时，孩子会说："不要扔！我想用它来做机器人的头或者做独木舟。"他们了解产品二次利用的价值。

所以，我认为节俭和当今时代形成了鲜明对比。现在，所有的产品都能更新换代。一得到酷炫的新玩具，我们就扔掉旧的。当时看来很爽，但长此以往就会出问题。因为当你扔掉物件时，它们就会进入垃圾填埋场。

垃圾填埋场一旦形成就很难消失，目前还在不断增加。现在我们每年有大约13亿吨材料进入堆填区。到2100年，这一数字将达到约40亿吨。所以我们应当从现在就开始节俭。

制造产品时我们会考虑使用什么材料，同时也要考虑使用寿命结束后什么时候可以回收利用。问题在于我们应该改变对"垃圾"这个词的看法，"垃圾"不再是一个肮脏的词，我们几乎消解了这一负面概念。我们所看到的只是资源，以及资源在产品间的不断流通和转化。

这一方面做得不太好的是建筑行业。其中一个原因是我们只考虑建造，却不考虑拆除的问题。我们不是拆解或拆除建筑物，而是直接摧毁。这是个大问题，因为美国垃圾填埋场中有三分之一都是建筑垃圾。我们应该想想怎么解决。有些做法可以减少建筑垃圾的产生。

比如，这些砖头是用建筑废料生产的，其成分包括玻璃、瓦砾和混凝土。把它们放进研磨机中加热，生产出的砖头又能用于建造。但这只是很小的一部分。

我希望我们能利用大数据和地理定位改变这种状况，把节俭的概念运用到建筑行业中。假如不远处正在拆毁一栋大楼，拆下来的这些材料中是否有些能用于建造这边的新建筑？这不就相当于保留了它们的自身价值？

让我们再看看其他行业是如何践行节俭的。现在许多行业都在思考如何解决生产废料这个问题。举个简单的例子：工业生产排放的废气。

许多冶金厂会在生产时排放大量的二氧化碳。我知道有一个叫Land Detector的公司目前在中国开设业务，很快也将拓展到南非。这家冶金厂可以收集70万吨工业废气，并把它们转换成40万吨乙醇，这相当于25万辆汽车一年所需的燃料。这就是有效利用生产废料的案例。

Text 4: The open letter by FAO Director-General on World Environment Day (excerpt)

Youth, including young professionals, who make up a large proportion of the global population, are and will continue to be disproportionately affected by the crises facing our planet, such as the impacts of climate change, ecosystem degradation, biodiversity loss, hunger and malnutrition, water scarcity, access to energy, and health for all. Without our immediate action, they will inherit an uncertain future.

Youth have always been a strong voice in calling for action, and they must continue to advocate for their future. Young people, with their commitment and passion, work on the frontlines, with the grassroots, making every effort to bring on board innovative ideas for a sustainable planet. They advocate for better policies, raise awareness on important environmental issues, and mobilize the public to take action to overcome some of our most pressing environmental challenges. Youth actively contribute to conservation and restoration efforts, often behind the scenes. The world needs to listen to the youth. To what they believe is needed to build and support a sustainable future. To work with them, and empower them as stakeholders, stewards and future leaders of the earth.

The recent XV World Forestry Congress in Seoul, hosted by the Government of the Republic of Korea in collaboration with the Food and Agriculture Organization of the UN, is an example of how the youth made their voice heard. While the global forest community discussed how to build a green, healthy and resilient future with forests, over 600 youth participated in consultations bringing their energy, motivation and vision to carry forward a constructive outcome reflected in a Youth Declaration: "Work with Us — Youth Call for Action". The Call asks for collaboration and support from all stakeholders to enhance the standard of, and access to, education and capacity development opportunities, decent work and employment, gender mainstreaming, access to finance, and participation in policy and strategy decisions at all levels. These are key enabling factors for elevating and strengthening the contribution, engagement and participation of youth and young professionals in the forest sector to help achieve internationally agreed global objectives and implement *the 2030 Agenda for Sustainable Development*.

The youth are catalysts for change who have the potential to transform our agri-food systems to make them more efficient, more inclusive, more resilient and more transparent. They are the global agents of change for better production, better nutrition, a better environment and a better life for all, leaving no one behind. We must ensure that youth are in the driver's seat of their future.

第十二章

专项练习

1. 习语口译练习

英译汉

（1）莎拉感到身体不适，决定留在家里不去上班。

（2）数学是他的软肋。

（3）工会已在最后一刻决定取消罢工。

（4）我已束手无策，不知道如何帮助他。

（5）你的好建议对他而言恐怕是对牛弹琴——他不会听的。

(6) 就议案的主题而言,大家都不是专家,确实是一个外行指导外行的情况。

(7) 他侥幸逃脱了秘密警察的追捕。

(8) 当粉丝发现偶像有不为人知的弱点时,祛魅的打击是巨大的。

(9) 房子的抵押贷款像一座大山,压得他喘不过气来。

(10) 削减预算所带来的威胁令剧院方面感到如临绝境。

汉译英

(1) Many celebrities are not talented players, but rely on day-to-day efforts to achieve a leap from quantitative change to qualitative change. This is the spirit of "a slow sparrow should make an early start" that we often say.

(2) The exam on Monday is very important for your future studies. Here I keep my fingers crossed and wish you all the best results!

(3) Everyone, please calm down, as the old saying goes: harmony brings wealth. It's better that we sit down together and have a detailed discussion.

(4) I'd been stuck in the old mindset for long before I was enlightened by your words just now. The solution seems rather clear now.

(5) This manufacturer was boycotted by consumers for selling expired food, and was later transferred to the Supervision Office by the relevant competent authority — losing the bait along with the fish.

(6) An army at a disadvantage can only escape by burning its own way of retreat and being determined to fight to the end.

(7) In terms of diplomacy, the pains brought by radical and reckless actions still linger, and China still remembers the admonition to hide our strength and bide our time.

(8) It is natural for parents to hold high expectations for their children, but be careful not to overwhelm them with too much burden.

(9) In order to cope with the turmoil in Iraq, the United States had to rob Peter to pay Paul and transfer troops from the battlefield in Afghanistan.

(10) Teachers should pay attention to the individual differences of students. Every child has different characteristics. How to motivate students to learn and teach them in accordance with their aptitude is the primary challenge for educators.

2. 俚语口译练习
英译汉

(1) —内森已经在做两份工作了。现在他又找了第三份,确实是有点打肿脸充胖子/贪多嚼不烂。

——的确,他应该悠着点。

(2)——你这学期成绩如何?

——不是自夸,我在班上的确名列前茅。

(3)——你打算给莎莉买什么生日礼物?

——不知道啊。我没有多少预算。

——也许我们可以集资,给她买点好东西。

(4)——不明白我数学怎么会不及格。

——你自己清楚有没有努力。如果想毕业,下学期必须面对现实重修。

(5)——你见过我的朋友艾米,对吧?

——嗯,我不确定,但这个名字听着耳熟。是去年去巴黎的那个女孩吗?

汉译英

(1) — Hi guys, as we don't have much time here, so I'm going to cut to the chase. We've been having some major problems in the office lately.

— Don't worry, please go straight, and we'll fully cooperate.

(2) — She must have had her head in the clouds when she made the reservations, because she can never afford such a luxury with the little she makes!

— Can't agree more, now she'd have to scrimp and save for several months.

(3) — John was born with a silver spoon in his mouth. His parents bought him everything he wanted and sent him to the best private schools.

— It's truly enviable!

(4) — Jane really has the Midas touch. Every business she starts becomes very successful.

— The process must be painstaking. It always requires talent and hard work to bring along the success.

(5) — What's your plan for tonight?

— I'd like to have dinner in the city but I'm not sure how the traffic will be so let's play it by ear.

3. 谚语口译练习

英译汉

(1) 五十步笑百步。

(2) 吃得苦中苦,方知甜中甜。

(3) 清心者自福。/好人有好报。

(4) 笑一笑,十年少;愁一愁,白了头。

（5）留得青山在，不怕没柴烧。

（6）学无坦途。/书山有路勤为径。

（7）要有学问，不耻下问。/久问成师。

（8）今日事，今日毕。

（9）知足者常乐。

汉译英

(1) The friendship between gentlemen is as pure as crystal./A hedge between keeps friendship green.

(2) Misfortune may be an actual blessing.

(3) Where there is a will, there is a way.

(4) Man's nature at birth is good.

(5) Money makes the mare go./Money talks.

(6) Better make friends than make enemies.

(7) A real man never goes back on his words.

(8) Know the enemy and know yourself, and you can fight a hundred battles with no danger of defeat.

(9) Modesty helps one go forward, whereas conceit makes one lag behind.

(10) Practice is the sole criterion for testing truth.

篇章练习

Text 1: 不必拘泥于使用英语

今天要跟大家讲的是关于语种消失和英语全球化的问题。我有一个朋友，她在阿布扎比教成年人英语。一天，她决定带学生们去花园教他们一些大自然用语。但是结果她反而学了所有当地植被的阿拉伯名称和它们的用途——药用的、妆用的、食用的、草药类的。那些学生从哪得到这些知识的呢？当然是从他们的祖父母那里，甚至是他们的曾祖父母那里。

但是，令人惋惜的是，今天很多语种正在以空前的速度消失。每14天就有一种语言消失。与此同时，现在英语无可争辩地成为全球性语言。这两者间有联系吗？我不知道。但是我知道我已目睹了很多变化。我被英国文化教育协会招聘到这里，同时招来的还有其他25个老师。我们是最早在科威特公立学校教书的非穆斯林。我们被请来教英语，因为政府想要发展国家现代化，让公民通过学习提高自己。当然，英国也因此得以收获可观的石油财富。

我目睹了英语教学是怎样演变的，从一个互惠的交流方式变成如今规模宏大的跨国生意。它不再只是学校里的一门外语课，也不再是英国特有的。对地球上每个说英语的国家而言，说英语已成为潮流。为什么不呢？毕竟，根据最新的世界大学排名，最好的教育在英国或者美国。每个人都想得到英语教育,但如果你的母语不是英语,首先要通过英语测试。

那么仅仅根据学生的语言能力就拒绝一个学生合适吗?一个天才的计算机科学家需要具备像律师一样的语言能力吗?我认为不必。我们做英语老师的总是否定他们,放一个禁止通行的标志,这就挡住了他们前进的道路。他们不能继续追寻梦想,除非已经掌握了英语。这么说吧,如果我遇到一个只会说荷兰语的人,他能治愈癌症,我会阻止他进入英国的大学吗?我想不会。但事实上我们正是这样做的。我们英语老师是"看门人"。你得先令我们满意,你的英语要足够好。这很危险,把很多权力交给了社会的一个小团体可能为诸多事务设障。

但是我听见你们说,"那科研呢?它们用的都是英语。"书是英语的,研究刊物是英语的。正是这样的自证预言让英语成为必须条件,于是现状就这样持续下去。那我问你,还需要翻译吗?想想伊斯兰的黄金时代,当时有很多翻译。他们把拉丁文和希腊语翻译成阿拉伯语和波斯语,然后又翻译成欧洲的日耳曼语和罗曼语。于是欧洲黑暗时代被点亮了。不要误会,我不是反对教英语,或是反对在座的英语老师。我支持我们有一种全球性语言,今天比过去任何时候都需要它。但是我反对用它设障。在600种语言中,我们难道真的只想让英语和中文成为主要语言吗?我们需要更多语言。那么又该如何划定界限?这个体制把知识和英语能力划等号,这是非常武断的。

当代知识分子是站在老一辈"巨人的肩膀"上发展起来的,而老一辈并不都具有英语能力,也不需要通过英语考试。爱因斯坦就是个典型。其实他在学校的时候是个需要补课的学生,因为他诵读有困难。他不必通过英语考试,因为1964年托福考试还没设立。而现在各种各样的英语测试已经泛滥,每年成千上万的学生参加这种考试。你我可能认为这些考试价格还算合理,但却令数百万穷人望而却步。所以一开始我们就把他们挡在了外面。

我的女儿从科威特回到英国。她已经在一所阿拉伯中学用阿拉伯语学了科学和数学。在英国的重点中学里,她要把所学的内容翻译成英语,而且她是最擅长这些科目的。这告诉我们,对于留学生而言,他们已经在本族语言中学会了这些知识,但我们却并未给予其足够认可。而当某一种语言消失的时候,我们甚至对这种语言中所包含的知识还一无所知。

我们不能让自己置身黑暗。让我们一起为多元化欢呼。重视你的语言,用它来传播优秀的思想。

Text 2: The Spring Festival traditions

The Spring Festival is the Chinese New Year. It reflects the great importance that Chinese people attach to their families. During the Spring Festival, they offer sacrifices to ancestors, travel back home for family reunion, and have a big feast on New Year's Eve. In the following days, people will pay visits to their relatives and friends, wishing each other good health and good fortune. It is a way to connect over and express best wishes for the coming year.

The Spring Festival also passes on traditional Chinese culture and art. People put on red couplets to add to the festive atmosphere, which embody the charm of Chinese calligraphy and poetry. The Spring Festival gala and other celebrations showcase folk art of different regions. And the Lantern Festival, celebrated on the 15th day of the first month of the lunar calendar, marks another important occasion. People put on colorful lanterns and solve the riddles on the lanterns as a brain teaser.

Nevertheless, the Spring Festival traditions are undergoing changes. In the past, people set off firecrackers and fireworks to ring in the new year, but now it is restricted in some parts of China to reduce air pollution and noise as well as to prevent fires. It is a custom for the elders to give lucky money in red envelopes to their children and grandchildren. But now many people send lucky money via WeChat to their families and friends living faraway, which is a new means to express best wishes.

Text 3: 茶的历史

神农是中国农业的发明者，这突出了茶在古代中国的重要性。考古证据显示茶起源于中国，距今6 000年左右，比法老修建吉萨大金字塔还早1 500年。早先的中国茶作物与现在遍及全球的茶树种类一致，但食用方法与现在却大不相同。茶最早作为蔬菜或用来煮粥，直到1500年前才从食品演变为饮品。彼时，人们发现加热和冲泡可以使这种树叶产生出复杂多变的口感。制茶方式经过了几百年的演化，形成了现在的标准流程，包括加热茶叶，压制成便携的茶饼，磨成粉末，冲入热水。这就是"抹茶"。抹茶文化风靡一时，独特的中国茶文化也由此产生。茶变成了诗歌和书籍的主题，成为了皇帝最喜爱的饮品。艺术家将其作为创作载体，在茶水泡沫中作画，与现在咖啡店的拉花颇有相似之处。

9世纪的唐朝，一位日本和尚将第一株茶作物带到日本。日本人最终形成了自己独特的品茶习惯，茶道由此诞生。14世纪的明朝，中国皇帝下令不再制作茶饼，而改用散茶工艺。此时，茶树种植仍为中国特有，因此，茶叶连同陶瓷和丝绸一起，成为中国出口的三大商品，为中国带来了巨大的政治和经济影响力。也正因如此，饮茶习俗当时遍及全球。

17世纪初，荷兰商人将大量的茶带到欧洲，饮茶风尚风靡一时。很多人认为，尊贵的葡萄牙女王凯瑟琳皇后1661年嫁给英国国王查尔斯二世后，将饮茶习惯带到了英国贵族阶层之中。当时的英国正忙于殖民扩张，日渐崛起成为世界领导力量。随着英国不断发展壮大，世界对茶的兴趣也日渐浓厚。1700年，欧洲市场上茶的价格已经达到了咖啡的十倍，但此时茶树仍仅在中国种植。茶叶贸易利润丰厚，就连世界上最快的船"飞剪船"都是因此而诞生的。西方贸易公司之间竞争激烈，都希望以更快的速度将茶运回欧洲以获取最多利润。

起初，英国用银币交换茶叶，但茶叶价格不断攀升，他们提出用鸦片进行交易。这引发了中国的公共健康问题：人们吸食鸦片成瘾。1839年，一位中国官员（林则徐）下令销毁大量英国运来的鸦片，以抗议英国鸦片贸易对中国的影响。

为进一步控制茶叶市场，英国东印度公司希望自行种植茶作物，因此委派植物学家罗伯特·福琼秘密前往中国盗取茶叶。他乔装打扮，踏上穿越中国山茶区的危险旅程，最终将茶树和经验丰富的茶工偷渡到印度大吉岭。从此，茶进一步传播开来，并迅速普及成为日常商品。如今，茶的饮用量仅次于水，位居世界第二。从甜味的土耳其红茶，到咸味的西藏酥油茶，饮茶方法之多，正如世界文化一样丰富多样。

Text 4: Artemisinin, discovery from the Chinese herbal garden

Malaria has been a deadly disease for humans since ancient times. Usually, people get malaria when infected mosquitoes bite them. Countless people have died from the disease. Thankfully, Chinese scientist Tu Youyou found an effective drug called *qinghaosu*, also widely known as *artemisinin*.

In 1969, Tu became the director of a national project to develop a drug against malaria. Her team took a unique approach by studying classical Chinese medicine texts. After examining more than 2,000 old remedies, Tu and her team collected over 600 plants and listed almost 380 potential remedies for malaria.

One remedy, which is 1,600 years old, uses sweet wormwood. Tu found it effective and tried to extract artemisinin from it for medicinal purposes. Initially unsuccessful, Tu returned to Chinese classical books and devised a low-temperature method to extract artemisinin and finally succeeded in 1972.

After her team showed that artemisinin could treat malaria in mice and monkeys, Tu and two of her colleagues volunteered to test the drug on themselves before testing on human patients. It turned out that artemisinin was safe and all the patients in the trial recovered. Gradually, artemisinin became the first-line treatment for malaria recommended by the World Health Organization (WHO), saving millions of lives around the world.

In 2015, Tu was awarded the Nobel Prize in Physiology or Medicine. Rather than taking all of the credit, she humbly acknowledged the controbution of her colleagues and the wisdom of traditional Chinese medicine. She once said, "Every scientist dreams of doing something that can help the world."

第十三章

专项练习

英汉段落1: 脏话

像抗生素一样，脏话也会因为用得太多而失去威力。有线电视让美国千家万户的客厅里回响起各种各样的脏话。这些脏话让你难为情了吗？如果没有的话，是不是因为你电视看太多了？

很难说电视上的脏话越来越多究竟是因为美国民众越来越常说脏话，还是说电视"污染"了美国人的话语。无论如何，结果是一样的：越来越多的美国人对脏话习以为常，甚至完全免疫了。禁忌在改变，那么脏话也必须改变。

有些禁忌消失了："天杀的"（damn）不再像原词"天谴"（damnation）那样让人想到地狱的烈火与硫磺。而社会变化带来了新的禁忌。美国民权运动之前，几乎人人都会使用一些基于种族、信仰或者性取向的贬低他人的绰号，一点也不会觉得遭受偏见。如今，这些词语成了禁忌。

英汉段落2：姓名

是时候质疑一个广为接受的社会习俗了。事实上这种习俗很难令人接受，而且在我们这个时代相当令人厌恶。为什么女人婚后要随夫姓？

历史上，随着人口增长，大多数人使用单名很容易混淆，因此才添加姓氏来区分。有的姓氏基于职业，比如Smith指的是铁匠，而Taylor指的是裁缝；有的基于地点，比如某人出生的村庄或城镇；还有的基于家族血统，即祖先选择的家族姓氏。9世纪时，英国普通法发展出女性法律身份的从属原则，这成了西方世界的标准做法：一位女性出生时其法律身份从属父亲，婚后则从属丈夫。后者意味着她的法律身份与其丈夫合并。也许"淹没"才是更合适的说法，因为从属意味着只有丈夫可以投票、拥有财产或是出席法庭。

这种荒谬的法律使得女性结婚时不得不冠以夫姓。如今女性结婚较晚，同时她们会以自己的名字获得学位、专业认证和丰富的工作经验，这种做法愈发显得荒谬。为了幸福的婚姻，女性必须忍痛放弃自我身份，在法律上更改她所有执照和证书上的名字，并且告知她的雇主、律师、医生和所有其他联系人。在谷歌与领英的时代，这代表着巨大的缺陷和惊人的职业障碍。

汉英段落1：Together for a shared future

"Together for a Shared Future" is another contribution made by Beijing, the first city to host both Summer and Winter Games, to the Olympic spirit and philosophy. Inspired by the core values of the Beijing 2008 motto "One World, One Dream", the 2022 slogan not only emphasizes inclusiveness, openness of the Olympic Games, but also stands as the world's common aspiration to work together for a better tomorrow.

"Together" symbolizes the resilience of humanity as a community with a shared future in the face of global challenges. It also points out that solidarity is the key to overcoming obstacles and creating a better future. The slogan also echoes the new Olympic motto "Faster, Higher, Stronger —

Together", highlighting the power of the Olympic movement to surmount difficulties and pave the way for sustainable development.

汉英段落 2: Urban planning

Since 2000, China has been investing in building the world's largest subway system. The lines are well-managed, punctual and reliable. Almost every urban resident can reach a subway station from home or office within 15 minutes. People don't have to live in crowded and expensive city centers to enjoy the benefits of urban clusters. Additionally, the bike-sharing system has addressed transportation issues. Now, in most Chinese cities, people can travel around without driving, which is crucial for building better cities in the future.

Meanwhile, the world's largest high-speed railway system is almost completed and is ready to connect most major cities in China. The next major infrastructure investment will be into a railway system that connects small cities with the larger core areas. The three major metropolitan regions, namely the Beijing-Tianjin-Hebei region, the Yangtze River Delta region, and the Pearl River Delta region, will become the largest urban clusters globally. This will alleviate the pressure on the metropolitans and enhance the transportation efficiency across the nation.

篇章练习

Text 1: "全球岩溶动力系统资源环境效应"计划

尊敬的各位同仁，

女士们、先生们：

值此"全球岩溶动力系统资源环境效应"计划启动之际，我很荣幸来到这里，并由衷地向各位致以鼓励和祝贺。

我们的星球面临着许多挑战：气候变化、人口增长、淡水匮乏、教育资源紧张，这些仅仅是其中很小的一部分。有些时候，这些问题看起来是那样难以逾越，但我坚信，随着人类能力和创新技术的提升，我们不仅能够迎接这些挑战，而且能够战胜这些难题。

地球上有许多非常脆弱的生态环境，其中之一就是我们宝贵的岩溶区。岩溶环境往往孕育着美妙的景观和神秘的洞穴，为多种多样的生物提供了庇护所，然而对于当地社区而言，它可能是非常艰苦的生存地。岩溶环境土壤贫瘠、岩石无法容纳地表水、地处偏远，这些都是当地人必须面对的挑战。我看到您的提案将对此展开研究，并为解决其中一些问题提出方案。

我很高兴看到我们许多经联合国教科文组织认定的世界地质公园和世界自然遗产都位于岩溶区，并且也通过联合国可持续发展目标来解决一些类似问题。我十分支持这项计划所设想的国际科学合作。我相信这种合作对于克服我们人类共同面临的难题至关重要。我坚信计划将取得巨大成功，也非常期待能听到有关项目进展和取得成功的好消息。

Text 2: 隐私

想象一下你有一把自己生活的万能钥匙。这把钥匙或是这串密码可以打开你家的前门、你的卧室、日记、计算机、电话、汽车和保险箱。你会到处制作备用钥匙并分发给陌生人吗？这可能不太明智——迟早会有人滥用它，对吗？那么，为什么你却愿意将你的个人数据提供给几乎任何管你要的人？

隐私是开启你最私密的那些方面的钥匙，这些方面让你成为你，也让你最为脆弱：你过去、现在和将来可能罹患的疾病，你的恐惧、失落和失败，你做过、说过、想过的最糟糕的事情，你的不足、你犯下的错、你受过的伤，你感到最羞愧的时刻，以及你醉到不省人事的那一晚。

将这把钥匙（也就是你的隐私）交给爱你的人，会让你享受亲密关系，他们会用这把钥匙来善待你。从某种程度上来说，与某人亲近意味着与其分享你的脆弱，并且相信这个人绝不会利用亲密关系带来的特权来加害你。爱你的人也许会用你的生日来为你组织一场惊喜派对；他们会记下你的品味来为你准备最棒的礼物；他们会考虑你内心最深处的恐惧来避免你受到惊吓。但是，并非所有能够接触你个人生活信息的人都是为你好的。欺诈者可能会利用你的生日来冒充你；公司可能会利用你的品味诱使你做出不明智的决定；敌人可能会利用你内心最深处的恐惧来威胁、勒索你。坏人会利用你的数据来达成自己的目的。隐私很重要，因为缺乏隐私会赋予他人压倒你的能力。

你可能会认为自己的隐私是安全的，因为你并不是什么名人，没什么特别的、有趣的或是重要的事情可让人看。别看轻自己啦。你有注意力，有思想，人人都在争夺它。他们想尽可能多地了解你，以便知道如何最好地分散你的注意力，即使这意味着剥夺你与亲人相处的美好时光或是睡眠等基本需求。你有钱，即使钱不算多，公司也希望你将钱花在他们身上。黑客渴望掌握敏感信息或图像，这样他们就可以勒索你。你去工作，企业想掌握雇员的一切信息，包括你是否可能会为自己的权利而战。你拥有一个身份，犯罪分子可以以你的名义犯罪，并让你担责。你有人际关系，是网络中的一个节点。你是某人的后代、某人的邻居、某人的老师或律师。通过你，他们可以联系到其他人。这就是为什么应用程序会要求访问你的联系人。你会发出自己的声音，所以各种机构都希望利用你成为他们在社交媒体和其他领域的喉舌。

Text 3: The Internet industry

Enterprises drive the growth of the Internet industry and propel scientific innovation and industrial transformation. It's fair to say they support the country's digital economy. Internet companies are rapidly expanding their business scope and competing to establish themselves in emerging high-tech industries, spawning new technologies, businesses, models, and services.

North America leads the world in Internet industry, and the United States is home to many leading Internet companies. Giants as Apple, Google, Microsoft, and Amazon are trend-setters of the global Internet scene. The rapid development of the Internet industry in Latin America provides a favorable environment for international Internet companies.

Europe's extensive language diversity and small population hinder the emergence of Internet giants. As a result, none of the world's top 20 Internet companies in terms of market value are based in Europe. The development of the Internet industry in Asia is uneven, with China, India, Japan, and South Korea being major players. Notably, China's Internet startups are growing rapidly.

Text 4: Remark at a seminar

It is my honor to participate in today's online seminar. First of all, on behalf of the Beijing 2022 Organizing Committee, I would like to extend my heartfelt thanks to Ambassador Sun and the Chinese Embassy in India for arranging this meaningful event. I would also like to thank the Indian Olympic Association and the Confederation of Young Leaders for your care and support for the Beijing 2022 Olympic Winter Games.

In less than a month, the much-anticipated Beijing 2022 Olympic Winter Games will begin, welcoming people from all over the world to celebrate this foremost international multi-sport event for winter sports together. In less than a month, the Olympic flame will again illuminate the National Stadium, or the Bird's Nest, as Beijing will become the first city in the world to have hosted both the Summer and Winter Games. We warmly welcome Olympic athletes from all countries and regions to participate in the Beijing 2022 Olympic and Paralympic Winter Games.

The Chinese government attaches great importance to the preparations for the Games. Since Beijing won the bid in 2015, President Xi Jinping has made five on-the-spot inspections to the Olympic venues and issued a series of important instructions, guiding our preparations for the Games. Eleven days ago, in his 2022 New Year Address, President Xi Jinping said that China will spare no effort to present a great Games to the world. The world is looking to China, and China is ready. This is a solemn commitment to the international community and a call for action for the Beijing 2022. A week ago, President Xi Jinping visited Beijing 2022 headquarters and several other venues again, inspiring our confidence and determination to successfully host the Games.

In the past six years and more, the Beijing 2022 Organizing Committee has been committed to its mission of hosting a "green, inclusive, open and clean" Games and delivering a "simple, safe and splendid" Games. We have pushed ahead with our preparatory work vigorously, orderly and effectively and have come a long way.

Dear friends, with the clock counting down to 24 days, we eagerly look forward to the opening of the Beijing 2022 Olympic Winter Games. We warmly welcome athletes from India and other parts of the world to participate in the Games. I am aware that an Indian alpine skier has been qualified for the Games. I sincerely wish him the best of his luck. I once accompanied several ministers and deputy ministers of the Ministry of Youth Affairs and Sports of India on their tours to inspect sports-related affairs in China. I could see the great importance India attaches to sports. I was deeply impressed by young people's passion for cricket in India. I also hope that dear Indian friends will stay engaged and support the Beijing 2022 Olympic Winter Games. We firmly believe that Beijing, as the world's first dual Olympic host city, will deliver a "simple, safe and splendid" Games to the world. Let us bear in mind the Olympic motto of "Faster, Higher, Stronger — Together"; let us join hands "Together for a Shared Future" and carry forward the Olympic spirit, promote friendship between the Chinese and Indian peoples and build a community with a shared future for humanity. Thank you!

第十四章

专项练习

1. 会议主题：线上教育

A: Good morning! Today we are honored to have Lacey Moore here with us. Lacey is an English teacher at Seven Lakes High School in Katy, Texas. With the rapid development of Internet technologies, our education system has shifted to distance learning. This is quite a shift in the education field. Most people look for information and advice about it on the Internet. So when did you start to use distance education, and how did you prepare for the shift?

B: 在我所在的地区，线上授课是从2020年3月23号开始的。我们只有十天左右的准备时间，多少有点力不从心。我们得处理来自各方的邮件，包括校监、校董事会、学生家长以及学生本人，还得迅速熟悉Canvas这一线上学习平台，而之前我从来没在这上面授过课。

A: Under some circumstances, due to the restraints of time and space, teachers can only teach online, and many teachers lack relevant experience. They are unfamiliar with online teaching platforms, and face many problems and challenges. Some even say that it is more difficult for them to start the live broadcast than to do ten math problems. Many also have trouble with their computers and networks. So what are the biggest challenges for you in this regard?

B: 对我来说，最大的困难是无法亲自帮助那些有特殊需要的学生。学生和家长对于线上学习充满恐慌，给我发了大量电子邮件，这是因为线上授课无法满足学生的特殊需要，而如果是线下授课，我就可以帮助他们了。我和一部分有困难的学生用Zoom进行了视频会议,希望帮助他们更好地适应线上学习、明确学习内容,这似乎有所帮助,但却给教师和学生带来了额外压力。

A: Online learning does bring challenges to teachers, but it has provided us with new ideas and methods for education and teaching. Besides, it enables teachers and students to set their own learning schedule, and there's the added flexibility that fits everyone's agenda. In your opinion, what are the other advantages of online learning?

B: 我认为积极的一面是,每个人都意识到了耐心以及时间管理有多重要。没有上下课铃声,学生必须学会自己安排作息时间表,自己对自己负责,他们也会因此受益终生。线上教学也让学生意识到能够与老师、同学一起在课堂学习是多么有意义。

A: We have just talked so much about the advantages, but every coin has two sides, and online learning is controversial as well. Some point to the lack of supervision in that students can easily be distracted by smartphones or other electronic devices. This way is not suitable for these students who lack self-discipline. So what do you think of the disadvantages of online learning?

B: 当然,线上授课也有很多消极影响。最大的问题可能是,明年开学时学生可能没有做好充分的准备。尤其是数学这类课程,他们每天都得学习新的技巧和策略,而这些技巧和策略可能在下周、下个月甚至是明年都会反复用到。有些学生线上学习时并不能掌握这些概念,未来他们可能会感到吃力,教师也必须得据此调整教学进度。

A: Thank you, Ms. Moore, for sharing with us your experience of online education. Sitting in the classroom allows more direct communication and engagement. It shows more empathy and that's what education is all about.

B: 是的,但无论如何它为我们打破了时空的限制,拓展了学校的边界,从一定程度上也推进了教育公平。我们都相信,线上教育不会取代面授,而只是一个补充。

2. 会议主题: 垃圾分类

A: The phrase "garbage sorting" has made several headlines and taken the Internet by storm with a deluge of memes. According to *Economist*, Shanghai generates 9 million tons of garbage annually, overtaking London. In the absence of an effective recycling mechanism, relying on scavengers to sift through the waste and recycle stations cannot cope with such a huge amount of trash.

B: 中国建起了数百座"转废为能"的工厂,还发起了"无废城市"计划。早在2000年,中华人民共和国住房和城乡建设部就指定了包括上海在内的8个地级市作为试点,展开垃圾分类。上海现行的垃圾回收制度是国内目前措施最具体、实施最广泛的。关键是,这个分类回收体系非常公开,而且有惩罚措施。

A: However, many working people find it hard to get their trash to designated dumping areas at the appropriate times. On Weibo, some posts show that people are hiring "garbage-sorters" to do it for them. A cup of unfinished milk tea is wet rubbish, the paper cup is dry rubbish, the straw and cover are plastic... Garbage sorting has helped me quit milk tea.

B：人们发现一些垃圾的分类和日常认知不大一样。比如鱼骨属于"厨余垃圾"，而棒骨却属于"其他垃圾"。玉米芯是"其他垃圾"而不是"厨余垃圾"，因为它不易降解。

A: Let us take a look at the garbage produced in takeaway industry. The growth of food delivery apps in China is flooding the country with takeout containers and bags. And the country's patchy recycling system isn't keeping up. The vast majority of this plastic ends up discarded, buried, or burned with the rest of the trash, researchers and recyclers say.

B：据科学家估计，2017年，中国的线上外卖业务造成了160万吨包装废弃物，比两年前增长了9倍，其中包括120万吨塑料盒、17.5万吨一次性筷子、16.4万吨塑料袋和4.4万吨塑料勺。

A: We can learn from Germany, the world's leader in waste recycling. It has the world's number one recycling system. The country has a quite sophisticated waste sorting system. There's the thing called Pfand in Germany, a certain portion of the price on a bottled drink that you get back if you return the bottle to a certified outlet.

B：垃圾分类政策可以使生活垃圾的再利用成本大大降低，因为消费者会把塑料和厨余垃圾分开，把食品容器冲洗干净后再扔进垃圾桶。这个政策也给其他发展中国家上了一课，建立现代垃圾管理系统的第一步就是要教育公众，让公众意识到回收利用是公民责任。

3. 会议主题：基因编辑

主持人：基因编辑几年前只不过是一个术语，而现在这一技术正全面发展，各国的科学研究和实验越来越多。今天，我们邀请到来自中国和美国的两位知名专家，从技术、安全和道德角度分享他们的观点。

A：先天性疾病会通过父母的基因传给后代，但利用基因工程，科学家可以阻止这些疾病传给胚胎。众所周知，基因突变会引发许多疾病和综合征，而基因编辑可能根治一些疾病。一旦这些疾病得以治愈，这将会是医疗科学史上的一大创举。

B: However, scientists still have a long way to go to completely figure out the genes relevant to various diseases. Even if gene editing could be safe and effective, it can't eradicate genetic diseases. For example, although Huntington's disease has been researched thoroughly, it is still hard to cure it. HD is caused by a repeated section of a gene, and more repeats mean worse symptoms and the number of repeats increases in successive generations. The dream is beautiful, but for now it remains a dream.

A：一个国家的未来掌握在下一代手中。通过出生前基因筛查，许多新生儿可以免受严酷的先天疾病。如果基因可以筛选，先天疾病就可以尽早治愈。这有助于国民身体健康，也有助于国家的发展。如果允许基因工程成为我国医疗实践的一部分，那么一些妨碍儿童发育的疾病也可以得到治愈，先天性缺陷可以得到治疗，甚至也许有一天，再也不会有人患先天性残疾。如果加以正确使用，基因工程可能带给人们真正的幸福。

B: But changing genes is not necessarily about creating a better future. No matter how precise we can edit genes, there are things that cannot be edited, let alone ensure safety. Most genes are multi-functional. Editing thousands of genes can put your body in an unpredictable situation. For example, eliminating the CCR5 gene can make people resistant to HIV, but it also makes them 13 times more likely to die from West Nile virus. In a word, eliminating a disease through gene editing may increase the risk of suffering from another disease, resulting in the opposite effect.

A：的确，毫无顾忌地使用基因编辑技术可能会产生意想不到的后果。但如果审慎研究和实验，基因编辑技术可以用于治愈细胞传播的疾病和生理障碍。这确实需要时间，但它将日趋成熟并得到广泛应用。

B: Even if gene editing is fully mature and the risks are under control, once the technology is promoted, it will bring serious social problems: those who want to become beautiful and smart can freely alter their genes or their offspring's, just like what we saw in the movie — eliminating the so-called weak genes and realizing gene customization. Our world is already doomed under racism, differentiations, intolerance towards people different from us, defined rules for beauty and everything we judge people on.

附 录

附录1：口译反思日志模板及说明

原　　文	我的译文	参考译文	分析与对策

原文：

本列中我们会录入音频的原文。许多音频素材配有文本（script），但是有的和实际音频有出入，例如进行了改编、缩写等，需要人工校对一下。尤其是一些正式会议的讲话稿在会后发布时都会进行一些修订，也就是我们从官方网站和新闻中获得的材料。

根据不同的任务类型，音频截段的时长有所不同：

a）主旨口译或复述不要求包括细节，重在训练如何把握篇章结构并进行逻辑分析，因此不宜过短，可以整篇听完后再进行，时长可达三、四分钟。

b）无笔记口译会鼓励学生尽量还原重要的细节，在文段大意和主要具体内容之间取得平衡。建议每段的长度适中，可以循序渐进，从最初的一两句话，到30秒以上，再到40秒或一分钟。

c）有笔记口译需要学生在分析与记录、脑记和笔记之间保持协调。笔记需要体现出主旨、逻辑关系，以及数字、专名等重要细节。截段的时长可以与无笔记口译一致。

我的译文：

本列需要转写自己所说的内容，包括填充词（fillers）、停顿、错误等。例如，较长的停顿可以用省略号表示，对填充词可以大致记录下其发音，各类口误、不准确的表述、奇怪的句式和搭配也都需要如实记录。需要注意的是，许多人在转写时都会不自觉地有"美化译文"的倾向，因此完成之后还需要复听核查，将那些"无心之失"补充上。这样才能正视自己的语言习惯，发现口译中的薄弱环节，从而有针对性地进行训练，减少口误、纠正口头禅。

参考译文:

本列在译后反思阶段完成。同学们复听原文之后可以自行重译,直至得出较为完善的译文。如果音频难度稍高,个别地方听了三、四遍还无法听懂,那么可能是存在重要生词或复杂的句式,可以对照原文文本,配合阅读以加强理解。有的素材可能配有参考译文,看似可以节省很多时间,但其实同学们自己重译的效果更佳。一方面是自己多了一次锻炼的机会,另一方面是因为许多译文是网友提供或机翻所得,意思未必准确,语言更谈不上流畅地道。因此,不管音频素材是否能够找到所谓的参考译文,我们都鼓励同学们自己做一遍。

分析与对策:

本列是反思日志的关键。在这栏中,同学们可以对材料的重点和难点进行分析,标注出自己翻译中的错误,回顾口译当时遇到的问题,思考今后遇到类似情况时应该如何处理。

翻译是不完美的艺术,而学生练习的译文普遍有多处错漏。所幸这里并不需要面面俱到,可以拣最重要的问题具体分析,或者分类概括自己的常见问题。

不同类型、难度和翻译方向的语篇,完成度和自我满意程度也有很大差异。因此同学们不必因为一段录音做得不理想就气馁,也不能由于材料比较简单、译出率较高而沾沾自喜。不同语段会暴露出来不同的问题,包括听辨、逻辑分析、词汇量、语法、笔记法,等等,我们应该摆正心态、一视同仁。

转写表格的下方还可以设一些开放型的问题,比如"本次遇到的困难""本次训练我学到了什么""下一阶段的训练目标"等。这部分的回答不在于长短,感悟多可以多写一些,没有特别的感觉也可以略过。

有笔记口译训练的反思日志还可以附上当次的口译笔记,并在"分析与对策"的部分结合笔记的情况来具体分析。例如笔记在格式上缺乏阶梯缩进、横向扩张,无法体现意群划分;笔记内容过多,信息零散但缺乏逻辑指示;笔记内容过少,细节记录不完整,等等。需要注意的是,笔记本身的详细程度和准确性并不是反思的主要内容,更重要的是听译文的效果,结合起来看笔记是否真正服务于口译任务。

附录 2：学生口译日志实例

材料标题：**Looking for a job? Highlight your ability, not your experience**

材料出处：**TED** 演讲

Part 1: Transcript

Source text	What I said	I should have said	Diagnosis
You know who I'm envious of? People who work in a job that has to do with their college major. Journalists who studied journalism, engineers who studied engineering. The truth is, these folks are no longer the rule, but the exception. A 2010 study found that only a quarter of college graduates work in a field that relates to their degree. I graduated with not one but two degrees in biology. To my parents' dismay, I am neither a doctor nor a scientist. Years of studying DNA replication and photosynthesis did little to prepare me for a career in technology. I had to teach myself everything from sales, marketing, strategy, even a little programming, on my own. I had never held the title of Product Manager before I sent my resume into Etsy. I had already been turned down by Google and several other firms and was getting frustrated.	有那么一群人，他们所做的工作就是他们大学所学的内容：记者学习新闻，工程师学习工程。那么实际上现在这些人，已经，不是主流了，已经成为了少数。根据一项2010年的研究表明，只有25%的大学生在毕业后做着与自己专业相关的工作。那么我呢，我拿了两个，生物学的学位，然而，和我父母意愿相违背的是，我并没有成为一名医生，也并没有成为一名科学家。我在过去那么多年里学的光合作用啊之类的内容，并没有，为我在后来在科技领域的工作起到什么作用啊。我自学了销售、市场……市场，等内容，那么在我还学了一点点编程。那么在进入易集之前，我……学习过产品经理相关的内容，此前我被谷歌等大企业拒绝了，那，也变得非常沮丧的。	知道我嫉妒什么样的人吗？那些做着和本科专业相关工作的人：读了新闻专业的记者，读了工程专业的工程师。但事实上，这种人已经成为了少数。一项2010年的研究表明，仅25%的大学毕业生毕业后所做工作与其专业相关。我拿了不止一个，而是两个生物学的学位，但并没有像我父母期望的那样成为医生或科学家。多年学习的DNA复制和光合作用对我后来在科技领域的工作帮助甚微。我只能自学内容、营销、策略，甚至还有一点点编程。在往易集投简历之前，我从没当过产品经理。此前我被谷歌和其他几家公司拒绝录用，十分沮丧。	**输入**：受听力水平局限，没能听出足够的信息：演讲者稍微有一些口音，有些地方我没能听懂，比如第一句就一个词都没听出来，另外还遗漏了信息点，比如"DNA replication"。 **输出内容**：出现误译，1) 将"held the title of Product Manager"译为"学习过产品经理相关的内容"，但实际应该是"从没当过产品经理"，其实应该是"营销"；3) "sent my resume into Etsy"误译为"进入易集之前"，其实只是"往易集投简历之前"，一方面是没听清，一方面没来得及记清楚；4) "and several other firms"自己由Google臆断为"大企业"，然而原文并没有这个信息点。 **输出语流**：不够流畅，1) 容易犹豫，断句奇怪，如"已经，不是主流了"、"并没有，为我此后在科技领域的工作起到什么作用"；2) 重复次数太多，译完"marketing"后纠结"strategy"是否需要与其合并，又重复了好几遍，大大影响语流，本可直接接上"等内容"，省略处理以提升流畅度，但反应不够快；3) fillers还是太多，用了非常多的"那么"、"那"。

续 表

Source text	What I said	I should have said	Diagnosis
The company had recently gone public, so as part of my job application, I read the IPO filings from cover to cover and built a website from scratch which included my analysis of the business and four ideas for new features. It turned out the team was actively working on two of those ideas and had seriously considered a third. I got the job.	易集这个公司不久前刚上市,那么……因此为了应聘,上市文件,我去看了他们的,上市文件,并且自己建了一个网站,在上面,记录了我对该公司的一些分析,并且总,总结出了4个……新……4个可能,即将投入的新,新方案。事实上,这个公司确实在为其中的两个方案做努力,并且准备开始……为第三,建设第三个方案,因此我也就顺利地拿到了这份工作。	易集这个公司不久前刚上市,因此为了应聘,我仔细阅读了公司的上市文件,还从零开始建了一个网站,记录了我对公司的分析和有关于新专题的四个想法。事实上,公司确实努力将其中两个想法付诸实践,并且认真考虑了第三个想法。我拿到了这份工作。	**输入:** 1)听力水平不够,许多内容没听明白,信息记录得不够完整,如"engineering manager"只记了"engineer",人名没有记全(而且日记的还不是挺);"WhatsApp"听成"Whatsup","built in the 20th century"听成"built since the 20th century"等;2)紧张情绪恶化听力事故,由于老想着前面漏记了不少信息,最后一句话实在是基本没听到,只零星地蹦出来"many occupations"和"human labor",最后只能结巴着模糊处理。
We all know people who were ignored or overlooked at first but went on to prove their critics wrong. My favorite story? Brian Acton, an engineering manager who was rejected by both Twitter and Facebook before cofounding WhatsApp, the mobile messaging platform that would sell for 19 billion dollars.	我们常常听说有一些人,他们一开始被低估,但后面却通过自己的努力证明了此前的预计是错误的。我最喜欢的故事是一位名叫布莱恩的工程师,他在被合歌、推特等大公司拒绝之后,与其他人合作并创立了Whatsup这个企业,并且最后,达,该,该,该企业达到了190亿美元的市值。	我技术经理布莱恩 • 阿克顿的经历。被推特和合歌拒绝录用后,他参与创立了WhatsApp,该移动通讯平台后的市值后来达到了190亿美元。	**输出内容:** 同样出现了误译,1)"Twitter and Facebook"与上一段混淆,译成了"合歌",推特",且主观添加了"等大公司"这个信息点;2)"I got the job"当时译为"因此我也就顺利地拿到了这份实实的工作,因此拿到了工作",但后来一想,这里可能说的是"我"为公司提供了四个方案,在入职后落实,实属主观误判因果关系,缺乏常识。
The hiring systems we built in the 20th century are failing us and causing us to miss out on people with incredible potential. The advances in robotics and machine learning and transforming the way we work, automating routine tasks in many occupations while augmenting and amplifying human labor in others.	我们自20世纪开始建立的这个,应聘体系,并没有达到我们想要的效果,反而让我们白白流失了许多人才。现在机器人自主学习的能力大,极大改变了我们的工作的内容,许多,许多重复的,以及许多的职业都受到了改变。人类劳动力的,应用受到了改变。	我们没能满足我们的期望,反而让我们白白流失了许多人才。机器人技术和机器学习的进步改变了我们的工作方式,使许多职业的常规任务自动化,同时增加了其他职业中的人力劳动。	**输出语流:** 十分不流畅,1)纠结表达,卡壳,如"ideas for new features"不知道如何表述,卡了半天挤出一个"可能,即将投入的新,新方案";2)断句奇怪,口吃,一部分原因因为紧张情绪。

续表

Source text	What I said	I should have said	Diagnosis
At this rate, we should all be expecting to do jobs we've never done before for the rest of our careers. So what are the tools and strategies we need to identify tomorrow's high performers? In search for answers, I've consulted with leaders across many sectors, read dozens of reports and research papers and conducted some of my own talent experiments. My quest is far from over, but here are three ideas to take forward. One: expand your search. If we only look for talent in the same places we always do — gifted child programs, Ivy League schools, prestigious organizations — we're going to get the same results we always have. Baseball was transformed when the cash-strapped Oakland Athletics started recruiting players who didn't score highly on traditionally valued metrics, like runs batted in, but who had the ability to help the team score points and win games. This idea is taking hold outside of sports. The Head of Design and Research at Pinterest told me that they've built one of the most diverse and high-performing teams in Silicon Valley because they believe that no one type of person holds a monopoly on talent. They've worked hard to look beyond major tech hubs and focus on designers' portfolios, not their pedigrees.	那么这样看来，我们此后，需要在我们的职业生涯中，做许多和我们此前做过的事情毫不相关的工作。那么有哪些方法和策略是我们可以用来寻找那些人才的呢？那么在我和各行各业许多……领导领域的领导者谈话，嗯，阅读了许多相关研究报告论文，并自己进行了一些关于人才的实验。我的探索自己关于人才的实验，但这里有三个想法可以参考。 第一点是，拓宽搜索的范围。在过去，我们总是从同样的渠道来寻找人才，从同样的项目，同样的学校，同样的那些组织去寻找，那么势必获得同样的结果。在棒球领域，他们开始去，寻找一些野路子的选手，这些选手，可能在传统的技巧，技巧上得分并不高，但他们可以帮助队伍得分，并且赢得比赛。那么这个在体育中运用的理念，也被拓展到了，其他行业的，应聘范围内。嗯……Pinterest的一，一位，额，领导者……跟我说，仪仪，他们公司相信，人才不是一类人。他们并不仅限于某一类的过程中，和他们的背景，出身。	照这样下去，我们都将在接下来的职业生涯中做我们从未做过的工作。那么，什么样的方法和策略能帮助我们寻找潜在的高绩效员工呢？为了回答这个问题，我咨询了许多领域的领导者，阅读了几十份报告和研究论文，并自己进行了一些关于人才的实验。我的探索还未结束，但这里有三个想法可以推进。 第一，扩大搜索范围。如果我们一直只在同样的地方寻找人才，即天才儿童项目、常青藤联盟学校、著名组织，我们将得到和以往一样的结果。资金紧张的奥克兰运动家队招募球员在上垒率等传统衡量指标上得分不高，但有能力帮助球队得分并赢得比赛的球员，使棒球这项运动发生了转变。这种想法拓展到了体育外的领域。Pinterest的设计与研究主管告诉我，他们建立了硅谷最多元化、绩效最高的团队之一，因为他们相信，人才并不单单出自某个类型的人。他们努力将目光投向主要科技中心以外，关注设计师的作品，而不是他们的出身。	输入：听力水平不够，许多内容没听明白，信息记录得不够完整，如"gifted child programs, Ivy League schools, prestigious organizations"全没听清楚，只记下了"programs""schools"和"organizations"，翻译时只能模糊处理为"同样的项目，同样的学校，同样的那些组织"；关于棒球的内容也只听出了个大概，"cash-strapped Oakland Athletics""like runs batted in"这类详细信息都没能记下；"The Head of Design and Research"这个职位没有记下，只联系上下文模糊处理为"领导者"，"they've built one of the most diverse and high-performing teams in Silicon Valley"这块内容也没记下，直接省略了，但其实还挺重要的。 输出内容：1）棒球那块的内容翻译得与原文差距较大。原文中，奥克兰运动队因资金紧张开始招募野路子选手，而翻译听起来像是整个棒球界不知为何就出现了这样的趋势，与原文偏差较大，不利于听众理解；2）Pinterest关注的是"设计师的作品"，但翻译变成了"应聘者的简历，和他们的能力本身"，"能力""倒还算模糊处理"，"简历"实属错译，理解时混淆了"resume"和"portfolio"。 输出语流：十分不流畅，主要还是上面提到过的纠结卡壳以及多用fillers的问题。

续 表

Source text	What I said	I should have said	Diagnosis
Two: hire for performance. Inspired by my own job experience, I cofounded a hiring platform called Headlight, which gives candidates an opportunity to shine. Just as teams have tryouts and plays have auditions, candidates should be asked to demonstrate their skills before they're hired. Our clients are benefiting from 85 years of employment research, which shows that work samples are one of the best predictors of success on the job. If you're hiring a data analyst, give them a spreadsheet of historical data and ask them for their key insights. If you're hiring a marketing manager, have them plan a launch campaign for a new product. And if you're a candidate, don't wait for an employer to ask. Seek out ways to showcase your unique skills and abilities outside of just the standard resume and cover letter.	第二点,根据表现应聘。那么根据我……受我个人经历启发,我与其他人,共同创立了……"车灯",这么一个平台,提供给求职者,一些机会,让他们能在求职过程中大放光彩。那么我们的平台就让这些求职者们,在被雇用前能够展示出自己的能力。这,与……这样我们的方法源于,此前的85年中进行的一项研究所获得的结果。研究表明,此类拥有……拥有此类能力的,人,能在应聘过程中成为佼佼者。如果你应聘的是数据分析师,那么你就给他提供一些你们过去的数据,让他,分析,并得出一些结论。如果你应聘的是经理,那么你就让他来,额,领号,包,领导,去领号,创,创立一项新产,午餐,宣传的活动。总之,别等应聘者,呃,别,别等雇用者问你是去求职者,那么你去寻找机会,去展示你的能力,而非让你的简历,只是平平无奇。	第二,按绩效招聘。受自己工作经验的启发,我与人合作创建了一个名为Headlight的招聘平台,为求职者提供展示自己能力的机会。就像团队有选拔赛,戏剧有试镜一样,候选人在被雇用之前应该被要求展示他们的技能。我们的客户从85年的就业研究中受益,研究表明,工作样本是成功的最佳预测因素之一。如果你想雇佣数据分析师,就给应聘者一份历史数据表格,询问关键见解;如果你想招聘一名营销经理,就让应聘者为新产品策划一场发布活动;如果你是求职者,别等雇主来问,想办法展示你独特的能力,而不只是呈现标准的简历和求职信。	**输入:** 听力水平不够,许多内容没听明白,信息记录得不够完整,如"launch"听成"lunch","Just as teams have tryouts and plays have auditions"没能记下,但这部分类比内容还挺重要的。另外,"which shows that work samples are one of the best predictors of success on the job"中,我在听的过程中主观将"sample"理解为研究样本,因此翻译过程中一直觉得自己漏听了修饰部分,纠结到底是什么样的样本,后来处理得与原意相差较远。 **输出内容:** 1) 出现误译,"standard resume and cover letter"应为"标准的简历和求信",而非"平平无奇的"。2) 平台名"Headlight"译成了"车灯",但其实还是不译为好。 **输出语流:** 十分不流畅,主要还是上面提到过的纠结卡壳以及多用fillers的问题。

Part 2: Challenges I encounter and things I learned this time

（1）听力理解：此次练习过程中，我仍然存在极大的听力问题，对词句的识别有一定困难，经常感觉听进耳朵的不是单个词组成的句子，而是一整块句子，要么根本无法识别，要么就得反应一下，在后一句的时间识别上一句的具体内容。这门课让我深刻意识到自己在听力能力方面的巨大漏洞，上次journal反馈过后，我开始针对该方面的薄弱找新闻材料做听写练习，但练习量肯定还远远不够，练习的频率也有待稳定，词汇有待进一步积累，希望接下来更加努力。

（2）笔记：（笔记是这学期里最能明显看到进步的地方了，虽说现在的记录还是问题很多，但是能明显看到格式较刚一开始有了质的变化，还挺开心的。）目前，我在笔记中的问题有记不完、笔记符号不熟练等问题，其中，"记不完"这一点具体来说，还是会下意识想拼全单词，拼几个字母又想起来拼不完，想要换个策略，但调整的方案还是比较迷茫，有时候没办法短时间内为每个语块想到对应的缩写或图案等替代者，可能得对短期记忆加强训练。

（3）表达：语流极其不流畅，经常有奇怪的断句、口吃、添加fillers的现象。虽然有时会有意识地想避免，但一紧张就控制不住，还是得多加练习。说实话，这次的练习蛮受挫的……但也让我意识到课下自己练习的时候还是缺乏针对性，也还是缺少练习量，基础打得不够扎实。

Part 3: My goal(s) for the next practice/stage

1. 在第一遍能听懂更高比例的内容。
2. 表达时能有意识地避免奇怪的断句，至少先顺利说完听到的内容。
3. 在做到简明扼要的同时，能提升笔记的完整度。